Lecture Notes in Computer Science 5272

Commenced Publication in 1973
Founding and Former Series Editors:
Gerhard Goos, Juris Hartmanis, and Jan van Leeuwen

T0223414

Juliana Freira   David Koop   Luc Moreau (Eds.)

Provenance and Annotation of Data and Processes

Second International Provenance and Annotation Workshop
IPAW 2008
Salt Lake City, UT, USA, June 17-18, 2008
Revised Selected Papers

 Springer

Volume Editors

Juliana Freira
David Koop
University of Utah, School of Computing
Salt Lake City, UT 84112, USA
E-mail: {juliana, dakoop@cs.utah.edu}

Luc Moreau
University of Southampton
School of Electronics and Computer Science
Southhampton SO17 1BJ, UK
E-mail: L.Moreau@ecs.soton.ac.uk

Library of Congress Control Number: Applied for

CR Subject Classification (1998): H.3, H.4, D.4, E.2, H.5, K.6, K.4

LNCS Sublibrary: SL 3 – Information Systems and Application,
incl. Internet/Web and HCI

ISSN   0302-9743
ISBN-10   3-540-89964-2 Springer Berlin Heidelberg New York
ISBN-13   978-3-540-89964-8 Springer Berlin Heidelberg New York

Springer is a part of Springer Science+Business Media

springer.com

© Springer-Verlag Berlin Heidelberg 2008

Typesetting: Camera-ready by author, data conversion by Scientific Publishing Services, Chennai, India
Printed on acid-free paper   SPIN: 12569199   06/3180   5 4 3 2 1 0

Preface

Computing has been an enormous accelerator to science and industry alike and it has led to an information explosion in many different fields. The unprecedented volume of data acquired from sensors, derived by simulations and data analysis processes, accumulated in warehouses, and often shared on the Web, has given rise to a new field of research: provenance management. Provenance (also referred to as audit trail, lineage, and pedigree) captures information about the steps used to generate a given data product. Such information provides important documentation that is key to preserving data, to determining the data's quality and authorship, to understanding, reproducing, as well as validating results.

Provenance management has become an active field of research, as evidenced by recent specialized workshops, surveys, and tutorials. Provenance solutions are needed in many different domains and applications, from environmental science and physics simulations, to business processes and data integration in warehouses. Not surprisingly, different techniques and provenance models have been proposed in many areas such as workflow systems, visualization, databases, digital libraries, and knowledge representation. An important challenge we face today is how to integrate these techniques and models so that complete provenance can be derived for complex data products.

The International Provenance and Annotation Workshop (IPAW 2008) was a follow-up to previous workshops in Chigago (2006, 2002) and Edinburgh (2003). It was held during June 17–18, in Salt Lake City, at the University of Utah campus. IPAW 2008 brought together computer scientists from different areas and provenance users to discuss open problems related to the provenance of computational and non-computational artifacts. A total of 55 people attended the workshop.

We received 40 submissions in response to the call for papers. Each submission was reviewed by at least three reviewers. Overall, 14 submissions were accepted as full papers, and 15 were accepted as short papers and demos. All accepted papers, short papers, and demos were invited for oral presentation at the workshop. Val Tannen (University of Pennsylvania) and Allen Brown (Microsoft Research) gave keynote addresses.

The workshop was organized as a single track event with paper, poster, and demo sessions interleaved. Slides and presentation materials can be found at http://www.sci.utah.edu/ipaw2008/agenda.html.

Immediately following IPAW 2008, a group of 22 researchers got together to discuss a proposal for an Open Provenance Model (OPM). The aim of OPM is to allow provenance information to be exchanged between systems, by means of a compatibility layer based on a shared provenance data model. The discussions were technical in nature, and touched upon fundamental notions such as provenance graphs, agents, alternate accounts, and permissible inferences.

A summary can be found at `http://twiki.ipaw.info/bin/view/Challenge/FirstOPMWork shopMinutes`. As a result of this workshop, a new version of the OPM was released, which is intended to be used in the next inter-operability exercise, the *Third Provenance Challenge*. Material related to OPM can be found at `http://openprovenance.org/`.

IPAW 2008 was a very successful event with much enthusiastic discussion and many new ideas generated.

We thank Microsoft Research for sponsoring the workshop banquet. We also thank the Program Committee members for their thorough reviews.

Juliana Freire

Luc Moreau

Organization

IPAW 2008 was organized by the Department of Computer Science, University of Utah.

Workshop Co-chairs

Juliana Freire   University of Utah, USA
Luc Moreau   University of Southampton, UK

Program Committee

Roger Barga   Microsoft Research, USA
Ken Brodlie   University of Leeds, UK
Peter Buneman   University of Edinburgh, UK
James Cheney   University of Edinburgh, UK
Min Chen   Swansea University, UK
Susan Davidson   University of Pennsylvania, USA
Paul Groth   ISI, USA
Beth Plale   Indiana University, USA
Carole Goble   University of Manchester, UK
Ian Foster   University of Chicago, USA
Juliana Freire   University of Utah, USA
Bertram Ludascher   UC Davis, USA
H. V. Jagadish   University of Michigan, USA
Marta Mattoso   UFRJ, Brazil
Simon Miles   King's College, UK
Luc Moreau   University of Southampton, UK
Jim Myers   NCSA, USA
Allen Renear   University of Illinois at Urbana-Champaign, USA
Margo Seltzer   Harvard University, USA
Claudio Silva   University of Utah, USA
Wang-Chiew Tan   UC Santa Cruz, USA
Jan Van den Bussche   Universiteit Hasselt, Belgium
Stijn Vansummeren   Universiteit Hasselt, Belgium
Daniel J. Weitzner   W3C

Web Co-chairs

Erik Jorgensen   University of Utah, USA
Tommy Ellkvist   Linköping University, Sweden

Local Organizers

David Koop   University of Utah, USA
Emanuele Santos   University of Utah, USA

Sponsoring Institutions

Microsoft Corporation, Redmond, WA, USA
Scientific Computing and Imaging Institute, University of Utah, USA
Springer, New York, NY, USA
University of Utah, Salt Lake City, UT, USA

Table of Contents

Invited Contribution

Provenance for Database Transformations

Val Tannen

University of Pennsylvania, USA

Database transformations (queries, views, mappings) and the languages in which they are expressed are of obvious interest in information management. They take apart, filter and recombine source data in order to populate warehouses, views, and analysis tool inputs. As they do so, we need to track the relationship between parts and pieces of the sources and parts and pieces of the transformations' output. This relationship is what we call database provenance.

This talk will present an approach to database provenance that relies on three observations. First, provenance definitions follow the constructs of the language in which queries/views/mappings are expressed. Second, provenance is a kind of annotation, and there exist approaches to annotated data that we can relate to. In fact, it can be argued that provenance is the most general kind of annotation, when properly viewed. Third, the propagation of annotation through most language constructs seems to rely on just two annotation operations: one when annotations are jointly used and one when they are used alternatively. We will see that this leads to annotations forming a specific algebraic structure, a commutative semiring.

The semiring approach works for annotations on standard relations, but also on nested relations (complex values), and unordered XML. It works for the positive fragment of relational algebra, nested relational calculus, unordered XQuery, and even for languages with recursion (Datalog). It turns out that specific semirings correspond to the approaches to provenance presented in previous work. Other semirings yield applications to incomplete/probabilistic data, and to access control in databases.

This is joint work with J. N. Foster, T. J. Green, and G. Karvounarakis.

J. Freire, D. Koop, and L. Moreau (Eds.): IPAW 2008, LNCS 5272, p. 1, 2008.
© Springer-Verlag Berlin Heidelberg 2008

Enforcing the Scientific Method

Allen L. Brown, Jr.

Health Solutions Group, Microsoft Corporation

Within Microsoft's Health Solutions Group we are engaged in the development of a platform to assist life sciences researchers—a class of extreme knowledge worker. We refer to this platform by the rubric, Pharos. Pharos has many objectives. One of the most important of those objectives is to supply an audit trail for research. This audit trail serves primarily to provide researchers and Pharos with a shared understanding of both the conduct of a scientific investigation and the results of a scientific investigation. But there are also other stakeholders in the audit trail, including regulatory agencies, funding agencies, tenure granting institutions and for-profit research managements. Put another way, Pharos is also concerned with the rigorous enforcement of the scientific method. In this presentation I will examine the roles and interplay of audited inference and audited workflow in constructing an audit trail.

J. Freire, D. Koop, and L. Moreau (Eds.): IPAW 2008, LNCS 5272, p. 2, 2008.
© Springer-Verlag Berlin Heidelberg 2008

Mapping the NRC Dataflow Model to the Open Provenance Model

Natalia Kwasnikowska and Jan Van den Bussche

Hasselt University and Transnational University of Limburg, Belgium

Abstract. The Open Provenance Model (OPM) has recently been proposed as an exchange framework for workflow provenance information. In this paper we show how the NRC data model for workflow repositories can be mapped to the OPM. Our mapping includes such features as complex data flow in an execution of a workflow; different workflows in the repository that call each other; and the tracking of subvalues of complex data structures in the provenance information. Because the NRC dataflow model has been formally specified, also our mapping can be formally specified; in particular, it can be automated. To facilitate this specification, we present an adapted set-theoretic formalization of the basic OPM.

1 Introduction

The Open Provenance Model (OPM) has recently been proposed as an exchange framework for workflow provenance information [1]. In order to validate this new framework, it is important to investigate how existing models and systems for provenance can be mapped to the OPM. In this paper, we do this exercise for a data model for workflow repositories which we recently introduced, called the NRC dataflow model [2].

The NRC dataflow model is a formally specified data model for workflows which emphasize data manipulation and data management. Hence we usually refer to such workflows as *dataflows*. The NRC dataflow model incorporates important aspects such as complex-data flow governed by expressions of the Nested Relational Calculus (NRC [3]); use of external services; formal representation of past executions; tracking of subvalues of a complex data structure in a past execution; and different dataflows in a repository that call each other. We will propose a representation in the OPM of all these features of our model. For example, to model the execution of one dataflow, called as a subdataflow in another dataflow, we use the interesting "accounts" feature provided by the OPM.

In this paper we assume familiarity with the OPM [1]. We will, however, give a set-theoretical formal definition of the OPM, adapted from the original set-theoretical formalization. We will use this definition to specify our NRC-to-OPM mapping formally.

This paper is organized as follows. In Section 2, we recall the basics of the NRC dataflow model. In Section 3, we give our formal definition of the OPM. In

J. Freire, D. Koop, and L. Moreau (Eds.): IPAW 2008, LNCS 5272, pp. 3–16, 2008.

Section 4, we describe the mapping from the NRC model to the OPM. We also show how an OPM description of an NRC dataflow execution can be augmented with information to track the provenance of a subvalue occurring in the final result of this execution.

2   The NRC Dataflow Model

In this section we present aspects of the NRC dataflow model that are relevant to workflow provenance information. For a more detailed description of the NRC dataflow model and repository we refer to the paper [2].

2.1   Specification of Dataflows in NRC

Consider the following computation, based on a real proteomics protocol [4]: "Given a set of raw data produced by a mass spectrometer in a proteomics experiment, and all its associated parameters, generate a list of proteins possibly identified in this experiment". We can express this computation in the following NRC dataflows:

dataflow $identify(data: \text{TMSdata}, p: \textbf{Parameters}): ProteinCandidateList$ is
    let $list :=$ for x in $data$ return
                    $\langle id: x.id, spectra: extract(x.file)\rangle$
    in $validation(search_1(list, p), search_2(list, p), search_3(list, p))$

dataflow $search(data: \text{TMSextracted}, p: \textbf{Parameters}): \text{AAlist}$ is
    for x in $data$ return
        $\langle id: x.id, aalist:$ for y in $x.spectra$ return $dbSearch(y, p)\rangle$

Each dataflow states its signature, i.e., the types for its input parameters and for its result. Dataflow $identify$ expects one parameter of type **Parameters** and one of type TMSdata. Type **Parameters** is a *base type*. Values of base types, called *base values*, are considered to be "atomic" to the operations in the dataflow. In our example, a value of type **Parameters** is an XML document conforming to a specific DTD. Type TMSdata is a *complex type*. Complex values are constructed using record and set constructions from base values, conforming to their type. For example, type TMSdata equals $\{\langle id: \textbf{Number}, file: \textbf{RawFile}\rangle\}$, that is, a set of records with first component labeled id, and second component labeled $file$. We use value $tmsInput$ of this type, illustrated in Fig. 1, as first input parameter to dataflow $identify$.

Both dataflows are composed of NRC expressions and *service calls*. NRC is a simple functional programming language [3], built around the basic operations on sets and records, with for-loops, if-then-else and let-statements as the only programming constructs. Service calls model all other actions in the dataflows. These can be calls to external services, such as NCBI BLAST or MASCOT search, but also calls to library functions provided by the underlying system,

$$tmsInput =
\begin{array}{|c|c|}
\hline
id & file \\
\hline
1 & \texttt{rawVial10} \\
2 & \texttt{rawVial11} \\
\vdots & \vdots \\
55 & \texttt{rawVial64} \\
\hline
\end{array}$$

$tmsOutput =$

protID	prob	evidence		
		peptide	score	spectrum
Protein$_1$	99	pep$_1$	9	spectrum$_{\text{vial}10,5}$
		pep$_2$	7	spectrum$_{\text{vial}23,2}$
		$\vdots$	$\vdots$	$\vdots$
		peptide	score	spectrum
Protein$_2$	96	pep$_8$	9	spectrum$_{\text{vial}57,3}$
		pep$_1$	8	spectrum$_{\text{vial}10,5}$
		$\vdots$	$\vdots$	$\vdots$
$\vdots$	$\vdots$		$\vdots$	

Fig. 1. Complex values of types, respectively, TMSdata and ProteinCandidateList

such as addition for numbers or concatenation for strings. Moreover, one dataflow can appear as a service call in another dataflow, thus becoming its *subdataflow*. Each service must be supplied with a signature describing the types of its input parameters and its result. In our example, dataflow *identify* uses the services

> $extract(raw : \textbf{RawFile}) : \{\textbf{TMSfile}\}$
> $validation(p_1 : \text{AAlist}, p_2 : \text{AAlist}, p_3 : \text{AAlist}) : \text{ProteinCandidateList}$

and also the services $search_1$, $search_2$, and $search_3$, all three with the same signature $(list : \text{TMSextracted}, p : \textbf{Parameters}) : \text{AAlist}$.

Before we can execute a dataflow, we not only need to provide values for its parameters, but we also need to provide meaning to called services by assigning them to actual services. In our example, in dataflow *identify*, we bind *extract* and *validation* to external applications `extract` and `validate`, and we bind services $search_1$, $search_2$, and $search_3$ to dataflow *search*. The latter becomes thus a subdataflow of *identify*. As *search* also contains a service call, namely, *dbSearch*, we now need to provide binding for that service for each call to *search* in *identify*: to external service `mascot` in the first, to external service `sequest` in the second, and to external service `xtandem` in the third. (These three external services stand for three database search engines frequently used in identification of mass spectra in proteomics research.) We sum up all these service call bindings in a data structure which we call a *binding tree*, shown in Fig. 2.

Suppose now that we have executed dataflow *identify* with value *tmsInput* for parameter *data* and file `PXML` for parameter p. Suppose that value *tmsOutput* has been returned (see Fig. 1).

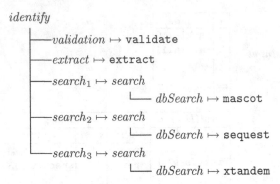

Fig. 2. Binding tree for dataflow *identify*

2.2   Past Executions of Dataflows

In order to keep a record of an execution of dataflow *identify*, it is not sufficient to store the input values, the result, and the binding tree for services. Indeed, the transient nature of the proteomics databases used by the search engines implies that also intermediate results must be stored. Since all NRC expressions are deterministic, only information about intermediate values of external services must be effectively stored. We naturally represent this information as a number of triples of the form (s, σ, v), where s is an occurrence of a service call in the dataflow, σ its *value assignment*, i.e., assignment of input values to parameters, and v the value produced by the service call.

For example, for the execution of dataflow *identify* from Sect. 2.1, we would store the service-call triples shown in Fig. 3.

There, *tmsExtracted*, $tmsRes_1$, $tmsRes_2$ and $tmsRes_3$ represent complex values produced in the corresponding step of the computation. As a matter of fact, a complete record of the entire past execution can be automatically derived from such triples, as we have shown elsewhere [2].

Caveat. The complete record of a past execution of some workflow (applied to certain input), leading to a final result, is commonly called the **workflow provenance** *of that result. In this paper, we refer to such a record as a* **run**.

In our model, a run is basically a set of triples like those for the service calls, except that now we have a triple for each occurrence of each subexpression in the dataflow. Note that, in particular, the final result value is also contained in the run, namely, in the triple for the entire top-level expression of the dataflow. Figure 4 shows a few examples of such additional triples that would be part of our example run of dataflow *identify*.

Of course, when a service call has been executed that was bound to a sub-dataflow, we necessarily also have a run of that subdataflow for the given values of its parameters. In our example, the three service-call triples for $search_1$, $search_2$ and $search_3$, will need to be linked to corresponding runs of the dataflow *search*.

service	assignment	value
extract	$data = tmsInput$ $p = \text{PXML}$ $x = \langle id : 1, file : \text{rawVial10} \rangle$ $raw = \text{rawVial10}$	$\text{spectrum}_{\text{vial10},1}$ ⋮ $\text{spectrum}_{\text{vial10},5}$
extract	$data = tmsInput$ $p = \text{PXML}$ $x = \langle id : 2, file : \text{rawVial11} \rangle$ $raw = \text{rawVial11}$	$\text{spectrum}_{\text{vial11},1}$ $\text{spectrum}_{\text{vial11},2}$ $\text{spectrum}_{\text{vial11},3}$
⋮	⋮	⋮
extract	$data = tmsInput$ $p = \text{PXML}$ $x = \langle id : 55, file : \text{rawVial64} \rangle$ $raw = \text{rawVial64}$	$\text{spectrum}_{\text{vial64},1}$ ⋮ $\text{spectrum}_{\text{vial64},13}$
$search_1$	$data = tmsInput$ $p = \text{PXML}$ $list = tmsExtracted$	$tmsRes_1$
$search_2$	$data = tmsInput$ $p = \text{PXML}$ $list = tmsExtracted$	$tmsRes_2$
$search_3$	$data = tmsInput$ $p = \text{PXML}$ $list = tmsExtracted$	$tmsRes_3$
validation	$data = tmsInput$ $p = \text{PXML}$ $list = tmsExtracted$ $p_1 = tmsRes_1$ $p_2 = tmsRes_2$ $p_3 = tmsRes_3$	$tmsOutput$

Fig. 3. Service-call triples from our example run

2.3   NRC Dataflow Repository Model

To summarize, if we want to have a complete record of an execution of a dataflow, we need to store the value assignment for its parameters, the binding tree for its services, all service-call triples of the run, and links to the runs of its sub-dataflows.

All this information, for different dataflows and executions, can be stored in a global dataflow repository. A conceptual schema illustrating the different entities that play a role in such a repository, and their relationships, is given in Fig. 5. There, mapping *internalcall* links runs of dataflows to the runs of its subdataflows. Given the identifier of a run of a dataflow, and a service-call triple from that run with the service bound to a subdataflow, the mapping will indicate the run identifier of the corresponding subdataflow run.

A very important integrity constraint is that the repository is *closed* by *internalcall*, i.e., if the repository contains a run of some dataflow, then it also

subexpression	assignment	value
let	$data = tmsInput$ $p = \text{PXML}$	$tmsOutput$
for	$data = tmsInput$ $p = \text{PXML}$	$tmsExtracted$
$\langle id, spectra \rangle$	$data = tmsInput$ $p = \text{PXML}$ $x = \langle id : 2, file : \texttt{rawVial11} \rangle$	id $spectra$ 2 $\texttt{spectrum}_{\text{vial11,1}}$ $\texttt{spectrum}_{\text{vial11,2}}$ $\texttt{spectrum}_{\text{vial11,3}}$

Fig. 4. Some run triples from our example run

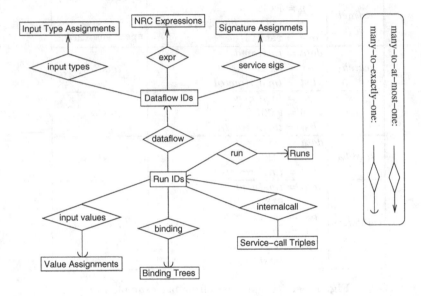

Fig. 5. E/R diagram of the NRC dataflow repository model

contains, for all its service-call triples, the corresponding runs of its subdataflows. Again, for a more detailed description of the repository and its constraints we refer to the paper [2].

3   Formal Definition of OPM Graphs

In this section we present a set-theoretic definition of the Open Provenance Model, adapted from the original timeless causality graph data model [1]. The main difference is in the treatment of account memberships, which we consider to be labels of nodes and edges, and as such we define the account-membership function *accountOf* to be part of an OPM graph. In our opion this is a cleaner formalisation; the original formalisation of accounts in OPM [1] seems flawed.

We also define an alternate as a set of accounts, rather then merely a pair of accounts. We believe this added generality can be useful in practice.

As we need only artifact nodes and process nodes to represent an NRC run in the OPM, we leave out agent nodes and their associated edges from the definitions.

All primitive sets are assumed to be pairwise disjoint. The set $OPMGraph$, as defined below, is the set of all possible OPM graphs.

$$
\begin{aligned}
ProcessId &: \text{primitive set containing all process nodes} \\
ArtifactId &: \text{primitive set containing all artifact nodes} \\
Role &: \text{primitive set containing all roles} \\
Account &: \text{primitive set containing all accounts} \\
Used &\overset{def}{=} ProcessId \times Role \times ArtifactId \\
WasGeneratedBy &\overset{def}{=} ArtifactId \times Role \times ProcessId \\
WasTriggeredBy &\overset{def}{=} ProcessId \times ProcessId \\
WasDerivedFrom &\overset{def}{=} ArtifactId \times ArtifactId \\
Alternate &\overset{def}{=} \mathbb{P}(Account)
\end{aligned}
$$

$$
\begin{aligned}
OPMGraph \overset{def}{=} \{ &\langle A, P, U, G, T, D, AL, accountOf \rangle \mid A \subset ArtifactId, \\
&P \subseteq ProcessId,\ U \subseteq P \times Role \times A,\ G \subseteq A \times Role \times P, \\
&T \subseteq P \times P,\ D \subseteq A \times A,\ AL \subseteq Alternate, \\
&accountOf : (A \cup P \cup U \cup G \cup T \cup D) \to \mathbb{P}(Account) \}
\end{aligned}
$$

Before we reformulate relevant aspects of the OPM according to the adapted definition, we introduce the following convenient notations for any given OPM graph $g = \langle A, P, U, G, T, D, AL, accountOf \rangle$:

$$
\begin{aligned}
A^g &\overset{def}{=} A & U^g &\overset{def}{=} U \\
P^g &\overset{def}{=} P & G^g &\overset{def}{=} G \\
Nodes^g &\overset{def}{=} A \cup P & T^g &\overset{def}{=} T \\
AL^g &\overset{def}{=} AL & D^g &\overset{def}{=} D \\
accountOf^g &\overset{def}{=} accountOf & Edges^g &\overset{def}{=} U \cup G \cup T \cup D \\
Elements^g &\overset{def}{=} Nodes^g \cup Edges^g
\end{aligned}
$$

Apart from $Nodes^g$, $Edges^g$ and $Elements^g$, the above notations may seem superfluous, but they will prove convenient when referring to several OPM graphs at the same time. Observe also that a $g \in OPMGraph$ is completely determined by $Elements^g$, AL^g, and $accountOf^g$. We will make use of this observation when defining new OPM graphs.

Edges and Equality of Edges. Note that any edge $e \in Edges^g$, for an OPM graph g, either belongs to

$$Used \cup WasGeneratedBy$$

and is then of the form $e = \langle x_1, r, x_2 \rangle$ with r some role, or belongs to

$$WasTriggeredBy \cup WasDerivedFrom$$

and is then of the form $e = \langle x_1, x_2 \rangle$. In both cases we introduce the notation $Src(e)$ to denote the source node of e, i.e., x_1, and $Dest(e)$ to denote the destination node of e, i.e., x_2. We also say that x_1 and x_2 are *incident* to e, and denote this by $isIncident(x_i, e)$ for $i = 1, 2$. Note that two causality edges are considered to be equal simply if they are equal in the mathematical sense, i.e., they are the same tuple.

Effective Account Membership. For a given OPM graph g, we define the function

$$effectiveAccountOf^g : Elements^g \to \mathbb{P}(Account)$$

as follows:

-   If $x \in Nodes^g$, then

$$effectiveAccountOf^g(x) = accountOf^g(x) \cup$$

$$\bigcup \{accountOf^g(e) \mid e \in Edges^g \text{ and } isIncident(x, e)\} .$$

-   If $e \in Edges^g$, then we simply put $effectiveAccountOf^g(e) = accountOf^g(e)$.
    (This latter definition may seem superfluous but will prove convenient in the definition of account views.)

The Union of Two OPM Graphs. Let g_1 and g_2 be two OPM graphs. We define the *union* of g_1 and g_2, denoted by $g_1 \sqcup g_2$, as follows:

$$Elements^{g_1 \sqcup g_2} \stackrel{def}{=} Elements^{g_1} \cup Elements^{g_2} ,$$

$$AL^{g_1 \sqcup g_2} \stackrel{def}{=} AL^{g_1} \cup AL^{g_2} ,$$

and $accountOf^{g_1 \sqcup g_2}$ is the point-wise union of $accountOf^{g_1}$ and $accountOf^{g_2}$.

Account Views. For a given OPM graph g and an account α, we now formally define the *account view* of g according to α, denoted by $view(g, \alpha)$, as follows:

-   $Elements^{view(g,\alpha)} \stackrel{def}{=} \{x \in Elements^g \mid \alpha \in effectiveAccountOf^g(x)\}$;
-   $accountOf^{view(g,\alpha)}$ is the restriction of $accountOf^g$ to $Elements^{view(g,\alpha)}$;
-   $AL^{view(g,\alpha)} \stackrel{def}{=} \{alt \cap ActAcc \mid alt \in AL^g\}$, where $ActAcc$ stands for the set of accounts that actually appear in the image (range) of $accountOf^{view(g,\alpha)}$.

Note that $view(g, \alpha)$ is again an OPM graph.

Legal Account Views. Before we formally define legal account views of an OPM graph, we point out that we can associate to any given OPM graph g a classical directed graph $DG(g) = (V(g), E(g))$ with set of vertices $V(g)$ equal to $Nodes^g$ and set of directed edges $E(g)$ equal to $\{(Src(e), Dest(e)) \mid e \in Edges^g\}$. Accordingly, we call g *acyclic* precisely when $DG(g)$ is.

Now for an OPM graph g and an account $\alpha \in Account$, the account view $view(g, \alpha)$ is considered to be *legal* when it is acyclic, and there do not exist two different edges in $G^{view(g,\alpha)}$ with the same source node, i.e.

$$\forall e_1, e_2 \in G^{view(g,\alpha)} : Src(e_1) = Src(e_2) \Rightarrow e_1 = e_2 .$$

Legal OPM Graph. An OPM graph is *legal* when all its account views are legal.

Alternate. For an OPM graph g and *alt* $\in AL^g$, we call *alt* an *alternate* in g, and we call each $\alpha \in alt$ an *alternative* in *alt*.

Legal Alternate. For an OPM graph g and an alternate *alt* $\in AL^g$, we call *alt* *legal* for g if

$$\bigcap_{\alpha \in alt} Nodes^{view(g,\alpha)} \neq \emptyset .$$

4   Mapping NRC Dataflow Runs to OPM Graphs

Recall that a run of an NRC dataflow is modeled as a table

$$R(subexpression, assignment, value)$$

holding triples of the form (e, σ, v), where e is an occurrence of a subexpression of the dataflow, σ the value assignment, and v the produced complex value. An important property of a run is that the pair (*subexpression*, *assignment*) is a key for the table R.

We now define an OPM graph g representing the information stored in R. To do so we first specify all nodes of g, then all the edges, and finally, the account membership function *accountOf* and set *Alternate*. The graph g will be a legal OPM graph. We introduce extra labels for the nodes of the graph g, such that the information contained in g will be sufficient to reconstruct R on the basis of its structure, and node and edge labels alone.

Process Nodes. First we specify the set P^g of all process nodes of g. As each triple in R actually describes one step of the computation, we need at least one process node for each triple. For most triples it is indeed sufficient to construct one process node. We can construct a unique ID for each node simply by using its corresponding triple as an ID:

$$P^g \stackrel{def}{=} \{[t] \mid t \in R\} .$$

We label each process node $[t]$, for $t = (e, \sigma, v)$, by e's top-level NRC operator (or service call).

The only exception are for-loops. In order to model the different parallel executions of the body of a for-loop (namely, one execution for each element of the set over which the for-loop operates), we split each process node $[t]$ as above, when e is a for-loop, into two process nodes $[dispatch, t]$ and $[collect, t]$.

So formally we redefine P^g as follows:

$$P^g \stackrel{def}{=} \{[t] \mid t = (e, \sigma, v) \in R \text{ and } e \text{ is not a for-loop}\}$$
$$\cup \bigcup \{\{[dispatch, t], [collect, t]\} \mid t = (e, \sigma, v) \in R \text{ and } e \text{ is a for-loop}\} .$$

Artifact Nodes. Next we construct the set A^g of all artifact nodes of g. As each triple in R contains the complex value produced by the corresponding step, we need one artifact node for each triple. We can again construct a unique ID for each node by using its corresponding triple as a part of its ID: for each triple $t = (e, \sigma, v)$ we have an artifact node with ID $[val, t]$; we label this node with the value v.

Moreover, each triple contains the value assignment, under which the corresponding step is performed. This value assignment is another artifact in our run. Thus, for each value assignment we create an artifact node, and we can use the value assignment itself as its ID.

We conclude that:

$$A^g \stackrel{def}{=} \{[val, t] \mid t \in R\} \ \cup \ \{[\sigma] \mid \exists e, v \colon (e, \sigma, v) \in R\} \ .$$

Edges. We now define the "was generated by" and "used" edges that play a role for a given process node $[t]$ with $t = (e, \sigma, v)$. Since for-loops and let-statements have a body that involves a local variable, these operators involve the extension of their value assignment with a new value for the local variable, and we must treat them separately.

So first assume e is not a for-loop or a let-statement. The general idea is that v is produced from the value, or values, that resulted from the constituent subexpressions of e. For example, if e is a record construction $\langle a\colon e_1, b\colon e_2 \rangle$, then v equals $\langle a\colon v_1, b\colon v_2 \rangle$ where v_1 (resp. v_2) is the result of ... e_1 (resp. e_2) under the same value assignment σ. We thus generate the edges shown in Fig. 6. Note the role **val** for the edge from v to e, and the role **env** (short for environment) for the edge from e to σ. (Indeed, σ provides the "environment" for the evaluation of e.) Note also the roles a and b that connect e to v_1 and v_2, which are in turn connected to e_1 and e_2 by edges with the role **val**. Clearly, e_1 and e_2 may have constituent subexpressions of their own, so the generation of edges continues

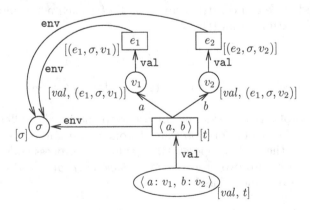

Fig. 6. OPM subgraph for a record construction operation

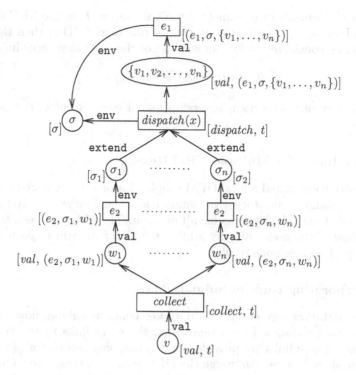

Fig. 7. OPM subgraph for a for-loop

from there. The generation of edges for other operators, except for-loops and let-statements, is analogous.

Now assume e is a for-loop of the form for x in e_1 return e_2. We recall from the semantics of NRC [2] the semantic rule for such an expression:

$$\frac{\sigma \models e_1 \Rightarrow \{v_1, \ldots, v_n\} \qquad \forall i \in \{1, \ldots, n\} : \sigma_i = extend(\sigma, x = v_i) \models e_2 \Rightarrow w_i}{\sigma \models \text{for } x \text{ in } e_1 \text{ return } e_2 \Rightarrow v = \{w_1, \ldots, w_n\}}$$

We then have the edges as shown in Fig. 7. Note the role **extend** for the edges from $dispatch(x)$ to the artifact nodes σ_1 through σ_n (the different value assignments for e_2). Again, e_1 and e_2 may have constituent subexpressions of their own, so the generation of edges continues from there. The construction of edges for a let-statement is analogous.

Since an NRC dataflow is basically a functional computation, each artifact is either used or generated by a step of the computation. Hence the set D^g of all "was derived from" edges is empty. Likewise, processes are only connected through artifacts that they either use or generate, so the set T^g of all "was triggered by" edges is also empty.

Accounts and Alternate. Finally we need to define account membership for all nodes and edges of the graph g. We believe that it is sufficient to assign a unique account for all elements of g, namely the ID of the run R in the NRC dataflow repository. Indeed, if g is a representation of run R with ID r, then the whole graph g can be considered to be "an account of the execution according to r":

$$\forall x \in Elements^g : accountOf^g(x) = \{r\} .$$

As there is only one account membership for all elements of g, the set AL is empty.

4.1 Amendment for Multiple NRC Runs

So far we have constructed a legal OPM graph g for one run R stored with ID r. As an NRC dataflow repository will contain many runs, we would like to be able to generate distinct OPM graphs for all of them. Therefore, we need to amend the identifiers of the nodes of g by adding the ID of the run to each of them: each node $[n]$ becomes node $[r, n]$.

4.2 Incorporating Runs of Subdataflows

In an NRC dataflow repository, if a dataflow contains subdataflows, then for each run of that dataflow in the repository, there are links to the runs of its subdataflows. These links are provided by the mapping *internalcall* (Sect. 2.3). In Fig. 8 we show how we can merge the OPM graphs of these runs. On the left we see the OPM subgraph of some run R, representing a service call f, with two actual parameter values v_1 and v_2 (produced by subexpressions e_1 and e_2), and the result value v of the call.

If f is bound to a subdataflow, the repository will contain the corresponding run R' of that subdataflow. In the OPM graph for R', we have a value assignment σ' containing the values v_1 and v_2 of the formal parameters x_1 and x_2. We also find back in this graph the artifact node representing the final result value of the subdataflow; this value obviously equals v. The nodes on the left (from the OPM graph for R) have account r, i.e., the ID of run R. The nodes on the right

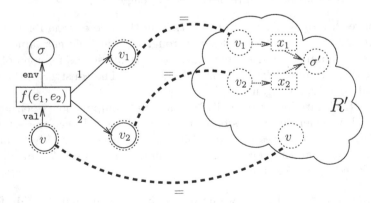

Fig. 8. Merging the OPM graph of a run R with the OPM graph of its linked run R'

(from the OPM graph for R') have account r', i.e., the ID of run R'. It is clear that account r' serves as a refinement of account r.

In order to obtain one combined OPM graph, we identify the left-hand nodes v_1, v_2 and v with the corresponding right-hand nodes v_1, v_2 and v. These identifications are shown by the thick dashed lines in the figure. Then we take the union of the two OPM graphs for R and R' (with nodes just identified taken only once). The identified nodes have both accounts r and r'.

Finally, we add the composite account (r, r') to all elements of the combined graph, and we add the set $\{r, (r, r')\}$ to AL. The account view of the graph according to (r, r') provides more details than the view according to r.

Now if the dataflow corresponding to R' contains a subdataflow of it's own, we can combine the OPM graph for R and R' with the OPM graph for the run linked by *internalcall* to that subdataflow, say a run R'' with ID r''. Then alternate $\{r, (r, r')\}$ can be extended to $\{r, (r, r'), (r, r', r'')\}$. The process can be repeated further, for each subdataflow found in the binding tree for R. The set AL of the final OPM graph will thus contain one alternate resulting from this process, its size bound by the depth of the binding tree for R.

4.3   Adding Subvalue Provenance to an OPM Graph

A major feature of the NRC dataflow model is that it can model the manipulation of complex data structures built as nested record and set constructions.

In the OPM mapping presented so far, the complex nesting structure of values is not yet represented. We can add this information by adding to the OPM graph a new account containing the structure information. Doing so also enables us to add "was derived from" edges in the OPM graph that track the *provenance* (or origin) of subvalues of complex data values.

Formal inference rules exist for the automatic generation of these provenance edges [2]. Since these inference rules are specific to the NRC dataflow model,

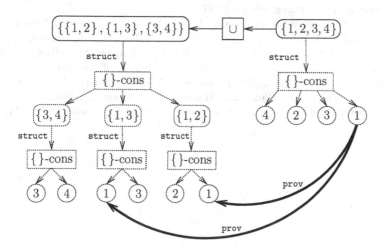

Fig. 9. Structure of complex values and provenance edges

and rely on the specific semantics of NRC operators on complex objects, they are not mere refinements of the OPM inference rules [1] for "was derived from" edges.

This is illustrated in Figure 9. The main account on top shows the OPM subgraph for a big union operation applied to the nested set $\{\{1,2\},\{1,3\},\{3,4\}\}$. The nested value structure account is shown in dotted lines. The thick lines show two subvalue provenance edges that can be be inferred by our provenance rules. The lines show that the value 1 produced by the big union operator comes from two different sets belonging to the nested set operated upon by the big union.

5   Conclusion

We believe the NRC dataflow model is important, because it provides fully formal definitions of the complex interactions that occur in a repository consisting of many different executions of many different, interrelated dataflows involving complex data structures.

In order to validate the NRC dataflow model, we found it important to map it to the Open Provenance Model, as that model has been especially designed as an exchange framework for workflow provenance information. Our mapping also serves as a validation of the OPM.

It is interesting to explore further how the OPM mapping we have presented here can also serve as a basis for visualization of NRC dataflow runs. Of course we also have to design an implementation.

References

1. Moreau, L., Freire, J., Futrelle, J., McGrath, R., Myers, J., Paulson, P.: The open provenance model. Technical Report 14979, University of Southampton, School of Electronics and Computer Science (2007)
2. Hidders, J., Kwasnikowska, N., Sroka, J., Tyszkiewicz, J., Van den Bussche, J.: A formal model of dataflow repositories. In: Cohen-Boulakia, S., Tannen, V. (eds.) DILS 2007. LNCS (LNBI), vol. 4544, pp. 105–121. Springer, Heidelberg (2007)
3. Buneman, P., Naqvi, S., Tannen, V., Wong, L.: Principles of programming with complex objects and collection types. Theoretical Computer Science 149, 3–48 (1995)
4. Dumont, D., Noben, J., Raus, J., Stinissen, P., Robben, J.: Proteomic analysis of cerebrospinal fluid from multiple sclerosis patients. Proteomics 4(7), 2117–2124 (2004)

Data Lineage Model for Taverna Workflows with Lightweight Annotation Requirements

Paolo Missier[1], Khalid Belhajjame[1], Jun Zhao[2],
Marco Roos[3], and Carole Goble[1]

[1] School of Computer Science, University of Manchester, UK
{pmissier,khalidb,carole}@cs.man.ac.uk
[2] Department of Zoology, University of Oxford, UK
jun.zhao@zoo.ox.ac.uk
[3] Faculty of Science, University of Amsterdam, NL
roos@science.uva.nl

Abstract. The provenance, or *lineage*, of a workflow data product can be reconstructed by keeping a complete trace of workflow execution. This lineage information, however, is likely to be both imprecise, because of the black-box nature of the services that compose the workflow, and noisy, because of the many trivial data transformations that obscure the intended purpose of the workflow. In this paper we argue that these shortcomings can be alleviated by introducing a small set of optional lightweight annotations to the workflow, in a principled way. We begin by presenting a baseline, annotation-free lineage model for the Taverna workflow system, and then show how the proposed annotations improve the results of fundamental lineage queries.

1 Introduction

Workflow technology is being increasingly adopted in e-science as a way to model and automate the enactment of scientific experiments, and more generally, to specify complex sequences of distributed data manipulation operations (retrieval, transformation and analysis) in a flexible and declarative way. The workflow shown in Fig. 1, for example, is designed to look for a list of diseases in response to a single input query consisting of clinical terms, for instance "Alzheimers disease +protein".[1] The output list is obtained by (i) retrieving relevant abstracts based on the query (Lucene-query), (ii) extracting protein names from the abstracts by means of a dedicated a named entity recognizer (NERecognize), and (iii) linking the proteins to disease names through the OMIM[2] disease database (extract_diseases-from-OMIM).

The final workflow output is certainly the most important product of this modelling and execution effort. If we intend to use it as a piece of scientific

---

[1] The example is due to one of the authors (Marco Roos). Full details are available through the myExperiment workflow repository and sharing facility: http://www. myexperiment.org.

[2] OMIM: http://www.ncbi.nlm.nih.gov/sites/entrez?db=omim.

J. Freire, D. Koop, and L. Moreau (Eds.): IPAW 2008, LNCS 5272, pp. 17–30, 2008.

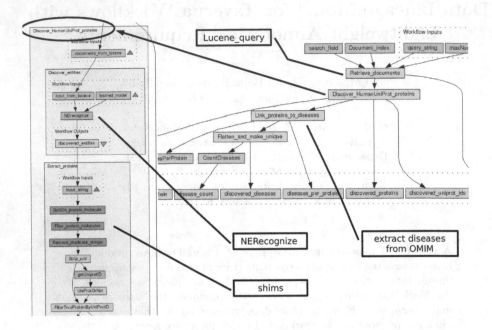

Fig. 1. Example Taverna dataflow, folded view (right) and unfolded selected sub-workflow (left)

evidence upon which more results will be built, however, we need to provide some proof of its soundness, i.e., by showing that such a sophisticated chain of data transformations and manipulations does indeed produce the intended result. This is not just a matter of debugging, but rather, of supporting the claim to reliability of the results. For instance, it is crucial for the experimenter to understand how proteins names were identified in the NErecognize step, if these automatically produced results are to be trusted. This suggests the need to use intermediate workflow data products as a way to explain the final result and to support any claim of reliability on it, for the benefit of both the experimenters and their community at large.

We use this example to motivate the need for collecting and analysing data provenance, broadly defined as "information that helps determine the derivation history of a data product, starting from its original sources" [16]. In this paper we focus specifically on *data lineage* obtained from one or more executions of a dataflow through multiple processors, i.e., the graph of data dependencies that account for an output value produced during the course of a dataflow execution. By *dataflow* we mean a workflow consisting only of data links, i.e., with no explicit control links between the nodes.

Issues of data lineage have been studied extensively in the context of data management in databases, originally with respect to the derivation of data elements as a result of relational operations [5], and, more recently, with the goal of helping resolve uncertainties in data, i.e., in the Trio project [3]. Despite this body of research, two main issues make the problem of capturing and presenting lineage information in the workflow context a challenging one. Firstly, a common assumption that underpins the work just mentioned is that the available data manipulation operations are limited to a well-founded set, i.e., a collection of relational algebra operators or data replication primitives. In contrast, workflows invariably include the invocation of services described only in terms of their access interfaces. It has been observed [4, 19] that the black-box nature of these services limits the specificity of the lineage information that can be captured by observing a workflow execution.

Secondly, a workflow is a detailed specification of a process that can be described, in abstract, as a set of interdependent data transformations, such as those listed in our early example. Nevertheless, the model of the data that the process operates upon is *remains latent* and is never made explicit as part of the process specification. If it were to be spelled out, a conceptual model designed from the top down to represent the data managed by our example workflow would probably include a handful of entities, such as "clinical term", "article abstract", "disease term", "protein name", along with logical associations amongst them. While one execution of the actual workflow does generate values that can potentially be used to populate the data model, doing so automatically is difficult, because the interesting values are part of a much larger collection of relatively irrelevant data products, that exist solely to enable the integration among the main data transformation steps.

While the adapters that produce these values should ideally disappear, along with their products, from a user-oriented view of the overall process, doing so requires an explicit abstraction mechanism. As an example, Figure 1 describes one possible mechanism for abstraction, available in Taverna [11, 15], Kepler [17], and other workflow systems, namely the nesting of workflows structures. The workflow shown in the right part of the figure actually consists of a number of sub-workflows, each rendered here as an atomic processor, while the left part shows the unfolding of one of those sub-workflows. At this finer level of detail we can see that only few of the processors, for instance NERecognize, actually perform interesting data transformations, while the remaining processors, known as *shims* [10], are adapters that must be there in order to perform mundane tasks. Note however that nesting is entirely optional and is perceived by many users more as a mechanism for reuse, rather than for abstraction. The lineage model described in this paper does not rely, and indeed does not benefit from, structural nesting, although this type of abstraction, central for example to the *Zoom* approach [4] mentioned below, is being considered as part of ongoing work.

Based on these observations, we argue that a desirable goal for a data lineage management system is to provide a variable level of specificity and abstraction, based on the specification provided by both workflow designers and consumers of the lineage information. The question is then, what is a reasonable trade-off between the effort required from users in order to create a complete specification, and the benefit in terms of precision of lineage information. We could, in an extreme case, transform all the black-boxes into "white-box" services by adding extensive annotations to describe their semantics. This would probably impose an unacceptable additional burden to the workflow designers, however. On the other hand, data lineage that is based exclusively on the workflow structure, i.e., its graph topology and the interface-level information about the services, is complete but it may contain too much irrelevant information that obscures the intended purpose of the workflow.

This paper explores the middle ground between these two extremes, focusing on a small set of lightweight annotations that add value to basic lineage information while requiring with little additional human effort. The analysis presented here underpins the current data lineage model for the Taverna workflow system, which will be used as a reference model throughout the paper. Specifically, our goal is twofold. Firstly, we define a simple, baseline model for annotation-free data lineage, and show that it is sufficient to answer lineage queries. Secondly, we introduce a small set of annotation types, in addition to user-defined constraints on the queries, and show their added value in terms of increased specificity and focus of the resulting lineage query results. The specific goals of the annotations are as follows:

- increase specificity, by explicitly declaring dependencies of output variables from input variables for each processor, including the fine-grained transformation of list-valued variables;
- increase focus, by letting users specify data lineage queries that select only relevant aspects of the workflow, for instance the few important processors alluded to earlier;
- enable space/time trade-offs when storing and querying lineage data. As pointed out recently [8], the size of provenance may easily outgrow the size of the data being computed by a workflow. We note that, if we instead knew that some of the workflow processors are stateless, then we would have the option to compute their transformation at lineage query time, as needed, rather than recording it explicitly. This is beneficial when the workflow includes many simple shims that add little computational cost to the query.

The lineage model described in this paper, including support for the proposed lightweight annotations, is currently being implemented as part of the Taverna provenance architecture.

2   Baseline Model for Capturing and Querying Data Lineage

In this section we lay the foundation for the lineage model, assuming that no information besides the workflow structure is available to collect and present data lineage. For this purpose we characterise a Taverna dataflow as a DAG where the nodes denote processors[3]. Throughout our discussion we are going to

---

[3] A full account of the formal syntax and structural semantics for the Taverna language can be found in [20].

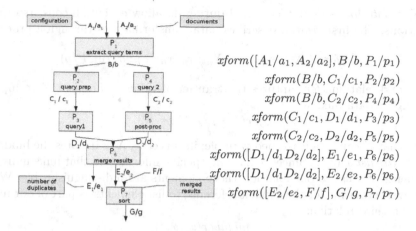

Fig. 2. Example dataflow with execution annotations, and corresponding lineage graph specification

use the generic workflow pattern of Figure 2, which, in particular, captures the topology of the real-life workflow presented earlier.

Each processor may have multiple inputs and outputs, each denoted by a distinct variable name. We write

$$\langle P, [X_1 : \tau_1 \ldots X_n : \tau_n], [Y_1 : \sigma_1 \ldots Y_m : \sigma_m]\rangle \tag{1}$$

to denote a node in the graph, representing a processor P with input variables $X_1 \ldots X_n$ and output variables $Y_1 \ldots Y_m$. Variables have a type, denoted here by τ_i and σ_j, which is either a simple type (**string**, **boolean**, etc.), or is a list of values, denoted $l(\tau)$. Lists can be nested, i.e., τ is either a simple type or itself a list. Nodes in the dataflow graph are connected through directed data links $\langle P_1, X_i, P_2, Y_j \rangle$ that transfer a value bound to output X_i from an upstream processor P_1 to the value bound to input Y_j of a downstream processor P_2. Note that this simple type system does not prevent the use of bulk or multimedia types, as strings can be used to hold references, typically URIs, to external objects.

The data lineage information captured during dataflow execution reflects the available knowledge regarding the dependencies of output variables from input variables, for each node of the form (1). Unless processors are annotated with specific dependency information, as discussed later in Section 3, we must assume that every output depends on every input. We write this as a set of functional dependencies, as follows:

$$X_1 \ldots X_n \rightarrow Y_1, \qquad X_1 \ldots X_n \rightarrow Y_2, \quad \ldots$$

When recording lineage information, we consider an instantiation of the dataflow graph consisting of:

- a binding of each variable X of type τ to a value x, denoted $X : \tau/x$, and
- a binding of each processor P to a process instance p, denoted P/p.

The *data lineage graph* captured during dataflow execution consists of three relations. The first, *xform*, describes data transformations through a processor:

$$xform([X_1 : \tau_1/x_1 \ldots X_n : \tau_n/x_n], Y_j : \sigma_j/y_j, P/p) \qquad (2)$$

A second relation *xfer* captures the transfer of value x of output X to input Y through a data link:

$$xfer(X : \tau/x, Y : \tau/x)] \qquad (3)$$

Note that X can be a list-typed variable; in this case, X/x denotes the binding of the *entire list* x to X. Since we have no specific information that links individual elements of a list to one another, those elements are indistinguisheable. We do, however, provision for the explicit reference to list elements as part of our model, using a third relation:

$$member(x_i, x, i) \qquad (4)$$

to indicate that value x_i appears at position i within list x. This can be used whenever there are good reasons to refer to individual members of a list, as described later (Section 2.1). In addition, we will use relation $isInput(X/x)$ and $isOutput(X/x)$ to denote the fact that X/x is an input (resp., output) to the entire workflow.

With this notation, the right side of Figure 2 shows the lineage graph for one sample execution of the dataflow on the left. Note that, without loss of generality, we have left the *xfer* relation implicit, assuming for simplicity that the variable names on corresponding outputs and inputs on a data link are the same (e.g. the output B of P_1 and the corresponding input into P_2). With this assumption, all *xfer* tuples are of the trivial form $xfer(X/x, X/x)$.

2.1   Explicit and Implicit Collections

As mentioned, each of the values in the example above may be a list. In fact, Taverna processors that manage lists can be described by the following patterns, where some of the variables have an explicit list type $l(\tau)$:

$$\langle P, [X : \tau], [Y : l(\sigma)] \rangle \qquad (5)$$
$$\langle P, [X : l(\tau)], [Y : \sigma] \rangle \qquad (6)$$
$$\langle P, [X : l(\tau)], [Y : l(\sigma)] \rangle \qquad (7)$$

These patterns reflect paradigmatic transformations: (5) is representative of a search service, where X is a search string and Y the result collection; (6) captures, among other things, aggregation functions, while (7) is appropriate for a filter (i.e., a selection of elements) or a sort operation on a list.

Characteristically, however, Taverna also allows for variables with simple type to be bound to a list. For instance, $X :$ `string` can be assigned a list of strings, $x = [x_1 \ldots x_k]$. Taverna manages this type cardinality mismatch by adding an implicit iterator on x, so that P is executed separately on each value x_i. Correspondingly, the output values y_i are collected into a list, which is then assigned

```
// compute a derivation tree
dt(V, DT) :- isInput(V), !,
             DT = derive(V, [], in).
dt(V, DT) :- xform(Vset, V, P),
             dt1(Vset, DTlist),
             DT = derive(V, DTlist, P).
dt1([], []).
dt1([V1 | Vrest], [DT | DTrest]) :-
             dt(V1, DT1),
             dt1(Vrest, DTrest).
```

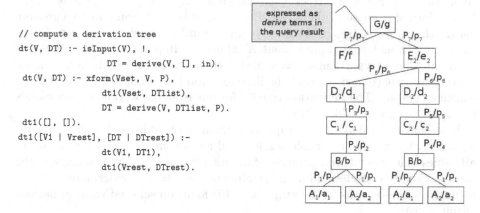

Fig. 3. A basic derivation tree computation in Prolog, and its output on a specific goal

to an output Y (also originally of type **string**). This case, where each element y_i depends only on the corresponding input x_i, is captured by the following tuples:

$$xform(X/x_i, Y/y_i, P/p_i), \quad member(x_i, x, i), \quad member(y_i, y, i), \quad i : 1 \ldots k$$

Thus, in Taverna this is equivalent to having n instances $p_1 \ldots p_n$ of a processor P, each responsible for one element x_i of x. This is a case where we can provide a more granular lineage data than would otherwise be possible in general.

2.2 Data Lineage Queries

The lineage graph collected during one execution supports a variety of queries, including some of those proposed as part of the First Provenance Challenge[4]. While a complete account of the query formulation is beyond the scope of this paper, it should be clear that useful queries involve traversing the lineage graph, a task that can be accomplished in a variety of ways. Consider for example the basic lineage query: "find all derivation paths for an output value (or any intermediate value), back to the input values that contribute to it during a specific execution". Its answer consists of the tree of paths, rooted at G/g, shown in Figure 3 (right). The graph-traversal algorithm that computes the tree is presented as a Prolog program on the left in the same figure[5]. Informally, the program computes a *derivation tree* for an input bound variable, say Y/y. The root of the tree is labelled Y/y. If Y/y is derived through a transformation of the form (2), i.e.:

$$xform([X_1/x_1 \ldots X_n/x_n], Y/y, P)$$

---

[4] http://twiki.gridprovenance.org/bin/view/Challenge/FirstProvenanceChallenge.
[5] Here we use Prolog for conciseness; however, this does not reflect the actual implementation for this and additional lineage queries supported by the lineage graph.

then node Y/y has n sub-trees, each rooted at X_i/x_i, expressing the fact that Y/y is derived from *all* of the X_i/x_i. Each such sub-tree is computed recursively using other *xform* tuples in the lineage graph, until we reach the input variables (i.e., the X/x such that tuple *isInput*(X/x) exists). In practice, a derivation tree is an unfolding of a particular traversal strategy on a lineage graph, in this case a bottom-up visit (remember that the lineage graph is a DAG, just as the original workflow graph). The derivation tree DT for our example workflow corresponds to the Prolog goal: dt(G/g,DT).

In a similar fashion we can support a number of additional queries; for instance, by traversing the graph in a forward fashion we can compute the set of all values that depend on a given set of inputs. Perhaps more interestingly, in the next section we consider adding constraints to these basic queries, namely to (i) focus on selected paths in the graph, and (ii) focus on selected transformations within a path.

3 Lightweight Annotations for Improving Lineage Data

The derivation graph described at the end of the last section exhibits some of the problems that we had stated informally at the beginning, namely:

- when services are black boxes, then we have to assume that all outputs depend on all inputs, for instance B/b depends on both A_1/a_1 and A_2/a_2; furthermore, each element in each output data collection depends on each element in all of the input collections;
- lineage derivation trees include shim services, i.e., P_2 and P_5, that add little to the understanding of the actual, latent data model that is implicit in the dataflow. In addition, the lineage data for all the shim transformations must be stored explicitly and dealt with in the same way as more critical workflow steps, although these processors usually perform mundane tasks. This additional space consumption does not translate into useful information to users.

To address these problems in a principled way, we propose a simple classification of annotation types that serve different purposes, namely *precision*, *focus*, and *optimisation* and are provided at different stages during experimentation, i.e., *workflow design*, *workflow execution*, and *lineage query*.

Precision: These annotations aim at improving the granularity and understandability of lineage derivation trees. We consider workflow design time annotations that:

1. Make a distinction among input variables according to their role during processing, i.e., between data that is used as part of the processor's computation, for instance a search string, and configuration parameters, e.g. the number of results returned by the search.
2. Refine the functional dependencies between inputs and outputs for individual processors. With reference to (2) on page 21, if the designer knew

that, say, Y_1 only depended on $X_1 \ldots X_k$, with $k < n$, then the first dependency would become $X_1 \ldots X_k \rightarrow Y_1$, resulting in more specific *xform* tuples, i.e., $xform([X_1/x_1 \ldots X_k/x_k], Y_1/y_1, P/p)$.

3. Assert a 1-1 mapping between elements of an input list and corresponding elements of an output list. When this additional information is available, as in the case of cardinality mismatch described earlier, lineage can be tracked at the level of individuals within a collection.

4. Explain the nature of aggregation functions. This amounts to stating, for example, that E_1/e_1 is the result of applying a function dupCount to the input lists D_1/d_1 and D_2/d_2. Note that this is a special case of a more general semantic annotation for processors, an interesting topic of current research.

We also consider additional information that may become available during workflow execution, and that is contributed either by the workflow enactor, or by the services themselves. This includes, for example:

- the information that implicit iterators have been applied to input collections to resolve some cardinality mismatch, and
- an explicit *permutation map* provided by a processor that performs a sort operation. Such a map allows the lineage service to refine the derivation graph by applying the inverse mapping to individual elements in the input/output lists.

Focus: These annotations provide users with a means to select relevant lineage information at lineage query time, namely by (i) suppressing some of the paths in the graph, for example those involving D_1 but not D_2, and (ii) specifying a subset of the processors of interest. In the example, it would be natural to focus on the query processors P_3 and P_4, while ignoring P_2 and P_5, for instance[6].

Optimisation: These annotations, specified at workflow design time, indicate that some of the processors are *stateless*, i.e., they are guaranteed to produce the same result when executed multiple times on the same input (unlike, for example, a query to a database that may change in time). When this is the case, the lineage service has a choice between materialising the lineage tuples corresponding to those processors' transformations, or re-executing the services themselves when the lineage tree is computed (under the realistic assumption that its implementation is available to the lineage service at query time). This is potentially beneficial for a number of small shim services that are computationally inexpensive.

Table 1 presents a summary of these annotation types (the specific annotation syntax is not relevant for the purposes of this paper). Although the framework in the table is fairly general and applicable to a variety of annotation options and workflow systems, we focus here on a few cases that are of direct interest to Taverna workflows. The last column of the table provides examples of the effect of each of these annotations.

---

[6] Taverna does include a basic feature that can be used as starting point, namely for tagging processors as "boring" so that they are excluded from the visual rendering.

Table 1. Summary of dataflow annotations types and their effect on lineage

Annotation type	Phase	Effect
Precision:		
refinement of functional dependencies between inputs and outputs	design	$xform([X_1/x_1 \ldots X_k/x_n], Y/y, P)$ replaced by: $xform([X_1/x_1 \ldots X_k/x_k], Y/y, P)$, $k < n$
parameter vs. data input distinction	design	$xform([A_1/a_1 A_2/a_2], B/b, P_1)$ replaced by: $xform(A_2/a_2, B/b, P_1)$ A_1/a_1 reported as separate context information instead
1-1 mapping on lists	design	$xform(B/b, C_2/c_2, P_2)$ replaced by: $xform(B/b_i, C_2/c_{2i}, P_2)$ for each i
type of aggregation functions	design	$xform([D_1/d_1 D_2/d_2], E_1/e_1, P_6)$ reported along with dupCount during query answering
implicit iteration over non-collection variables	execution	equivalent to 1-1 mapping, only implicit
explicit permutation maps for list sorting processors	execution	a permutation map containing: $\Pi(E/e_{2i}) = G/g_j$ justifies the derivation: derive$(G/g_j, [E/e_{2i}], \_)$
Focusing:		
path suppression	lineage query	disregard some of the lineage paths, e.g. $P_6 \rightarrow P_5 \rightarrow P_4 \rightarrow P_1$ not considered
processor selection	lineage query	only report on derivation through, say, P_3 and P_4.
Optimisation:		
stateful vs. stateless processors	design	If P_1, P_2, P_5, P_6, P_7 are stateless, then the only required materialisation of lineage is now: $xform(B/b, C_2/c_2, P_4)$ $xform(C_1/c_1, D_1/d_1, P_3)$

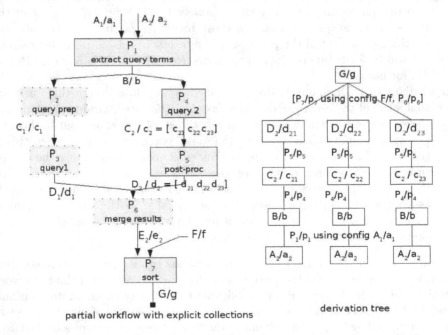

partial workflow with explicit collections

derivation tree

Fig. 4. Derivation tree obtained using additional annotations and user selection

Let us now consider their effect on our example workflow graph, specifically:

(1) A_1, F are configuration parameters
(2) P_5 provides a 1-1 mapping between input and output lists
(3)   Any path containing P_3 should be excluded from the derivation tree
(4)   Processor P_6 should be excluded from the derivation tree.

Figure 4 (left) shows a new version of the workflow graph, where the nodes that will be ignored according to (3) and (4) are shown in dotted lines. The derivation tree from G/g back to the input A_2/a_2 is shown on the right. Note that F/f and A_1/a_1 are now mentioned only as part of the processor configuration, and that G/g now appears to be derived from D_2 through a two-nodes path involving P_7 as well as P_6. Also, since we know that P_5 maps each element c_{2i} of its input list C_2 to the corresponding element d_{2i} in D_2, we can make the derivation from c_{2i} to d_{2i} explicit in the tree, resulting in the three branches shown in the figure (this fine granularity does not extend to B/b nor to G/g).

4   Discussion and Conclusions

The work presented in this paper stems from the hypothesis that a model for describing the lineage of workflow data products can improve in precision by adding a few, selected annotations to the workflow, both at design time and at execution time. Furthermore, a simple selection of relevant processors by the users when formulating lineage queries can be effective in presenting lineage data at a suitable level of abstraction. We have proposed a simple classification of lightweight annotation types and have demonstrated their impact by comparing a derivation tree obtained as the results of a typical lineage query, with the equivalent derivation tree obtained using a baseline, annotation-free data model for lineage in Taverna.

A number of well-known workflow management systems for scientific applications have been proposed which collect and exploit provenance information for different purposes. These include enabling partial, "smart" re-runs of previously executed workflows (Vistrails [7] and Kepler [1]), debugging workflows (Kepler [1]), and comparing experiment results (Karma [18])). Hidders *et al.* [9] describe a formal functional model of *dataflow repositories* using the Nested Relational Calculus [6] (NRC). The authors show how, for dataflows described using NRC, the lineage of any occurrence of a value that appears during the course of a workflow execution can be specified using the same formalism, in terms of a path across the dataflow model. This interesting reference model could, potentially, be adopted as a starting point for our own model of data lineage. This would entail showing that Taverna workflows can be expressed using the NRC-based dataflow model, so that the provenance inference rules defined therein can be applied. Indeed it would be interesting, but beyond the scope of our current work, to investigate how the model can be used to describe the types of annotations that we propose in this paper, and their effect on the computation of lineage paths.

It is important to emphasize that, in this paper, we are not claiming any specific element of novelty with respect to the provenance models and management systems just mentioned: tracking "raw" data lineage on a dataflow graph is, after all, a well-defined problem with known solutions, as the cited research shows. Here we focus instead on the problem of specifying and exploiting additional properties that may be known about the graph components, to bring added value to provenance users. In this respect, the *Zoom* system [4] is perhaps the closest in spirit to our efforts. Zoom lets users define personalised "composite modules" that are abstractions of the concrete workflow, by way of grouping some of its components and then selecting the relevant groups. The system then provides answers to provenance queries that are consistent with the abstraction level chosen by the user. The type of abstraction envisioned by the authors is similar to that described in Figure 1, i.e., by modular composition.

In a similar vein, Miles *et al.* [12] propose a mechanism for narrowing the cope of provenance queries. In this proposal, *p-assertions* are used when provenance is collected as a way to document the relationships among items of provenance metadata. In particular, one can use p-assertions to specify causal, functional, or other kinds of relationships. Provenance queries are then scoped based on these p-assertions types.

In contrast to both these approaches, we envision a distinction among processors that is independent of any grouping/nesting feature, and is instead based on the contribution of individual processors to the "latent data model", as we have described it earlier.

The only work to our knowledge that considers the use of semantic annotations for analysing workflow provenance is by Miles *et al.* [13], where a method for validating scientific experiments is proposed. The validation entails reasoning over collected data provenance and the semantic descriptions of the services that compose the workflows. Its goal is to ensure that the experiments are enacted correctly, and that the results they deliver are of value. Using this method, for example, a user is able to check that the intermediate data delivered by a given service operation belongs the appropriate domain, e.g. "protein". It is worthwhile noting that this proposal assumes that semantic annotations of web services are always available. However, practice shows that semantics annotations are a scarce commodity in general [2]. With this in mind, the solution we propose is incremental in that semantics annotations are not mandatory inputs for analysing the lineage of workflow results. Rather, they are used for improving the analysis and facilitating the interpretation of the lineage results.

Finally, although the systems mentioned above define a variety of different data lineage models, a consensus has recently begun to emerge among different groups towards a common model for workflow provenance. The result is an initial version of the Open Provenance Model (OPM) [14], a conceptual model that describes provenance using a pre-defined set of entities and relationships. This is an interesting reference schema onto which we hope to map our lineage model (a detailed comparison between the lineage model proposed in this paper and the OPM is beyond the scope of this paper).

The work presented in the paper is still in progress and forms the core of the provenance architecture for Taverna, with support for a range of queries, both on a single workflow execution and across executions. A mapping of the Taverna lineage model to the Open Provenance Model is also in the plans.

References

1. Altintas, I., Barney, O., Jaeger-Frank, E.: Provenance collection support in the Kepler scientific workflow system. In: Moreau, L., Foster, I. (eds.) IPAW 2006. LNCS, vol. 4145, pp. 118–132. Springer, Heidelberg (2006)
2. Belhajjame, K., Embury, S.M., Paton, N.W., Stevens, R., Goble, C.A.: Automatic annotation of web services based on workflow definitions. ACM Transactions on the Web 2(2) (2008)
3. Benjelloun, O., Das Sarma, A., Halevy, A.Y., Theobald, M., Widom, J.: Databases with uncertainty and lineage. VLDB J. 17(2), 243–264 (2008)
4. Biton, O., Cohen-Boulakia, S., Davidson, S., Hara, C.: Querying and managing provenance through user views in scientific workflows. In: Procs. Internation. Conference on Data Engineering (ICDE) (April 2008)
5. Buneman, P., Khanna, S., Chiew Tan, W.: Why and where: A characterization of data provenance. In: Van den Bussche, J., Vianu, V. (eds.) ICDT 2001. LNCS, vol. 1973, pp. 316–330. Springer, Heidelberg (2000)
6. Buneman, P., Naqvi, S.A., Tannen, V., Wong, L.: Principles of programming with complex objects and collection types. Theor. Comput. Sci. 149(1), 3–48 (1995)
7. Callahan, S.P., Freire, J., Santos, E., Scheidegger, C.E., Silva, C.T., Vo, H.T.: VisTrails: visualization meets data management. In: SIGMOD Conference, pp. 745–747 (2006)
8. Chapman, A., Jagadish, H.V.: Issues in building practical provenance systems. IEEE Data Eng. Bull. 30(4), 38–43 (2007)
9. Hidders, J., Kwasnikowska, N., Sroka, J., Tyszkiewicz, J., Van den Bussche, J.: A formal model of dataflow repositories. In: Cohen-Boulakia, S., Tannen, V. (eds.) DILS 2007. LNCS (LNBI), vol. 4544, pp. 105–121. Springer, Heidelberg (2007)
10. Hull, D.: Description and classification of shims in ^{my}grid. Technical report, University of Manchester (2006)
11. Hull, D., Wolstencroft, K., Stevens, R., Goble, C., Pocock, M.R., Li, P., Oinn, T.: Taverna: a tool for building and running workflows of services. Nucleic Acids Research 34, W729–W732 (2006)
12. Miles, S.: Electronically querying for the provenance of entities. In: Moreau, L., Foster, I. (eds.) IPAW 2006. LNCS, vol. 4145, pp. 184–192. Springer, Heidelberg (2006)
13. Miles, S., Wong, S.C., Fang, W., Groth, P.T., Zauner, K.-P., Moreau, L.: Provenance-based validation of e-science experiments. J. Web Sem. 5(1), 28–38 (2007)
14. Moreau, L., Freire, J., Futrelle, J., McGrath, R., Myers, J., Paulson, P.: The Open Provenance Model (December 2007)
15. Oinn, T., Addis, M., Ferris, J., Marvin, D., Senger, M., Greenwood, M., Carver, T., Glover, K., Pocock, M.R., Wipat, A., Li, P.: Taverna: A tool for the composition and enactment of bioinformatics workflows. Bioinformatics, 3045–3054 (November 2004)

16. Simmhan, Y.L., Plale, B., Gannon, D.: A survey of data provenance in e-science. SIGMOD Rec. 34(3), 31–36 (2005)
17. Simmhan, Y.L., Plale, B., Gannon, D.: A framework for collecting provenance in data-centric scientific workflows. In: ICWS, pp. 427–436 (2006)
18. Simmhan, Y.L., Plale, B., Gannon, D.: Towards a quality model for effective data selection in collaboratories. In: Proceedings of 22nd International Conference on Data Engineering Workshops, pp. 72–72 (2006)
19. Chiew Tan, W.: Provenance in databases: Past, current, and future. IEEE Data Eng. Bull. 30(4), 3–12 (2007)
20. Turi, D., Missier, P., De Roure, D., Goble, C., Oinn, T.: Taverna Workflows: Syntax and Semantics. In: Proceedings of the 3rd e-Science conference, Bangalore, India (December 2007)

A Logic Programming Approach to Scientific Workflow Provenance Querying

Yong Zhao[1] and Shiyong Lu[2]

[1] Microsoft Corporation, Redmond WA
[2] Department of Computer Science, Wayne State University, Detroit, MI
yozha@microsoft.com, shiyong@wayne.edu

Abstract. Scientific workflows have become increasingly important for enabling and accelerating many scientific discoveries. More and more scientists and researchers rely on workflow systems to integrate and structure various local and remote heterogeneous data and services to perform *in silico* experiments. In order to support understanding, validation, and reproduction of scientific results, provenance querying and management has become a critical component in scientific workflows. In this paper, we propose a logic programming approach to scientific workflow provenance querying and management with the following contributions: i) We identify a set of characteristics that are desirable for a scientific workflow provenance query language; ii) Based on these requirements, we propose FLOQ, a Frame Logic based query language for scientific workflow provenance, iii) We demonstrate that our previous relational database based provenance model, *virtual data schema*, can be easily mapped to the FLOQ model; and iv) We show by examples that FLOQ is expressive enough to formulate common provenance queries, including all the provenance challenge queries proposed in the provenance challenge series.

1 Introduction

Today, scientists use scientific workflows to integrate and structure various local and remote data and service resources to perform various *in silico* experiments to produce scientific discoveries. As a result, scientific workflows have become the de facto cyberinfrastructure upper-ware for e-Science and an efficient environment for computational thinking. A scientific workflow is a formal specification of a scientific process, which represents, streamlines, and automates the steps from dataset selection and integration, computation and analysis, to final data product presentation and visualization. A Scientific Workflow Management System (SWFMS) supports the specification, execution, re-run, and monitoring of scientific processes.

Provenance management is essential for scientific workflows to support scientific discovery, reproducibility, result interpretation, and problem diagnosis, while such a facility is usually not necessary for business workflows. Provenance metadata captures the derivation history of a data product, including the original data sources, intermediate data products, and the steps that were applied to produce the data product. Although

J. Freire, D. Koop, and L. Moreau (Eds.): IPAW 2008, LNCS 5272, pp. 31–44, 2008.

several provenance storage and query models have been developed [17], they are based on query languages designed for other data types such as relational data, XML data, and Semantic Web data that are not specifically tailored for scientific workflow provenance. While it is still not clear which provenance model is most suitable for workflow provenance query representation and processing, we argue that a provenance query language should have the following characteristics: 1) The language should be based on a well-defined semantics to represent computations and their relationships, since only with such formalism in place can we define the model and syntax for representing and querying workflow provenance; 2) The language should be able to define, query, and manipulate data structures, as they are essential components of workflows, on which various operations are performed; 3) The language should have declarative syntax for both computation and data declarations and flexible query specification; 4) The language should allow the composition of simple queries into more complex queries; and 5) The language ideally should support inference capability for provenance reasoning.

Based on these requirements, we propose FLOQ, a Logic Programming (LP) approach to workflow provenance representation and querying. We use Frame Logic (F-Logic) [16] as the theoretic foundation and base our implementation on the FLORA-2 system [24]. Moreover, we demonstrate that our previous relational database based provenance model, *virtual data schema*, can be easily mapped to the FLOQ model, and show by various examples that FLOQ is expressive enough to formulate common provenance queries, including all the provenance challenge queries proposed in the provenance challenge series. Although the logical programming approach is not innovative by itself, we hope the introduction of such an approach into the provenance community can stimulate and motivate further research in this direction.

The rest of the paper is organized as follows. In Section 2, we briefly introduce Frame Logic and the FLORA-2 system. In Section 3, we show the mapping of the virtual data schema into Frame Logic, and the logic programming representation of the sample fMRI workflow used in the provenance challenges. In Section 4, we demonstrate the expressiveness of FLOQ. In Section 5, we discuss implementation issues and related work. Finally in Section 6, we draw our conclusions.

2   Frame Logic and FLORA-2

Frame Logic [16] provides a logical foundation for frame-based and object-oriented languages. It has a model-theoretic semantics and a sound and complete resolution-based proof theory. F-Logic combines clean and declarative semantics; expressiveness and powerful reasoning provided by deductive database languages; and rich data modeling supported by its object-oriented data model.

FLORA-2 [24] is both a LP language and an application development environment. The language is a dialect of F-Logic with meta-programming extensions (HiLog) [5] and logical updates (Transaction Logic). The implementation is built on top of the powerful and efficient XSB inference engine [20]. In the following, we introduce some of the key features of F-Logic using the FLORA-2 language syntax:

Objects and properties

    Zhao[name -> "Yong Zhao", affiliation -> UChicago]

    Lu[name-> "Shiyong Lu", affiliation->WSU, teaches(2008)->{CS300, CS501}]

    UChicago[name-> "University of Chicago", location-> Chicago]

    WSU[name-> "Wayne State University", location-> Detroit]

The above examples define two people and their associated universities, where **->** denotes the value of an attribute or method.

Class or Schema information

A set of similar objects can be categorized into a class. An F-Logic program can also represent the structural information of a class and its type signature (types for method arguments and results):

    Employee[name *=> string, affiliation *=> University]

    Faculty[teaches(integer) => Course]

    University[name => string, location => City]

The above examples define a few classes and their type signature, where **=>** denotes the type of the method of the class, and ***** indicates that the signature can be inherited by a subclass. The original F-Logic distinguishes between functional (**=>**) and set-valued (**=>>**) methods. In FLORA-2 it has been simplified to use only set-valued methods. However, cardinality constraints can be specified, and {0:1}=> corresponds to functional methods.

Class hierarchy and Class membership

    Faculty::Employee

    Zhao:Employee

    Lu:Faculty

    UChicago:University

    WSU:University

In the example, *S::C* denotes that *S* is a subclass of *C*, where *O:C* denotes that O is a member (instance) of C. Since the signature of *Employee* is defined as inheritable, *Faculty* gets the signature from it.

Predicates

In F-Logic, predicate symbols can be used in the same way as in predicate logic (e.g. Datalog). Information expressed by predicates can usually also be represented by frames. For instance, the *location* method of *UChicago* can be alternatively represented as:

    Location(UChicago, Chicago)

Rules

Rules define the deduction process. Based upon a given set of facts, rules provide the mechanism to derive new information. Rules encode generic information of the form

    rule head :- rule body

The rule body specifies the precondition that must be met, and the rule head indicates the conclusion.

To give an example:

?U[offers(?Y)->?C] :- ?F[teaches(?Y)->?C],?F[affiliation->?U]

The above rule specifies that if a faculty member *F* teaches a course *C* in year *Y*, and the person is affiliated with university *U*, then we conclude that the university *U* offers the course *C* in year *Y*.

Other features
FLORA-2 programs also allow the combined and nested specification of the above definitions, for instance

Lu[affiliation->WSU[name-> "Wayne State University"]]:Faculty

It also supports path expression where

Lu.affiliation

would result in *WSU* - the value of the method *affiliation* of object *Lu*.

It also provides aggregation functions such as average, count, max, etc. For instance:

?N = count{?C[?Y]|Lu[teaches(?Y)->?C]}

The above query counts the number of courses taught by *Lu* in each year. Due to space limitation, we do not give the details of these features; interested readers can look at the online tutorials for FLORA-2.

3 Mapping Virtual Data Schema to F-Logic

To illustrate how existing provenance systems can be mapped to and thus benefit from our logical programming approach, consider the following example. The virtual data schema [26] models the various relationships that exist among *datasets*, *procedures*, *calls* (to procedures), *workflows* (a set of dependent calls) and *invocations* (the actual executions of a specific call on physical resources), as well as *annotations* that associate metadata to these entities. Originally, the virtual data schema was interpreted as a relational model and implemented as a relational database in the virtual data system (VDS) [11]. Recently, we have evolved the schema and adapted it to the XML Dataset Typing and Mapping (XDTM) model [18], and integrated it into the Swift system [25].

XDTM is a data integration model that allows logical dataset structures to be specified separately from their physical representations so that workflows can be defined to operate on cleanly typed datasets. It also provides a mapping mechanism to map these logical structures to physical data access when a workflow is scheduled to execute. Swift is a fast, scalable and reliable Grid workflow system that builds on the XDTM data model, it combines a simple scripting language called *SwiftScript* for concise, higher level specification of complex parallel computations, and an efficient workflow engine to schedule the execution of large number of parallel tasks onto distributed and parallel computing resources. In Swift, all datasets are typed, and procedures take typed inputs and produce typed outputs, workflows are represented as a set of procedure calls, and their execution sequence is determined by data dependencies.

In this section, we show that the virtual data schema can also be modeled from an object oriented (OO) perspective, and it can be represented naturally in F-Logic. We

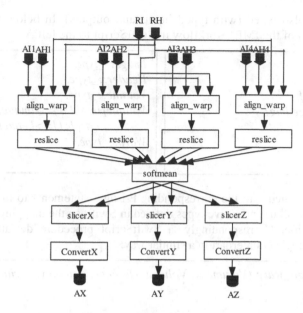

Fig. 1. Sample fMRI workflow

also demonstrate via the sample fMRI workflow that our SwiftScript declarations of the workflow can be easily mapped into F-Logic programs. The details about the sample fMRI workflow can be found at the first provenance challenge site [10]. We only give a brief description of the workflow here for clarity purpose. The workflow graph is shown in Fig. 1. The inputs to the workflow are a set of *brain images* (Anatomy Image 1 to 4) and a single *reference brain image* (Reference Image), and each image has an associated header file with metadata in it. The outputs are a set of atlas graphics. The stages of the workflow are as follows:

Firstly, each brain image is spatially aligned to the reference image using *align_warp*. The output is a warp parameter set defining the spatial transformation to be performed (Warp 1 to 4). For each warp parameter set, the actual transformation of the image is done by *reslice*, which creates a resliced image of the original brain image with the configuration defined in the warp parameter set. All the resliced images are then averaged using *softmean*, producing a 3D atlas image. The averaged image is sliced along a plane in x, y, and z dimensions respectively into a 2D atlas using a program called *slicer*, and lastly, each 2D atlas is converted into a graphical atlas image using (the ImageMagick utility) *convert*.

In the OO model, datasets all have *types*, and each dataset is an instance of its type. Procedures have typed signature, and each call is an instance of a procedure. To distinguish these different types, we firstly define a few base classes in F-Logic:

> _type
> _procedure
> _anno

And use them to represent dataset types, procedures and annotations. SwiftScript is a typed workflow language. Datasets are typed (with structural definition), and procedures are also typed (with typed inputs and outputs). In below we show the type declarations of the fMRI workflow in SwiftScript to the left.

```
type Image;
type Header;
type Volume {
        Image img;
        Header hdr;
}
type Warp;
```

```
Image::_type.
Header::_type.
Volume::_type.
Volume[img{1:1}=>image,
        hdr{1:1}=>header].
Warp::_type.
```

This gets translated into the corresponding F-Logic statements to the right. Since FLORA-2 covers all the primitive types defined in Swift, so the mapping is a straight-forward translation. Correspondingly, a SwiftScript procedure declaration can be mapped to its F-logic counterpart in a similar way:

```
(Warp w) align_warp (Volume iv, Volume reference, string overwrite)
{
}
```

```
align_warp::_procedure.
align_warp[iv=>Volume, reference=>Volume,overwrite=>string, w=>Warp].
align_warp[input->{iv,reference}, output->w].
```

The script defines a procedure called *align_warp*, which takes two volumes, a string option, and produces a warp file (which defines the spatial transformation to be performed to warp an input image to the reference image). The F-Logic program defines it as a class with its type signature. In order to capture whether a dataset is an input or output, we define two extra behavior attributes *input* and *output* for the procedure. The other procedures in the sample workflow can be mapped in the same manner and we omit the details. Now the call to a procedure (shown below in the top) is translated into F-Logic (shown in the bottom) as follows:

```
Volume vol1;
Volume std_vol;
Warp w1 = align_warp (vol1, std_vol, 'y');
```

```
vol1:Volume.
std_vol:Volume.
w1:Warp.
align_warp_uuid[iv->vol1, reference->std_vol,overwrite->'y', w->w1].
align_warp_uuid:align_warp.
```

Firstly the dataset declarations are translated into instance specifications of their corresponding types, and they are then supplied as values to the procedure inputs and outputs. Note that we generate a unique id for the call, and the call is an instance of its procedure class. For the calls, we want to find out which datasets are the inputs and outputs, instead of the parameter names. This can be achieved as follows:

?I[in->?D] :- ?I[?P->?D],?C[in->?P],?I:?C.
?I[out->?D] :- ?I[?P->?D],?C[out->?P],?I:?C.

What the rules specify is that: if an instance *I* of a class *C* has a parameter *P*, and *P* is an input (or output) parameter with value *D*, then *D* is an input (or output) dataset to the instance *I*.

An invocation record captures the execution environment that a call is executed. It typically has information such as the execution host, start time, duration, exit code, memory usage, and stats of the input and output files. We model a record as an F-Logic object, and give an example below:

align_warp_inv_uuid[call->align_warp_uuid,
         host-> "uchost",
         arch-> "ia64",
         start_time-> "2008-02-14T09:55:33"^^_dateTime,
         duration-> "00:29:55"^^_duration ,
         exit_code->0].

For annotations, since we allow the association of metadata to any of the virtual data entities, including dataset types, datasets, procedures, procedure parameters, calls, invocations, the mapping is not as straightforward as the other ones. There are many ways to map an annotation into F-Logic. For instance, each annotation can be modeled as a predicate. But as annotations to an annotation should also be supported so that we can track the provenance of the annotation itself, we need to model the annotation as an object. We define a base class _anno, and each annotation is declared to be an instance of this base class. An annotation object takes the form as follows:

annotation_key [on(object, part, ...)->annotation_value]:_anno.

For instance, if we want to annotate the procedure *align_warp* with *model=nonlinear*, the annotation is specified like this:

model[on(align_warp)-> 'nonlinear']:_anno.

With these simple mappings, we can already pose some interesting queries to the system. For instance, the following query can find all the types defined in the workflow.

Q: *?X::_type.*
A: *?X = Image*
         ?X = Header
         ?X = Volume

         ...

Find all procedures that take Volume as a parameter:

Q: *?X[?Y=>Volume]::_procedure.*
A: *?X=align_warp*
         ?Y=iv

         ?X=align_warp
         ?Y=reference

```
align_warp_1[iv->vol1, reference->std_vol, overwrite->'y', w->w1] : align_warp.
align_warp_2[iv->vol2, reference->std_vol, overwrite->'y', w->w2] : align_warp.
align_warp_3[iv->vol3, reference->std_vol, overwrite->'y', w->w3] : align_warp.
align_warp_4[iv->vol4, reference->std_vol, overwrite->'y', w->w4] : align_warp.

reslice_1[w->w1, ov->svol1] : reslice.
reslice_2[w->w2, ov->svol2] : reslice.
reslice_3[w->w3, ov->svol3] : reslice.
reslice_4[w->w4, ov->svol4] : reslice.

softmean_1[iv->{svol1,svol2,svol3,svol4}, ov->atlas] : softmean.

slicer_1[iv->atlas, dimension->'x', ppm->'atlas_x.ppm'] : slicer.
slicer_2[iv->atlas, dimension->'y', ppm->'atlas_y.ppm'] : slicer.
slicer_3[iv->atlas, dimension->'z', ppm->'atlas_z.ppm'] : slicer.

convert_1[from->'atlas_x.ppm', to->'atlas_x.jpg'] : convert.
convert_2[from->'atlas_y.ppm', to->'atlas_y.jpg'] : convert.
convert_3[from->'atlas_z.ppm', to->'atlas_z.jpg'] : convert.
```

Fig. 2. F-Logic Program for the Sample fMRI Workflow

Find procedure calls that ran on *ia64* processors:

Q: ?[call->?X, arch-> "ia64"].
A: ?X=align_warp_uuid

In Fig. 2 we show the specification of the sample fMRI workflow mapped to F-Logic terms, but omitting the detailed structural information about the datasets and procedures involved.

4   FLOQ Query Examples

In our virtual data query model, three major query dimensions were identified: (1) lineage information obtained by interrogating the patterns of procedure calls, argument values, and dependencies in the workflow graphs that describe the indirect nature of the production of a given data object; (2) prospective and retrospective provenance data, as provided by records of procedure definition, procedure arguments, and runtime invocation recording; and (3) metadata annotations that enrich this application-independent schema with application-specific information. In this section, we show the expressiveness of the FLOQ approach using extensive examples drawn from our single- and multi-dimensional queries and some of the core provenance challenge queries.

Lineage Queries: One of the key capabilities of a provenance system is to query the derivation history (lineage) of a data product, i.e. from which datasets this product is derived and by what procedures, and what datasets can be further derived from this product and by using what kind of procedures. These lineage relationships can be easily represented in F-Logic using the following predicates:

DirectlyDerived(?X, ?Y) :- ?Proc[in->?X, out->?Y],?Proc:_procedure.
Derived(?X,?Y) :- DirectlyDerived(?X,?Y).
Derived(?X,?Y) :- Derived(?X,?Z), Derived(?Z,?Y).

The first predicate specifies that if a procedure *Proc* takes *X* as an input, and produces *Y* as an output, then *Y* is directly derived from *X*. The second predicate defines the transitive closure of the derivation relationship, finding all *Y* that can be directly or indirectly derived from *X*. Now if we want to find what datasets can be derived from the dataset *vol1*, or what datasets are involved to derive the data product *atlas*, we can simply pose the following queries:

Q: Derived(vol1, ?X).
A: ?X=w1, svol1, atlas, atlas_x.ppm, atlas_x.jpg, atlas_y.ppm, ...

Q: Deirved(?Y, atlas).
A: ?Y=svol1, svol2, svol3, svol4, w1, w2, w3, w4, vol1, vol2, ...

Similarly, if we want to track what procedures are used to process a dataset and its derived datasets, we can define:

ConsumedBy(?X, ?P) :- ?P[in->?X], ?P:_procedure.
ConsumedBy(?X, ?P) :- DirectlyDerived(?X, ?Y),ConsumedBy(?Y, ?P).

As we can observe, these logic based derivation rules follow very closely to our natural thinking and are easy to define and understand.

In contrast, a relational database based approach usually requires a more strictly defined schema such that procedures cannot be specified column-wise (they have various parameters), causing lineage queries to use expensive self-joins [23]. Since not all DBMS support recursion, such queries may have to be implemented in stored procedures that involve complex programming. Our XML based approach in VDS still required a pre-defined XML schema to write template-based queries, although the XQuery engine did provide the flexibility to join across multiple schemas and query recursively. We list the XQuery program to find all derived datasets in below for comparison purpose, and it is obvious that the query is less intuitive than the F-Logic counterpart.

```
declare namespace v='http://www.griphyn.org/chimera';
declare function v:lfn_tree($lfn as xs:string) as item()* {
        let $d := //derivation[.//lfn[@file=$lfn][@link='input']]
        return ( $lfn,
            for $out in $d//lfn[@link='output']/@file return v:lfn_tree($out))
};
let $f := v:lfn_tree('vol1');
return distinct-values($f)
```

Virtual Data Relationship Query: Virtual data relationship refers to the bindings between dataset types, procedures, calls, invocations, and the queries focus on the attributes of such entities. The query of "find all the procedures that have an input of type *Volume* and an output of type *Warp*" can be formulated as:

$$?Proc[input->?X, output->?Y]:\_procedure,$$
$$?Proc[?X=>Volume, ?Y=>Warp].$$

Similarly, the query of "find all calls to procedure *align_warp*, and their runtimes, with argument *reference=std_vol* that ran in less than 30 minutes on non-*ia64* processors" can be formulated as:

$$?Inv[call->?C, duration->?d, not arch->"ia64"],$$
$$?d<= "00:30:00"^{\wedge\wedge}\_duration,$$
$$?C[reference->std\_vol]:align\_warp.$$

Annotation Queries: Annotation queries can be used to find any application specific information about various virtual data entities, such as procedure description and data curation, and to discover certain procedures and datasets by their associated metadata. The query of "show the values of all annotation predicates *developerName* of procedures that accept or produce an argument of type *Volume* with predicate *Mode = nonlinear*" is formulated as:

$$developerName[on(?Proc)->?Name],$$
$$?Proc[?=>Volume]::\_procedure,$$
$$Model[on(?Proc)->'nonlinear'].$$

Aggregation Queries: Aggregation queries can perform basic statistical mining over the provenance information, which can be useful for reporting purpose and anomaly detection. For instance, one of the following queries identifies jobs run unusually long, and the other one does a monthly tally of the total jobs run in a year. The query of "find all the align_warp invocations that ran three times longer than the average run time" is formulated as:

$$?X=avg\{?d\backslash?Inv[call->?C, duration->?d], ?C:align\_warp\},$$
$$?Inv[call->?C, duration->?d], ?C:algin\_warp,$$
$$?d > 3* ?X.$$

To list the total number of jobs run in each month of 2007, we use the query:

$$?X=count\{?Inv[?M]\backslash ?Inv[start->?T],$$
$$?T[\_month->?M]@\_basetype, ?T[\_year->2007]@\_basetype\}.$$

Provenance Challenge Queries: Several provenance challenge queries are already discussed in previous sections, including Q1, Q6 (lineage), Q4 (relation), Q5, Q8, and Q9 (annotation). We discuss the rest of the queries below.

Q2: Find the process that led to Atlas X Graphic, excluding everything prior to the averaging of images with softmean.

This query is similar to the lineage queries, here, we are tracing back to a dataset's source. We can follow similar logic to answer this query:

$$ProducedBy(?X, ?P) :- ?P[out->?X], ?P:\_procedure.$$
$$ProducedInBetween(?X, ?Y, ?P1, ?P2) :- ProducedBy(?X, ?P1),$$
$$Derived(?Y, ?X), ConsumedBy(?Y, ?P2).$$

Basically the rule specifies that if a dataset X is the output of procedure $P1$, and X is somehow (directly or indirectly) derived from another dataset Y, which is the input of procedure $P2$, then we stop tracing back. The query can be posed as:

> Q: ProducedInBetween('atlas_x.jpg', ?Y, ?P, softmean).
> A: ?P = convert, slicer, softmean
>   ?Y = altas_x.ppm, atlas, svol1, svol2, svol3, svol4

Q3. Find the Stage 3, 4 and 5 details of the process that led to Atlas X Graphic.

We can track the depth of derivation by slightly modifying the definition of *ProducedBy*, and add the depth information in the rules:

> *ProducedBy(?X, ?P, ?D) :- ?P[out->?X], ?P:_procedure, ?D is 1.*
> *ProducedBy(?X, ?P, ?D) :- DirectlyDerived(?X, ?Y), ProducedBy(?Y, ?P, ?D0), ?D is ?D0 + 1.*

The rules specify that if a dataset X is directly produced by a procedure P, then the depth of derivation is 1; otherwise if X is directly derived from a dataset Y, and Y is produced by P at some depth $D0$, then the depth of derivation for P and X is $D0$ plus 1. Now the query can be posed as:

> Q: ProducedBy('atlas_x.jpg', ?P, ?S), ?S >=3, ?S=<5.
> A: ?S = 3, ?P = softmean
>   ?S = 4, ?P = reslice
>   ?S = 5, ?P = align_warp

When there are multiple paths that can be traced back from a data product, we can define the depth as the longest path to that data product. The rules would be slightly more complex, but still follow the same idea. The rules also require the workflow to be acyclic, which is the case in Swift. Otherwise, we may go into an infinite loop.

Q7. A user has run the workflow twice, in the second instance replacing each procedure (convert) in the final stage with two procedures: ppmtopnm, then pnmtojpeg. Find the differences between the two workflow runs.

Q7 turned out to be quite challenging for most of the teams. There were only one or two teams that could tackle this query. Using FLOQ, we can use the predicate for Q2 to find the answers to this query:

> Q: ProceducedInBetween('atlas_x.jpg', ?Y, ?P, softmean).
> A1:   ?P=convert, slicer, softmean
> A2:   ?P=pnmtojpeg, ppmtopng, slicer, softmean

The solutions to *?P* in the two cases would identify the differences exactly as they are, and also find the different intermediate datasets that have been produced.

Modification Queries: Modification queries allow the ability to couple queries with updates to define new procedures, annotations, and work requests, for instance, changing a procedure argument, replacing a procedure in a workflow, or editing a subgraph of a workflow. It is worth noting that FLORA-2 also supports updating the knowledge base, such as inserting and deleting facts and rules on-the-fly, and the updates can also be conditional, i.e. based on some rules. In our case, we can specify that for each call to *convert*, we insert two consecutive calls *ppmtopnm* and *pnmtojpeg*, and then delete the calls to *convert*, in this way, the workflow is transformed into a new one with similar functionality.

5 Discussions and Related Work

Provenance management has become an important functionality for most scientific workflow management systems [2,8]. The Kepler system implements a *provenance recorder* [1] to record information about a workflow run, including the context, data derivation history, workflow definition, and workflow evolution. The my-Grid/Taverna system [22] uses Semantic Web technologies for representing provenance metadata at four levels: process, data, organization, and knowledge. Two levels of ontologies are used. A domain-independent schema ontology is used to describe the classes of resources and the properties between them that are needed to represent the four levels of provenance. A domain ontology is used to classify various types of resources such as data types, service types, and topic of interest for a particular domain. The VisTrails system [12] supports provenance tracking of workflow evolution in addition to data derivation history. In VisTrails, workflow evolution provenance is represented as a rooted tree, in which each node corresponds to a version of a workflow, and each edge corresponds to an update action that was applied to the parent workflow to create the child workflow. The above provenance systems are tightly coupled with their scientific workflow environments. A couple of stand-alone provenance systems have also been developed, including the PReServ system [13] and the Karma system [21]. PReServ supports the recording of interaction provenance, actor provenance, and input provenance with the Provenance Recording Protocol (PReP), which specifies the messages that actors can asynchronously exchange with the provenance store to support provenance submission.

The recent Open Provenance Model [19] effort tries to identify key relationships in data provenance systems, such as the transitive relationship of derivation, and in the mean time maintains openness about the alternative views that different users may have over the same data production process. Although the actual model and query language implementations are not yet discussed, we think a logic-based approach is natural to explore. Existing provenance systems have chosen to use different technologies for provenance querying, of which relational databases, XML, and RDF are three representative approaches [17]. For relational database based approach, persistence and indexing are the obvious advantages, however, it is difficult to define and integrate different schemas for different entities involved in the provenance space, and the queries for cross-entity joins and transitive relationships are not easy to write and extend. XML/XQuery based approaches also allow to define schemas and provide more flexibility in such definitions (can be semi-structured), yet, they lack the extensibility to define deductive rules, such that different use cases have to be implemented as different query templates. RDF/RDFS based approaches support interoperability and inference, but the triple style assertions make knowledge representation flat, requiring a lot more statements to define class and schema information. RDF/RDFS based approaches also lack the deductive rule engine, and as a matter of fact, many RDF systems choose to use an F-Logic system as its inference engine. OWL and some flavors of Description Logic are also candidates for knowledge representation, however, they focus more on the Class-level (T-Box) relationships, and do not have the expressiveness in instance level knowledge representation, and they also lack the reflective inspection capabilities (query schema, rule definitions themselves) presented in F-Logic. Again, they often engage an F-Logic system as their inference engine too [15].

Previously, F-Logic has been applied to workflow verification [9] and program query [14], they share some similarities to our approach, as all need to represent workflow and program structure to some extent. Our work can be actually extended to provide type checking (for instance, a procedure call needs to supply the right type of datasets to the procedure parameters) that is done programmatically in Swift, and if we choose to put more detailed information about Swift programs into the knowledge base, we can perform verification and program query, and even workflow scheduling within the FLORA2 engine using transaction logic.

While XSB has been shown to be highly efficient, scalability is an issue for large-scale provenance management, as the whole knowledge base may not fit into memory. We plan to address this issue by 1) developing a partitioning scheme for provenance data so that different portions of provenance information are loaded into memory dynamically as needed; 2) investigating database persistence techniques [7] for logic programs where tables can be stored externally in relational databases and loaded on-demand.

6 Conclusions and Future Work

In summary, we have described FLOQ, our Frame Logic based approach to representing and querying the virtual data provenance model, and we have demonstrated that our previously identified provenance problems and challenges can be addressed by this approach. Our Swift workflow definitions can be mapped to F-Logic programs in a straightforward manner, and provenance queries can be written and extended with great expressiveness and flexibility. For future work, we plan to 1) extend the translations of other SwiftScript program declarations to F-Logic and enable type checking and workflow structure querying. We can also apply F-Logic to type inference, so that procedure signatures can be derived instead of explicitly specified, which can further simplify SwiftScript; and 2) generalize the logical programming descriptions and apply them to more general workflow provenance problems, not limiting to the virtual data schema defined in the Swift system.

References

1. Altintas, I., Barney, O., Jaeger-Frank, E.: Provenance collection support in the Kepler Scientific Workflow System. In: Moreau, L., Foster, I. (eds.) IPAW 2006. LNCS, vol. 4145, pp. 118–132. Springer, Heidelberg (2006)
2. Biton, O., Boulakia, S., Davidson, S., Hara, C.: Querying and Managing Provenance through User Views in Scientific Workflows. In: ICDE 2008 (2008)
3. Bose, R., Foster, I., Moreau, L.: Report on the international provenance and annotation workshop (IPAW 2006). SIGMOD Records (September 2006)
4. Buneman, P., Khanna, S., Tan, W.-C.: Why and Where: A Characterization of Data Provenance. In: International Conference on Database Theory (2001)
5. Chen, W., Kifer, M., Warren, D.S.: HiLog: A Foundation for Higher-Order Logic Programming. Journal of Logic Programming 15(3), 187–230 (1993)
6. Clifford, B., Foster, I., Voeckler, J., Wilde, M., Zhao, Y.: Tracking Provenance in a Virtual Data Grid. Journal of Concurrency and Computation, Practice and Experience (2007)
7. Costa, P., Rocha, R., Ferreira, M.: Tabling Logic Programs in a Database. In: Proceedings of the 21st Workshop on (Constraint) Logic Programming, WLP 2007 (2007)

8. Davidson, S., Boulakia, S., Eyal, A., Ludäscher, B., McPhillips, T., Bowers, S., Anand, M., Freire, J.: Provenance in Scientific Workflow Systems. IEEE Data Eng. Bull. 30(4), 44–50 (2007)
9. Davulcu, H., Kifer, M., Ramakrishnan, C.R., Ramakrishnan, I.V.: Logic based modeling and analysis of workflows. In: Proceedings of the Seventeenth ACM SIGACT-SIGMOD-SIGART Symposium on Principles of Database Systems, June 01 - 04. PODS 1998, Seattle, Washington, United States (1998)
10. http://twiki.ipaw.info/bin/view/Challenge/FirstProvenanceChallenge (June 2006)
11. Foster, I., Voeckler, J., Wilde, M., Zhao, Y.: Chimera: A Virtual Data System for Representing, Querying, and Automating Data Derivation. In: 14th Conference on Scientific and Statistical Database Management (2002)
12. Freire, J., Silva, C.T., Callahan, S.P., Santos, E., Scheidegger, C.E., Vo, H.T.: Managing Rapidly-Evolving Scientific Workflows. In: Moreau, L., Foster, I. (eds.) IPAW 2006. LNCS, vol. 4145, pp. 10–18. Springer, Heidelberg (2006)
13. Groth, P., Miles, S., Tan, V., Moreau, L.: Architecture for Provenance Systems. Technical report, University of Southampton (October 2005)
14. Hajiyev, E., Verbaere, M., de Moor, O.: CodeQuest: Scalable Source Code Queries with Datalog. In: Thomas, D. (ed.) ECOOP 2006. LNCS, vol. 4067, pp. 2–27. Springer, Heidelberg (2006)
15. Kattenstroth, H., May, W., Schenk, F.: Combining OWL with F-Logic Rules and Defaults. In: International Workshop on Applications of Logic Programming to the Web, Semantic Web and Semantic Web Services (ALPSWS 2007) (2007)
16. Kifer, M., Lausen, G., Wu, J.: Logical Foundations of Object-Oriented and Frame-Based Languages. Journal of the ACM 42, 741–843 (1995)
17. Moreau, L., et al.: The First Provenance Challenge, Concurrency and Computation, Practice and Experience (2007)
18. Moreau, L., Zhao, Y., Foster, I., Voeckler, J., Wilde, M.: XDTM: XML Dataset Typing and Mapping for Specifying Datasets. In: European Grid Conference (2005)
19. Open Provenance Model (March 2008), http://twiki.ipaw.info/bin/view/OPM
20. Rao, P., Sagonas, K.F., Swift, T., Warren, D.S., Freire, J.: XSB: A System for Efficiently Computing Well-Founded Semantics. In: Fuhrbach, U., Dix, J., Nerode, A. (eds.) LPNMR 1997. LNCS, vol. 1265, pp. 2–17. Springer, Heidelberg (1997)
21. Simmhan, Y., Plale, B., Gannon, D.: A Performance Evaluation of the Karma Provenance Framework for Scientific Workflows. In: Moreau, L., Foster, I. (eds.) IPAW 2006. LNCS, vol. 4145, pp. 222–236. Springer, Heidelberg (2006)
22. Stevens, R., Zhao, J., Goble, C.: Using provenance to manage knowledge of In Silico experiments. Briefings in Bioinformatics 8(3), 183–194 (2007)
23. Terracina, G., Leone, N., Lio, V., Panetta, C.: Experimenting with recursive queries in database and logic programming systems, Theory and Practice of Logic Programming. Cambridge University Press, Cambridge (2007), doi:10.1017/S1471068407003158
24. Yang, G., Kifer, M., Zhao, C.: FLORA-2: A Rule-Based Knowledge Representation and Inference Infrastructure for the Semantic Web. In: Second International Conference on Ontologies, Databases and Applications of Semantics (ODBASE), Catania, Sicily, Italy (November 2003)
25. Zhao, Y., Hategan, M., Clifford, B., Foster, I., Laszewski, G.V., Raicu, I., Stef-Praun, T., Wilde, M.: Swift: Fast, Reliable, Loosely Coupled Parallel Computation. In: IEEE International Workshop on Scientific Workflows (SWF 2007). Collocated with SCC (2007)
26. Zhao, Y., Wilde, M., Foster, I.: Applying the Virtual Data Provenance Model. In: Moreau, L., Foster, I. (eds.) IPAW 2006. LNCS, vol. 4145, pp. 148–161. Springer, Heidelberg (2006)

Recording the Context of Action for Process Documentation

Ian Wootten and Omer Rana

School of Computer Science, Cardiff University, UK

Abstract. In reviewing evidence about real world processes, being aware of the context in which activities within such processes are performed enables us to make more informed judgements. It is necessary to distinguish between the environment in which a process occurs, and the sequence of activities which form part of the description of that process. Each of these types of information is complementary to understanding the other and therefore making associations between them is also important. Our work has been exploring the use of *context* whilst documenting a process and working toward a solution which incorporates the two. We present an approach to automatically relating properties of workflow actors to the documentation of the process within which these actors are involved.

1 Introduction

Context plays a crucial role in support of evidence for a given argument. Statements which are taken 'out of context' could face criticism from those who note such omissions as a distortion of the original intended meaning. There are a number of definitions of context in distributed systems – Brown [1] defines context to be the elements of a user's environment which the computer knows about. Dey and Abowd [2], refer to context as "any information that can be used to characterize the situation of entities (i.e., whether a person, place or object) that are considered relevant to the interaction between a user and an application, including the user and the application themselves". Therefore the amount of information we have about context affects how we interpret the event we have observed. Similarly, the way in which we interpret the recording of some data may be altered based on the context in which it has been generated.

We use Groth et al.'s view on provenance [3] as the process which led to a piece of data, and that such processes may be described using evidence represented in the form of process documentation. In service oriented architectures we believe that the context of an action or sequence of actions may be provided by each actor involved in execution of a process. Records of context may exist outside of the notion of a process or the control of a client and this makes later interpretation based on review of both difficult. Our work has been exploring the use of context in the documentation and structuring of such evidence. Known relationships between a process and its context will be different depending on the application, and it may not always be possible to document both in open,

J. Freire, D. Koop, and L. Moreau (Eds.): IPAW 2008, LNCS 5272, pp. 45–53, 2008.

loosely coupled architectures. In this paper we present a system which documents both the sequence of actions which describe a process and the situation in which those actions took place, enabling both navigation of process documentation and prediction of future actor properties. The rest of this paper is organised as follows: in section 2 we review the relevant literature in the area of context as relating to provenance systems and describe our motivation. In section 3 we describe our model of the context of actions upon an actor, followed by a description of the architecture we have adopted in section 4 and a demonstration of its implementation in section 5. Finally in section 6 we conclude.

2   Background and Motivation

Provenance is important for scientists to be able to record information in order to, for example, ensure experiments are performed correctly and to be able to repeat processes which produced interesting results. As many disparate activities may be involved in such a process, without such recording it is difficult to determine precisely how results have been reached. Several solutions have been developed to capture provenance or enable applications to be *provenance aware*, e.g. in Bioinformatics[11] or Chemical Sciences[9]. The Oxford English dictionary describes context as: *the circumstances that form the setting for an event, statement or idea.* For actors in a service oriented system, documenting a process involves describing each of those steps which comprise it. Research to date has widely addressed documenting messages which are sent between actors[3] as these typically indicate invocation of some functionality. Other actions commonly include the actions of scientists who control such systems, which may be documented in a more ad-hoc manner. Recording single events does not however describe properties or conditions which hold true for the actor over a given period of time. We refer to such properties as a description of the *context* of the action, where the action is the function being performed by a particular entity. A universal agreement on the content of process documentation representing context submitted by actors has not yet been reached. Attempts to provide a generic schema for what is to be recorded as context have so far proved to be fruitless, with the Grid Provenance project[1] choosing not to adopt any formal structure for the state of actors during a process. This is due to the diversity in the types of use cases that are required to be satisfied for all those domains which have unique provenance requirements. Such diversity has led to scientists building a variety of tools able to capture specific contextual data. Recently, the Open Provenance Model has been developed to enable sharing of provenance data amongst different systems that adopt it [8]. In this model, data representing context could be considered *artifacts* as they are immutable pieces of state. As yet, no systems are known to have implemented the model and no formal representation of the model has been specified, but work is ongoing. The model we present focuses less on what the content of this contextual data may be and

---

[1] http://www.gridprovenance.org

more on how those elements are represented and recorded over time, to be of use during queries of process documentation.

3   Modeling the Context of a Process

We record *process documentation* about past processes to understand what has occurred following invocation of a workflow [3]. In order to document the context of these processes, a set of variables associated with each actor is recorded during workflow execution. The value taken by these variables at any time constitutes the *state* of that actor. It is possible for an actor to progress through a number of different states over a period of time, indicated by a difference in the value of any one of the states variables. When a state changes for an actor, a *state transition* is said to occur from the previous to following state. We assume when state transitions are documented that an actor is only involved in one process at a time.

An example of deriving a number of states from a given set of variables (v_1, v_2, v_3) is given in figure 1(a) with a finite state machine representing the states mined from the data shown in figure 1(b). Here we see that although some common values exist for each variable (such as the value of v_3) a change in any variable can lead to a state change.

State	Observation Time	v_1	v_2	v_3
s_1	1164277522	4.71	13084	2.56
s_2	1164282522	4.71	15698	2.56
s_3	1164287522	4.00	15698	2.56

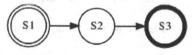

(a) Deriving unique states from variables   (b) FSM of variable data

Fig. 1.

In the scenario of a service based architecture, the most interesting states are those which occur within the interval when a request message was sent to a service and the associated reply. In this period, the actor's observed state may be documented as a part of any process documentation that is recorded for a process. State is documented using details of the time intervals over which that state applies (i.e start and end times). This means it is possible to mine series which describe the same property as being true over a number of non-overlapping intervals. In figure 2(a) we demonstrate how thresholds are used to segment the measurements of a variable[4], to determine when it was in one of a number of pre-defined ranges. Each of these properties which hold true for a state is documented within a *pattern*. The pattern is an array of values which has the same number of elements as variables that are measured, with each individual element holding a reference to the range which applies. By looking at two series segmented from variables, (as in figure 2(b)) we are able to determine the unique patterns (and hence states) and the times over which they apply. As an example, consider the first highlighted section of figure 2(b). The first two rows correspond to segmented variable measurements and the third indicates over which intervals various combinations of the segmented series applied. Our resultant (state) series therefore describes the periods over which each variable is described as high, medium or low. So for the example, the state series tells us both variables were initially low, whilst a short while later the first variable changed to be within the medium range. The final row indicates the patterns for each state (which correspond to the original ranges), with the upper value indicating the range applying for the series in 2(a).

States observed upon an actor are assumed to be an effect of the request (cause) event from which the observation interval begins. This is in order to support prediction of future actor properties - which would be impossible without causal knowledge.

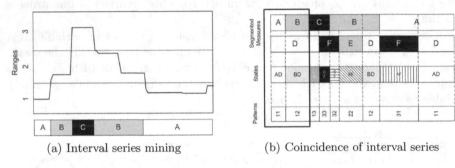

(a) Interval series mining   (b) Coincidence of interval series

Fig. 2. Mining unique context series from numeric time series

Particular focus has previously been paid to documenting the set of events which comprise a process, without discussion of whether any one of these events may hold causal relationships with properties and conditions holding true for longer than a single point in time. By adopting a representation capable of recording intervals we hope to capture such knowledge.

4   Documenting Context in Service Based Architectures

We use the PreServ software created at the University of Southampton to capture assertions of provenance to a repository known as a *provenance store* [3]. This software has been built in response to a large variety of requirements gathered from numerous domains such as bioinformatics, high energy physics and medicine [5]. PreServ breaks up process documentation into three sub-categories of assertion known as *p-assertions*. Interaction p-assertions document message exchange between services, relationship p-assertions document the causal dependencies between events or data items and actor state p-assertions document the state an actor is in at a given point in time during a process. Dividing documentation into these three types means that parts of it may be recorded by each of the actors which were involved in a process to a repository common to all. PreServ is suitable as a capture mechanism for assertions of state as it does not prescribe their contents, instead leaving it up to specific applications to define this. This leaves us free to specify our own XML representation of state and assert this to storage.

Our implementation of a system capable of automatically documenting state makes use of a State Assertion Registry (StAR) co-located with a service [10]. StAR is implemented as a Java library and acts as a wrapper to the service, enabling it to dynamically record assertions of provenance according to a policy file. StAR represents a benefit to the scientist in capturing assertions automatically.

Data is collected and *segmented*[4] to one of a set of possible values. This segmentation uses thresholds based on average values of the variables previously observed. The segmented value corresponds to an element within the pattern for a particular state as described in section 3. We use techniques from the Time Series Knowledge Representation (TSKR) [6] to determine the intervals over which the segmented series coincide with one another as shown in figure 2(b). Details of these series are then used as the content of an actor state p-assertion, along with a complete pattern description indicating all those conditions which hold over the series. Following recording of documentation, any actor may be query the provenance store.

A user can determine future states for a process based upon the states previously documented within a provenance store. For all states which are related to the same event, a transition table listing the probability of state transition given that observed event may be calculated. The most likely next state for an actor is the one with the highest probability value given to the current state. In cases where the two states (predicted and actual) do not match we use a similarity measure to find how similar those states are. It is a simple distance measure of each corresponding pattern value, shown in equation 1, where q and r are the two patterns being compared and p and t are the number of items in the patterns and the number of possible values for each of those items. The total number of possible states is p^t, though for any given process run not all states may be observed.

$$s = 1 - \frac{\sum_{n=0}^{p} |q_n - r_n|}{p \times (t - 1)} \tag{1}$$

The distance between two states therefore is the total measured error between each of the states pattern elements, divided by the maximum total distance possible for error on each of those elements. Our measure differs slightly from a distance measure such as the Levenshtein distance as such a measure is unable to distinguish between the degree of change in any one of our pattern elements, just that elements differ. As pattern elements correspond to numerically ordered ranges in our model, taking account of the difference in these elements is important. The overall similarity of a process against a comparison process is calculated from the product of the similarities of each state. This similarity value gives us a single measure of how similar the conditions under which each of the actors involved were operating were for two processes.

5   Evaluation

We now demonstrate two uses of documenting actor state for a process; 1) attempting to predict future actor properties for processes based on previously documented ones and 2) Reducing manual navigation of process documentation based on comparison of states over the monitored intervals. The workflow we use to demonstrate this was the subject of both the first and second provenance challenges [7]. It is used to create population-based brain atlases from high resolution anatomical data from the Functional Magnetic Resonance Imaging (fMRI) Data Center[2]. We use StAR to automatically record assertions of interaction and state to a provenance store for each of the services in the workflow. We focus on the last two services in the workflow, which convert an averaged brain image (determined from the average of intensities of MRI scans) gathered from a collection of high resolution anatomical data into graphics files showing slices of the brain. Actor state assertions identify the interval over which the actor is invoked (between request and response messages) based upon TSKR mined series from the segmented values using three variables: bytes in per second, one minute load average and the amount of buffered memory.

Each of the services in the workflow is hosted separately on a IBM JS20 blade machine (2 x 2.1GHz, 1.5GB RAM) and the provenance store for each of them is a Sun x2100 machine (1 x 2.2GHz, 4GB of RAM). When the workflow executes, a single action is performed by each of the services used and a set of states are recorded for it. We perform the process 1000 times, delaying subsequent invocations to allow the systems to recover. We do this as features observed in the variables may continue for longer than just the duration of a single action. For our state prediction evaluation, results are based on this experiment being performed twice.

Prediction of Future Actor Properties. A scientist is able to build a likely model for future properties using a transition table (as described in section 4) for each action. A state prediction is made for each actor after a single process is executed, based upon the last known state of that actor and the most common transition observed. Figure 3 shows the percentage of matches for predicted states to actual ones for our approach along with a history based and simple monte-carlo prediction. Each point represents the match rate for a single actor in the process. All machines consistently predicted states at a reasonably high success rate (50-85%), which was always above that of the monte-carlo predictions. The average trend indicates that as more transitions are observed, state becomes more difficult to predict in the future. This is due to the increased complexity of the model which is built when more transitions are found. It is likely that a more sophisticated analysis of the transition pattern leading to a state could further increase this success rate. Using this approach, the scientist executing the process is able to form a hypothesis detailing the most likely states to occur for each actor during future invocation of each action.

---

[2] http://www.fmridc.org/

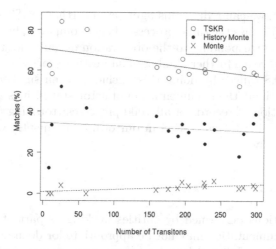

Fig. 3. Match rate of predicted states to those observed

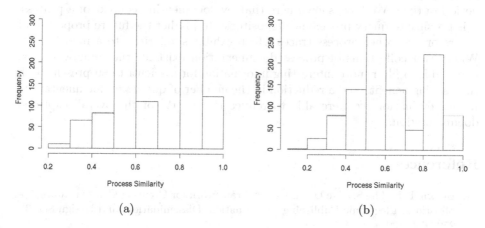

Fig. 4. Distribution of process similarity values when compared to model process

Reduction of Manual Process Documentation Navigation. We demonstrate reduction of navigation performed by a scientist by determining the similarity of a single state for each action within the process against that observed in a "comparison process", with our results shown in figure 4(a). The total similarity of a process (as defined in section 4) is the product of multiplying each of these similarities for each action. The scientist may then use these distances as a filter to locate the most interesting processes from a large collection of process documentation. Our results in figure 4 show the distribution of process similarity values. For our scenario, we are able to see that the total documentation to be navigated is reduced dramatically when searching for either those processes with a high or low similarity (≥ 0.9 or ≤ 0.4). This corresponds to 12% and 8% of all of the documentation recorded. If we look at the lowest similarity

processes ($\leq$0.3), we can reduce this figure even further to 1% of all documentation. Figure 4(b) shows the same processes being compared, but with an average
similarity value corresponding to the observation of multiple states within each
invocation. We reveal a further number of interesting processes within the 0.1-0.2
range and 0.7-0.8 ranges by doing this, including even smaller subsets of documentation. Without the documentation of actor states, it is perfectly feasible
that the navigation of records of all 1000 processes (totalling 56MB's worth of
XML documentation to be queried in our own experiments) would have to be
navigated manually.

6   Conclusion

In modeling actions performed by entities working as part of a process, strict
event-based documentation may not be appropriate for documenting all process
features. Instead, an interval based representation – such as the one presented
in this paper, better represents observation of properties which hold true over a
period of time. We have shown here that by documenting context of a process,
it is possible to query provenance repositories to predict the future properties of
actors or find other process traces which exhibit similarities to a model trace.
Where vast collections of process documentation exist for the same workflow,
being able to filter more interesting information for a scientist can present both
time saving benefits and a reduction in the number of queries of documentation.
In our evaluation we were able to reduce this to 1% of the overall captured
documentation.

References

1. Brown, P.J.: The Stick-e Document: A Framework for Creating Context-aware Applications. Electronic Publishing - Origination, Dissemination, and Design 8(2/3),
   259–272 (1995)
2. Dey, A.K., Abowd, G.D.: Towards a Better Understanding of Context and Context-
   Awareness. In: Workshop on The What, Who, Where, When, and How of Context-
   Awareness. ACM Press, New York (April 2000)
3. Groth, P., Miles, S., Moreau, L.: PReServ: Provenance Recording for Services. In:
   Proceedings of the UK OST e-Science second All Hands Meeting 2005, AHM 2005
   (2005)
4. Keogh, E., Chu, S., Hart, D., Pazzani, M.: Segmenting Time Series: A Survey and
   Novel Approach (1993)
5. Miles, S., Groth, P., Branco, M., Moreau, L.: The requirements of using provenance
   in e-Science experiments (January 01, 2006)
6. Moerchen, F.: Algorithms for time series knowledge mining. In: KDD 2006: Proceedings of the 12th ACM SIGKDD international conference on Knowledge discovery and data mining, pp. 668–673. ACM, New York (2006)
7. Moreau, L., Ludäscher, B. (eds.): The First Provenance Challenge. Concurrency
   and Computation: Practice and Experience 20(5), 409–418 (2007)

8. Moreau, L., Freire, J., Futrelle, J., McGrath, R., Myers, J., Paulson, P.: The Open Provenance Model (December 2007), http://eprints.ecs.soton.ac.uk/14979/

9. Myers, J.D., Pancerella, C.M., Lansing, C.S., Schuchardt, K.L., Didier, B.T., Goble, C.N.A.: Multi-scale Science: Supporting Emerging Practice with Semantically Derived Provenance (March 06, 2006)

10. Wootten, I., Rajbhandari, S., Rana, O.: Automatic Assertion of Actor State in Service Oriented Architectures. In: ICWS 2007, pp. 655–662 (2007)

11. Zhao, J., Goble, C.A., Stevens, R.: An Identity Crisis in the Life Sciences. In: Moreau, L., Foster, I. (eds.) IPAW 2006. LNCS, vol. 4145, pp. 254–269. Springer, Heidelberg (2006)

User-Centric Annotation Management
for Biological Data

Qinglan Li, Alexandros Labrinidis, and Panos K. Chrysanthis

Advanced Data Management Technologies Laboratory
Department of Computer Science,
University of Pittsburgh,
Pittsburgh, PA 15260, USA
{qinglan,labrinid,panos}@cs.pitt.edu

Abstract. Annotations play an increasingly crucial role in scientific exploration and discovery, as the amount of data and the level of collaboration among scientists increases. Although all such systems are implemented to take user input (i.e., the annotations themselves), very few systems are user-centric, taking into account user preferences on how annotations should propagate and be applied over data. In this paper, we propose to treat annotations as first-class citizens for biological data management by presenting a *user-centric, view-based annotation framework*, called ViP. Under the ViP framework we consider user preferences over the time semantics of annotations (by supporting future annotations) and over the network semantics of annotations (by supporting both implicitly-defined and explicitly-defined annotation propagation paths). In addition to novel functionality, we describe a novel caching technique which enables ViP to outperform the state of the art. We also propose to demonstrate our prototype implementation of the ViP framework. As part of the demo, we propose on the one hand to highlight the user-interface/functionality of our system and on the other hand to visualize the server/behind-the-scenes aspect.

1 Introduction

We are witnessing an accelerated pace of discovery and innovation in science research. This is true across all sciences, from gene sequencing and drug discovery to weather modeling and the exploration of the Universe. Without a doubt, data management is playing a pivotal role in scientific exploration nowadays. In addition to efficiently managing the tsunami of experimental data generated, data management also facilitates effective collaboration among scientists, by recording *data provenance* and by supporting *annotations* [2, 3]. Data provenance essentially keeps track of where the data is coming from (and what transformations it has been through), whereas annotations enable users to record additional information about the data stored (and propagate this information to all "related" data items).

There are a lot of projects that deal with annotation propagation and management, for example, DBNotes [2], Mondrian [5], ULDB [1], bdbms [4], and MMS [7]. Our interest in this research area came from our participation in the Center for Modeling Pulmonary

J. Freire, D. Koop, and L. Moreau (Eds.): IPAW 2008, LNCS 5272, pp. 54–61, 2008.

Immunity (CMPI)[1]. Our group is responsible for the design and development of the *data sharing platform* (DataXS), where experimental data, analysis, and models will be shared among project participants. In such a diverse setting, the ability to record annotations and propagate them to all related data items and interested parties is crucial to the success of the project.

As part of the design process and during the implementation of our first prototype, we were able to identify two distinct *usage patterns* which are not handled by the current state of the art. This led to the development of the ViP annotation framework [6], whose main contribution is to give users the ability to specify *when*, *to what/how*, and *for whom* a user's annotations will be visible and/or propagated (in addition to specifying the actual annotations). Towards this, the ViP framework utilizes *views* both as a specification mechanism and as a user-interface mechanism.

Support for user-centric time semantics for annotations. For example, assume that we have a microarray scanner which was mis-calibrated on a certain day. When this is first discovered, we want to be able to annotate all experimental data in the system accordingly, but also do this for all data that would fall in this category, but are entered in the system later. Since users have different understanding/explanations of why/how certain biological process unfold, it is possible that they want to personalize the time setting of such annotations (i.e., whether they would applied just now, or also in the future). Most current systems do not support annotations that are also valid in the future (Table 1). The only exception is MMS [7], which always supports future time semantics (i.e., without giving the user the option to choose). We refer to this feature as "*user-centric time semantics*".

Support for propagation of annotations in user-defined ways. For example, provide the ability to "link" related data items together, so that an annotation on one of them would be visible to the other one and vice-versa. Most annotation-enabled systems propagate annotations along data provenance paths. In other words, annotations are propagated over existing implicit annotation propagation paths between source data and derived data (i.e., driven by the database schema and data transformations). Although this can happen over multiple derivation levels, it fails to capture relationships between data items that do not share a common "ancestry" in the database. As we have witnessed from our involvement in the CMPI project, this can happen often in biological databases. To address this, ViP builds explicit paths for annotation propagation. It also allows users to protect data privacy on these paths, that is, each user can have his or her own paths to propagate annotations. Since these paths can form a network, we refer to this feature as "*user-centric network semantics*". Although existing systems support implicit annotation propagation paths, none except for our proposal supports explicit, user-defined annotation propagation paths (Table 1).

---

[1] The Center is a joint effort between the University of Pittsburgh, Carnegie Mellon University, and the University of Michigan, bringing together experimentalists and modelers to study pulmonary immunity in response to three bio-defense pathogens (the influenza A virus, Mycobacterium tuberculosis, which causes TB, and Francisella tularensis, the bacterium responsible for tularemia).

Table 1. Standard Annotation Management Features Comparison

Standard Features	DBNotes[2]	Mondrian[5]	ULDB[1]	bdbms[4]	MMS[7]	ViP[6]
Annotation	Yes	Yes	Confidence	Yes	Yes	Yes
Provenance	Yes	Yes	Lineage	Yes	Yes	Yes
Time Semantics:						
· Implicitly-defined	No	No	No	No	Yes	Yes
· Explicitly-defined	No	No	No	No	No	Yes
Network Semantics:						
· Implicitly-defined	Limited	Limited	Limited	Limited	Yes	Yes
· Explicitly-defined	No	No	No	No	No	Yes
Propagation Type	Eager	On-demand	On-demand	Eager	On-demand	Hybrid
Annotation Storage	Naive	Naive	x-relations	Anno. table	q-type	A-table
Scalability	Small	Medium	Medium	Medium	Large	Large
Query	pSQL	Color algebra	TriQL	A-SQL	Predicate	ViP-SQL

Table 2. User Centric Annotation Management Features Comparison

User-centric Features	DBNotes[2]	Mondrian[5]	ULDB[1]	bdbms[4]	MMS[7]	ViP[6]
Time Semantics:						
· Valid Time	No	No	No	No	No	Yes
Network Semantics:						
· Propagation Method	Yes	No	No	Limited	No	Yes
Access Control:						
· Annotations	No	No	No	Limited	No	Yes
· Annotation Views	No	No	No	No	No	Yes
· Annotation Paths	No	No	No	No	No	Yes

Contributions: This research project has both theoretical and practical contributions as follows:

- based on our experience from a real system implementation, we propose new annotation propagation methods, suitable for biological data,
- we propose user-centric features that enable users to personalize annotation propagation, and
- we propose to use views as a user-interface and also as the formal mechanism to optimize the implementation of the new annotation propagation features.

Roadmap: In the next section we briefly describe the main aspects of the ViP framework. In Section 3 we present the implementation of our prototype. In Section 4 we provide an overview of the different components of our prototype system along with the demonstration highlights. We conclude in Section 5 and acknowledge in Section 5.

2   The ViP Framework

To the best of our knowledge, ViP brings user-centric features in many aspects that are not considered in most related works as shown in Table 2.

2.1   User-Centric Time Semantics

User-Centric Time Semantics: During our involvement in the CMPI project, we observed that *experimental data was almost always entered in the database in an order different than the one it was generated*. In fact, even data about the same experiment could be entered at completely different times, since more than one lab were involved in generating the data (for example, one lab would generate the luminex data whereas a different lab would produce microarray data for the same tissues). Looking at annotations, this means that if one wanted to annotate data from a particular experiment with an observation about the tissues, it would **not** be enough to do this once, as additional experimental data may be added into the database later (which would not automatically "inherit" the annotation).

To address this, we proposed the concept of *valid time* for annotations and for annotation paths (which we describe next). This is specified by the user for each annotation and works in tandem with using *database views* to describe the annotation targets. Using views allows us to declaratively describe the data to be annotated instead of simply enumerating them. Combined together, we can set, for example, the valid time for an annotation to be $[now, \infty)$ which means that the annotation will be applied to matching items now and also in the future.

When we consider the time dimension of annotation propagation, we can easily distinguish four different cases:

1. *now* only (e.g., mark all the data that have been processed until today),
2. *now* + *future* (where an annotation is propagated to data items currently in the database, and also to those that are added in the database in the future, e.g., the typical calibration experiment mentioned above),
3. *future* only (e.g., all the files until today have been fixed, but all files submitted in the future should be marked accordingly),
4. *future interval* only (e.g., for one week after the Daylight Saving Time show an annotation that reminds scientists to make sure they have accounted for Daylight Saving Time in experiment settings). It also be able to start from now.

The cases above present the four *valid time* usages in User-centric Time Semantics of ViP.

2.2   User-Centric Network Semantics

The second usage pattern that we observed during our involvement in the CMPI project was that *there exist many relationships, or paths, between data items that cannot be inferred by the existing database schema*. Such links materialize because, for example, tissues from multiple, unrelated experiments are processed together, in a single assay (for example, on a single plate that needs to be filled up to minimize costs).

To address this, ViP enables users to specify explicit *annotation paths*, linking data items together. Annotations should be propagated along these paths, reaching "related" data items, as specified by users. Since these paths are essentially forming a network, we refer to this feature as *"user-centric network semantics"*.

ViP enables users to specify the propagation method. In DBNotes [2], users can specify *custom* propagation scheme to bind the source and target tuples while there is a join operation, so that the annotations that are associated to the source tuples will be propagated to the target tuples. ViP provides a stronger and more complex scheme, that is, we propose to empower users to specify *explicit paths* between data items, thus establishing additional annotation propagation paths. Such explicit paths are defined using views as follows:

- given a source view, V_s and a destination view, V_d
- an explicit annotation propagation path $V_s \rightarrow V_d$ is defined, such that any annotation that is added in a member of V_s must be propagated to all members of V_d.

3   Implementation Highlights

3.1   Implementation Using Views

We propose to use the concept of *database views* as the building block to implement the technologies mentioned above. Database views can be used to describe (at a high-level) the results of a database query. For example, instead of attaching a comment about mis-calibration to individual files (and miss files that are added in the future), using views enables the system to record this annotation in a single location (the view) and to also associate this annotation with files matching the view definition in the future.

Views enable us to build a specialized cache for storing annotations (and may also storing annotation propagation paths), thus improving performance.

3.2   User-Centric Access Control

We advocate that scientific annotation must have a strong user-centric component. First of all, much of the data is not public, so appropriate access controls need to be in place for the raw data, and the annotations on them. Secondly, even for public data, the annotations are often private, since they reflect additional analysis that is not ready to be made available to all. Thirdly, in many cases, even the way that raw data are associated (i.e., by specifying explicit paths for annotation propagation) corresponds to private information that should not be made public. Given all these reasons, the ViP framework includes a strong user-centric access control module.

Some systems consider the *access control* on the data level, or even on the update authorization part [4]. Instead, we propose to fully support this feature in a broader domain, both on annotations and on annotation paths. Individual users have different annotation views and paths. We support arbitrary user hierarchies. This is different than traditional access control, since access control on annotation views (given user-centric time semantics) and on annotation paths (given user-centric network semantics) essentially means who can "execute" the annotation propagation mechanism and not on the data itself.

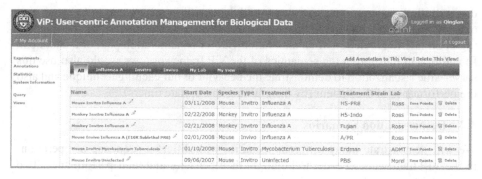

Fig. 1. Annotation Views

4 Prototype Highlights

4.1 User Interface

The ViP framework relies heavily upon the concept of *database views* to declaratively describe annotations and annotation paths[2]. Clearly, users are not expected to provide view definitions in SQL. In our ViP framework, a user can easily specify filtering conditions to locate certain data items. This functionality enables users to specify views using a point and click interface (Figure 1); these views can be trivially used to support user-centric time and network semantics.

In particular, we will showcase the following ways of adding annotations (i.e., defining *annotation views*):

- A set of conditions used for filtering results is used in its entirety (exact match); this is implemented in "Save View" tab functionality as well as annotation definition functionality in our system.
- If the set of conditions are not enough to adequately describe the set of data to be annotated, then we will allow the user to provide additional constraining predicates (typically a date range).
- To also support a simplified interface, we will also enable the user to just specify the list of data items to annotate (i.e., enumerate).

We will also showcase adding of explicit annotation paths, by providing the above *view definition* abilities as a two-step process (for specifying the from and the to "nodes" of the explicitly-defined annotation path).

Finally, we should be able to annotate specific data items directly (which could trigger annotation propagation across pre-established annotation paths).

4.2 Visualization

We believe it is absolutely crucial to be able to visualize how the ViP framework works in order to demonstrate it. Towards this, we will produce a server-side visual monitor

---

[2] The MMS system [7] advocated the use of views for metadata management; our system is targeting annotations (i.e., a special case of metadata), but on the other hand is significantly extending their proposal with additional semantics.

that will display appropriate statistics for all data items in our system (e.g., number of queries, annotations, and query time). This would allow us to illustrate what is happening upon insertion/deletion of an annotation view or an annotation path or a data item. In addition to illustrating the semantics of the ViP framework, we would also use this server-side visualization to demonstrate the behavior of our caching technique and also the performance of the system (by maintaining appropriate timers).

4.3 Demonstration Scenarios

We will demonstrate many different scenarios with different sequence of operations in the ViP framework in order to highlight their behavior and their performance. Two characteristic examples are as follows.

Annotation Views
- Define an annotation view V (e.g., all experiments performed on June 15, 2008) with a specific annotation tag T and visualize it at the server
- Query an item that belongs to V; it should have tag T
- Insert a new item D that should match V's definition and visualize it
- Query item D; it should also have "received" tag T

Annotation Paths
- Establish an annotation path from V_1 to V_2 (e.g., all experiments performed on June 15, 2008 should be linked to experiments performed on June 16, 2008 because all tissues were transferred) and visualize it at the server
- Query a data item that belongs in V_2; it should have no annotations
- Add annotation (e.g., tag TT) to a data item that belongs to V_1
- Query the same data item from V_2; it should have "received" tag TT

5 Conclusions

The proposed ViP framework provides a novel view-based annotation propagation scheme. It also brings user-centricity throughout annotation propagation, applied in time and network semantics. ViP utilizes views both as a specification mechanism and as a user-interface mechanism, and employs caching techniques for improved performance compared to the state of the art.

Acknowledgements

Research of the project is supported by NIH-NIAID grant NO1-AI50018. We would like to thank Chad Spensky for his help in designing the user interface.

References

1. Benjelloun, O., Sarma, A.D., Halevy, A.Y., Widom, J.: ULDBs: Databases with uncertainty and lineage. In: Proc. of the VLDB, pp. 953–964 (2006)
2. Bhagwat, D., Chiticariu, L., Tan, W.-C., Vijayvargiya, G.: An annotation management system for relational databases. In: Proc. of the VLDB, pp. 900–911 (2004)

3. Buneman, P., Khanna, S., Tajima, K., Tan, W.-C.: Archiving scientific data. ACM Transaction Database System 29(1), 2–42 (2004)
4. Eltabakh, M.Y., Ouzzani, M., Aref, W.G.: Bdbms – a database management system for biological data. In: Proc. of the CIDR (2007)
5. Geerts, F., Kementsietsidis, A., Milano, D.: Mondrian: Annotating and querying databases through colors and blocks. In: Proc. of the ICDE, pp. 82–92 (2006)
6. Li, Q., Labrinidis, A., Chrysanthis, P.K.: ViP: a user-centric view-based annotation framework for scientific data. In: Ludäscher, B., Mamoulis, N. (eds.) SSDBM 2008. LNCS, vol. 5069, pp. 295–312. Springer, Heidelberg (2008)
7. Srivastava, D., Velegrakis, Y.: Intensional associations between data and metadata. In: Proc. of ACM SIGMOD Conference, pp. 401–412 (2007)

A Model for Sharing of Confidential Provenance Information in a Query Based System

Meiyappan Nagappan and Mladen A.Vouk

North Carolina State University,
Raleigh, NC 27695, USA
{mnagapp,vouk}@ncsu.edu

Abstract. Workflow management systems are increasingly being used to automate scientific discovery. Provenance meta-data is collected about scientific workflows, processes, simulations and data to add value. There is a variety of workflow management tools that cater to this. The provenance information may have as much value as the raw data. Typically, sensitive information produced by a computational processes or experiments is well guarded. However, this may not necessarily be true when it comes to provenance information. The issue is how to share confidential provenance information. We present a model for sharing provenance information when the confidentiality level is decided by the user dynamically. The key feature of this model is the *Query Sharing* concept. We illustrate the model for workflows implemented using provenance enabled Kepler system.

Keywords: Provenance, Confidentiality, Workflow management tools.

1   Introduction

The provenance collection approach in workflow support systems can be flow based, annotation based, or a combination of both [4]. Workflow systems execute scientific simulations and secure the output data in order to maintain confidentiality/privacy and ownership of the sensitive data. Most of them, however, do not have any mechanisms in place for maintaining the confidentiality of provenance information. Here we use the term confidentiality as defined in ISO/IEC-17799[11]:*ensuring that information is accessible only to those authorized to have access.*Building the provenance collection system with such a mechanism should be the priority from the very beginning [13]. Security and confidentiality must be considered in an integrated context. For example, one must implement security to ensure confidentiality of the information. Security is a process or tactics that ensures that the desired level of confidentiality can be an outcome [9].

While confidentiality of provenance information is important, so is the sharing of information among collaborators. Most of the scientific projects are highly collaborative projects. Often the collaborators are in different research labs in the country, and sometimes even in different countries. They may be working

J. Freire, D. Koop, and L. Moreau (Eds.): IPAW 2008, LNCS 5272, pp. 62–69, 2008.

together on the same approach, or may be taking different approaches to scientific discovery. Provenance data throws a lot of light onto a particular scientific problem, process, and the data it produces. It can discover a knowledge nugget that needs to be shared among all collaborators, and some that need to be shared sparingly. Hence provenance information of these projects is unlike any other data-centric application. Provision of mechanisms for confidentiality, like the ones in other similar system, should not restrict the sharing of provenance data with trusted collaborators. For example, scientist A is the owner of runs 1,2, and 3 of a scientific simulation. Each of the runs produced a set of provenance data viz. R1, R2 and R3 respectively. User A wants to share subsets of R1, R2 and R3, with Scientists B and C. Each of these subsets can be different from the others. An appropriate mechanism should enable easy sharing of data either on a per run basis, or on a per user group basis, or individually. The goal of the current work is to develop a model, in the context of the provenance for scientific simulations, that

- Enables an easy sharing of the provenance data.
- Does not compromise the confidentiality of the provenance data.
- Allows for dynamic changes in the confidentiality levels.

The specific focus is on the systems that use Kepler [1] for scientific workflow automation and management. Kepler workflows are composed of a set of actors (processes) forming, in more complex situations, generalized activity networks [3], [8]. The order of execution of these actors depends on the nature of the problem (workflow) being solved and the Model of Computation (MoC) used to execute the workflow [6], [12]. These MoC's (or process schedulers) are called directors in Kepler. One version of Kepler implements a provenance collection mechanism [3], [12]. We describe it in more detail in Section 2.

2   Provenance in Kepler

The workflow support system we have been using is Kepler [1]. There is a version of Kepler that directly supports provenance recording. The Kepler Provenance Recorder (PR) is described in [3], [6], [12]. PR implements the Read-Write-State reset (RWS) trace information (flow-based provenance) first introduced in workflow systems in [6]. The recorder captures the flow of data objects between the ports of actors. The reads(consume), and writes(emit) done by an actor are captured as provenance. Also, events such as the 'flushing' of the state of the actors is captured. It generates a unique token id for every token consumed/emitted by an actor. Each execution of the workflow is assigned a unique id too. An implementation model is described in section 4. The PR is designed so that we need not edit any of the Kepler actors. It is similar to a Kepler director in that it is configured in the same way, but it is different in the fact that it does not control the workflow, rather it just listens to it (in that sense it is more akin to the Kepler debugging facilities that allow detailed workflow tracing). When the Kepler PR actor is included into a workflow, it automatically collects the provenance data by listening to the ports of all the actors in the workflow.

We propose to slightly modify the RWS relational tables in order to achieve our goal. The relational tables in our model are: *usersTable (username, workflow name, run id, annotation), actorTable (run id, actor id, port id, annotation), traceTable (port id, token, event, annotation), tokenTable (token, object, annotation), objectTable(object, value, type, annotation)*. This is very similar to the provenance relations described in [12]. The difference is that here we have introduced an annotation field in each relation and the *usersTable* relation for keeping tack of the owner of a run. This enables capture of the provenance that was recorded by their RWS PR. However, the annotation field in each of the above relations will get its value from the user only, and not from Kepler.

3   An Implementation Model

In this section we describe a model that can accommodate the sharing of confidential provenance information in a scenario where the confidentiality level changes dynamically. Here we try to reach the goal stated above through five sub goals. The Model is being implemented in a system being built by DOE Scientific Data Management Center [2], [17]. Fig. 1 illustrates the architecture. The details of this figure are discussed in the following text.

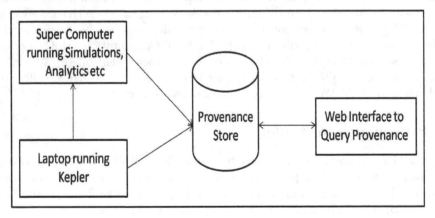

Fig. 1. Top-level architecture view of our Model

3.1   Sub Goal 1: Data Ownership

We need to ensure that the person who generates the simulation data would be the owner of the original provenance data. To achieve this we use a three tiered (Client-Application Logic-Database) approach and build role based access control in the application logic layer. When collecting provenance the client would either be the workflow management system or the scripts and simulation applications running in the super computer, or other affiliated analytics resources. The recording API is the application logic layer and makes sure that the information from the clients are stored in the appropriate tables of the schema. Also there is an authentication service that verifies the user. Thus the data in the provenance schema is indexed by the user and a particular run id.

In order to view this data, we use a Web Application (WA). Here the client is the Web Interface (WI) and the Query API is the application logic. Here too we have an authentication service that will authorize the user. Since the data is indexed by user, the query API is able to fetch a particular user's data. Each user has multiple runs under their username [5]. They pick the one they want to see the provenance data for. The query API will execute some of the default queries only on the dataset for this particular run and for this particular user. Then the user who launched this query can refine the dataset as they please. This is similar to the role based access available in many database applications.

3.2 Sub Goal 2: Editing and Audit Trail

The access privileges to the database are restricted to prevent any unwarranted use of provenance data. Once the data is created, users cannot delete or update any of the provenance information. But they can modify annotation fields of the records in the provenance relations and the *queryTable* relation. The prevention of edits to the data is important not just for audit purposes. Another major reason is to maintain consistency. A collaborator should not get a different dataset when he/she executes shared queries at different times. This can be possible only if the owner is not allowed to delete any provenance data. Only an administrator may delete this data. But all superuser actions also must be logged. A trail for this must be maintained for audit purposes. A system that tracks the changes that happen to database relations would suffice for this purpose. Even though users cannot delete the provenance data they can, through the annotation fields, comment on the accuracy of the provenance data. Thus by using access privileges in modern database systems we are able to achieve this sub goal.

3.3 Sub Goal 3: Data Annotation

The annotation field in the *queryTable* relation and the other relations may be updated from the WA. They can annotate the datasets regarding any inaccuracies or interesting findings. They may update only the annotation field in the provenance relations and the *queryTable* relation. The users when sharing can choose not to share the annotations. Annotation in itself is a form of user specified meta-data. Thus annotations help in differentiating the useful provenance information without deleting the inaccurate data, as well as add user level meta data to the results. Thus through the WA we are able to achieve this sub goal.

3.4 Sub Goal 4: Data Sharing

The ability of researchers to share their provenance data with their colleagues in an easy manner is probably as important as the confidentiality of this data. We introduce the notion of **query sharing** for this purpose. A logged-in user will be able to see data in the WI of the WA. If the scientist finds the provenance data that they currently see as interesting and wants to share it, he/she can do so by saving the query that created that dataset and sharing it with collaborators. This is analogous with the WYSIWYG concept. Here it is: What You See Is What You Want to Share(WYSIWYWTS): The relation *queryTable (Query ID, Saved by, Saved for, Query, Timestamp, Allow Cascading, Revoke Active)* is used to save the queries, and the relation *annotTable (UserID, Query ID, Annotation, Viewable)* is used to store the annotation for the data set that is to be shared. The WA provides saving of the query that created the dataset. The scientist who wants to share the data can choose to annotate the dataset. For example if User U1 wants to save the dataset of run Rx and share it with User U2, then the entry in the queryTable relation would look like this: *(QID, U1, U2, Select Query similar to the above one, timestamp, A binary 1/0 for whether cascading of should be allowed or not, A binary 0/1 if the collaborator has access currently or not).* They can also choose to annotate the dataset by making an entry in the *annotTable* relation. A typical entry would be *(UID, QID, Any relevant annotation to the dataset, A binary 1/0 if the collaborator should see the annotation or not)*

The collaborator, when logged in to the WA, will be able to see, give the right access rights, all their data in the hierarchical fashion above. In a separate tab they will also be able to see the queries (possibly not the actual query itself, but rather the *Query ID, annotation, timestamp, saved by and saved for* columns). This is done by the WA which will pass the user-id of the currently logged-in user and one of the Query API's will fetch all the entries in the *queryTable* where the user id matches the user id in the saved by or saved for columns and the corresponding entries in the *annotTable* if the *viewable* attribute is set to 1.

A user selects a query to run. Then the user sees the data. If the user wants to refine the query the user can do so as required. The queries are built for refining acts only on the dataset that was shared and not on the whole database. By abstracting the execution of the query to an API that will manage whose data is to be accessed, we restrict the user from seeing data that is not meant to be seen. As an extra measure, we could encrypt the query attribute of the *queryTable* relation in the database, to protect the data in case the *queryTable* in the database gets compromised. The saved query is not shown to the users and can be use in an execute-only mode.

The *cascade* attribute in the *queryTable* is used either allow or deny a collaborator from passing the shared information to another person. The *revoke* attribute is used to remove access to a particular query from a particular user by the owner of that query. Also they can save interesting subsets of the provenance information for themselves too. In this case saved by and saved for attributes in the queryTable will be the same as the owner. A collaborator in our model though may not be able to annotate individual pieces in a shared dataset. They can only annotate the dataset as a whole. For this they would make an entry into the annotTable. If they want the owner to view their annotations then they would set the *viewable* attribute to 1.

A user can thus give others access to all their data, or to a particular dataset, or a particular part of a particular dataset. Thus the granularity to which the user wants to share data depends on the user. Each time the user can decide to share a different piece of the dataset without editing any rule set for access control. Also the entire chosen dataset can be shared by saving a single query instead of sharing each record in the dataset or saving a copy of the whole dataset. Thus with the help of the *Query Sharing* concept we are able to achieve the fourth sub goal too.

As we can see, the query sharing concept is very similar to stored procedures. Both have the same overhead. But by saving queries in a table we extend their scope to add more meta-data to the saved query which would not be possible in stored procedures. Now, let us discuss why the data sharing concept would be better than any other solution given the following constraints:

− Dynamically decide what to share: Due to this constraint we are not able to build the logic of the query in the application layer. Since applications are static, the users would not be able to able to add a new query for a subset of the dataset that should be shared.
− Size of the set of information to be shared is large: Since the datasets are large, and so are the subsets of information, we may not be able to share copies with the collaborators.
− Subset of information rather than individual records: The data users share are subsets. If we were to use a high level language to control access, then the users would have to individually pick the cells in the subset that they want to share. The large size, and the fact that they can be thought of as atomic piece of information, would make the process of individually picking cells too time consuming.

Thus given these constraints our query sharing solution scales well(as only one row is added for each subset to be shared), and also it is very flexible(just a click away from sharing a subset).

3.5 Sub Goal 5: Data Audit and Verification

The inclusion of auditing in the model is to maintain accuracy of the data. Users with malicious intent may not tamper with the data if they know that it is going to be audited and that auditors have sufficient information to find any such use. Thus authenticated auditors are users who can view the original data, provenance data, and annotations. They are to be provided with sufficient information for auditing. The provenance relations have annotations in them for the auditors to verify the data against. Also the *queryTable* relation has timestamps in it for the auditors to find any discrepancy in the sharing of data. Finally since all the edits to the database had a trail, any missing information can be accounted for by the auditors. Thus by collecting and having access to all this information the auditors can catch any malicious use of data.

Hence by meeting these five sub goals we are ale to achieve the main goal of sharing provenance information at any level of confidentiality.

4 Limitations and Conclusions

The implementation model we have presented has some limitations. For example, it is query-centric. Only provenance systems that store data in databases and fetch them using queries can use this approach effectively. Another limitation is that the model requires automatic run-time provenance collection. The user is still allowed to annotate the data and create manual provenance, but not to modify original records. This provides a considerable level of integrity for the originally (and automatically) collected data, but perhaps less oversight for manually added annotations. Also to be noted is that only owners of the provenance data can freely annotate any part of the dataset. The collaborators can only annotate the entire shared subset and not any individual part in it. Even in automatic provenance collection systems we could face the security and privacy problems discussed in [7].

With more and more emphasis being laid on provenance data collection in scientific workflow applications [14], [15], the issue of sharing provenance with varying levels of confidentiality becomes increasingly important. We believe that the simple model described in this paper is able to ensure considerable level of confidentiality of provenance data, as well as sharing of it amongst trusted collaborators. The data sharing technique described in this paper allows for users to change the level of collaboration dynamically. This model addresses the integrity, confidentiality and availability, and ownership responsibility issues raised in [10], and [18]. But this model does not address the issues arising due to long term storage and scalability of provenance data discussed in [18]. There are some systems like PASS [16] that are used to provide security using provenance data. But there is not much research in the field of securing provenance data, providing confidentiality and enforcing privacy policies.

Acknowledgments

This project is funded in part by the DOE SciDAC grant DE-FC02-01ER25809 and the IBM SUR program. I would like to thank the SPA group of the SDM Center for their collaboration. I would also like to thank Dr.Yu and Dr.Sherriff, and graduate students Vinod Arjun, Lucas Layman, Aaron Massey, and Andy Meneely for discussions and insights into the various aspects of this research.

References

1. Kepler development and download site, http://kepler-project.org/
2. Scientific Data Management Center, http://sdm.lbl.gov/sdmcenter/index.html
3. Altintas, I., Barney, O., Jaeger-Frank, E.: Provenance Collection Support in the Kepler Scientific Workflow System. In: Moreau, L., Foster, I. (eds.) IPAW 2006. LNCS, vol. 4145, pp. 118–132. Springer, Heidelberg (2006)
4. Barga, R.S., Digiampietri, L.A.: Automatic Generation of Workflow Provenance. In: Moreau, L., Foster, I. (eds.) IPAW 2006. LNCS, vol. 4145, pp. 1–9. Springer, Heidelberg (2006)

5. Barreto, R., Critchlow, T., Khan, A., Klasky, S., Kora, L., Ligon, J., Mouallem, P., Nagappan, M., Podhorszki, N., Vouk, M.: Managing and Monitoring Scientific Workflows through Dashboards. In: Poster # 93, at Microsoft eScience Workshop Friday Center, University of North Carolina, Chapell Hill, NC, October 13 - 15, p. 108 (2007)
6. Bowers, S., McPhillips, T., Ludeascher, B., Cohen, S., Davidson, S.B.: A Model for User-Oriented Data Provenance in Pipelined Scientific Workflows. In: Moreau, L., Foster, I. (eds.) IPAW 2006. LNCS, vol. 4145, pp. 133–147. Springer, Heidelberg (2006)
7. Braun, U., Garfinkel, S., Holland, D.A., Muniswamy-Reddy, K.-K., Seltzer, M.I.: Issues in Automatic Provenance Collection. In: Moreau, L., Foster, I. (eds.) IPAW 2006. LNCS, vol. 4145, pp. 171–183. Springer, Heidelberg (2006)
8. Elmaghraby, S.E.: Activity Networks: Project Planning and Control by Network Models. Wiley-Interscience, New York (1977)
9. Griffiths, P.P., Wade, B.W.: An authorization mechanism for a relational database system. ACM Transactions on Database Systems 1(3), 242–255 (1976)
10. Hasan, R., Sion, R., Winslett, M.: Introducing secure provenance: problems and challenges. In: Proceedings of the 2007 ACM workshop on Storage security and survivability, pp. 13–18. ACM, Alexandria (2007)
11. ISO/IEC 17799. Information technology – Security techniques – Code of practice for information security management (2000) (Rev. 2005), http://www.iso.org/iso/en/prods-services/popstds/informationsecurity.html
12. Ludaescher, B., Podhorszki, N., Altintas, I., Bowers, S., McPhillips, T.: From Computation Models to Models of Provenance: The RWS Approach. Concurrency and Computation: Practise and Experience 20(5), 507–518
13. McGraw, G.: Building secure software: better than protecting bad software. Software, IEEE 19(6), 57–58
14. Moreau, L., Foster, I.: IPAW 2006. LNCS, vol. 4145. Springer, Heidelberg (2006)
15. Moreau, L., Ludäscher, B.: Concurrency and Computation: Practice & Experience – Special Issue on the First Provenance Challenge. Wiley, Chichester (2007)
16. Muniswamy-Reddy, K.-K., Holland, D.A., Braun, U., Seltzer, M.I.: Provenance Aware Storage Systems. In: Proceedings of the 2006 USENIX Annual Technical Conference, p. 4 (June 2006)
17. Nagappan, M., Altintas, I., Chin, G., Crawl, D., Critchlow, T., Koop, D., Ligon, J., Ludaescher, B., Mouallem, P., Podhorszki, N., Silva, C., Vouk, M.: Provenance in Kepler-based Scientific Workflow Systems. In: Poster # 41, at Microsoft eScience Workshop Friday Center, University of North Carolina, Chapell Hill, NC, October 13 - 15, p. 82 (2007)
18. Tan, V., Groth, P., Miles, S., Jiang, S., Munroe, S., Tsasakou, S., Moreau, L.: Security Issues in a SOA-Based Provenance System. In: Moreau, L., Foster, I. (eds.) IPAW 2006. LNCS, vol. 4145, pp. 203–211. Springer, Heidelberg (2006)

Kepler/pPOD: Scientific Workflow and Provenance Support for Assembling the Tree of Life[*]

Shawn Bowers[1], Timothy McPhillips[1], Sean Riddle[1],
Manish Kumar Anand[2], and Bertram Ludäscher[1,2]

[1] UC Davis Genome Center, University of California, Davis
[2] Department of Computer Science, University of California, Davis

Abstract. The complexity of scientific workflows for analyzing biological data creates a number of challenges for current workflow and provenance systems. This complexity is due in part to the nature of scientific data (e.g., heterogeneous, nested data collections) and the programming constructs required for automation (e.g., nested workflows, looping, pipeline parallelism). We present an extended version of the Kepler scientific workflow system to address these challenges, tailored for the systematics community. Our system combines novel approaches for representing scientific data, modeling and automating complex analyses, and recording and browsing associated provenance information.

1 Introduction

The National Science Foundation's Assembling the Tree of Life (AToL) initiative funds systematists investigating the phylogenetic relationships of groups of organisms, with the ultimate goal of reconstructing the evolutionary origins of all life. AToL projects range from the study of particular sets of organisms (e.g., using morphologial features or sequencing the genetic material of specimens) to the development of new computational approaches. Success of the AToL program, however, also depends on addressing significant informatics challenges. For instance, there is no straightforward way to integrate data collected by different AToL projects, to test hypotheses against all data collected so far, or to begin to reconstruct the entire Tree of Life based on AToL data and results. Further, the details of how the results of these projects were obtained—from the observations of specimens through the inference and evaluation of phylogenetic relationships—are often difficult to determine. Not only is the provenance of specimens, observations, and computed results hidden within the data management infrastructure of each AToL project, many of the details required to reconstruct how results were obtained or to trace them back to primary observations are not recorded reliably.

The pPOD project (http://www.phylodata.org) aims at addressing these informatics challenges by developing (1) a common data model encompassing the data types used in the various AToL projects; and (2) methods for recording information about specimens, and relating this data and metadata to the results of phylogenetic analyses.

---

[*] This work supported in part through NSF grants IIS-0630033, OCI-0722079, IIS-0612326, DBI-0533368, and DOE grant DE-FC02-01ER25486.

J. Freire, D. Koop, and L. Moreau (Eds.): IPAW 2008, LNCS 5272, pp. 70–77, 2008.
© Springer-Verlag Berlin Heidelberg 2008

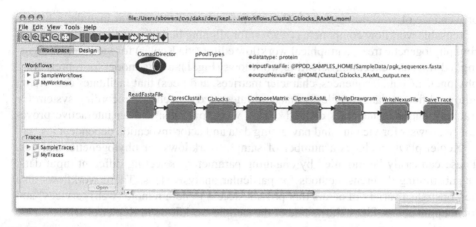

Fig. 1. A workflow in Kepler/pPOD with actors to read and parse FASTA files, compute multiple sequence alignments using Clustal, eliminate poorly aligned regions with Gblocks, create character matrices, infer phylogenetic trees using RAxML, draw resulting trees, and save outputs

For the latter, our aim is to provide a mechanism to record and maintain a continuous processing history for all data and computed results across multiple analysis steps. These steps are often carried out using a wide variety of scripts, standalone applications, and remote services. This paper reports on our solution to this problem, i.e., of recording the provenance of results derived using heterogeneous software systems for phylogenetic data analysis.

Kepler/pPOD[1] is an extension of the Kepler scientific workflow system [1] for automating phylogenetic studies, orchestrating and routing data between invocations of local applications and remote services, and tracking the dependencies between input, intermediate, and final data objects associated with workflow runs. Kepler/pPOD uses the COMAD workflow design paradigm [2], which has built-in support for processing nested data collections in an assembly-line manner, complex dataflow constructs such as loops and subworkflows, and an efficient, fine-grained method for capturing and representing comprehensive data provenance. Thus, COMAD is well-suited for automating phylogenetic workflows, often yielding simpler and more reusable workflow designs [3] when compared with existing approaches [4,5,6,7] (e.g., that often employ "adapters" or "shims" between actors). In the remainder of this paper, we describe Kepler/pPOD, focusing on its use of COMAD and its support for recording, representing, and navigating provenance information.

2   The Kepler/pPOD System

Kepler/pPOD is a customized distribution of the Kepler scientific workflow system designed specifically to support phylogenetic data analysis. The goal of the current version of the system is to provide an easy-to-use desktop application that allows researchers to create, run, and share phylogenetic workflows as well as manage and explore the

---

[1] Kepler/pPOD can be downloaded at http://daks.ucdavis.edu/kepler-ppod

provenance of workflow results.[2] The main features of the system include: a library of reusable workflow components (*actors*) for aligning biological sequences and inferring phylogenetic trees; a graphical workflow editor (via Kepler) for viewing, configuring, editing, and executing scientific workflows (Fig. 1); a data model for representing phylogenetic data (sequences, character matrices, and trees) that facilitates conversion among different data and file formats; an integrated provenance recording system for tracking data dependencies created during workflow runs; and an interactive provenance browser for viewing and navigating data and actor-invocation dependencies.

Kepler/pPOD includes a number of sample workflows for phylogenetic analyses. These can easily be modified by changing parameters, selecting different input data, or substituting different methods for particular analysis steps. These workflows also demonstrate a variety of actors that provide access to both remote (web) services[3] and local applications. Fig. 1 shows one of the sample workflows in Kepler/pPOD.

2.1   The Computation Model of Kepler/pPOD

Kepler uses a graphical block-diagram metaphor for representing workflow specifications (i.e., workflow graphs). Blocks represent *actors* that carry out particular steps in an analysis, and connections among blocks represent dependencies between actor invocations. Kepler distinguishes between the workflow graph and the *model of computation* (MoC) used to interpret and enact the workflow. Workflow authors explicitly select a MoC by choosing a *director* (Fig. 1), which specifies whether a workflow is scheduled as, e.g., a process network (PN) or a synchronous dataflow network (SDF) [8]. Most Kepler actors used in PN or SDF workflows are *data transformers*, which consume input tokens and produce *new* output tokens on each invocation.

Kepler/pPOD includes a new director for *collection-oriented modeling and design* (COMAD) workflows, where actors and their connections are significantly different from those in PN or SDF. Instead of assuming that actors transform all input data to output data, COMAD employs an **assembly-line** processing style: COMAD actors (*coactors*, or *actors* for short) can be thought of as workers on a virtual assembly line, each contributing its part to the construction of the workflow products. In a physical assembly line, workers only "pick" relevant parts from the conveyer belt, letting irrelevant parts pass by for downstream processing. Coactors work analogously, recognizing and operating on data relevant to them as specified by a *read scope* parameter, adding new data products to the data stream, and allowing irrelevant data to pass through undisturbed. Thus, unlike actors in other workflow systems, actors are *data preserving* in COMAD where data *flows through* serially connected coactors rather than being consumed and produced at each stage.

An advantage of the assembly-line approach of COMAD is that one can put information into the data stream that could be represented only with great difficulty in traditional PN or SDF workflows. For example, COMAD embeds special tokens within the data stream to delimit collections of related data tokens. Because these *delimiter tokens* are paired, much like the opening and closing tags of XML elements (as

---

[2] Note that it is also possible to run the Kepler workflow engine separately from the workflow editor, allowing Kepler/pPOD to also support additional deployment configurations.

[3] E.g. CIPRes RESTful services, http://www.phylo.org/sub_sections/portal/

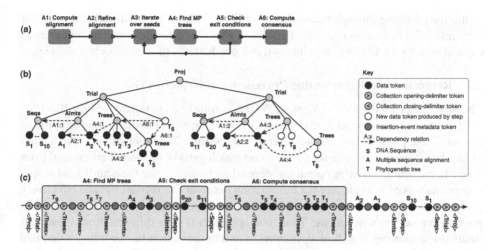

Fig. 2. A snapshot of a workflow run: (a) example workflow; (b) logical organization of data at a point in time during the run; (c) tokenized version of the collection structure where three actors are working *concurrently* on different parts of the data stream. Nested collections organize and relate data objects from domain-specific types (DNA sequences, alignments, phylogenetic trees). A *Proj* collection containing two *Trial* sub-collections is used to pipeline multiple sets of input sequences through the workflow. Provenance events (insert-data, insert-collection), insertion dependencies, and deletions (from the stream) are added directly as metadata tokens to the stream (c).

shown in Fig. 2), collections can be nested to arbitrary depths. This generic collection-management scheme allows actors to operate on collections of elements as easily as on single data tokens. Similarly, *annotation tokens* can be used to represent metadata for collections or individual data tokens, or for storing within the data stream the provenance of items inserted by coactors (see Fig. 2). The result is that coactors effectively operate not on isolated sets of input tokens, but on well-defined, information-rich collections of data organized in a manner similar to the tree-like structure of XML documents.

Another advantage of COMAD, compared to conventional dataflow approaches, is that COMAD workflows are generally more robust to change and easier to understand. For instance, inserting a new actor into a workflow or replacing an existing actor with a new version is straightforward, i.e., structural modifications to other parts of the workflow are not required. Similarly, while in traditional approaches maintaining collections of data and routing data to multiple actors requires the use of low-level control-flow constructs and associated actor connections, the same workflow in COMAD is often linear (as in Fig. 1). Thus, the intended function of a workflow can often be more easily understood, e.g., simply by reading the actor names in "assembly line order." Kepler/pPOD includes a library of coactors from which systematists can easily compose new workflows with minimal effort. For the same reason, the sample workflows in Kepler/pPOD can be easily modified to employ alternative methods for particular steps, extended with additional analysis steps, and concatenated with other workflows.

Fig. 2 illustrates a number of details of the COMAD approach, showing the state of a COMAD run at a particular point in time, and contrasting the logical organization of the data flowing through the workflow in Fig. 2(b) with its tokenized realization at the same point in time in Fig. 2(c). This figure also illustrates the pipeline-concurrency capabilities of COMAD by including two independent sets of sequences in a single run.

2.2   Recording and Representing Provenance in Kepler/pPOD

The provenance model used in Kepler/pPOD is unique (e.g., compared to [7,9,10,11,6]) in that it takes into account nested data collections, pipeline parallelism (in addition to the usual task parallelism), and actor scope expressions. The latter capture which parts of the data stream are visible for an actor and which parts of the output are created from them. In particular, no actor output can depend on items *outside* the actor's read scope. Our primary goal is to capture the information necessary to reconstruct and effectively present the derivation history of scientific data products, thereby supporting the main provenance needs of scientists. Thus, our approach is also different from those that focus on supporting workflow development and optimization by recording a detailed log of workflow events (e.g., execution time, invocation time-stamps, resources used); but similar in this way to efforts focusing on "scientist-oriented" provenance [9,11].

Recording Provenance Events.   Provenance is captured during a workflow run by coactors, each of which places special provenance tokens directly into the token stream (Fig. 2) as needed to record its actions. Three types of provenance tokens are used to represent distinct provenance-related events during workflow execution. Actors add *insertion tokens* to the stream for each new data and collection item they produce. An insertion token consists of (1) the actor *invocation-id* used to produce the (data or collection) item; (2) the *token-id* of the produced item; and (3) a set of *token dependencies*, i.e., the collection- and data-token identifiers within the read-scope that contributed to the insertion of the item and that were input to the actor invocation. Similarly, actors add *deletion tokens* for each data and collection item they remove from the stream. A deletion token consists of (1) the actor invocation-id that removed the data or collection item; and (2) the token-id of the item that was removed. To maintain the dependencies between data products, our system simply tags removed items as deleted, preventing downstream actors from using deleted items, while retaining these items in the stream for later use by the provenance system.

   Kepler/pPOD exploits nested data collections to help minimize the number and size of provenance tokens added to the token stream. In particular, insertion and deletion events are recorded at the highest node in the tree where they apply, and implicitly cascade to collection descendents. Insertion dependencies are applied in a similar way. For example, in Fig. 2, each alignment in an *Almnts* collection implicitly depends on each sequence in the corresponding *Seqs* collection, as indicated by the dependency between the two collections. In certain cases, actors also add *invocation-dependency* tokens to the stream that specify an ordering relation between two actor invocations. Specifically, invocation dependencies are added when actor invocations insert data or collection items that depend on a collection that was modified by a previously invoked actor. Here, a collection is considered modified when a data or collection node is added or removed (either a direct child or a descendent).

   The result of running a Kepler/pPOD workflow is represented in an execution *trace*, an XML representation of the data and collections input to and created by a workflow

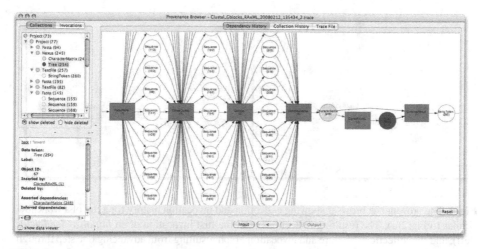

Fig. 3. The provenance browser of Kepler/pPOD showing the *integrated* dependency graph for a run of the workflow specified in Fig. 1

run, the parameter values used for configuring actors, and each of the provenance tokens added by actor invocations. Each trace is assigned a unique id by the system, and trace files are organized in the workspace according to their corresponding workflows. Traces created from previous runs can also be used as input to workflows. In such cases, the system creates a new trace for the new run, referencing the input trace and thus linking to the provenance of the previous run. Kepler/pPOD can be used in this way to capture data dependencies across multiple workflow runs.

Constructing Provenance Graphs. Two types of provenance graphs are computed for displaying provenance information within Kepler/pPOD. These graphs are constructed directly from execution trace files. An *actor invocation graph* consists of actor-invocation nodes and directed invocation-dependency edges. An edge $B:1 \rightarrow A:1$ in an invocation graph states that the first invocation of actor A was (logically) invoked prior to the first invocation of B, implying that $A:1$ produced an item used by $B:1$, or more generally, $A:1$ modified a collection used by $B:1$. A *data dependency graph* consists of nodes representing data items and directed edges representing insertion dependencies. Each edge is additionally labeled by the corresponding insertion invocation. An edge labeled $A:1$ from D_3 to $\{D_1, D_2\}$ states that data item D_3 was produced by the first invocation of actor A from data items D_1 and D_2. Thus, D_1 and D_2 were "input" to $A:1$, i.e., they were within the read scope of the invocation. Data dependency graphs in Kepler/pPOD can distinguish items that depend only on a subset of the data input to an invocation. This is often the case, e.g., for actors that implement non-strict (i.e., "streamable") functions such as sliding-window algorithms.

The COMAD provenance model can be used to derive additional information, e.g., the set of collections input to a workflow run can be determined by selecting the collection and data items that were not inserted by actors and by removing any deletion tags. Similarly, the structure of a collection can be recreated at different points in the execution history, e.g., before or after a given set of actor invocations.

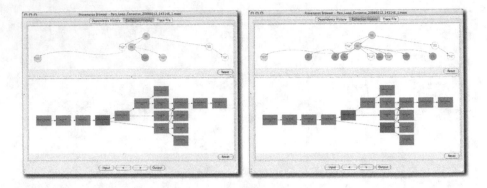

Fig. 4. The provenance browser showing collection and invocation history for a run of a workflow similar to Fig. 2(a): The resulting collections after the first invocation of an *Initialize Seed* actor (left); and the collection structure and invocation graph resulting from advancing one step through the execution history (right).

2.3   Displaying and Browsing Provenance in Kepler/pPOD

Within Kepler/pPOD, users can easily browse and navigate execution traces. The provenance browser, shown in Fig. 3, can be run directly from within Kepler/pPOD (e.g., by opening a trace file), or alternatively as a standalone application. The left-side of the browser displays the data, collections, and actor invocations of the workflow run, as well as a simple HTML navigation pane that displays details about these items. The browser also displays three different graphical views of the execution trace: (1) the *dependency history*, which combines the data-dependency and actor-invocation graphs; (2) the *collection history*, which shows how the various collections of a run were constructed (Fig. 4); and (3) the invocation graph (Fig. 4). Users can select and display the details of each item in a view (including the underlying data represented by a token, e.g., the particular sequence alignment or phylogenetic tree), and all of the views are synchronized. For instance, the selection of a data item in the dependency history also selects the corresponding item in the collection history. Using the browser, users can also incrementally step forward and backward through execution history, incrementally displaying (i.e., revealing or hiding elements, depending on navigation direction) the collection and data-dependency histories. This feature allows users to start from the input of the workflow and incrementally move forward through actor invocations to the final output. Similarly, it is possible to start at the output and navigate to the input, as well as move forward or backward at any point in between. The views in Fig. 4 are especially useful for analyzing how the structure of collections evolved throughout a workflow run; whereas the view of Fig. 3 more explicitly shows the steps and dependencies involved in generating data products.

3   Conclusion and Future Work

Kepler/pPOD supports the automation of phylogenetics workflows and the recording and visualization of data provenance for individual workflow runs. The system combines and implements our previous work on COMAD [2] and provenance [12], together with the new application presented here for browsing provenance traces and incrementally navigating execution histories. AToL projects will involve many interrelated workflows, where data produced during workflow runs commonly will be used as input to subsequent runs of different workflows, and workflows will be run multiple times with different parameterizations and on different input data sets. These projects also include tasks that cannot be fully automated between workflow runs, and the provenance of data products must be tracked across such manual data management tasks. We plan to extend Kepler/pPOD with *project histories* [13] for tracking data dependencies across multiple workflow runs and accommodating data management activities performed between runs. This will allow AToL researchers to organize their projects and data as they desire, while maintaining a continuous record of how results were obtained via a combination of manual operations and automated scientific workflows.

References

1. Ludäscher, B., et al.: Scientific workflow management and the kepler system. Concurrency and Computation: Practice & Experience 18(10), 1039–1065 (2006)
2. McPhillips, T., Bowers, S., Ludäscher, B.: Collection-oriented scientific workflows for integrating and analyzing biological data. In: Leser, U., Naumann, F., Eckman, B. (eds.) DILS 2006. LNCS (LNBI), vol. 4075, pp. 248–263. Springer, Heidelberg (2006)
3. McPhillips, T., Bowers, S., Zinn, D., Ludäscher, B.: Scientific workflow design for mere mortals. In: FGCS (to appear, 2008)
4. Majithia, S., Shields, M.S., Taylor, I.J., Wang, I.: Triana: A graphical web service composition and execution toolkit. In: ICWS (2004)
5. Oinn, T., et al.: Taverna: Lessons in creating a workflow environment for the life sciences. Concurrency and Computation: Practice & Experience 18(10), 1067–1100 (2006)
6. Bavoil, L., Callahan, S.P., Scheidegger, C.E., Vo, H.T., Crossno, P., Silva, C.T., Freire, J.: VisTrails: Enabling interactive multiple-view visualizations. In: IEEE Visualization (2005)
7. Altintas, I., Barney, O., Jaeger-Frank, E.: Provenance collection support in the kepler scientific workflow system. In: Moreau, L., Foster, I. (eds.) IPAW 2006. LNCS, vol. 4145, pp. 118–132. Springer, Heidelberg (2006)
8. Lee, E.A., Sangiovanni-Vincentelli, A.L.: A framework for comparing models of computation. IEEE Trans. on CAD of Integrated Circuits and Systems 17(12) (1998)
9. Moreau, L., Ludäscher, B. (eds.): Computation and Concurrency: Practice and Experience, vol. 20(5). Wiley, Chichester (2008)
10. Moreau, L., Freire, J., Futrelle, J., McGrath, R., Myers, J., Paulson, P.: The open provenance model. Technical Report 14979, University of Southampton (2007)
11. Biton, O., Boulakia, S.C., Davidson, S.B.: Zoom*userviews: Querying relevant provenance in workflow systems. In: VLDB (2007)
12. Bowers, S., McPhillips, T.M., Ludäscher, B.: Provenance in Collection-Oriented Scientific Workflows. Concurrency and Computation: Practice and Experience (2007)
13. Bowers, S., McPhillips, T.M., Wu, M., Ludäscher, B.: Project histories: Managing data provenance across collection-oriented scientific workflow runs. In: Cohen-Boulakia, S., Tannen, V. (eds.) DILS 2007. LNCS (LNBI), vol. 4544, pp. 122–138. Springer, Heidelberg (2007)

Using Visualization Process Graphs to Improve Visualization Exploration

T. J. Jankun-Kelly

Department of Computer Science and Engineering
James Worth Bagley College of Engineering
Mississippi State University, MS 39762, USA
tjk@acm.org

Abstract. Visualization exploration is an iterative process of setting parameters, rendering, and evaluating results. This process can be recorded and analyzed in order to make visualization exploration more efficient and more effective. This work describes methods for visualizing the visualization process using new visualization process graphs; several visualization process relations are introduced to construct these graphs. These methods were used to analyze and improve a network routing visualization, and the results of this analysis are presented. Through this analysis, redundant exploration was quickly identified and eliminated.

1 Introduction

During the visualization process, a user iteratively explores a very large space of visualization parameters in order to discover results of interest. The search of this space can be costly—especially for expensive visualization techniques. It is vital that visualization systems be designed to streamline the exploration process, but support for this sort of optimization is not common. To understand and improve visualization exploration, a user's session must be recorded and analyzed. Unnecessary and expensive re-exploration could then be identified, suggesting ways to improve the visualization interface. Visualization process graphs, depictions of different characteristics of the user's exploration, can be used to perform this analysis, leading to improved systems. This form of provenance analytics is chiefly aimed at system designers, though there are potential uses by users as well.

This work describes new methods for extracting visual representations of the visualization process. Visualization sessions are themselves visualized using the process graphs introduced here. The formalism for constructing these graphs—visualization process relations—can also be used to directly analyze aspects of the visualization sessions. As a motivating example, a case study of how visualization graphs were used to improve a network visualization tool (the OASCBrowser [1]) is discussed. The OASCBrowser looks a changes of autonomous systems (ASes) via colored lines connecting ASes to IP addresses; clusters of these indicate anomolies. The graphs were used as a "visual profiler" to detect cycles and similar redundancies. This example illustrates how the process graphs can be used to make visualization more efficient.

J. Freire, D. Koop, and L. Moreau (Eds.): IPAW 2008, LNCS 5272, pp. 78–91, 2008.

2   Background

Both scientific and information visualization can be described as an iterative process of data-filtering, visual mapping, and rendering with user interaction. Several approaches have been taken to present the history of the iterative exploration to the user. Where present, most visualization history depictions are linear graphs of next-previous relations (such as the Zoom Graphs in Polaris [2]). A more sophisticated history mechanism can be found in GRASPARC [3]. GRAS-PARC presents a tree of branching parameter settings in a problem solving environment which includes visualization. The tree is used to step back to any previous simulation setting and branch the exploration. Finally, some novel visualization user interfaces present the visualization result provenance to the user, either as a depiction of the entire visual parameter space [4], a tabular projection of that space [5], a parallel coordinates depiction of the space [6], or an interactive graph of visualization derivations [7]. Additional work has extended the depiction to include changes in the visualization's construction [8]. Recent work has also informally evaluated how to better measure the effectiveness of the visualization process [9, 10].

The previous works focused mainly on showing the history of the visualization or problem solving processes. However, for analyzing the visualization process, history alone is not sufficient. Often, there are relationships between the results and other elements of the visualization session which are vital to its understanding. The visual database exploration (VDE) work by Lee [11, 12] has identified these elements for database exploration; Lee's work encapsulates multi-result relationships based upon database structural metadata. The VDE Model also uses graphs to display process information for database exploration; lessons from the VDE work are applied here. For visualization exploration, the P-Set Model of visualization exploration [13] was developed. The P-Set Model formalizes the visualization process and discusses relationships between results and the parameters which generate them; the details of these relationships are provided in the next section. The current work extends the P-Set Model by expanding the two process graphs previously discussed (the history and derivation graphs) and introducing two new process graphs (difference and containment graphs). In addition, a set of metrics and heuristics to evaluate these graphs is discussed. Taken together, the graphs and measures provide a framework for improving visualization tools such as the OASCBrowser system.

2.1   The P-Set Model for Visualization Exploration

Visualization process graphs depict links between different results in the session. These links are dependent upon the underlying model describing the visualization process. While the graphs discussed here could be distilled from other models of visualization exploration, the P-Set Model is used for the purposes of this work.

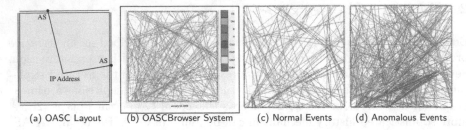

(a) OASC Layout　　(b) OASCBrowser System　　(c) Normal Events　　(d) Anomalous Events

Fig. 1. The initial Origin AS Change (OASC) Event visualization system, the OASCBrowser [1]. The ASes initiating an event (aligned around the square) are connected to the affected IP addresses within the square. Color indicates change type. Normal activity appears as a random collection of lines; anomalies in routing are detected by browsing through dates and active events types looking for correlated lines.

The P-Set Model of visualization exploration formalizes the iterative visualization cycle by describing a user's interaction with a visualization system. During such interaction, a user manipulates parameter values to form a parameter set (a *p-set*); a p-set is a collection of parameter values of different types (such as the date and active event parameters used by the OASCBrowser). Created p-sets are used to generate new results. A p-set, combined with a *visualization transform* (the operation which creates results), uniquely identifies a result; a result can be recreated given a p-set and transform. By recording how p-sets are derived from previous p-sets, the P-Set Model captures the salient details of the exploration process.

For each result generated during visualization exploration, four items are stored: a timestamp, parameter derivation information, p-set derivation information, and result derivation information. This four-tuple is known as a *derivation*. The timestamp indicates when the derivation was performed; it is possible for multiple results to be generated during the same timestamp as a consequence of a single user interaction. The parameter and p-set derivations describe which previous parameters and p-sets were used to create the new parameters and p-sets. Finally, the created results are identified by the p-sets and transforms used in their creation; the p-sets used must have been created via the parameter and p-set derivations. In this manner, each explored result is encoded by the model. Each of the four elements in a derivation will be used to form different visualization process graphs.

3　Relations and Graphs for Visualization Analysis

Visualization process graphs encode different relationships between results, parameters, and p-sets explored during a visualization session. These relationships are based upon different properties of these elements—when they were generated, what parameters they share, etc. In this section, four *visualization process relations* are introduced that are in turn used to define the process graphs.

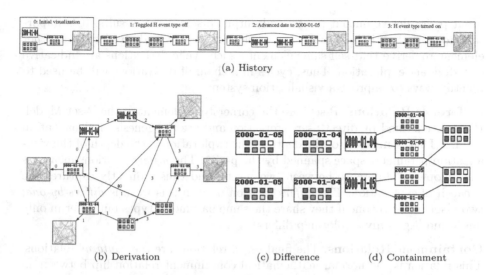

(a) History

(b) Derivation   (c) Difference   (d) Containment

Fig. 2. Visualization process graphs for a OASCBrowser session. There are two parameters types in the graphs: dates and displayed OASC events. In the example, one event type was turned off, the next date's data was loaded, and finally all event types were toggled on again.

3.1 Visualization Process Relations

Four classes of visualization relations are used in this work: *history, derivation, difference,* and *containment.* Each relation is a boolean function over two elements in a visualization session; the function is true if the corresponding relation holds. Most of these operations relate parameters, p-sets, or results. Derivations, however, are vital to most of these relations, determining if a relation holds or not.

History Relation. The history relation imposes a linear temporal ordering upon the derivations in a session. This *follows* relation holds between two derivations if the latter derivation immediately follows the former (i.e., their timestamps differ by one). Since a derivation encapsulates several sets of parameter, p-sets, and results, this relation also imposes an ordering on these elements. The *follows* relation will be used to compose history information with derivation information from the *derives* relation.

Derivation Relations. In an individual P-Set Model derivation, four things occur. First, parameters are taken from existing p-sets to be modified. These *input parameters* are manipulated by the user to create *output parameters.* These output parameters are then applied to an *input p-set* from a previous result to create an *output p-set.* Finally, this output p-set is applied to a visualization transform to generate a result image. Each of these stages imposes a relationship between the two entities—i.e., the input parameters derive the output parameters. Thus, there are five *derives* relations: P-sets derive input parameters, input parameters derive output parameters, output parameters derive output p-sets, input p-sets derive output p-sets, and output p-sets derive results. It is important to note that it is possible for an element that was derived from another element to derive that self-same element—such cyclic derivations are indicative of redundant exploration. Thus, cycles in a chain of derivations will be used to identify ways to improve a visualization system.

Difference Relations. P-sets are the cornerstone element of the P-set Model. P-sets are formed by direct user interaction and are the genesis of visualization results. Thus, a measure of the depth of the exploration is the depth of the visualization parameter space spanned by the p-sets. The *differs* relations measures the amount of difference between two p-sets, and thus indirectly captures the breadth of exploration. The *differs* relation used in this work is *differs-by-one*; two p-sets differ by one if they share the same parameter types but differ in only one value (e.g., only a colormap differs).

Containment Relations. The final set of relations are the *contains* relations. This relation is the normal mathematical containment relationship between an item and a set. In this context, the relation holds between a parameter and a p-set (if the parameter is contained within the p-set) or a parameter and a result (if the parameter is contained within the p-set used to generate that result). Similar to the *differs* relation, the containment relation measures the depth of exploration. If a single parameter value is shared among many p-sets, then further exploration could be facilitated by using a different parameter value for those same p-sets.

Using Visualization Process Relationships. Each set of relationships highlights different aspects of the visualization process. Though parameter derivation information is not present in the history relation, it gives a clear sense of the flow of time during the visualization process. The derivation relations provide a sense of parent-child relationships; this relationship could be combined with the history relation or used without. Combined, the *derives* and *follows* relations could identify how a result or p-set was first created. Alone, the *derives* relation details how that result/p-set was used in subsequent exploration. Finally, the difference and containment relations give a sense of the depth of exploration during the process. Shallow spanning trees of graphs using this relation signify a visualization process that did not deeply search the space of parameter values while deep or broad spanning trees could suggest lack of focus. In fact, using these relations to build graphs is a powerful method for performing visualization session analysis. This idea will be explored in-depth next.

3.2   Visualization Process Graphs

Each visualization process relation has a corresponding visualization process graph; these graphs visually summarize the relations. The graphs introduced here are similar in purpose and properties to the graphs of the VDE model. However, these graphs are tailored to visualization exploration. In addition, the difference and containment graphs have no analog in the VDE work. To illustrate the process graphs, Figure 2 will be used as an example; for an explanation of the OASCBrowser system used in the example, refer to Figure 1 and Section 4.

History Process Graph. The history process graph (Figure 2a) provides a visual overview of the temporal ordering of results. Each element in the sequence is a derivation that was generated by the user in a single operation. These elements are drawn from the domain and range of the *follows* relation. History can be displayed graphically using vertices representing the derivation and directed edges representing time.

The history graph is a line connecting each derivation; in interfaces that expose session information, this is the type of graph usually displayed. To be more informative, derivations components within a single time-step can be included (such as in Figure 2a). The parameters, p-sets, and results within a derivation are ordered based upon the *derives* relation: Inputs are sources while results are sinks in the derivation subgraphs. Thus, each derivation is depicted as a sequence of parameter, p-set, and result derivations. For example, node 2 in the figure clearly shows how the date from the previous result's p-set was changed from January 4, 2000 to January 5, 2000 to create a new p-set and result for the following day's events. Note, though the same p-set or parameter may be used in different derivations, each derivation's subgraph possesses a unique node for its p-set or parameter instance. This prevents edges between nodes belonging to different derivations (i.e., different time-steps); such relations are the purview of the derivation graph discussed next.

Like the OASCBrowser system, most visualization systems have derivations with only one input p-set, one input and output parameter, and one generated result. This occurs because most of these interfaces cannot manipulate more than one parameter, cannot utilize more than the immediately preceding p-set, and cannot generate more than one result at a time. A system which relaxes these constraints, such as the Image Graph [7], would have correspondingly more complex derivation information such as multiple input p-sets or created results.

Derivation Process Graph. The history process graph is insufficient for describing the relationships between results, parameters, and p-sets. Over the course of an exploration session, different parameters from the same p-set may be used to create multiple results. In addition, a result may be visited more than once. These relations are not explicitly present in the history graph. The derivation process graph captures this information (Figure 2b).

A derivation process graph is constructed from three types of nodes: parameters, p-sets, and results. For each derivation, an edge exists between two nodes if the former derives the latter according the the *derives* relation. Unlike the history graph, there is only one node per parameter, p-set, or result. Thus, nodes may have multiple incoming or outgoing edges due to derivations involving that node at different time-steps. To disambiguate these edges, they are labeled with the corresponding derivation's timestamp.

The derivation graph succinctly summarizes the ancestor-descendent relations within the visualization session; paths in the graph correspond to sequences of derivations. Landmark parameters and p-sets are easily identified by possessing a large number of incoming and outgoing edges. In addition, redundant exploration is identified by p-sets nodes with multiple incident edges with distinct time-stamps. Such edges indicate that the p-set was visited by multiple user interactions, re-creating its associated result each time. Analysis of Figure 2b shows that there was no redundant exploration (every p-set was explored only once) while one parameter was used twice (the parameter signifying that all OASC event types were displayed, lower left corner of Figure 2b).

Difference and Containment Process Graphs. The p-set difference graph and the p-set containment graph highlight the depth of exploration whereas the other graphs highlight the structure of the exploration. A difference process graph (Figure 2c) connects two p-sets if they vary by a certain number of parameter values; all difference graphs in this paper connect p-sets that differ by only one parameter. Each partition in these graphs represents similar results. The more clusters there are, the larger the explored parameter space. In Figure 2c, there are two partitions of the graph based upon parameter type—the top/bottom partition separate p-sets by which event types are displayed, while the left/right partition separates the dates explored. The number and size of such partitions are proportional to the size of the parameter space explored. Many, small partitions indicate a broad exploration of several different parameter types while few, large partitions correspond to a session with significant depth in one parameter.

Containment graphs (Figure 2d) depict how the explored p-sets are composed from the explored parameters: An edge exists between a parameter and a p-set if the parameter belongs to the p-set. The relative number of parameters of different types and p-sets are another indicator of the depth of exploration. Parameter types which dominate the exploration are easily spotted by how they outnumber the other parameter type nodes. If the number of p-sets dominates the graph, then the parameter space was highly explored. In Figure 2d, every valid combination of parameter values generated was explored during the session.

Using Visualization Process Graphs. Visualization process graphs serve two functions: They provide an overview of the visualization process and allow that process to be analyzed. The history and derivation graphs are most useful in the former application; the last three are vital for the latter. The history graph, augmented with derivation information, could be used as a browser over the visualization session; the Image Graph can be considered an implementation of a subset of this graph. Like the Image Graph, the history graph could be made interactive. This interaction would provide a sophisticated mechanism to build results from previous results. Such a system is beyond the scope of this discussion.

Several methods for analyzing visualization process graphs have already been introduced (i.e., looking at the number of incident edges to a p-set with differing time-stamps in the derivation graph). These methods can be formalized via *visualization process metrics*. Each metric is a function over a graph, node, or edge and summarizes properties of the graph; the properties relate to characteristics of the exploration. Previously, Lee [12] developed a set of metrics for the VDE model; we adapt some of them and introduce several new ones. The metrics introduced here are tailored to visualization exploration, and measure statistics relevant to such exploration:

- *Importance Metric.* For a given node in a derivation process graph, the important metric counts the degree of the node—the total number of incoming and outgoing edges. Nodes with a higher degree were derived by or derived multiple results in the exploration session, and thus were integral to that process. For the sample session, the p-sets which derived the second and third results have the most importance; however this difference is not significant (the next importance value is only one less than the maximum).

- *Redundancy and Efficiency Metrics.* For a given derivation process graph, the redundancy metric counts the number of incident edges to any p-set which have different time-stamps. This metric could be applied directly to p-sets to count the number of times the p-set was re-explored. Recall that p-sets, combined with visualization transform, uniquely identify a result; thus, a measure of the redundancy of one is a measure of the redundancy of the other.

  Given a redundancy value, a measure of efficiency can be derived. The inefficiency of a session is the ratio of the redundant edges to the total number of p-set derivation edges in the derivation graph; the efficiency is one minus this number. For the sample session, the efficiency was 100%—no p-set was explored more than once.

- *Depth Metric.* The value of the depth metric is the maximum number of neighbors of any node in the p-set difference graph. This value is also the size of the largest cluster in the difference graph. Since each node in this cluster must differ by only one parameter type, the sub-space of the parameter space spanned by this type was well explored. For the sample session, the depth value was 2 parameter settings.

- *Breadth and Coverage Metrics.* The breadth of a visualization session is defined as the number of p-sets explored during the session—the more p-sets generated, the larger the explored visualization parameter space. A more meaningful measure is coverage; this is the number of p-sets explored over the possible number of valid p-sets in the session. This value can be calculated from the containment graph: The total number of valid p-sets for a single visualization transform is the product of the count of parameter values nodes for the transform's associated parameter types (e.g., if there are 3 dates and 2 selections of events, there are 6 possible valid p-sets); the total number of valid p-sets is the sum of the valid p-sets for each transform. For the sample session in Figure 2d, the coverage was 100% since there were two parameters values for each of the two parameter types and four explored p-sets. While the coverage metric is useful for understanding the extent of the exploration, is not necessarily a measure of its effectiveness—not all combinations of parameter values are equally meaningful.

These metrics provide heuristics to evaluate a visualization system. Assuming that the re-exploration of results is costly and should be avoided, systems should strive for a high efficiency (limiting redundancy). If a certain parameter has a high depth value, it suggests that a means to more quickly explore this sub-space of the visualization parameter space could be beneficial. While process graphs do not capture every characteristic of a visualization system (such as its running-time or memory efficiency), they capture the essential properties of explorations using that system. The use of the graphs and their associated will be explored in more depth in the following section.

4   Case Study: Improving the OASCBrowser

The OASCBrowser [1] is a tool for visually detecting anomalies in internet routing information (Figure 1). The tool displays different types of changes to ownership of autonomous systems (ASes)—groups of hosts on the Internet. The different types of changes (called *OASC events*) are labeled with different colors. The colored lines connect ASes along the edge of a square to points within the square corresponding to the IP address affected by the change. The tool allows a user to browse through recorded dates with different types of AS changes highlighted. Anomalies are found by visually searching the dates for unusual patterns—normal behavior appears random while abnormal behavior appears as correlated lines.

The user can manipulate two different parameter settings for the OASCBrowser: The currently displayed date, and which OASC events to display. There are eight event types; the display of each can be individually toggled. The OASCBrowser does not provide a history mechanism—only the last result may be manipulated by the user. Thus, to compare a previous result, a user must recreate its parameter settings manually. As will be demonstrated, this leads to significant inefficiency during exploration.

4.1   Example Session and Analysis

Several visualization sessions were analyzed; all showed similar behavior. In an exemplar session, a range of OASC events between August 1st and August 22nd, 2000 were visualized. During this exploration, three sets of anomalies were discovered: A pair of correlated anomalies near August 1st, a major anomaly and its correction between the 14th and 17th, and another pair of correlated events on the 21st. In the session, 61 parameters and 76 p-sets and results were generated. Since there was only one visualization transform (the OASC Event visualization), there is a one-to-one correspondence between p-sets and results.

Figure 3 depicts the derivation, containment, and difference graphs for this session. For clarity, the derivation graph has been collapsed into a different (but equivalent) view of the session that shows only result derivations. Since there is a one-to-one correspondence between these two graphs (as there is only visualization type), the graphs are isomorphic.

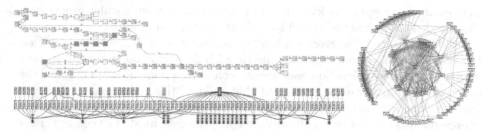

Fig. 3. Visualization process graphs for the original OASCBrowser viewing events during August 1–22, 2000. Top-left: Result derivation. Bottom-left: P-Set Containment. Right: P-set Difference.

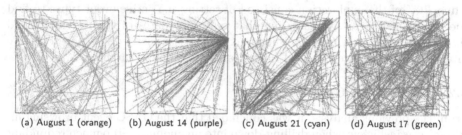

(a) August 1 (orange)   (b) August 14 (purple)   (c) August 21 (cyan)   (d) August 17 (green)

Fig. 4. Landmark results in the example exploration session. Each is highlighted in the graphs in Figure 3 using the given color. The August 1st and 21st results show two correlated anomalies each; each pair of events is of different types. The August 14th result shows anomalous events that are later corrected by events on the 17th.

Several observations can be made from the session's process graphs. First, there are several cycles in the exploration. The cycles occur in three portions of the derivation graph: The upper half (the August 1st anomalies), the lower left (the major anomaly between August 14th and 17th), and the lower right of the graph (the August 21st anomalies). In fact, the three most important results in the derivation graphs (according to the importance metric) correspond to these three anomalies (Figure 4a–c, outlined in orange, purple, and cyan respectively in Figure 3). For the August 1st and 21st anomalies, it is telling that each important result displays the two correlated events together; the derivation graph shows that these results were generated multiple times while the user toggled the two events on and off in order to isolate them.

The exploration of the August 14th anomaly is more complex. Upon initial inspection, the visualization is flooded with H (green) events. However, further analysis shows that the cause of these corrective events is one AS's OS (purple) events; these events correspond to the result highlighted in the figures. The exploration cycle here is complex for several reasons. First, there are the multiple anomalous events (the H and OS events) on the August 14th date; this causes the toggling seen before. However, there is a another set of anomalous H events three days later from the same AS (Figure 4d, highlighted in green in Figures 3); these are another set of corrective events. In the exploration session, the user compared the 14th and

17th events by stepping back and forward in time and changing which events were displayed. This caused the nested loops in the derivation graph.

As demonstrated, the given exploration session was inefficient: It has 70% efficiency according to our efficiency metric with 28 redundant derivations—over a quarter of the exploration was spent recreating previous results. From the difference graph, it can be confirmed that most of this redundant exploration was over one parameter type, the displayed events—most of the outer clusters represents toggling active events while keeping the date fixed. The center cluster represents p-sets stepping through time. The distribution of parameter values in the containment graph also supports the inefficient parameter exploration conclusion. The parameter corresponding to rendering all event types (bold border in the upper middle of the figure) covers 30% of the p-set nodes in the graph. Thus, 70% of the exploration consisted of setting the active event types to find the events of interest. Considering that only four dates of the 22 viewed had significant anomalies, this parameter exploring is unneeded. A more effective interface would reduce the need for excessive parameter searching.

4.2   The Refined OASCBrowser

From the previous analysis, it was concluded that the OASC event browsing interface was inefficient when drilling-down into an anomaly—too much redundant activity was spent toggling through the parameter values to find the event types of interest. The occlusion of the events was determined to be the cause of this toggling; analysts could not perceive specific events when exploring an anomaly. However, the ability to show all the event types simultaneously in one image was found useful to quickly spot when anomalies occur. Thus, a new interface was designed that showed both the overview visualization and visualizations for each of the event types concurrently (Figure 5, see Teoh [14] for details). By using multiple views, unneeded parameter generation is avoided.

Figure 5 depicts the process graphs for the exploration of the August 1st–22nd, 2000 events using new the interface. The new interface does improve the exploration, though it does not remove all inefficiencies. The difference graph

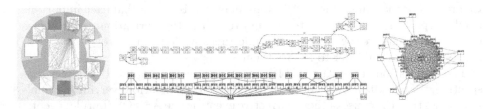

Fig. 5. The refined OASCBrowser interface (showing the anomalous events of August 14th, 2000) and corresponding process graphs for the exploration of August 1–22, 2000. The new interface displays the combined OASC event view in addition to a view for each individual event; events from the surrounding dates are also shown. This reduces the amount of redundant exploration compared to the original interface. Middle-Top: Result Derivation. Middle-Bottom: P-Set Containment. Right: P-Set Difference.

shows that the exploration was more dense; the majority of the p-sets only changed their date parameter. Because the new interface allowed users to drill-down to individual events directly, more interactions were spent exploring the dates than the event types. The containment graph corroborates this finding; it shows that only 30% of the parameter exploration focused on individual anomaly types. Since the majority of dates did not have anomalies, this exploration is more in line with the actual data, unlike the original interface.

While the new interface does reduce the need for excessive parameter manipulation, it still suffers from inefficiency. For the given session, the overall efficiency is 56%, less than that of the original interface. If the results exploring the August 14–17 events are excluded, the efficiency rises to 85%, an improvement over the original browser. This signifies that for correlated anomalies on the same date (such as the August 1st and 21st anomalies), the new interface is more efficient—fewer derivations are needed to drill-down to individual events. However, the new OASCBrowser does not solve the problem of comparing anomalies from different dates; a user is still required to re-explore the intervening date's results. Further interface refinement could address this issue.

5 Discussion

Analyzing a user's process via the process graphs allowed us to improve the OASCBrowser. The graphs clearly identified cycles in exploration and reinforced some issues we had previously identified. It is important to note the the exact metrics are user dependent—each user will have slightly different patterns—so aggregate or holistic examination of the different sessions will be required. All users of the tool in our case study were familiar with it, so the question of how novice and expert sessions vary is still open.

The P-Set Model explicitly captures changes in parameters, not in other aspects of the visualization. For systems such as the OASCBrowser which are not modular (i.e., not extendable by adding new components or by changing the visualization pipeline), the P-Set Model is adequate. For modular visualization environments, the P-Set Model can capture interactions with complete pipelines, but not explicitly capture changes within the pipeline. Extensions to capture pipeline changes are possible so long as the model is derivational—modifications to the more transaction-based approach used in VisTrails [8] is conceivable initial approach. In this sort of model, the visualization transform of a p-set would refer to complete transforms which would be built/modified by the transform model. Annotation of such changes (e.g., why the user performed an operation) is easily added by capturing it and using an RDF-like model [15] to extend the XML representation [13].

While the metrics presented are agnostic to the number of parameters used in the visualization, the graph-based representation may need to be condensed or collated in some fashion. This is especially true for the difference relation: More possible parameters will explode the number of possible nodes. An intelligent clustering scheme would elide individual nodes to display only groups of interest. For very long sessions, a similar graph summarization approach would be needed for the containment and derivation relations. Such condensation is especially important if the graphs are to be used by users directly; only more recent derivations will be typically of interest, and chains of non-branching derivations could be summarized.

6 Conclusions

The provenance of the visualization process is complex. To gain an understanding of visualization sessions—and perhaps a better understanding of the data originally visualized—this information needs to be visualized. Four graphs examining different parts of the visualization process were presented, and an in-depth example demonstrated the uses of this kind of analysis.

There are several potential applications for the work presented here. Visualizations of the visualization process give insight into the process and the interfaces used. The analysis of both OASCBrowser interfaces suggested areas of refinement, and a quantifiable improvement was observed for the refined interface. Similar analysis could be performed on other visualization systems. Other potential uses include communicating results and exploration sessions to collaborators, validation of sessions, and navigation of the visualization parameter space during exploration.

6.1 Future Work

As mentioned, one area of further study is the development of additional relations and metrics for visualization process analysis. Of interest is the identification and quantifying of the common patterns within process graphs. If quantified, a data-mining system could then be used to automatically identify these patterns and call attention to them when displaying the process. This automation would assist in the understanding of the visualization process. Besides improving the visualization interface, this analysis could also be used to perform usability studies utilizing the metrics presented here.

Another avenue of research is the integration of visual analysis tools with visualization systems. During the visualization, the user could also be presented with visualization process graphs summarizing the exploration. This depiction could help in parameter space navigation and be used as a history tool to return to different results in a manner similar to the Image Graph.

Acknowledgments

The author would like to thank Kwan-Liu Ma and Soon Tee Teoh for their input and discussion and for access to the original OASC visualization tool. Melanie Tory feedback on an initial draft of this work are appreciated. GraphViz from AT&T Research was used to generate the graph images.

References

1. Teoh, S.T., Ma, K.L., Wu, F., Zhao, X.: Case study: Interactive visualization for internet security. In: Proc. of 13th IEEE Conference on Visualization (Vis 2002), pp. 505–508 (2002)
2. Stolte, C., Tang, D., Hanrahan, P.: Multiscale visualization using data cubes. IEEE Trans. on Visualization and Computer Graphics 9(2), 176–187 (2003)
3. Brodlie, K., Poon, A., Wright, H., Brankin, L., Banecki, G., Gay, A.: GRASPARC–A problem solving environment integrating computation and visualization. In: Proc. of the 4th IEEE Conference on Visualization (Vis 1993), pp. 102–109 (1993)
4. Marks, J., Andalman, B., Beardsley, P.A., Freeman, W., Gibson, S., Hodgins, J., Kang, T., Mirtich, B., Pfister, H., Ruml, W., Ryall, K., Seims, J., Shieber, S.: Design Galleries: A general approach to setting parameters for computer graphics and animation. In: Proc. of ACM SIGGRAPH 1997, pp. 389–400 (1997)
5. Jankun-Kelly, T.J., Ma, K.L.: Visualization exploration and encapsulation via a spreadsheet-like interface. IEEE Trans. on Visualization and Computer Graphics 7(3), 275–287 (2001)
6. Tory, M., Potts, S., Möller, T.: A parallel coordinates style interface for exploratory volume visualization. IEEE Trans. on Visualization and Computer Graphics 11(1), 71–80 (2005)
7. Ma, K.L.: Image Graphs—A novel approach to visual data exploration. In: Proc. of the 10th IEEE Conference on Visualization (Vis 1999), pp. 81–89, 513 (1999)
8. Bavoil, L., Callahan, S.P., Crossno, P.J., Freire, J., Scheidegger, C.E., Silva, C.T., Vo, H.T.: Vistrails: Enabling interactive multiple-view visualizations. In: Proc. of the 16th IEEE Conference on Visualization (Vis 2005), pp. 135–142 (2005)
9. Perer, A., Shneiderman, B.: Integrating statistics and visualization: case studies of gaining clarity during exploratory data analysis. In: Proc. of CHI 2008, pp. 265–274 (2008)
10. Shrinivasan, Y.B., van Wijk, J.J.: Supporting the analytical reasoning process in information visualization. In: Proc. of CHI 2008, pp. 1237–1246 (2008)
11. Lee, J.P., Grinstein, G.G.: An architecture for retaining and analyzing visual explorations of databases. In: Proc. of the 6th IEEE Conference on Visualization (Vis 1995), pp. 101–108 (1995)
12. Lee, J.P.: A Systems and Process Model for Data Exploration. PhD thesis, U. of Mass. Lowell (1998)
13. Jankun-Kelly, T.J., Ma, K.L., Gertz, M.: A model and framework for visualization exploration. IEEE Trans. on Visualization and Computer Graphics 13(2), 357–369 (2007)
14. Teoh, S.T., Jankun-Kelly, T.J., Ma, K.L., Wu, S.F.: Visual data analysis for detecting flaws and intruders in computer network systems. IEEE Comp. Graph. and Applications 24(5), 27–35 (2004)
15. Lassila, O., Swick, R.R.: Resource Description Framework (RDF) Model and Syntax Specification. Technical report, World Wide Web Consortium (1999), http://www.w3.org/TR/REC-rdf-syntax

Implementation and Evaluation of a Protocol for Recording Process Documentation in the Presence of Failures

Zheng Chen and Luc Moreau

School of Electronics and Computer Science
University of Southampton, Southampton, SO17 1BJ, UK
{zc05r,L.Moreau}@ecs.soton.ac.uk

Abstract. The *provenance* of a particular data item is the process that led to that piece of data. Previous work has enabled the creation of detailed representation of past executions for determining provenance, termed *process documentation*. However, current solutions to recording process documentation assume a failure free environment. Failures result in process documentation not being recorded, thereby causing the loss of evidence that a process occurred. We have designed F-PReP, a protocol to guarantee the recording of process documentation in the presence of failures. This paper discusses its implementation and evaluates its performance. The result reveals that it introduces acceptable overhead.

1 Introduction

The *provenance* of a data product refers to the process that led to that data product [6]. Previous work [6] has enabled a computer-based representation of a past process for determining provenance, i.e., *process documentation*. A dedicated repository, *provenance store*, is used to persistently maintain process documentation. For scalability reasons, process documentation may end up distributed in multiple stores, linked by pointers. Using the pointer chain, distributed process documentation can be retrieved from one store to another.

A generic recording protocol, PReP [6], has been developed to record process documentation in Grids. It has been used in many applications, e.g., aerospace engineering [8], fault tolerance in distributed systems [15], and biodiversity [14]. Grids are large-scale heterogeneous environments, where failures may happen. Failure rates as high as 30% have been reported [13]. In this context, reliable recording of documentation can become very challenging, given that the documentation produced in a process can be of the order of terabytes [5].

PReP, however, does not specify a well-defined behavior to record process documentation in the presence of failures. For example, a provenance store may not be available and network connection may be broken. The consequences are that documentation fails to be recorded in provenance stores and the pointer chain is broken, separating distributed documentation into isolated islands in provenance stores. A scientific application, to be described in this paper, used

J. Freire, D. Koop, and L. Moreau (Eds.): IPAW 2008, LNCS 5272, pp. 92–105, 2008.
© Springer-Verlag Berlin Heidelberg 2008

PReP to record process documentation in the presence of simulated failures. By analyzing the contents of provenance stores after the application completes, we find that the quality of documentation recorded using PReP is poor, as demonstrated in Fig. 1 and Fig. 2. In Fig. 1, as failure rate increases, a large proportion of process documentation fails to be recorded. Fig. 2 reveals the increase in the number of dangling links, i.e., pointers to other provenance stores that were supposed to record part of process documentation but did not, and in the number of isolated documentation islands.

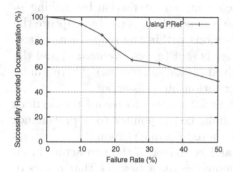 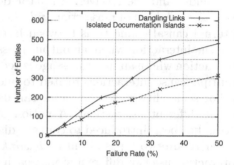

Fig. 1. Loss of documentation records in provenance stores

Fig. 2. Dangling links and isolated islands in provenance stores

Process documentation of poor quality cannot be utilized by applications. We now draw a parallel between the documentation of a process and a particular type of evidence in a legal setting, testimony. The absence of testimony from eyewitnesses to a crime scene makes it difficult for juries to make a judgment about whether to believe the claims provided by a suspect. Similarly, poor quality process documentation is not acceptable in the applications that rely on process documentation to verify the provenance of their data products, as key evidence that a process occurred may have been lost.

To guarantee the recording of *high quality*, i.e., complete and connected, process documentation in Grids where failures may occur, we have extended PReP and designed a recording protocol, F-PReP. F-PReP provides remedial actions and a novel component, Update Coordinator. It has been formalized as an abstract state machine and its correctness has been proved in [4].

The contribution of this paper is the extensive evaluation of this novel protocol. Our evaluation is conducted at several levels. First, we measure the throughput of the provenance store and update coordinator. We demonstrate that the update coordinator is not a performance bottleneck. Second, we benchmark the recording performance of F-PReP. The results show that its remedial actions introduce small overhead (below 10%). Third, we investigate the performance impact on the execution time of a scientific application. We find that PReP and F-PReP have similar impact on application execution when there is no failure. In tests with failures, the recording overhead of F-PReP varies depending on configurations. Lessons are learned on achieving good performance in the case of failures. Our results also show that the problems in Fig. 1 and Fig. 2 do not exist when using F-PReP to record process documentation.

2   Protocol Outline

2.1   Terminology

A process is modeled as a set of interactions between actors [6]. Each *interaction* is concerned with one application message exchanged between two actors, i.e., the sender and the receiver. An actor documents an interaction by making *p-assertions*. A kind of p-assertion, *relationship p-assertion*, is used to capture the internal causal connections between interactions within the scope of an actor, i.e., the interaction where an output message is sent (*effect interaction*) and the interaction where an input message is received (*cause interaction*). There can be multiple cause interactions related to one relationship p-assertion.

For scalability reason, an actor can use various stores to record p-assertions about different interactions. A notion of link, i.e., a pointer to a provenance store, has been introduced to connect distributed documentation [6].

There are two types of links: *viewlink* and *causelink*. If the two actors in an interaction use two different stores, each actor records a *viewlink* that points to the provenance store where the opposite party recorded its p-assertions about that interaction. Therefore, both views of an interaction can be retrieved by navigating from one store to the other. The causelink is used in relationship p-assertion. If the p-assertions that represent a cause interaction are recorded in a different provenance stores, a *causelink* is embedded in the relationship p-assertion, indicating which provenance store the p-assertions representing the cause interaction are stored in. A relationship p-assertion is recorded in the context of its effect interaction, describing the causes that led to the effect.

2.2   Failure Assumptions

Provenance stores may crash, i.e., they halt and stop any further execution, and can be restarted from their latest consistent state[1]; messages to/from provenance stores can be lost, reordered but not duplicated in communication channels; an actor has several alternative provenance stores to use. We do not consider the failures of actors and the exchange of application messages, since they are application dependant and the application should provide its own fault tolerance mechanisms to ensure its availability and reliable communication.

2.3   Protocol Outline

F-PReP[4] has been designed to meet the following requirements:

- *Guaranteed Recording.* After a process finishes execution, the entire documentation of that process must eventually be recorded in provenance store(s).

---

[1] The provenance store has been implemented as a stateless web service with a database storage system. Hence the latest consistent state refers to the initial state of the service and the latest checkpointed state of the database.

– *Viewlink Accuracy.* Viewlinks recorded for each interaction of a process must eventually be accurate. Each must point to the store where the other actor in the same interaction recorded p-assertions documenting that interaction.
– *Causelink Accuracy.* Causelinks recorded during a process must eventually be accurate. Each must point to the store where p-assertions about the corresponding cause interaction were recorded.
– *Efficient Recording.* Recording p-assertions and taking remedial actions should be efficient and introduce minimum overhead.

Fig. 3 demonstrates an example of message exchanges in F-PReP. The default provenance stores that the sender and receiver use are $PS1$ and $PS2$, respectively. The sender and receiver create p-assertions documenting the interaction where an application message app is exchanged (Step 1). Asynchronously, they submit all their p-assertions about the interaction and a viewlink[2] in a single message, record, to their provenance store. Before delivering a record message, an actor checks all the relationship p-assertions in the message and updates incorrect causelinks in order to meet *Causelink Accuracy* requirement.

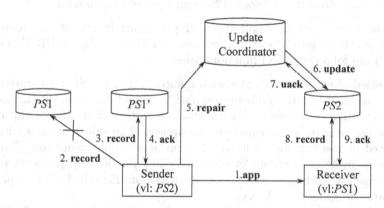

Fig. 3. An example of message exchanges in F-PReP

An actor sets a timeout when waiting for an acknowledgement ack immediately after it sends a record to a provenance store (Steps 2, 8). A provenance store acknowledges a record by means of an ack message, only *after* it has successfully recorded the content of record in its persistent storage. If an ack is not received before a timeout, an actor can conclude that failures may have occurred; it can then resend the same record to the actor's default store or an alternative store (Step 3). However, the use of an alternative store leads to incorrect causelinks or viewlinks, hence requiring an update. In the example of Fig. 3, the receiver's viewlink to $PS1$ becomes incorrect.

We introduced an update coordinator to facilitate viewlink updating. An update coordinator is necessary since both sender and receiver may issue a repair

---

[2] We assume the sender and receiver know their viewlink to $PS2$ and $PS1$, respectively, by means of built-in knowledge.

request in an interaction. This cannot be achieved by direct update of the other actor's provenance store, because at that moment, one does not know which store the opposite actor is actually using. In Fig. 3, the sender requests the co-ordinator (Step 5) to help update the receiver's viewlink in $PS2$ (Step 6). After updating a viewlink, $PS2$ returns an acknowledgement message uack (Step 7).

We assume *the update coordinator does not crash*. We can use the traditional fault-tolerance mechanisms such as replication to ensure its availability. This is feasible since a coordinator maintains only a small amount of information, as illustrated later. However, it is not feasible to replicate provenance stores which usually maintain a large amount of process documentation. Because replication, although sophisticated, comes with a significant cost due to the preservation of the *one-copy equivalence* property [11].

3   Implementation

The implementation of F-PReP involves three parts: Provenance Support Library (F-PSL), Provenance Store (PS), and Update Coordinator.

F-PSL includes a set of Application Programming Interfaces to create and record p-assertions into a provenance store. F-PSL extends the PReP-oriented PSL with the following novel functionalities:

(1) Remedial actions that cope with failures. First, F-PSL resubmits record messages according to the policies specified by a configuration file, including a list of alternative stores. Second, it maintains a history of the use of alternative stores during an actor's participation in a process. This information is currently maintained in memory and deleted when an application completes. Third, F-PSL checks an actor's causelinks when recording relationship p-assertions and updates them according to the history information. Fourth, F-PSL requests a coordinator to update viewlinks.

(2) Multithreading for the creation and recording of p-assertions. F-PSL enables the concurrent creation and recording of p-assertions during application execution. An application's requests for creating p-assertions are queued to be processed by a creation thread. Created p-assertions are also kept in a queue (in the form of record messages) before being submitted to a store by a recording thread. Basic flow control is provided in the form of queue management.

(3) A local file store for temporarily maintaining p-assertions. If recording p-assertions significantly degrades an application's performance, p-assertions can be maintained locally and submitted later. We employ Berkeley DB Java Edition database (BDB) as the local file store for its ease of installation.

PS has been implemented as a Java Servlet and deployed in the Apache Tomcat Servlet container[1]. It supports several types of backend data stores. Our implementation and experiments were based on BDB. We extend the current implementation of PS in terms of the following aspects:

(1) Disk cache. A PS *persistently* caches a received record message to disk before providing an acknowledgement[3], and at a later stage processes the record message and stores p-assertions. This caching mechanism delays actual message processing and hence saves on the overhead of processing messages.

(2) Update Plug-In. PS has been designed to facilitate convenient integration of new features through the use of plug-ins. A new plug-in, Update Plug-In, is implemented to receive update requests from the coordinator and update requested view links.

Update Coordinator is implemented as a Java Servlet and deployed in the Tomcat container. It receives a repair request from an actor and maintains the requested information in a local file store before sending an update message to a provenance store to update a requested view link.

Only minimum information is maintained for each repair request: the identity of the destination store that needs to be updated, and the identity of the store that successfully recorded the requesting actor's record message for a given interaction. The maintained information is used to cope with the case where both actors in an interaction request to update the other's viewlink in that interaction. The internal behavior of the coordinator and the management of maintained request information are detailed in [4].

Similarly to PS, the coordinator persistently caches received repair requests in its local file store, and at a later stage processes these requests to save on the overhead of processing messages. An actor continues its execution after receiving a response indicating its repair request has been cached in the coordinator. BDB is also employed as the file store.

An application can utilize multiple coordinators in its process. When using more than one, any two actors exchanging an application message must share the same one in order to ensure VIEWLINK ACCURACY requirement. The identifier of a coordinator can be built in actors or exchanged to other actors in the application message app.

4 Performance Evaluation

Our experiments were run on the Iridis Computing Cluster at the University of Southampton. Iridis contains several sets of nodes (i.e. computers). Nodes used in the experiments each have two Single Core AMD Opteron processors running at 2.2 GHz and 2 GB of RAM. Provenance store and update coordinator were run on nodes each with 4 Dual Core AMD Opteron processors running at 2.4 Ghz and 2 GB of RAM. In the experiments with failures, one coordinator was employed, installed on a node of the cluster. All nodes are connected by Gigabit Ethernet. All applications used in the evaluation were written in Java and were run using the Java 1.5.0 05 64-bit Server Virtual Machine.

---

[3] The PS in PReP, though caching a record message into BDB before replying an acknowledgement, does not force the message into disk by flushing operating system's buffers, thus having a risk of losing p-assertions if operating system fails.

Since failures are non-deterministic in nature and typically very hard to predict, a generator was used on an actor's side to inject random failure events, i.e, failure to submit a record message to a provenance store or failure to receive an acknowledgement from a provenance store before a timeout. The presence of such an event triggers an actor to take remedial actions. The generator generates a failure event based on a failure rate, i.e., the number of failure events that occur during a total number of recordings. Given a timeout, the generator postpones generating a failure event until the timeout expires. The advantage of using a failure generator is that it enables us to fully control the number of failures that may occur so as to investigate the correlation between recording performance and failure rate.

Our evaluation was conducted at three levels. First, we measured the throughput of the provenance store and update coordinator. We also investigated how the contention for the coordinator affects an actor's recording performance when the number of recording actors increases. Then, we benchmarked the recording performance of F-PReP without considering contention. Third, we investigated F-PReP's impact on the execution time of a scientific application. In each level, we performed two experiments: failure-free experiment and experiment with failures. A comparison with PReP was made in the failure-free experiment. In our evaluation, when we say recording p-assertions using F-PReP or PReP, we mean their respective client side library, F-PSL or PSL, was used, and the provenance store was configured with or without disk cache, respectively.

4.1   Throughput Experiment

Provenance Store. In Section 3, a *disk cache* mechanism is introduced as the default setup of a provenance store in F-PReP. This means the store forces every received record message into disk before providing an acknowledgement in order to maintain the durability of p-assertions. However, this mechanism may sacrifice a provenance store's throughput (i.e. the number of p-assertions accepted in a period of time).

We performed two failure-free tests with and without *disk cache* enabled, respectively. On each node, we created up to 16 threads (i.e., clients) recording 10k p-assertions at the same time. An MPI based test harness was used in the experiments to guarantee that all clients were run in parallel. Given that an experiment is allowed to use up to 32 nodes in the Iridis environment, we can have 512 clients simultaneously recording p-assertions into a provenance store. P-assertions are recorded with a new record message created for each p-assertion. All p-assertions were directly created and submitted to a provenance store without using threading.

Fig. 4 shows the results. In both setups, the provenance store's throughput levels off, where about 212,200 and 176,000 10k p-assertions are accepted in a 10 minute period in the setup *without disk cache* and *with disk cache*, respectively. This means a store's throughput decreases by 20% due to enabling disk cache.

Update Coordinator. We also measured the coordinator's throughput (i.e. the number of repair requests accepted in a period of time) with up to 512

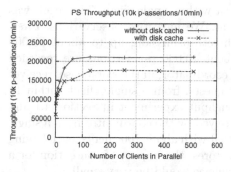

Fig. 4. Provenance Store Throughput   **Fig. 5.** Coordinator Throughput

clients simultaneously sending repair messages to an update coordinator. To save on the cost of network connection, 100 repair requests were sent to a coordinator in a single message. Fig. 5 shows that a coordinator can accept up to around 30,000*100 repair requests in a 10 minute period. This means there were 30,000*100 recording failures in 10 minutes, which is unlikely to see in applications.

4.2 Throughput Experiment with Failures

This experiment investigated: (1) the impact of contention for a coordinator on a client's recording performance[4]; (2) the tradeoff between resending a record message to the same provenance store and to an alternative store.

We conducted two experiments where a single client and 128 clients kept recording 10k p-assertions into one provenance store in a 10 minute period. Various failure rates (5%, 10%, 16%, 20%, 25%, 33% and 50%) were considered. We did not consider failure rates beyond 50% because it is not realistic [13]. Another provenance store was employed as the alternative store. One coordinator was used in the experiments and 100 repair requests were sent in a single batch. Since the more failures the more repair requests[5], failure events were immediately generated without considering timeouts to maximize the number of repair requests that could be sent to the coordinator within 10 minutes.

There exists a tradeoff between using the same provenance store or an alternative one when resubmitting a record message. Retransmitting messages to the same provenance store can tolerate transient failures, such as message loss. However, if a provenance store has crashed and is to be recovered after a long period of time, resending messages to the same store is not a good solution. On the other hand, the use of an alternative store, though provides guaranteed recording, ends up with an actor's causelinks or another actor's viewlink incorrect. This introduces additional cost of updating links. We compared the two approaches in our experiments.

---

[4] The impact of contention for a provenance store has been studied in [6].
[5] Recall that a repair request is produced after a record message is successfully recorded into an alternative store.

Fig. 6 shows the result in the experiment with a single client. The result was averaged from five runs of the experiment. We have two observations. First, when using the alternative store in each retransmission, up to about 20,000 repair requests are produced (because about 40,000 p-assertions are recorded when failure rate is 50%). This means the coordinator, in the worst case, receives 200 batches, each containing 100 repair requests, from a single client within 10 minutes. According to coordinator's throughput experiment in Section 4.1 and the fact that the 200 repair batches are received by the coordinator from a single client all across 10 minutes, we can imply that with about 100 clients, each having its own provenance store and alternative stores, the impact of contention for a coordinator on a client's recording performance would be very small.

The second observation is that resending messages to the same provenance store can record more p-assertions than to an alternative store, assuming that only transient failures are present. This is because the use of an alternative store requires extra actions to update links.

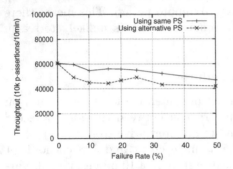 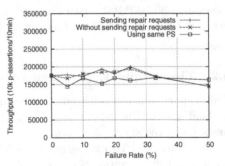

Fig. 6. Throughput experiment (single client)

Fig. 7. Throughput experiment (128 clients)

Fig. 7 shows the result when 128 clients record p-assertions into one provenance store in the presence of failures. This experiment considers the contention for a provenance store as well as potential contention for a coordinator. We also have two observations. First, communicating with the coordinator does not affect total throughput. This implies that the contention for a coordinator is negligible (It can be calculated that up to about 750 repair batches are sent to the coordinator from 128 clients in 10 minutes.). Second, using an alternative store, in general, results in more p-assertions recorded than using a same store to resend p-assertions. This is because the use of an alternative store helps to balance the load of recording p-assertions (especially when failure rate is 25%), though introducing additional cost of updating links.

From these experiments, we have two conclusions. First, the coordinator is scalable and the impact of its contention on a client's recording performance is very small or negligible. Since our implementation supports the use of multiple coordinators, we believe the introduced component, update coordinator, does not affect an application's recording performance. Second, to achieve a better recording performance, an alternative store should be employed after resending messages to a same provenance store has failed for certain times.

4.3   Benchmark Experiments

We now investigate the recording performance of a single actor without considering contentions. All the benchmark experiments were run with one client recording p-assertions into one provenance store. All p-assertions were directly created and submitted to a provenance store without using threading.

Failure-free Experiment. The experiment compares F-PReP to PReP in a failure-free environment. We measured the time to record 10,000 10k p-assertions. To minimize the impact of network connection overhead, 100 p-assertions were shipped in a same record message. Measurements were taken after recording a record message. Fig. 8 summarizes the record time. The graph displays an average from ten trials. From the figure, we have two observations:

(1) The provenance store without using disk cache, i.e., in the setup *using PReP*, periodically flushes 900 p-assertions from its operating system buffers into disk. This means if the provenance store's operating system crashes, up to 900 10k p-assertions may be lost.

(2) The average time to record 100 10k p-assertions is 198.8ms and 174.4ms using F-PReP and PReP, respectively. Therefore, F-PReP has an overhead of 13.8% compared to PReP. We note that in an application, the impact of F-PReP on the application's performance is similar to that of PReP, as illustrated later in the application experiment. This similarity benefits from the use of multithreading to asynchronously record p-assertions.

Experiment with Failures. In Section 4.2, we measured a client's recording performance in the presence of failures in terms of throughput. However, we did not consider the overhead of updating causelinks. Updating causelinks matters only when a relationship p-assertion is to be recorded. In this experiment, we

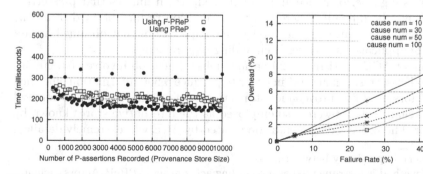

Fig. 8. Time to record 100 10k p-assertions   **Fig. 9.** Overhead of taking remedial actions

approximated the maximum overhead of taking remedial actions by measuring the record time of relationship p-assertions.

In F-PReP, the more causes a relationship p-assertion has, the longer it takes to check and update causelinks. Therefore, we increased the number of causes from 10 to 100.

Given a number of causes, several tests were conducted with various failure rates (5%, 25% and 50%). For each failure rate, the p-assertions about cause interactions of a relationship p-assertion were recorded prior to measuring the recording time for the relationship p-assertion itself. In order to measure the actual cost of remedial actions by means of record time, failure events were immediately generated without considering timeouts. We deployed another store as an alternative store, which was used in the retransmission of a relationship p-assertion. Repair requests were sent to a coordinator in batch sizes of 100.

Fig. 9 summarizes the results in terms of overhead. The measurements were taken after recording 100 relationship p-assertions. We can observe a maximum overhead of 10% for taking remedial actions, when compared to the record time when no failure occurred. Broadly speaking, the overhead increases linearly with the increase in failure rate. We note that since it takes much longer time to record a relationship p-assertion with larger number of causes, the overhead of taking remedial actions becomes relatively small in the settings with more causes. Therefore, we observe the smallest overhead in the setting with 100 causes.

4.4 Application Experiment

This experiment aims to investigate F-PReP's recording performance in a scientific application, the Amino Acid Compressibility Experiment (ACE), which has been detailed in [6]. ACE attempts to find possible new relationships between amino acids by investigating the information theoretic properties (e.g., information efficiency) of their computational representations.

ACE is chosen because of its general properties representing a range of workflow applications. First, it can be used to answer a range of provenance queries. Second, it is high performance and fine grained, which implies that p-assertion recording may be difficult. Therefore, the evaluation result obtained from this difficult application can imply a worst case complexity of that obtained from a large set of applications with less demanding requirements.

One run of ACE consisted of 20 parallel jobs[6]. Each job involved 54, 000 interactions between seven actors[7] in order to produce 4,500 information efficiency values. Actors used five provenance stores to record process documentation and these provenance stores were also employed as the alternative stores known by each actor. The process documentation created by ACE was extremely detailed;

---

[6] There is no dependency between jobs.

[7] A local method is instrumented as a recording actor using F-PReP. Actors exchange messages by means of method calls without network connections. They record p-assertions documenting the messages they receive and send to contribute to the process documentation of an information efficiency value.

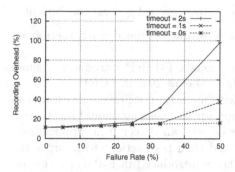
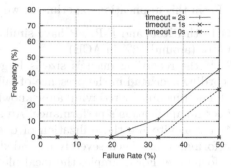

Fig. 10. Recording overhead of F-PReP   **Fig. 11.** The frequency of a queue in full capacity

the steps used to compute each result were recorded. The recorded process documentation could effectively answer all the use case questions in [6].

Each job produced 108,000 record messages, each containing about 10Kb p-assertions on average. To minimize network connection overhead, both record messages and repair requests were sent in batches of 100 each. Multithreading for creation and recording p-assertions was used in all tests. Various failure rates (5%, 10%, 16%, 20%, 25%, 33% and 50%) were considered. When taking remedial actions, a randomly selected alternative store was used in each resubmission.

We also investigated the impact of timeout on an application's performance. We studied three timeouts, 0s, 1s and 2s. The timeout, 0s, provides an extreme case, where a failure event occurs (or is detected) very quickly.

The application runtime is the average of the runtime of all parallel jobs from five runs of ACE. The runtime of an application without recording p-assertions is 22:24 (in the format $mm{:}ss$). When no failure occurs, the application runtime using PReP and F-PReP are 24:58 and 25:07, respectively. Therefore, the recording overheads of PReP and F-PReP are similar (about 12%). This benefits from the use of multithreading to asynchronously record p-assertions[8].

The asynchronous approach allows an application's p-assertions to be queued before being shipped to a provenance store. F-PReP has provided a flow control mechanism in queues to avoid exhausting memory. P-assertions cannot be queued until there is space in the queue. This may however affect the application's performance, since the application is postponed occasionally in order to reduce the speed of creating p-assertions when the queue becomes full frequently.

Our results in Fig. 10 and Fig. 11 demonstrate the correlations among application performance, failure rate, timeout and queue utilization. In Fig. 10, the recording overhead slightly increases as the failure rate increases in all timeout setups. However, it is sharply increased at certain points. Fig. 11 shows how often a queue is in a full capacity when a new batch of record messages is to be enqueued. It clearly reveals that the sharp increase in the recording overhead in Fig. 10 results from the flow control mechanism.

---

[8] Multithreading was also used in the tests of PReP.

From this application experiment, we can draw several general conclusions:

(1) Both PReP and F-PReP have similar recording overhead when there is no failure (around 12% in ACE);

(2) If the recording queue's size is large enough, F-PReP introduces a small recording overhead in the presence of failures (below 20% in ACE);

(3) The timeout for receiving an acknowledgement from a provenance store can affect an application's performance. An appropriate timeout should be chosen.

(4) By monitoring the utilization of queues, we can detect if an application's performance has been severely degraded and then take actions to improve the performance. For example, the local file store introduced in F-PSL can be automatically employed for temporarily maintaining p-assertions[9], when the frequency of the queue in maximum capacity reaches a certain threshold, e.g., 40%.

Query. After each run of ACE in the presence of failures, we also queried the provenance stores to further verify the quality of documentation recorded by F-PReP. The results showed an equal number of documentation records in the stores and records produced in ACE. In addition, no isolated island or dangling link is found, and distributed documentation of the process that led to an information efficiency value can always be retrieved in its entirety.

5   Related Work and Conclusion

Several provenance frameworks have emerged in the past a few years, e.g., Karma [12], PASOA [6]. Some workflow systems also provide provenance collection functionalities, e.g., Kepler [2]. From an analysis of these works, the issue of recording process documentation in the case of failures has not been discussed. Xu et. al. [15] have proposed a framework to tolerate failures occurring in service-oriented systems. Their approach relies on provenance information recorded in the presence of failures, which would benefit from F-PReP.

There is not much work on performance study related to provenance. Performance evaluations of PReP are presented in [7,6]. A detailed comparison on recording and querying performance between Karma and PReServ is seen in [12]. Extensive performance evaluations have been made on techniques to reduce the amount of storage required for process documentation [3]. There has been a performance study on PASS [10], an automatic provenance collection and maintenance storage system at the operating system level. None of these evaluations considers failures.

In this paper, we have evaluated a protocol, F-PReP, for recording process documentation in the presence of failures. In a failure-free environment, it has similar impact on an application's performance as PReP does. Although it introduces overhead in the presence of failures, we believe the overhead is still acceptable given that it can record *high quality* process documentation.

We are currently investigating how to create process documentation when an application has its own fault tolerance schemes to tolerate application level

---

[9] When using a local file store, the recording overhead was about 42% in our test.

failures. In future work, we plan to make use of the process documentation recorded in the presence of failures to diagnose failures.

References

1. Apache tomcat. User guide,
   http://tomcat.apache.org/tomcat-5.5-doc/index.html
2. Altintas, I., Barney, O., Jaeger-Frank, E.: Provenance collection support in the kepler scientific workflow system. In: Moreau and Foster [9], pp. 118–132
3. Chapman, A., Jagadish, H.V.: Efficient provenance storage. In: SIGMOD Conference (June 2008)
4. Chen, Z., Moreau, L.: Recording process documentation in the presence of failures. In: Butler, M., Jones, C.B., Romanovsky, A., Troubitsyna, E. (eds.) Methods, Models and Tools for Fault Tolerance. LNCS. Springer, Heidelberg (accepted, 2008)
5. Gagliardi, F., Jones, B., Grey, F., Bgin, M.E., Heikkurinen, M.: Building an infrastructure for scientific grid computing: Status and goals of the egee project. Philosophical Transactions of the Royal Society A: Mathematical, Physical and Engineering Sciences 363(1833), 1729–1742 (2005)
6. Groth, P.: The origin of data: Enabling the determination of provenance in multi-institutional scientific systems through the documentation of processes. Phd thesis, University of Southampton (2007)
7. Groth, P., Miles, S., Weijian Fang, S. C. Wong, K.-P. Zauner, and L. Moreau. Recording and using provenance in a protein compressibility experiment. In: Proceedings of 14th IEEE International Symposium on the High Performance Distributed Computing (HPDC), pp. 201–208 (2005)
8. Kloss, G.K., Schreiber, A.: Provenance implementation in a scientific simulation environment. In: Moreau and Foster [9], pp. 37–45
9. Moreau, L., Foster, I. (eds.): IPAW 2006. LNCS, vol. 4145. Springer, Heidelberg (2006)
10. Muniswamy-Reddy, K.-K., Holland, D.A., Braun, U., Seltzer, M.I.: Provenance-aware storage systems. In: USENIX Annual Technical Conference, General Track. USENIX, pp. 43–56 (2006)
11. Ozsu, M.T., Valduriez, P.: Principles of Distributed Database Systems, 2nd edn. Prentice-Hall, Englewood Cliffs (1999)
12. Simmhan, Y.L., Plale, B., Gannon, D., Marru, S.: Performance evaluation of the karma provenance framework for scientific workflows. In: Moreau and Foster [9], pp. 222–236.
13. Tierney, B., Schopf, J.: The cedps troubleshooting architecture and deployment on the open science grid. Journal of Physics: Conference Series 78 (2007)
14. Wootten, I., Rajbhandari, S., Rana, O.F., Pahwa, J.S.: Actor provenance capture with ganglia. In: CCGRID, pp. 99–106 (2006)
15. Xu, J., Townend, P., Looker, N., Groth, P.: Ft-grid: a system for achieving fault tolerance in grids. Concurrency and Computation: Practice and Experience 20(3), 297–309 (2008)

Provenance and the Price of Identity

Adriane Chapman and H.V. Jagadish

University of Michigan, Ann Arbor, MI USA
{apchapma,jag}@umich.edu

Abstract. As developers acknowledge that provenance is essential, more and more datasets are attempting to keep provenance records describing how they were created. Some of these datasets are constructed using workflows, others cobble together processes and applications to manipulate the data. While the provenance needs are the same, the inputs and set of processes used must be kept, the identity needs are very different. We outline several identification strategies that can be used for data manipulation outside of workflows. We evaluate these strategies in terms of time to create and store identity, and the space needed to keep this information. Additionally, we discuss the strengths and weaknesses of each strategy.

1 Introduction

Workflow systems [1,2,4,10,17,19,24,25,26] provide a framework for users to map out a set of inputs and a series of processes to manipulate that input. In the First Provenance Challenges [19], the given inputs were a set of brain images, and a set of reference brain images. A series of processes such as "align_warp" and "softmean" were arranged in a particular order to output a set of graphics. As the workflow runs on a set of data, provenance information captures the details of what happened to that data. In most of these systems, particularly the ones which utilize myGRID [11,12,18,26], the notion of data identity is firmly established and rigorously attended to. For example, in the Taverna workflow system [26], every computed data product is given a Taverna identity. This strict notion of identity in provenance is essential for data reuse and distribution of resources.

However, as the world at large achieves a greater understanding for the need of maintaining provenance, more and more hand-built systems are attempting to store provenance. These systems and datasets are built outside traditional workflow frameworks. Many times, these systems and datasets are a series of processes applied in a particular order to a set of inputs, exactly as a workflow would, but without the rigid, and helpful but occasionally overwhelming, workflow framework. In other words, an "implicit" workflow is followed to create a desired outcome. Some examples of these, hand-made systems are:

- The creation of MiMI [15]: A set of classic protein interaction sources are transformed, merged and annotated into one cohesive dataset.
- The creation of the Linguist Search Engine [23]: Sentences are culled from the web. These sentences are then run through a series of parsing, tokenization and part of speech tagging processes. The end result is a database of sentences that linguists can query using sentence syntax.

J. Freire, D. Koop, and L. Moreau (Eds.): IPAW 2008, LNCS 5272, pp. 106–119, 2008.

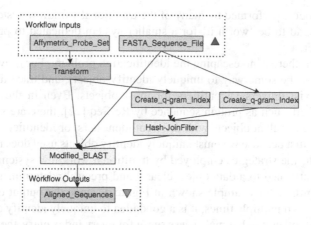

Fig. 1. The MANIPULATIONs used by miBLAST [16] to align probe and DNA sequences

A more in-depth example of a system, and how it strings together many processes workflow-style, is explored below.

Example 1. *miBLAST [16] finds sequence alignments between 25bp Affymetrix Probe sets and published gene sequences, and is 10x faster than a traditional BLAST search. Figure 1 shows a simplified breakdown of the processes used. First, probe sequence data from an Affymetrix probe is transformed into a specific format. Then, a q-gram index with specified word size is then built on the Query Set of Affymetrix probes. A q-gram index, with specified word size, is also built for the Database Set of sequences. These two indexes are then input into a Hash-Join Filter Module that outputs a set of (Query Set, Database Set) pairs based on word overlap. This set of paired sequences are then fed into a modified BLAST. Instead of doing a sequence comparison between every Query Sequence and every Database Sequence, only sequence comparisons between sequences in a (Query Set, Database Set) pair occur.*

We would like to re-iterate that while the drawing in Figure 1 is the same as is used by many workflow systems, miBLAST is not created using a traditional workflow. Instead a human user, with a clear goal in mind, runs a set of data through a series of processes.

Many of the systems used to create a dataset are only interested in the final product, and not on any intermediate data produced. If these systems wish to record provenance information, what do they need to do? Obviously, there needs to be some storage system, and some way, even if it is hand-entry, to capture the provenance information [13]. A trickier topic that needs to be addressed by each provenance-capturer centers around identity. How should they identify data products or intermediates, so that the final provenance store can accurately trace what happened to a data item?

As stated earlier, traditional workflow systems have a rigid, fail-safe method of making sure that all intermediate objects can be identified and located. Thus the final version can easily trace through a series of manipulations and intermediate data products if necessary. However, this notion of identity may be overkill for these smaller hand-made systems that do not care about intermediate data reuse or resource distribution.

In fact, the protocols performed by many of the traditional workflow systems may add too much overhead to be 'worth it' for a smaller system dedicated to producing one particular dataset.

At some level, there is no escaping the identification problem. For provenance to be useful, there must be some way to uniquely identify objects, and trace their changes. There do not exist universal identifiers for most objects. Even in the few that are uniquely identified, such as protein sequence by RefSeq [22], there are still problems with overlap of equivalent objects with different identifiers, or identifiers being deprecated. However, just because we must uniquely identify objects used does not mean that we are limited to the strategies employed by traditional workflow systems, as long as the provenance attached to a data object clearly and precisely determines the object's history. In the miBLAST example shown in Figure 1, since the output of the Transform process is used multiple times, it is a good idea to uniquely identify all data items produced. On the other hand, it makes less sense for every index entry, the data product of Create_q-gram_Index, to be uniquely identified; the index is only used once, and is easily re-created. Moreover, the provenance attached to each data item in the index will uniquely identify the original sequence used to create it, thus clearly and precisely determining the data item's history.

In this work, we examine the costs and benefits that different identity strategies can afford. We lay out the few assumptions and definitions we use in the rest of this work in Section 2. Section 3 documents and explains the methods currently used when dealing with data and identity. In Section 4, we evaluate these methods. Finally, we discuss implications, related work and conclusions in Sections 5–7.

2   Foundations

Throughout this work, we call the basic logical data unit a *data item*. Data items may be tuples in a relational table, elements in XML, objects of arbitrary granularity in an OODB, etc. One data item may completely include, overlap with, or be totally disjoint from another data item. A data item contains a set of *features*. A data item that is a tuple contains features that are attributes; a data item that is an XML element contains features that are child elements or attributes. Each feature is associated with a data value. Features can be single or multi-valued. A *dataset* is comprised of a set of data items.

We restrict our discussion of identity to the provenance found within systems that perform a series of modifications upon a set of data; we do not look at annotation [3,27] or lineage [21] system needs. Moreover, we wish to be more general than standard explicit workflow systems [1,2,4,10,17,19,24,25,26], and also include systems that are built by "implicit" workflows: workflows that refer to a series of steps executed by a user with a specific goal in mind, but without using a workflow system. For example, a series of relational database queries, or a set of batch files run over some data can be considered an implicit workflow. Indeed, while drawn using a standard workflow representation, miBLAST in Figure 1 is actually an implicit workflow, with the series of processes held together by some hand-written wrapping code. For both explicit and implicit workflow systems, we assume there is an input, a manipulation on that input, and an output. The output may then be used as input to another manipulation. Additionally, we look at the effects of identity on fine-grained provenance, i.e. provenance that can be attached at the dataset, data item or feature level.

A MANIPULATION is a basic unit of processing in a workflow, explicit or implicit. Each MANIPULATION takes one or more datasets as input and produces a dataset as output. We write $M(D^{I_1}, D^{I_2}, ...) = D^O$ to indicate that MANIPULATION M takes datasets D^{I_1}, D^{I_2}, etc as input to generate data set D^O as output.

In short, a MANIPULATION is a discrete component of a workflow, and uses a set of specific features from the input dataset. Processes can be mapped into MANIPULATIONS. For example, a MANIPULATION from the Provenance Challenge [19] is:

Manipulation 1. *Softmean Takes a set of re-sliced images and headers, and produces a single image and header using the average of the files contents.*

An instance of a MANIPULATION applied to a specific data item we call a *manipulation*. We write $m(d^{I_1}, d^{I_2}, ...) = d^O$, where $d^{I_1} \in D^{I_1}$, $d^O \in D^O$, etc. m is an instance of M applied to specific data items d^{I_x} within dataset D^{I_x}. For example, an instance of Create_q-gram_Index with a word size of four is applied to the probe probe1 results in an index entry of {atgc, probe1}.

While a data item is the object in the final result set after all MANIPULATIONS have been performed, we will utilize the following terms: a *intermediate* data item is a data item that is created by a MANIPULATION and utilized by another MANIPULATION(s); an *input* data item is the initial input from the base data into any MANIPULATION; the set of *intermediate* and *input* data items is collectively referred to as *involved* data items.

Regardless of how the information is actually stored, the provenance records we are dealing with contain the following information (for a data item in our running example):

$$(1)$$

This can be stored as a series of RDF triplets, a relational table, etc. The important point is that there is a record of the MANIPULATIONS that produced a data item, and it is possible to trace back to the input data item(s).

Finally, we would like to separate the concerns of "storage" and "identity", although they are intricately entwined. "Storage" denotes that a data item has been saved and stored for possible reuse. "Identity", in this work, means that a data item has been uniquely characterized and is immutable. If the data item then changes, a new identity must be assigned. If a data item is stored, it must also have an identity in order to retrieve it. However, data items not stored may also be identified for ease of provenance notation.

3   Current Available Strategies

Within this work, we aim to explore a broad range of techniques to identify input and intermediate data items within a provenance store. We believe there is no one universal 'correct' way to tackle the problem of identifying involved data items. In an attempt to highlight when and where each strategy should and should not be used, we look at four very general classes of involved data item identification and any special algorithms they may need.

3.1 Strong Identification

In a very coarse-grained approach, provenance is only associated at the file-level. Consider a possible identification strategy that will work across many systems: machine_name + path_name. Since every file by definition has a unique path name on a unique machine, this strategy will uniquely provide identity for coarse-grained objects.

In many workflow systems such as [12,26] that are run with myGRID, every involved data item, not just file, is given a unique identifier. For example, in [28] an LSID of the form URI:urn:lsid:mygrid.ac.uk:data:49841:1 is assigned to every data product, and describes: a prefix, an authority, the authority-specific data namespace, the object identifier and the object version. This LSID is assigned by an authority who maintains responsibility for ensuring that the data item is immutable. For instance, for the workflow in Figure 1 a unique id would be generated and stored with the data product for all data products from transform, Create_q-gram_Index, etc. This level of data product identification is necessary within a workflow context, where each MANIPULATION does not pass data to the next MANIPULATION , but instead writes out data items, which the next MANIPULATION is directed by the workflow system to take as input. Obviously, it is possible to create a provenance record that both associates all MANIPULATIONs with a data item, and can trace back to the source input data items.

3.2 Strong Identification with IDSet

In [28], the use of an IDSet identifier is discussed to facilitate the use of sets and aggregation. In this system, data items are assigned an LSID as usual. Whenever an aggregation step occurs, the output set of that aggregation is tagged with an ID containing references to all of the ids of the component data items. In our running example, every data product from every component would be identified and stored as discussed above. The only difference would be for the data product of the Hash-Join Filter Module which is an aggregation of entries from the Query Set and the Database Set. The id strategy in this case would be a unique id for the (Q1, D1) pair, that would also contain the unique identifiers of Q1 and D1. Again, because all intermediate data items are being IDed and stored, it is possible to associate all MANIPULATIONs with a data item, and trace back to the source input data items.

3.3 Intermittent Identification

Some results of MANIPULATIONs are only ever used by a unique subsequent MANIPULATION. For example, the results of the Create_q-gram_Index component are only every used by the Hash-Join Filter component. In this case, it may not be necessary to identify and store every intermediate result. We can effectively store:

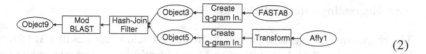

$$(2)$$

Of course, this does mean that if an intermediate result, $Object2$, is not id-ed and stored, and is later needed by a different MANIPULATION, either the intermediate result must be re-computed, or the MANIPULATION is out of luck. However, to preserve the ability to trace back to input data items, we must be aware of certain restrictions.

Intervals between Identification. If there is a long line of MANIPULATIONs that take in no other input but the output of a single previous MANIPULATION, then it may be beneficial to store occasional, intermediate results. For every intermediate result stored, there exists a closer point from which non-stored data items may be recomputed.

Aggregations. In [8], it is shown that in certain cases, some intermediate results must be identified and stored for Aggregation results, if the provenance of a particular data item is to be traced back through the aggregation step in ASPJ queries. Moreover, as discussed later, if only intermittent data items are IDed and stored, if a MANIPULATION later needs the results of a previous MANIPULATION whose data items have not been stored, that MANIPULATION (and any MANIPULATIONs prior to it that have not also been IDed and stored) must be re-run. Because an aggregation MANIPULATION can take in data items that may have been produced by a series of MANIPULATIONs , such as HashJoin Filter in Figure 1, the costs of re-running can be explosive. As such, a good rule of thumb is to identify and store data items before use in an aggregation.

Workflows and Intelligent Users. If a workflow exists, then a simple traversal of the workflow before running will determine all intermediate data items that must be identi-fied and stored to be used in a subsequent MANIPULATION. For instance in our exam-ple, it is readily apparent that the output of the transform component will be used not only for Create_q-gram_Index but also the Modified_BLAST MANIPULATION. These data items should be identified and stored. If a workflow does not exist, all is not lost. An organized user who has a clear goal in mind is almost as good as a workflow, and is likely to know when a particular intermediate output will be reused. Unfortunately, many users are disorganized and run scripts in a haphazard manner. Even worse, often users who wish for intermediate data products are different from those who produced the data. In these cases, intermittent identification may not be the best strategy.

3.4   Initial Identification

An even more extreme way to reduce the number of identifications made would be to label just the input data items. All subsequent intermediate data items are never stored or identified. For example, merely uniquely identifying the input probe and database sequences. The same problem as in Intermediate Identification occurs, in which any intermediate data item that is reused must be recomputed, as stated in re-running below.

3.5   Recreating Intermediate Data Items

The re-creation of intermediate results discussed below requires that MANIPULATIONS be deterministic. Both Intermittent and Input Identification strategies may require intermediate re-creation.

Reverse Transformations. Using reverse transformations we can work backwards from a known, identified and stored data item to a prior non-identified or stored intermediate result. [8,9] show that certain types of MANIPULATIONS can be traced backwards. In particular Select-Project-Join queries require no intermediate results, while Aggregate-Select-Project-Join (ASPJ) queries require selective intermediate results to be stored. For more complicated MANIPULATIONS outside the realm of standard relational operators, a reverse transformation must be explicitly included by the user. Unfortunately, since users rarely take the trouble to define a reverse transformation, we exclude the possibility of using reverse transformations in our evaluation of strategies.

Re-running. As long as the input data items and MANIPULATIONS used are stored, the MANIPULATIONS are deterministic and not dependent upon non-repeatable events (such as occurring exactly at noon PST on Valentine's Day 1956), then it is possible to re-run all MANIPULATIONS until the needed intermediate data items are produced. If there are intermediate data items that have been identified and stored, it is possible to re-run using these checkpointed data items as a starting point. This option should be carefully thought through before application, however. Consider a SUM over all book prices in a database. If the database is updated prior to re-running, the re-created intermediate results will be incorrect. In other words, re-running is only an option if the MANIPULATION is deterministic and the data either a) is unchangable, or b) is checkpointed at a previous, re-runnable step.

4   Evaluation

To illustrate the effects of data product identification and storage, we took a real workflow from [14] and, as shown in Figure 2, abstracted each MANIPULATION as: a) an aggregator (aggregate); b) producing data items used only by 1 other MANIPULATION (manipulation); c) producing data items used by multiple MANIPULATIONS (reuse). To facilitate visualizing just how much identity choices matter, we have set up every manipulation in the workflow to output a constant number of data items. For every identification strategy, we run the workflow three times, changing the number of data items used and output between 100, 1,000 and 10,000. Figure 3 contains the set of identity strategies we explored.

   Each manipulation was created as a black box with a fixed constant time. Because we only wanted to test the identity component inherent in data manipulation, the manipulations themselves do nothing but sleep for the requisite amount of time and output a new set of data items. An input set of data items is created and fed through the workflow in Figure 2. For Strong ID (S), the data products are sent to an external authority after each manipulation. For Strong ID + IDSet (SS), the same practice occurs, but after

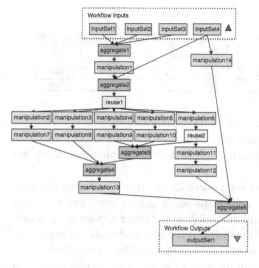

Fig. 2. The series and type of MANIPULATIONs used in the experiments. This workflow is a abstraction of the one found in [14].

S	Strong ID
SS	Strong ID with IDSet
IW	Intermittent ID Storage with prior Workflow knowledge
IAI(2)	Intermittent ID Storage with pre-Aggregation ID Storage and Interval ID Storage every 2 MANIPULATIONs
IAI(3)	Intermittent ID Storage with pre-Aggregation ID Storage and Interval Storage every 3 MANIPULATIONs
IA	Intermittent with Aggregation
I	Input Stored Only

Fig. 3. The strategies employed in all experiments, and their reference codes in the Figures

every aggregation step, we also build a unique id for the aggregated data item containing all of the input data item ids. Then, we test a series of Intermittent identification strategies. The first of these, Intermittent ID Storage with a known workflow (IW), acts as if a complete workflow is known in advance, and thus any data items that are used in an aggregation, or will be used in multiple MANIPULATIONs are identified and stored. The next three strategies use Intermittent ID Storage, but without advance workflow knowledge. IAI(2) and IAI(3) store object identification before every aggregation MA-NIPULATION and after every two or three MANIPULATIONs respectively. Finally, Input only ID storage (I) only identifies and stores the input objects.

All experiments were run on a Dell workstation with Pentium 4 CPU at 2GHz with 640MB RAM and 74.4GB disk space with Windows XP. The algorithms were implemented as a Java application. The external object authority was implemented using a mySQL database.

4.1 Pros and Cons

First, we would like to explore some of the pros and cons of each approach in a little more detail. Table 1 contains a breakdown of how each strategy can handle specific situations. With the proper provenance information, all strategies are able to trace back to the input data items. If the provenance structure contains:

$$\text{Object9} \leftarrow \boxed{\begin{array}{c}\text{Mod}\\\text{BLAST}\end{array}} \leftarrow \boxed{\begin{array}{c}\text{Hash-Join}\\\text{Filter}\end{array}} \begin{array}{c} \nearrow \boxed{\begin{array}{c}\text{Create}\\\text{q-gram In.}\end{array}} \leftarrow \text{FASTA8} \\ \searrow \boxed{\begin{array}{c}\text{Create}\\\text{q-gram In.}\end{array}} \leftarrow \boxed{\text{Transform}} \leftarrow \text{Affy1} \end{array} \tag{3}$$

Table 1. The abilities of each general identity strategy

	Strong	Strong & IDSet	Intermittent	Input Only
Can trace back to original source data	Yes	Yes	Yes	Yes
Intermediate Data Items can be reused by other applications	Yes	Yes	Maybe	No
Processes can be distributed across machines	Yes	Yes	Maybe	No
Lightweight Implementation	No	No	Yes	Yes

In other words, for every data item, there must be an explicit statement about the input data items, even if records of intermediate data items are not maintained. This is a very different approach than the one found in [8,9] in which the input data items are computed, not stored.

The Strong identification strategies do have a major leg-up over the other techniques: sharing. Because every intermediate data item is stored, these data items can be reused by other MANIPULATIONs within an implicit workflow and other applications. Moreover, because every data item is uniquely identified, it is easier to distribute running the various MANIPULATIONs of an implicit workflow over many different machines.

However, the Intermediate and Input identification strategies do have one significant strength over the Strong approaches: ease of implementation. Consider how many of the datasets created via implicit workflows are actually made. A dataset is ingested, and process1 is applied to it. The results are written to a file. That file is then read in by process2 and new results are written to a file. etc. This is essentially the Input Only Identification strategy. While the data items are stored between MANIPULATIONs in this scenario, they are not identified. Changing this habit and forcing developers to constantly call an external authority for identification is an uphill battle. However, adding an identification step at a few points, such as ingestion, is an easy and lightweight step to take.

4.2 Time and Space

Figure 4 shows the effects of choice of identification strategy on provenance capture time and storage space. The difference between Strong techniques (S), (SS) and

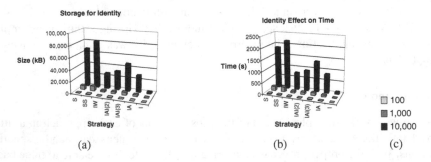

(a)   (b)   (c)

Fig. 4. The effect of Identity Strategy on space and time while running the workflow found in Figure 2. (a) The size of the provenance store for each strategy. (b) How long each identification strategy takes. (c) Legend for the size of the input set. i.e. every MANIPULATION in Figure 2 takes in 100, 1,000, or 10,000 objects.

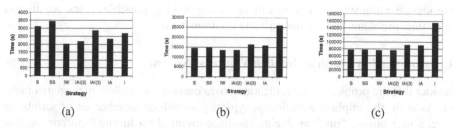

Fig. 5. The time for each identity strategy, particularly non-strong strategies, is related to how long it takes to re-run a manipulation. Manipulation execution times are set to a constant of (a) 1 minute, (b) 10 minutes, and (c) 1 hour.

Intermittent techniques, (IW), (IAI(2)), (IAI(3)), (IA), is expected since more effort is needed to log every data item produced for the Strong techniques. Unexpected, however, is the size of the difference. For the workflow in Figure 2, utilizing strong techniques is almost twice as expensive in time and space as a basic Intermittent approach. Thus for users and applications that do not require reuse of intermediate data, Intermediate and Input identification strategies are extremely attractive.

Additionally, we would like to point out that the choice of Intermediate identification strategy is important, and is dependent upon the implicit workflow. In Figure 4, we show two Intermediate identification options that store data item identity after set intervals, IAI(2) and IAI(3). In theory, IAI(3) should be faster and smaller to use than IAI(2). However, given the workflow in Figure 2 with which these strategies were utilized, the opposite is the case in both time and space. A quick glance at the workflow shows an Aggregate MANIPULATION almost every two MANIPULATIONs . Thus, for this workflow, IAI(2) is almost equivalent to IA. Unfortunately, because IAI(3) blindly stores results every three MANIPULATIONs , it is out of sync with the automatically stored pre-aggregation identities, and many more identities are stored.

However, this is not the entire story. The numbers reported in Figure 4 were created using MANIPULATIONs that were instantaneous. This is rather deceptive, and fairly unlikely. In Figure 5, we show how each strategy performs with different length MA-NIPULATIONs. With fast MANIPULATIONs , on the order of 1 minute or less, Intermediate and Input Strategies do much better than the Strong Strategies. However, as the MANIPULATIONs get longer and near 10 minutes, the difference is less striking. When the MANIPULATIONs take an hour to run, the Strong Strategies are the clear winners with respect to time. This trend is because of the need to occasionally re-run MANIP-ULATIONs to get intermediate results for Intermediate and Input Strategies. Whenever a data item is reused by a different MANIPULATION in the Strong Strategies, it can be easily retrieved. However, in the Intermediate and Input strategies, the data item cannot be reused without being recomputed.

5   Discussion

Until now, we have merely explored the types of identification strategies available to users of implicit workflow systems. However, there are several open issues about *using* these identification strategies. While there are a myriad of possible topics, we discuss two distinct problems and lay out possible solutions below.

5.1   Identification within an Implicit Workflow System

Consider that the problem of identification arises outside a workflow management system. As such, the implicit workflow is typically a cobbled together set of scripts, or worse, a user hitting "run", analyzing results, copying data, hitting "run" on another program, etc. How do you enforce proper data identification in these scenarios?

This is a difficult problem that requires either the automation of identification or a change in user behaviour. While a user may be willing to change enough to recognize that keeping proper identification is important, it is naïve to expect users to become organized, identifying, data custodians overnight. As such, some mechanism must be put into place that automatically provides data identification for disorganized users.

The logical answer to this problem is to teach the user how to use a workflow management system. Again, breaking all the bad-computation habits may be asking too much from the poor user. Is there a middle ground? A possible sketch would be a modified 'terminal' (e.g. xterm, terminal, dos-prompt), that looks the same as the user's default execution environment, but quietly keeps track in the background of the scripts run. Any identification strategy discussed above could be implemented behind such a system, transparent to the user.

5.2   Identification Across Disparate Workflow Systems

A separate problem occurs when dealing with data across multiple systems that were not designed to work together. For instance, a user wishes to integrate data produced through multiple distinct workflow systems. What identification strategy should be employed? While we see multiple possible methods for dealing with this, we shall discuss just one.

While using multiple workflow systems, if integration and homogeneous identification is the goal, then a possible strategy is utilizing one system as the "master" identifier. Anything from another system that is semantically or syntactically the same could be mapped to the same identifier in the "master" system. Anything from another system that cannot be mapped can be given a 'new' identification by the "master" system. Obviously there are pros and cons to this approach. We merely wish to point out an open problem, and provide the base for a discussion on it.

6   Related Work

Provenance needs, applications and types are incredibly diverse. There has been work studying lineage [7,8,9,21], annotations [3,27], capturing provenance [5,20] and a range of forms, events, etc. Moreover, there has been work in creating provenance stores during workflow execution [1,2,4,10,17,19,24,25,26]. The Provenance Challenge [19] explored the requirements these workflow systems needed to adhere to in order to produce useful provenance stores.

Identity and Provenance needs in a workflow system were explored in [28]. This work built IDSet on top of the Taverna [26] workflow system. The workflow systems [1,2,4,10,17,19,24,25,26] are reliant upon the Strong identification strategy. This allows them to reuse intermediates data items and easily go back to intermediate states. Additionally, it enables them to distribute processes across the grid [11,12,18,26] if applicable. Moreover, [2] explore identification strategies for entries in a cache that allow: data sharing, correct computation of the full object, and re-execution of only changed steps.

Finally, [5,6] discuss enabling users to collect provenance records of their actions. By requiring users to utilize a particular tool, information is captured about user actions on provenance-unaware systems. This is similar to the strategy outlined in Section 5.1.

7   Conclusions

In this work, we focus on the provenance generated by "implicit" workflows; workflows created by a user with a specific goal, but outside a workflow framework. In particular, we study the needs for identification of data items in these systems. Unlike workflow systems [1,2,4,10,17,19,24,25,26] that are required to identify and keep all intermediate data items, many systems, [15,16,23] for example, do not need intermediate data. It is still imperative that they maintain provenance, and the provenance can be used to trace back to a data item's origin, but there is no need to keep intermediate data items.

We explore a set of identification strategies: Strong, Strong with IDSet, Intermittent and Input Only. Each of these identification strategies have strengths and weaknesses in terms of intermediate support, provenance capture time and storage space. We show that Strong identification is preferred not only for workflow style systems, but also for systems with long-running processes, where the "do over" time is large. On the other hand, we outline cases in which Intermittent and Input Only identification strategies would be preferable.

Acknowledgments

Thanks to Luc Moreau for his correspondence, which inspired this work. This work was supported in part by NSF grant number IIS 0741620 and by NIH grant number U54 DA021519.

References

1. Barga, R.S., Digiampietri, L.A.: Automatic capture and efficient storage of escience experiment provenance. In: Concurrency and Computation: Practice and Experience (2007)
2. Bavoil, L., Callahan, S., Crossno, P., Freire, J., Scheidegger, C., Silva, C., Vo, H.: VisTrails: Enabling interactive multiple-view visualizations. In: IEEE Visualization, pp. 18–26 (2005)
3. Bhagwat, D., Chiticariu, L., Tan, W.-C., Vijayvargiya, G.: An annotation management system for relational databases. In: VLDB, pp. 900–911 (2004)
4. Bowers, S., McPhillips, T., Wu, M., Ludäscher, B.: Project histories: Managing data provenance across collection-oriented scientific workflow runs. In: Cohen-Boulakia, S., Tannen, V. (eds.) DILS 2007. LNCS (LNBI), vol. 4544, pp. 122–138. Springer, Heidelberg (2007)

5. Buneman, P., Chapman, A., Cheney, J.: Provenance management in curated databases. In: ACM SIGMOD, pp. 539–550 (June 2006)
6. Buneman, P., Chapman, A., Cheney, J., Vansummeren, S.: A Provenance Model for Manually Curated Data. Provenance and Annotation of Data edition. LNCS, pp. 162–170. Springer, Heidelberg (2006)
7. Buneman, P., Khanna, S., Tan, W.-C.: Why and Where: A characterization of data provenance. In: ICDT, pp. 316–330 (2001)
8. Cui, Y., Widom, J., Wiener, J.L.: Tracing the lineage of view data in a data warehousing environment. In: ACM Transaction on Database Systems, TODS (2000)
9. Cui, Y., Widom, J.: Lineage tracing for general data warehouse transformations. In: VLDB, pp. 41–58 (2001)
10. Digiampietri, L., Medeiros, C., Setubal, J.: A framework based on web service orchestration for bioinformatics workflow management. Genet. Mol. Res. 4(3), 535–542 (2005)
11. Foster, I., Vockler, J., Wilde, M., Zhao, Y.: The virtual data grid: a new model and architecture for data-intensive collaboration. In: CIDR (2003)
12. Groth, P., Miles, S., Moreau, L.: PReServ: Provenance recording for services. In: Proceedings of the UK OST e-Science second All Hands Meeting 2005, AHM 2005 (2005)
13. Groth, P., Miles, S., Moreau, L.: A Model of Process Documentation to Determine Provenance in Mash-ups. In: Transactions on Internet Technology (TOIT) (2008)
14. Howison, J., Wiggins, A., Crowston, K.: eResearch workflows for studying free and open source software development. In: IFIP 2.13 (2008)
15. Jayapandian, M., Chapman, A., Tarcea, V.G., Yu, C., Elkiss, A., Ianni, A., Liu, B., Nandi, A., Santos, C., Andrews, P., Athey, B., States, D., Jagadish, H.V.: Michigan Molecular Interactions (MiMI): Putting the jigsaw puzzle together. Nucleic Acids Research, D566–D571 (January 2007)
16. Kim, Y.J., Boyd, A., Athey, B.D., Patel, J.M.: miBLAST: Scalable evaluation of a batch of nucleotide sequence queries with blast. Nucleic Acids Research 33(13), 4335–4344 (2005)
17. McPhillips, T., Bowers, S., Ludäscher, B.: Collection-oriented scientific workflows for integrating and analyzing biological data. In: Leser, U., Naumann, F., Eckman, B. (eds.) DILS 2006. LNCS (LNBI), vol. 4075, pp. 248–263. Springer, Heidelberg (2006)
18. Miles, S., Groth, P., Branco, M., Moreau, L.: The requirements of recording and using provenance in e-science experiments. Journal of Grid Computing 5(1), 1–25 (2007)
19. Moreau, L., Ludäscher, B., et al.: The First Provenance Challenge. Concurrency and Computation: Practice and Experience (2007), http://twiki.ipaw.info/bin/view/Challenge/SecondProvenanceChallenge
20. Muniswamy-Reddy, K.-K., Holland, D.A., Braun, U., Seltzer, M.I.: Provenance-aware storage systems. In: USENIX Annual Technical Conference, pp. 43–56 (2006)
21. Mutsuzaki, M., Theobald, M., et al.: Trio-One: Layering uncertainty and lineage on a conventional DBMS. In: CIDR, pp. 269–274 (2007)
22. Pruitt, K.D., Tatusova, T., Maglott, D.R.: NCBI reference sequence (RefSeq): a curated nonredundant sequence database of genomes, transcripts and proteins. Nucleic Acids Research, D501–D504 (2005)
23. Resnik, P., Elkiss, A., Lau, E., Taylor, H.: The web in theoretical linguistics research: Two case studies using the linguist's search engine. In: 31st Meeting of the Berkeley Linguistics Society, pp. 265–276 (February 2005)
24. Scheidegger, C.E., Vo, H.T., Koop, D., Freire, J., Silva, C.: Querying and re-using workflows with vistrails. In: SIGMOD (2008)
25. Simmhan, Y., Plale, B., Gannon, D.: A framework for collecting provenance in data-centric scientific workflows. In: ICWS (2006)

26. Taverna (2008), http://taverna.sourceforge.net/
27. Wang, Y.R., Madnick, S.E.: A polygen model for heterogeneous database systems: The source tagging perspective. In: VLDB, pp. 519–538 (1990)
28. Zhao, J., Goble, C., Stevens, R.: An Identity Crisis in the Life Sciences. Provenance and Annotation of Data edition. LNCS, pp. 254–269. Springer, Heidelberg (2006)

Towards Provenance-Enabling ParaView

Steven P. Callahan[1,2], Juliana Freire[1,2], Carlos E. Scheidegger[2],
Cláudio T. Silva[1,2], and Huy T. Vo[2]

[1] VisTrails, Inc.
[2] Scientific Computing and Imaging Institute, University of Utah
{stevec,cscheid,csilva,hvo}@sci.utah.edu, juliana@cs.utah.edu

Abstract. Currently, there are no general provenance management systems or tools available for existing applications. Our goal is to develop provenance technology that is flexible and adaptable to the wide range of requirements of software applications. By consolidating provenance information for a variety of applications, we can provide a uniform environment for querying, sharing, and re-using provenance in large-scale, collaborative settings. In this paper, we describe our framework for provenance-enabling existing applications. Our approach is applicable to a variety of software systems that are process driven. As a concrete example, we describe a working plug-in for an open source application in scientific visualization.

1 Introduction

Computers are now extensively used throughout science, finance, engineering, and medicine. Advances in data mining, computational geometric modeling, imaging, and simulation allow researchers, engineers, and artists to build increasingly complex models and generate unprecedented amounts of data. Hedge funds use simulations to construct accurate risk and return assessments for portfolios. Oil & Gas companies heavily depend on simulations for various tasks, including exploration and pipeline transport. Clinical medicine has become increasingly dependent on procedures that include simulations from data acquired directly from the patient through magnetic resonance imaging (MRI), Computed Tomography (CT), and other computerized exams. Even areas of the entertainment industry have been greatly impacted by the use of computers to design complex computer models and scenes for movies and video games. A major problem that these disciplines face is the management of this data and the processes that were used to generate the data.

Currently, ad-hoc approaches for capturing the provenance of exploratory computational tasks are used in the scientific and engineering community. For example, laboratory notebooks are commonly used to track changes in parameters or processes. However, ad-hoc approaches have serious limitations. In particular, scientists and engineers need to expend substantial effort managing data and recording provenance information. The absence of detailed provenance makes it hard (and sometimes impossible) to reproduce and share results, to solve problems collaboratively, to validate results with different input data, to understand

J. Freire, D. Koop, and L. Moreau (Eds.): IPAW 2008, LNCS 5272, pp. 120–127, 2008.

the process used to solve a particular problem, and to re-use the knowledge involved in the data analysis and generation processes. In addition, it limits the
longevity of the data products—without precise and sufficient information about
how the data product was generated, its value is greatly diminished. The growing demands for compliance to varying industry and governmental regulations
and standards also requires detailed audit trails of data sources and workflows
(tasks) executed.

Originally motivated by the needs in the scientific domain, the VisTrails provenance technology [3] and the infrastructure it provides is general and applicable
to a wide range of applications that involve complex computational processes.
Whereas our initial development focused on provenance management for tasks
developed within a workflow system, our goal in this paper is to show that the
same infrastructure can be used to *provenance-enable existing applications*, without requiring them to be integrated within a workflow system. One of the major
advantages of this approach is that users will be able to leverage provenance
using the same applications and environments that they are used to.

1.1 Related Work

There are important distinctions that set our work apart from previous approaches to provenance. Notably, our focus is on interactive applications that
provide graphical user interfaces. Although there has been previous works on
provenance-enabling such applications, these have proposed application-specific
solutions (see e.g., [1]). In contrast, the plug-in infrastructure is general and can
be integrated with any application that exposes its undo-redo stack.

There has also been work proposing general provenance solutions that can
be combined with arbitrary systems. The Earth System Science Workbench
(ESSW) uses scripts to wrap legacy systems so that their inputs and outputs can
be transparently gathered [4]. The Provenance-Aware Service-Oriented Architecture (PASOA) was designed to support provenance capture in a service-oriented
environment [5]. It requires that services be instrumented to produce assertions
which detail, for example, how different services interact and which data item
they manipulate and derive. Like PASOA and ESSW, our approach also requires
applications to be instrumented, however the purpose of this instrumentation is
to obtain access to existing applications' undo-redo capabilities. Furthermore,
the approaches used in PASOA and ESSW were designed for services and batch-
oriented programs. In contrast, our infrastructure can be combined with both
interactive and batch oriented system.

2   A Process-Driven Provenance Model

VisTrails introduced a change-based model to capture provenance and display
it in a history tree called a *vistrail* [2]. Here we describe a generalized version of
this provenance model that is adaptable to a variety of settings.

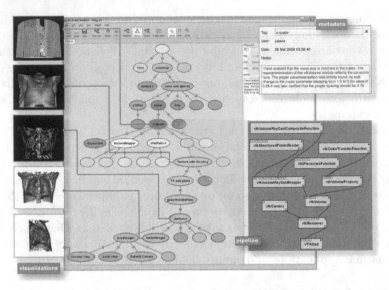

Fig. 1. The version tree stores the complete history of the actions performed by a user. Each node corresponds to a state in the application, the edges show how the actions are ordered to achieve these states.

2.1   Change-Based Provenance

In an application, as the user makes changes to the state of the application through a user interface, the provenance mechanism records those changes. Instead of storing a set of application states, the change-based model stores the operations, or actions, that are applied to the application (e.g., slicing a volume or editing a parameter in a scientific visualization system). This representation is both simple and compact—it uses substantially less space than the alternative of storing multiple instances or *versions* of the state. In addition, it enables the construction of an intuitive interface that allows users to both understand and interact with the history of the application states through these changes. A tree-based view allows a user to return to a previous version in an intuitive way, to undo bad changes, to compare different workflows, and to be reminded of the actions that led to a particular result. Figure 1 shows an example of a vistrail created through computational workflows.

The change actions are represented as a rooted tree VT in which each node corresponds to a *version* of the application state, and each edge between nodes d_p and d_c, where d_p is the parent of d_c, corresponds to the action applied to d_p which generated d_c. This is similar to the versioning mechanism used in Darcs [8]. More formally, let DF be the domain of all possible states of the application, where $\emptyset \in DF$ is a special empty state. Also, let $x : DF \to DF$ be a function that transforms one state into another, and $\mathcal{D}$ be the set of all such functions. A vistrail node corresponding to a workflow d is constructed by composing a sequence of actions, where each $x_i \in \mathcal{D}$:

$$d = (x_n \circ (x_{n-1} \circ \ldots \circ (x_1 \circ (\emptyset))\ldots))$$

This change based representation is general in that the actions can be captured at different granularities and they can be made to match the semantics of a specific application. In particular, it can be readily applied to create Provenance Explorer plug-ins for existing applications.

3 Capturing, Representing, and Re-playing Provenance

Our change-based representation of provenance is easily incorporated into existing applications that provide a mechanism for controlling the actions that are being performed by a user via a graphical interface. The model-view-controller paradigm [6] is an architectural pattern used in software engineering that decouples the user interface (view) from the domain-specific logic and access (model) using an event processor (controller). This software engineering paradigm is frequently used in large projects to increase the flexibility and reuse of code. As the user interacts with a view that is generated based on the current model, a registered handler or callback is triggered in the controller. The controller then updates the model so that the view can be recreated. Since all the events that are generated by the application pass through one event handler, capturing and replaying then is performed either by modifying this controller directly, or by intercepting and fabricating the events via the callback mechanism.

Our Provenance Explorer is an application that runs along-side the main application. Provenance is captured during user interactions with the main application using a custom solutions for the application. This provenance is passed to and from the Provenance Explorer via a Communication API. The details of these steps are provided in more detail in this section.

3.1 Capturing Actions

The implementation of the action-based provenance in the VisTrails system is specific to the actions that occur while creating and editing workflows in the VisTrails Builder. These actions include adding and deleting modules and connections, and changing parameter values. For other applications, our Provenance Explorer needs to be able to handle a more general action type. Conceptually, the model supports actions at varying granularities or semantic levels, from basic mouse button presses to complex sets of operations (such as copying and pasting a set of actions). The level of granularity that an action may take needs to be application specific.

In general, applications that take advantage of the model-view-controller paradigm have a mechanism for storing and re-using actions: the undo and redo operations. In a scientific visualization system, for instance, with *undo* a user should be able to walk through the steps they took to create an image, albeit backwards. Although undo does not capture the complete exploration process nor does it persist across sessions, it provides valuable context for granularity of actions. The designers of the software have already determined the granularity of actions by designing the undo stack. The undo stack of an application may individually capture single mouse events or keyboard strokes if they are needed to recreate of the state. Furthermore, interactions performed by the user may cause multiple actions to be performed, which the undo stack will store as one step. We capture actions at the same granularity in which the undo stack does. In fact, in practice it is simpler to capture actions as they are being added to the undo stack instead of where they are handled by the controller. Obviously, this depends on the completeness and availability of the undo/redo mechanism in the application.

In some applications, access to the controller is limited, the undo mechanism captures state instead of actions, or the undo mechanism does not provide the actions that are required for full reproducibility. In these cases, it is necessary to compute actions based on the previous and next states, s_p and s_n, respectively. Using the application's model of the state, the difference $s_p - s_n$ can easily be computed as the set of changes that take s_p to s_n. These changes can then be stored much more efficiently and uniformly as actions in our provenance model.

3.2   Representing Actions

Once the actions have been captured from the application, we use our Communication API to pass them on to our Provenance Explorer, which is an independent application running on its own thread. The Communication API uses sockets to send and retrieve actions from the application's controller to Provenance Explorer's controller. These actions that move across the socket are simply strings that represent the commands that have been captured or are to be executed by the main application. When the Provenance Explorer receives a new command, it creates an action that contains the command along with additional metadata that is either automatically and manually created. Automatically created metadata includes the date and time the command was executed, the user who created it, a unique identifier for the action, and the identifier for the action that preceeds it. Other metadata such as annotation notes or a tag to label the action can be added by the user in the Provenance Explorer interface.

The set of actions stored in the Provenance Explorer, or vistrail, is represented in XML as is described by the following partial schema given in a terse form:

```
type Vistrail =
  vistrail [@version, @id, @name, Action*, annotation? ]
type Action =
  action [ @date, @user, @id, @parentId, @command, tag?,
           annotation? ]
```

This is a more general form of the original VisTrails schema [2] that was used to capture the limited number of actions that are available within the VisTrails Builder (i.e., adding/deleting workflow modules, adding/deleting connections, and changing parameter values). This schema has also been extended to store vistrails in a variety of available relational database management systems as well.

Visually, a vistrail is shown in the Provenance Explorer as a history tree of actions that can be tagged, annotated, and queried using our graphical user interface.

3.3 Re-playing Actions

When the user interacts with our history tree by selecting a version, the Provenance Explorer uses the Communication API to send actions back to the main application. The set of actions to reproduce a version in the tree are serialized by compiling all the commands in each action from the top of the tree to the current selected node. The main application receives these actions, clears the current state, and uses the actions either as a series of events that are executed by the controller or as direct updates to the model state. By returning to a previous version in the history tree, then making changes in the main application, it is possible to branch the tree. In this way, the actions performed by a user are never lost, even though they would be with a normal undo stack.

During interaction with the main application, the user may still want to use undo/redo as is provided by that application. It is important to allow this interaction so that we minimize disruption to the normal workflow of the user. The undo and redo operations can be hijacked so that they trigger the current version in the Provenance Explorer to change by walking up (undo) or down (redo) the history tree. This allows a complete history tree of the provenance to be captured even if the user has visual component of the Provenance Explorer interface disabled.

4 Case Study: ParaView

ParaView [7] is an open-source, multi-platform application designed to visualize data sets of size varying from small to very large. The project started in 2000 as a collaboration between Kitware and Los Alamos National Laboratories. The current version, ParaView 3.0, was released in May 2007. ParaView is quite popular, and is downloaded over 10,000 times a month. The system is used by researchers and engineers in both industry and academia.

Figure 2 shows ParaView together with the Provenance Explorer, transparently capturing the complete exploration process. This Provenance Explorer was implemented by inserting monitoring code in ParaView's undo/redo mechanism, which captures changes to the underlying pipeline specification. Essentially, the action on top of the undo stack is added to the vistrail in the appropriate place, and undo is reinterpreted to mean "move up the version tree". The current version of the Provenance Explorer captures all of the changes to the pipeline. However, some changes of state are not related to the pipeline and ParaView does not store these in the undo stack. For example, the position of the camera is not stored there. In fact, it is quite common for 3D applications to not store navigation in the undo/redo stack (just like word processors typically do not store which page the user is looking at in undo stacks). In this sense, it would

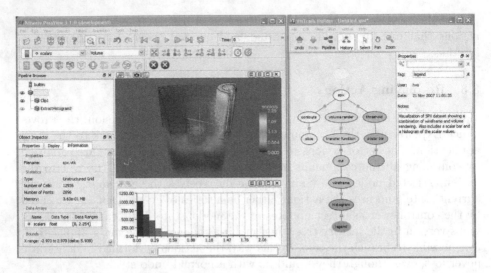

Fig. 2. A screenshot of ParaView (left) with the provenance captured by VisTrails and displayed as a version tree in a separate window (right). This preliminary prototype taps into ParaView undo/redo mechanism to capture the exploration process.

arguably be incorrect to interpret view changes as actions that generate new versions.

If, however, capturing these interactions is really required, more sophisticated approaches are necessary. The latest version of ParaView introduced "Lookmarks", which capture the complete underlying pipeline of a visualization. Unlike in VisTrails, however, Lookmarks need to be manually set by the user during the exploration process. Lookmarks can be serialized, allowing a visualization to be reproduced at a later time. This mechanism for capturing the pipeline and state of the application exposes a wider class of actions for our Provenance Explorer. We are currently implementing a version of the infrastructure that combines the undo/redo stack inspection with Lookmark information, in order to capture this potentially missing information.

5   Discussion

In the VisTrails system, provenance is used for more than version tracking and persistence. Specifically, there are some operations on particular version that can be cast as operations over the set of stored actions. For example, VisTrails allows users to compare two different workflows by looking at a sequence of actions that takes one workflow into the other [3]. This sequence of actions is presented analogously to a workflow, which allows users to look at the result in the same way they look at regular workflows. It would be interesting to extend this principle to third-party applications. For example, the difference between two visualizations in ParaView should be presented as a single visualization, superimposing and highlighting the differences between the two versions.

VisTrails also allows users to build workflows by analogy [9]. The technique involves identifying the differences between two workflows a and b and remapping this sequence of actions so it can be applied to a different workflow c. It originally involves computing an approximate graph matching between a and c. In a general case, the remapping would have to be specifically tailored for each application, but the general algorithm would still apply.

Finally, our broader goal is to provide a uniform platform for capturing, querying, and reusing provenance from many applications. To this end, we intend to develop the infrastructure that allows other developers to quickly and easily incorporate our Provenance Explorer as a plug-in to their own applications.

Acknowledgments. This work was funded by the Department of Energy grant FG02-08ER85157 and SciDAC (VACET and SDM centers), the National Science Foundation (grants IIS-0746500, CNS-0751152, IIS-0713637, OCE-0424602, IIS-0534628, CNS-0514485, IIS-0513692, CNS-0524096, CCF-0401498, OISE-0405402, CCF-0528201, CNS-0551724, IIP-0712592), and IBM Faculty Awards (2005, 2006, 2007, and 2008).

References

1. Becker, R.A., Chambers, J.M.J.M.: Auditing of data analyses. SIAM Journal of Scientific and Statistical Computing 9(4), 747–760 (1988)
2. Callahan, S., Freire, J., Santos, E., Scheidegger, C., Silva, C., Vo, H.: Managing the Evolution of Dataflows with VisTrails (Extended Abstract). In: IEEE Workshop on Workflow and Data Flow for Scientific Applications, SciFlow (2006)
3. Freire, J., Silva, C.T., Callahan, S.P., Santos, E., Scheidegger, C.E., Vo, H.T.: Managing rapidly-evolving scientific workflows. In: Moreau, L., Foster, I. (eds.) IPAW 2006. LNCS, vol. 4145, pp. 10–18. Springer, Heidelberg (2006)
4. Frew, J., Bose, R.: Earth system science workbench: A data management infrastructure for earth science products. In: Proceedings of SSDBM, pp. 180–189 (2001)
5. Groth, P., Jiang, S., Miles, S., Munroe, S., Tan, V., Tsasakou, S., Moreau, L.: An architecture for provenance systems. Technical report, ECS, University of Southampton (2006)
6. Krasner, G.E., Pope, S.T.: A description of the model-view-controller user interface paradigm in the smalltalk-80 system. Journal of Object-Oriented Programming 1, 26–49 (1988)
7. Paraview, http://www.paraview.org
8. Roundy, D.: Darcs, http://abridgegame.org/darcs
9. Scheidegger, C.E., Vo, H.T., Koop, D., Freire, J., Silva, C.T.: Querying and creating visualizations by analogy. IEEE Transactions on Visualization and Computer Graphics 13(6), 1560–1567 (2007)

Application of Provenance for Automated and Research Driven Workflows

Tara Gibson, Karen Schuchardt, and Eric Stephan

Pacific Northwest National Laboratory,
P.O. Box 999, Richland, WA, USA
{Tara.Gibson,Karen.Schuchardt,Eric.Stephan}@pnl.gov

Abstract. Provenance has recently become a popular topic for workflow execution environments but it is also relevant to other applications, such as long-running, user-driven "research workflows", problem solving environments, and data streaming (data analysis) environments. This paper presents a number of use cases where provenance can play an important role in understanding how data was derived, how decisions were made, and enable sharing of data from a variety of sources. We break down the requirements elucidated by our use cases and discuss our experiences in applying an existing provenance system to these use cases.

Keywords: provenance, metadata, use cases, workflow.

1 Introduction

Science relies on intermediate results to guide future research; every result needs to be supported with detailed records of its derivation (provenance). At the same time, science is becoming more complex, involving both manual and automated pipeline processing steps, and consequently records are more difficult to maintain. Adding to this complexity, simulations and experiments often need to be analyzed together. This creates a challenge for scientists who need integrated views of the different types of provenance records associated with computation, experimentation, and analysis. The existing method for capturing data derivation, traditional laboratory notebooks, suffers from the mismatch between media (paper versus electronic). Electronic laboratory notebooks fill an important niche but are often not used and usually capture only a manual record of research within a desktop publishing type environment. Our vision is to go one step further, automatically providing a very detailed recording of any complex scientific processes.

Documenting the scientific process requires an architecture designed to record, store, manage, and access the provenance describing the scientific process [1]. While the topic of provenance has gained interest in the computer science community it is at a relatively early stage of investigation and application. For example, Simmhan, et. al [2], recently surveyed the use of provenance in e-science applications. Based on the projects surveyed, provenance is typically implemented as an application extension,

J. Freire, D. Koop, and L. Moreau (Eds.): IPAW 2008, LNCS 5272, pp. 128–135, 2008.

rather than a component that can be applied to many systems. Chapman et al. [3] provided a useful set of general requirements based on tracking provenance while combining and manipulating protein interaction data. Based on these requirements as well as those described by Miles et al. [1] we define a set of requirements which apply to a provenance architecture. Many of these requirements were drawn from automated workflow implementations with an emphasis on a Service Oriented Architecture (SOA) architecture. To complement this research, we explore the requirements gathered from use cases related to both automated and user-driven workflows and data systems. From these motivating use cases, we introduce new requirements for consideration while confirming many existing requirements. In the remainder of this paper, we present our use cases (section 2), describe the requirements resulting from our analysis (section 3), and we compare our findings to other state-of-the-art provenance architecture requirements.

2   Use Cases

The following use cases are derived both from direct experiences on projects that have provenance needs and from conducting interviews with scientists across diverse domains. We present the use cases in two categories: automated workflow, and user-driven research workflow. Each use case is described in a moderate amount of detail and is accompanied by a summary of the applicability of provenance for that context. Requirements are presented as a synthesized list in the next section.

2.1   Automated Workflow

U1. Sensor Analysis Pipelines. Intrusion detection systems currently have production network sensors deployed at 30 sites around the country. These sensors monitor a combined network data volume of approximately 30 TB per day for malicious activity. Attacks must be detected as they occur in order to stop intruders from gaining entry and damaging sensitive systems. To enable this detection, aggregation and summarization techniques are applied to compress the data streams into manageable volumes. A component-based (SOA-based) messaging and integration architecture for creating analytical pipelines is used to provide anomaly detection and analysis by following a general pattern of processing stages; ingest, aggregation, signature generation, anomaly detection, context analysis, and data visualization.

The anomaly detection stage is responsible for using statistical and heuristic methods for automatically determining whether a given signature should be considered a significant event. As algorithms are improved, the pipeline may be rerun on the same data to compare the affects of the changes on the identification of significant events. In this context, provenance can be used to review incidents, understand why they were marked as significant, and analyze the impact of changes to the algorithms. This is a different model of provenance capture for workflow than others we are familiar with in that it becomes important to save provenance only for notable events. Additionally, due to the volume of data processed, the provenance capture mechanism must not incur significant delay in the pipeline performance.

U2. Predictive Biology. System's Biology research relies on the collection and analysis of massive amounts of complex biological response and genetic data with the goal of identifying signatures that define, or are predictive of, biological systems and their response to perturbation. Automated workflow is used for gene set enrichment calculations using KEGG pathways and Gene Ontology (GO) terms. A second workflow is being developed to automate the quality control and normalization of Microarray data. This process retrieves data from an external source, and sends it to a machine capable of performing the statistical calculations using R scripts.

In these contexts, provenance allows users to validate the results of past workflows and examine the full derivation of a result. Additionally, since public data sources such as KEGG and GO are constantly changing as new research is added and curated by the community, provenance can track the information about the data source (such as version) to understand differences in results that occur over time. Provenance can also be used to determine which analysis have been run and on which data sources/versions.

U3. Protein Interaction Discovery. Proteins have largely been studied as independent units of function. However, most proteins cooperate with one another in the form of higher level functions, referred to as protein complexes or pathways. A deeper understanding of protein interactions help scientists understand how proteins work together. Protein interaction databases play a vital role in helping identify protein complexes that may ultimately share the same characteristics in two different organisms. The hope is that by discovering characteristics within one organism, searching protein interaction in another organism may lead to similar types of behaviors.

Biologists continually go through a painstaking and time consuming process to manually access distributed data sources, merge the data sets in some way, and perform analyses on the data. For example, the question *"What proteins correspond to genes that are up-regulated at 3hr and 4hr in my microarray data, and which proteins are they known to interact with?"* illustrates the need to correlate experimental results derived from a microarray experiment and compare them to various public protein interaction databases. Answering this question requires several major steps suitable to workflow automation techniques. In this case, provenance can again be used to compare workflow executions to understand the impact of data or algorithm changes on the final result. To do so, it is useful to capture intermediate query results that can vary based on database version, and have an effect on later steps in the workflow.

2.2 User-Driven Research Workflow

We apply the term research workflow to a group of use cases where the goal is to document data derivation and provenance of long-running and at times ad-hoc user-driven research activities.

U4. Subsurface Modeling. Subsurface modeling employs computerized mathematical models to explore complex physical systems that cannot be easily or cost effectively investigated through experiment. When applied to environmental remediation, the goal might be to model processes to understand how contaminants react and move through the environments. Developing this understanding necessarily involves running numerous (tens or hundreds of) related simulations. The research process typically involves running a small number (often one) of simulations, analyzing results and deciding what to do next. There is usually a derivation relationship among the simulations; that is, a researcher will explore along one line of investigation, then go back and explore along another line perhaps branching multiple times within a given line of investigation. A key aspect of this process is that there are many branches of investigation with complex relationships between simulations and across branches.

In current practice, this type of study is maintained in a directory structure with simple metadata naming conventions on directories. However the relationships are not tracked. Weeks later, the detail of the relationships between simulations becomes difficult to recall, even by the researcher performing the simulations. To collaborators, it is undecipherable. In this context, provenance can be used to record the complex relationships between simulations, document branches of investigation, and enable a user to organize and understand their overall process. It can also be used to decide on next steps, present customs views that reduce the complexity, repeat a sequence of steps with different initial conditions, and search for simulations based on detailed context information typically found only in the data files.

U5. Comparative Analysis. The study of complex computational biology and computational chemistry simulations is pursued with the goal of improving the understanding of complex protein interactions. Scientists make extensive use of several high-performance computational tools to produce and analyze data and ultimately to design protein-based scaffolds for environmental cleanup. This can, in principle, be achieved by performing a wide array of simulations of several protein variants under a variety of physico-chemical conditions (pH, temperature, ionic strength). Data for published work must typically be retained for five years.

The research workflow for this problem contains few steps, but numerous simulations and iterations. Once a collection of simulations is complete, visualization tools are used to analyze candidate simulation trajectories exhibiting particular behavior under a variety of conditions. Based on the chosen candidate trajectories, provenance can be used to answer important questions such as: what simulations were used in my comparative analysis, and what simulations and analysis were used in my cited research. Additionally, a researcher will want to quickly access important summary information about simulations (who ran them, under what conditions) and analyses (why was a particular line of investigation followed), and gain direct access to the data files.

U6. Archive Data Mining and Sharing. The Environmental and Molecular Sciences (EMSL) facility houses a variety of high performance experimental and computational resources dedicated to environmental molecular sciences research. The facility has an archive with hundreds of terabytes of data essentially treated as a large file system. There is growing recognition of the value of documenting the data to improve overall effectiveness of the facility. Early versions of the archive required and enforced the use of metadata. However, this requirement was too onerous and effectively discouraged use of the archive. Collection of metadata must therefore be lightweight, customizable, and optional. Further, it is often important to track the relationships between experiments or between experiments and computations. For example, Nuclear Magnetic Resonance (NMR) experiments may be run on samples and computer models used to determine the 3D structure. It is desirable to capture those relationships in searchable, browse-able, notebook type form.

In this context, provenance and metadata can be used to answer important questions such as: what experiments have already been run and under what conditions, what research has been conducted on particular organisms, by whom, with what equipment, what data is available, and how is it related to other experiments?

Harvesting technology is ideal in such an environment, particularly if it can be readily customized and if mechanisms for describing relationships are provided.

3 Use Case Findings

From these use cases, we derived a set of requirements, both functional and non-functional. The full derivation of these requirements, which is beyond the scope and available space for this paper, is based on our detailed discussions and experiences. However, we cross reference the connections between them in the list below and highlight what we view as new requirements and other unique aspects of our findings.

R1.   Record (and query) arbitrary information about individual processes, data that moves between processes, and the relationships between them (U1-U6)

R2.   Record enough information to enable references of data regardless of size or location (U2-U6)

R3.   Extract and record customized file metadata for context searching (U4, U6)

R4.   Record only the provenance from significant events and the processes and data that led to the identification of the event (U1)

R5.   Identify processes, experiments, or data as a collection of related work and allow users to record arbitrary annotations and define new relationships. (U1-U6)

R6.   Record provenance of high throughput pipelines with minimal impact on performance (U1)

R7.   Determine who ran a particular process, under what conditions, and which settings were used (U1-U6)

R8.   Determine if an analysis or experiment has previously been run (U2, U6)

R9.   Identify data generated from a particular process (U1-U6)

R10. Retrieve information to be presented for application specific views (U2, U3)

R11. Identify contextual information and results from access to dynamically changing data sources and versions used in an analysis (U2, U3)

R12. Examine full derivation of the result or significant event (U1-U3)

R13. Determine where a process/data was used for data that should be regenerated due to an algorithm or data source change (U2)

R14. Query for derivation graph, filtering on level of detail (U1-U6)

R15. Compare multiple runs of the same workflow execution (differentiated by data source or software module versions) to analyze the effects of the changes(U1-U3)

R16. Retrieve process documentation to re enact an experiment or workflow using new inputs or parameters (U3-U5)

From the list of requirements we identify the following highly abstracted core capabilities:

- Record data about process, data, relationships
- Group items together for comparison
- Record arbitrary metadata
- Standards-based search capability
- Examine process and data that led to result
- Identify the overall impact on a workflow due to changes in process/data.

Our goal in examining such diverse use cases is to verify the core capabilities applicable to virtually all use cases and to understand the extension points and design constraints necessary to support important, but non-universal capabilities. These core capabilities show great overlap with those the requirements described in Miles et. all. [1]. We also identified several requirements which we view as new additions to published capabilities. While these additions do not affect the core capabilities of a provenance architecture, they represent design considerations that impact may APIs or system design. R3 is one such case. Provenance and metadata stored within existing files (which may include who, what, when information, references to source files, and application specific contextual information), must be extracted and made accessible to satisfy query requirements. This is particularly important when provenance is applied to ad hoc research workflows where the ability to capture process information is more constrained.

Another new requirement, R4, involves storing only the significant provenance in a workflow, this applies particularly to data streaming environments. To capture all data in such an environment would essentially duplicate the original data stream and overwhelm the system both in scalable storage and query interpretation. These requirements suggest a transaction-oriented capability where a provenance record can be constructed during execution and committed only when a positive identification of significant event is made. R6 introduces the non-functional requirement for minimal overhead associated with a provenance capture mechanism in an automation environment. Critical systems processes need to proceed as efficiently as possible and provenance should not interfere with this in any way. This suggests the need for an asynchronous recording mechanism. Finally, in R14, we identify the need to reduce the data derivation graphs (at query time) to the level of detail necessary to its end purpose. A powerful view filter would support filtering based on arbitrary metadata about either process or data. The Open Provenance Model (OPM) has also made a point of providing for multiple graph descriptions or 'accounts' [4]. This is described as offering different levels of explanation for such execution, such sub graphs are also known as alternate accounts.

4 Experiences

The exploration of the described use cases and requirements presented us with challenges which we needed to adapt to a generic architecture. To meet these challenges we altered our previous architecture as described in Schuchardt, et. all [5] with several modifications, We adopted the use of RDF for its support of graph queries, arbitrary relationships and metadata, and standards. We also developed a transaction oriented API, as needed by R4, and incorporated several of the key ideas of the OPM into our existing model. Below are a number of other challenges that we encountered while studying the use cases.

Data Overload: Even with desired view capabilities, in automated systems it is still possible to capture too much meaningless provenance, overloading the database technology. An example of this is the protein interaction discovery workflow, which was implemented on an automated workflow platform with a plug-in mechanism designed to capture provenance when any minor event occurs. We found that by ingesting every minor call within the workflow engine, that we were quickly flooded with too much detail. For this reason, workflow systems need design time control to manage the level of detail captured.

Client Side Filtering: No capabilities for server side view filtering exist at this time. For efficiency reasons, some applications thus developed client-side graph filtering capabilities to fulfill the requirement.

User Views: General tools/browsers are useful for capabilities such as simple browsing, but for most use cases, specific interfaces are required. The view desired by each application can vary greatly in level of detail or interpretation. For use cases such as subsurface modeling, a more extensive classification may be desired to represent the nuances between various actions. To resolve this, the provenance model could be extended to describe various types of actions, such as a compute job versus a data transfer. Among other things, this classification can be used to filter views where certain types of actions are more interesting to the end user and to group related research.

Language Bindings: Our initial implementation of a provenance API was in java but several of our use cases required other languages (python, C++). A general provenance system should support multiple language bindings or a standard protocol (e.g. REST) that can easily be accessed in any language. In the latter case, a language wrapper is still necessary to reduce the burden of adding provenance to a system.

Scalability: Server scalability quickly became an issue for both Sensor Analysis (U1) and Archive Data Mining (U6). To support the full number of datasets that can be encountered in either use case, we must have a storage solution that can scale to billions of triples or support queries and relationships across multiple (federated) stores.

Augmentation: We encountered numerous examples where users would like to go back and augment the provenance record. For example, when a user publishes a paper using results generated by a workflow, they will want to later go back and associate the paper with the provenance record. In simulation environments, some users want to identify and annotate processes, data or entire sub graphs with notes and analyses or manually make associations within or between different sub graphs.

5 Conclusions

Our use case studies have documented compelling examples of the benefits that provenance can provide for a diverse set of domains. Reviewing these use cases has given us a sense of similarity between nearly all workflows, and allowed us to validate a number of existing requirements of a provenance system, as well as present several new ones. To support several of these new requirements, we envision revisiting our provenance model as well as ensuring better interoperability with the OPM, we also plan to improve the API, using standardized recording protocols and adding multiple language bindings. By applying these requirements to our architecture we expect to produce an adaptable, effective system for the support of various domains.

Acknowledgement

The research described in this paper was conducted under the Laboratory Directed Research and Development Program at the Pacific Northwest National Laboratory, a multiprogram national laboratory operated by Battelle for the U.S. Department of Energy under Contract DE-AC05-76RL0 1830. The research in subsurface workflows is supported by the U.S. Department of Energy's Office of Science under the Scientific Discovery through Advanced Computing (SciDAC) program.

References

1. Miles, S., Groth, P., Branco, M., Moreau, L.: The Requirements of Using Provenance in e-Science Experiments. J. Grid Comput. 5(1), 1–25 (2007)
2. Simmhan, Y.L., Plale, B., Gannon, D.: A survey of data provenance in e-science. SIGMOD Rec. 34(3), 31–36 (2005)
3. Chapman, A., Jagadish, H.V.: Issues in Building Practical Provenance Systems. IEEE Data Eng. Bull. 30(4), 38–43 (2007)
4. Moreau, L., Freire, J., Myers, J., Futrelle, J., Paulson, P.R.: The Open Provenance Model. In: Luc Moreau at Workshop on Principles of Provenance, Edinburgh, Scotland, November 20 (2007)
5. Schuchardt, K.L., Gibson, T.D., Stephan, E.G., Chin, G.: Applying Content Management to Automated Provenance Capture Concurrency and Computation. Practice & Experience 20(5), 541–554 (2007)

Using Provenance to Improve Workflow Design

Frederico T. de Oliveira[1], Leonardo Murta[1,2], Claudia Werner[1], and Marta Mattoso[1]

[1] COPPE/ Computer Science Department
Federal University of Rio de Janeiro (UFRJ)
{ftoliveira,werner,marta}@cos.ufrj.br
[2] Instituto de Computação
Universidade Federal Fluminense (UFF)
leomurta@ic.uff.br

Abstract. With the popularity of scientific workflow management systems (WfMS), workflow specifications are becoming available. Provenance support in WfMS can help reusing third party code. Browsing can be done through queries instead of ad-hoc search on the Web. Finding dependencies among programs or services through provenance queries, without tool support, is not a trivial task. Due to the huge number of program versions available and their configuration parameters, this task may be heavily error prone and counterproductive. In this work we propose a recommendation service that aims at suggesting frequent combinations of scientific programs for reuse. Our recommendation service is designed to work over WfMS that provide provenance on workflow specification and execution logs. We have based our service on software components reuse and data mining techniques, and implemented a prototype with Vistrails WfMS.

1 Introduction

Workflow management systems are getting more complicated and providing more functions. Each day, more services are available and their combinations become more complex. Scientific workflows are based on the automation of scientific processes in which scientific programs are associated, based on data and control dependencies. Frequently, these scientific programs are third party code, shared by scientists from a common domain. Aiming at reusing these programs, the scientist browses public execution scripts to see how the program should be parameterized to his specific needs. With the popularity of scientific workflow management systems (WfMS), workflow specifications are also becoming available.

Provenance support in WfMS can help reusing third party code. Browsing can be done through queries instead of ad-hoc search on the Web. Despite that, reusing a scientific program often involves reusing complementary programs. Finding dependencies among programs or services through provenance queries, without tool support, is not a trivial task. Due to the huge number of program versions available and their configuration parameters, this task may be heavily error prone and counterproductive. Automating those tasks can reduce errors and improve reliability. Even if a powerful

J. Freire, D. Koop, and L. Moreau (Eds.): IPAW 2008, LNCS 5272, pp. 136–143, 2008.

workflow provenance support is provided, such as the management of workflow versioning of Vistrails [1], identifying adequate combinations can be time consuming and may involve designing complex queries. Current e-Science infrastructures provide the capability to combine services from a diverse set of providers in a variety of ways. However, they can only be exploited by a minority of specialists who are familiar with workflow composition systems, programming paradigms, distributed infrastructures and complex problem solving environments [2]. In this work we propose a recommendation service that aims at suggesting frequent combinations of scientific programs for reuse. Our recommendation service is designed to work over WfMS that provide workflow specification databases or workflow execution logs. We have based our service on software components reuse and data mining techniques, and implemented a prototype that works with Vistrails.

Our prototype consists on a recommendation system based on a collaborative filtering approach [3]. This recommendation system let users discover useful workflows components and how they can be combined. According to collaborative filtering approach, collected provenance histories are used to recommend a set of candidate services that may be useful to individual scientists.

This work is organized as follows. In section 2, we present the background of our research, containing an overview of workflow and some related work and related techniques. We describe our approach in section 3 and the usage of our prototype in section 4. Finally, we conclude our work presenting some advantages of recommendation in workflow design and some future work in section 5.

2 Background

The scientific workflow design process still occurs in an ad-hoc manner, driving to irreproducible results due to absence of predefined processes or methods. In some cases, the workflow is not explicit because the scientists directly connect programs to perform the experiment, hindering the comprehension of the whole process. In other cases, despite the existence of a WfMS that manages the interaction of the programs and services necessary to perform the experiment, no systematic method is used throughout its design.

In this section we present an overview on the benefits component-based workflow, software reuse and component-based software development, and collaborative filtering can provide to workflow design.

2.1 Software Reuse and Component-Based Software Development

Software reuse is the process of creating software systems from existing software [4]. It encompasses two main perspectives, which are development **for** reuse and development **with** reuse. Software development **for** reuse aims to produce assets that can be reused later. On software development **with** reuse, assets are coupled to the system under development. Reusable assets represent any product derived from software development, for example, source code, components, test cases, etc.

Component-based software development is a technique for software reuse that focus on reusing well defined components, produced via an independent process [5]. Component-based software development uses components, interfaces and connectors as first-class entities to structure software systems. Components, which are reusable assets [6], make use of interfaces, described in a contractual manner, to interact with the remaining software elements [7]. Connectors are responsible for performing the binding among components.

When component-based software development is in place, the software development teams can be classified by their roles in the process. Some teams are in charge of developing components. These teams, named producers, produce reusable components that serve to others. Other teams, named consumers, are in charge of developing systems by reusing existing components. Finally, there are some hybrid teams, which act as both producers and consumers. They reuse existing components to produce more other components.

The component-based software development process is currently supported by a variety of methods. The most well known and adopted are Catalysis [6], UML Components [8], and KobrA [9]. However, besides the existence of these methods, components must be sufficiently widespread to allow their reuse and composition in different contexts, as it is expected from workflow tasks and services [10].

There are already some exiting work that apply reuse to the conception of workflows. De Roure and Goble [2] address several issues to promote workflow reuse. One of them is the recommendation of workflow and services, which is a vital part of enabling sharing through discovery by other scientists and it is also a part of communicating know-how. For instance, Taverna has made over 3500 bioinformatics orientated operation available to its users, and it would probably get benefits from recommendation systems.

2.2 Component-Based Workflow

Zhuge [11] proposes an approach to the development of component-based workflow system through integrating the characteristics of software component. On this approach, the user combines workflows components, which are business process units, to build a complete business process. Workflow components are defined as a workflow process that describes a category of complete business process units, Compared with traditional workflow development, the component-based workflow system has the following potential advantages [11]:

- Lower complexity: a complex workflow can be transformed to a workflow component hierarchy, where each workflow component has the lower complexity than the whole workflow;
- Reusability: a workflow component can be safely reused by any other workflow component or tasks through its access interface;
- Adaptability: component modifications or new component additions will not influence the other components;
- Connectivity: different components can be easily connected;

- Maintainability: components can be maintained at run time if the maintenance can be finished before its execution, increasing the adaptability of the workflow;
- Error localization: workflow definition errors and execution errors occur within components, enabling the checking mechanism to localize them; and
- User's acceptability: workflow components encapsulate domain business process units, so it can be more easily checked and used.

These advantages have a business scenario in mind. However, they may be extended to scientific experiments also. For example, Vistrails components are called modules and Kepler components are called actors.

Despite the documentation available through provenance, it is not systematically used in the design of scientific workflows. On section 3, we expose how our approach can use provenance to help workflow design.

2.3 Recommendation Systems and Collaborative Filtering

Recommendation systems apply data mining techniques to the problem of helping user find the items they would like to purchase at E-Commerce sites by producing a predicted likeliness score or a list of the top recommended items for a given user [12].

The Collaborative Filtering is considered a key technology of recommendation systems, which provide the user with a set of candidate items that may be useful or preferable to the individual user, from a large amount of items [3]. In other words, collaborative filters help people make choices based on the opinions of other people.

For example, in the e-commerce scenario, if a customer searches for the book "The Secret" at an online store, the store recommends other products, like The Secret: 2008 Day-to-Day Calendar, The Secret Soundtrack, etc.

We can also map some concepts adopted in e-commerce domain into concepts concerned to scientific domain. Table 1 illustrates those mapping.

Table 1. E-commerce concepts mapped into scientific experiments concepts

Domain	Concepts			
E-commerce	Customer	Cart	Product	Preference
Scientific Experiment	Scientist	Workflow	Component	Context

Similarly, to help scientists design workflows, we propose a tool to recommend services and task that are more likely to be used by the scientist.

3 Workflow Process Recommendation in Vistrails

In addition to the reuse of components in isolation, we aim to reuse the most common relations between them, increasing productivity and quality of workflow design. Our recommendation service is designed to work over WfMS that provides provenance on histories of workflow specification and execution logs, as Vistrails WfMS does. Based on the collaborative filtering approach, collected histories are used to recommend the

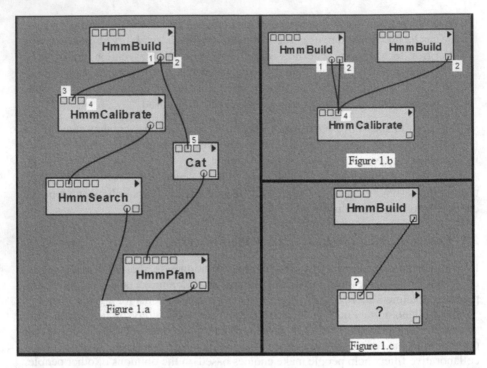

Fig. 1. Component recommendation example in the bioinformatics domain. Ports 1 and 2 are the output ports DestinationDir and StdOut, respectively. Ports 3, 4 and 5 are the input ports SourceDir, HmmPath and Dir, respectively.

scientist a set of candidate components that may be useful to the workflow under design. We propose to infer the need of a component and proactively recommend that component to the scientist.

First, we parse the workflows files to extract the relations between two components. Those relations are mapped into a database table, containing the components, the port that they are connected and the workflow itself. Then, each time a scientist adds a component to his current workflow, the tool automatically analyses the database and recommends the most relevant components previously connected to this one, and indicates how they can be connected.

For example, Figure 1 illustrates parts of some existing bioinformatics workflows. These workflows employ the use of some workflow components, such as "HmmBuild", "HmmCalibrate", and "Cat". These components are connected in different ways in these workflows. Assuming that scientists need to conceive new workflows, if they add the component "HmmBuild" to a new workflow, it is possible to automatically infer that "HmmCalibrate" and "Cat" may also be needed in this new workflow. Moreover, it is also possible to detect how "HmmCalibrate" and "Cat" connect to the existing components in the new workflow, based on how they were connected in previous workflows.

Besides suggesting related workflow components, we can also extract some metrics that provides support to the scientist on selecting the appropriate workflow components. For instance, in the example shown in Figure 1, the recommendation confidence metric regarding connecting the "HmmBuild" StdOut port to HmmPath port from "HmmCalibrate" is 40%. Moreover, the recommendation confidence metric regarding adding component "Cat" after adding component "HmmBuild" is 20%. It is possible to notice that our recommendation confidence metric consists of the conditional probability of selecting a component ("HmmCalibrate" or "Cat", in our example), assuming that another component is also selected ("HmmBuild", in our example).

Finally, in Figure 2 we present the algorithm used to detect the related components and compute the recommendation confidence metric.

```
#populating the database
load_workflow(wf.file):
    for connections in wf.file:
        source_component = get_source_component( connections )
        source_port = get_source_port( connections )
        destination_component = get_destination_component( connections )
        destination_port = get_destination_port( connections )
        insert_database( source_component, source_port, destination_component, destination_port, wf_name )

#recommending components
insert_new_component( component ):
    first_list[ source_port, destination_component, destination_port ] = select_all_where_source_component( component )
    recommendation_list[ source_port, destination_component, destination_port, weight ] = {"", "", "", "", 0}
    for tuple in first_list:
        for recommendation_tuple in recommendation_list:
            if ( recommendation_tuple.source_port == tuple.source_port )
            AND ( recommendation_tuple.destination_component == tuple.destination_component )
            AND ( recommendation_tuple.destination_port == tuple.destination_port ):
                recommendation_tuple.weight = recommendation_tuple.weight + 1
            else:
                recommendation_tuple.add( tuple )
    total_weight = compute_total_weight( recommendation_list )
    for recommendation_tuple in recommendation_list:
        show_recommendation ( recommendation_tuple , (recommendation_tuple.weight / total_weight)% )
```

Fig. 2. Algorithm for component recommendation

4   Usage Details

Preliminary ideas on these recommendation techniques have been implemented and incorporated to the Vistrails WfMS. By parsing the XML files that store versions of workflows we were able to evaluate and recommend.

Figure 3 illustrates the prototype working inside Vistrails, based on the previously discussed example shown in Figure 1. When the user adds the module HmmBuild to his workflow, the tool automatically recommends two other modules that may be connected to this one: "HmmCalibrate" and "Cat". The first row means that port StdOut of HmmBuild has been connected to port HmmPath of HmmCalibrate in 40% of previously designed workflows. The recommendations are on the bottom right corner of figure 3.

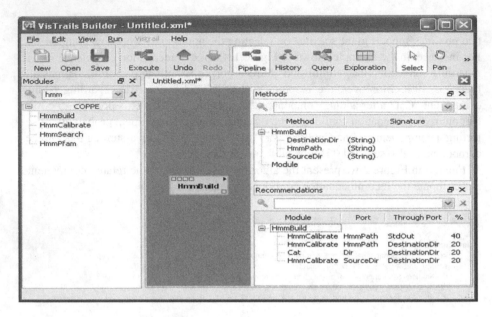

Fig. 3. Recommendation Prototype in Vistrails

5 Conclusion

In this paper, we presented a recommendation system for suggesting the reuse of pre-existing scientific workflow components during the conception of new workflows. We expect that this approach may help to propagate the benefits of software reuse and component-based development to the context of scientific workflows.

However, we could detect some limitations of our approach. The current version of our prototype recommends only a subsequent component based on previously used connection. Now, we are aiming to improve the approach recommending a component investigating the whole path. We also believe that specifying a context to each workflow will help doing a better recommendation. For instance, if a scientist is designing a bioinformatics workflow, connections that come from others bioinformatics workflows should have a higher weight and then more relevance in the recommendation list. At last, we are considering using the number of workflows executions to establish a higher weight to more used workflows.

As a future work, we intend to analyze other possibilities regarding recommendation algorithms in the next prototype versions and perform some structured evaluations to quantify the benefits provided by our approach.

Acknowledgments

This work was partially funded by CNPq.

References

1. Scheidegger, C., Koop, D., Santos, E., Vo, H., Callahan, S., Freire, J., Silva, C.: Tackling the provenance challenge one layer at a time. Concurrency and Computation: Practice and Experience (2007)
2. De Roure, D., Goble, C.: MyExperiment - A Web 2.0 Virtual Research Environment. In: International Workshop on Virtual Research Environments and Collaborative Work Environments, Edinburgh, UK (May 2007)
3. Sarwar, B.M., Karypis, G., Konstan, J.A., Riedl, J.: Item-Based Collaborative Filtering Recommendation Algorithms. In: Proc. of the 10th International World Wide Web Conference (WWW10), Hong Kong, pp. 285–295 (2001)
4. Krueger, C.W.: Software Reuse. ACM Computing Surveys 24(2), 131–183 (1992)
5. Brown, A.W.: Large Scale Component Based Development. Prentice Hall PTR, Englewood Cliffs (2000)
6. D'Souza, D., Wills, A.: Objects, components, and frameworks with UML: The catalysis approach. Addison-Wesley, Reading (1998)
7. Szyperski, C.: Component Software: Beyond object-oriented programming. Addison-Wesley, Reading (2002)
8. Cheesman, J., Daniels, J.: UML Components: A Simple Process for Specifying Component-Based Software. Addison-Wesley, Reading (2000)
9. Atkinson, C., et al.: Component-Based Product Line Engineering with UML. Addison-Wesley, Reading (2001)
10. Ludäscher, B.: Scientific workflow management and the Kepler system. Concurrency and Computation: Practice & Experience, 2006 18(10), 1039–1065 (2006)
11. Zhuge, H.: Component-based workflow systems development. Decision Support Systems 35(4), 517–536 (2003)
12. Hill, W.: Recommending and Evaluating Choices in a Virtual Community of Use. In: Conference on Human Factors in Computing Systems (1995)

Job Provenance – Insight into Very Large Provenance Datasets*

Software Demonstration

Aleš Křenek[1,2], Luděk Matyska[1,2], Jiří Sitera[1], Miroslav Ruda[1,2],
František Dvořák[1], Jiří Filipovič[1], Zdeněk Šustr[1], and Zdeněk Salvet[1,2]

[1] CESNET z.s.p.o., Zikova 4, 160 00 Praha 6, Czech Republic
[2] Institute of Computer Science, Masaryk University,
Botanická 68a, 602 00 Brno, Czech Republic
`First.Last@cesnet.cz`

Abstract. Following the job-centric monitoring concept, Job Provenance (JP) service organizes provenance records on the per-job basis. It is designed to manage very large number of records, as was required in the EGEE project where it was developed originally.

The quantitative aspect is also a focus of the presented demonstration. We show JP capability to retrieve data items of interest from a large dataset of full records of more than 1 million of jobs, to perform non-trivial transformation on those data, and organize the results in such a way that repeated interactive queries are possible.

The application area of the demo is derived from that of previous Provenance Challenges. Though the topic of the demo — a computational experiment — is arranged rather artificially, the demonstration still delivers its main message that JP supports non-trivial transformations and interactive queries on large data sets.

1 Introduction

Provenances are usually used to provide insight in the history of a particular piece of data. In the context of computational experiments they also serve as a source of additional information when results are out of expected bounds, grouped in new ways or organized in patterns not encountered previously. Systems like Job Provenance (JP) [1,2], which keep track of a potentially huge number of executed jobs [3,4,5], are able to either guarantee or to repute that the computational experiment itself was properly executed and correct data were used.

In the proposed demonstration, we will show how the JP can be used to manage large amount of provenance data in a parametric study that is able to easily generate millions of provenance records, thus getting easily out of the range of conventional analysis methods.

* This work has been supported by Czech research intents MSM6383917201 and MSM0021622419. Job Provenance was developed in the EU EGEE-II project, INFSO-RI-031688.

J. Freire, D. Koop, and L. Moreau (Eds.): IPAW 2008, LNCS 5272, pp. 144–151, 2008.

2   Demonstration Scenario

2.1   Evaluated Computational Experiment

The demonstration is based on the conclusions of the study [6], which compares normal aging vs. Alzheimer's disease. Image processing workflow of this study was used for both previous Provenance Challenges[1].

A critical step in this study is measurement of volume of seven regions of interest in the brain. In [6] this step is done manually, by an expert human operator. Our demonstration assumes development of a software tool to replace this manual step with an automated procedure. Then the topic of the demo is a computational experiment of evaluating and calibrating the tool — sweep over available datasets and the whole space of possible parameter settings.

We extend the original workflow with the acquirement of annotations of the softmeaned image. It is implemented either as the human action (for reference), or by invoking the hypothetic automated tool we evaluate.

The parametric study sweeps over 100 sets of available patient images, as well as the following parameters of the processing:

- The *order of the warping model* (-m argument of `align_warp`) has a significant impact on the computational complexity, therefore it makes sense to examine an overall sensitivity to it. Moreover, as each of the four input images is acquired with different MRI scan settings, the sensitivity can be different, therefore all four instances of the parameter have to be examined independently. We sweep those in 4 distinct steps: 3, 6, 9, and 12.
- We assume that the core of the hypothetical automated measurement of the volume of the regions of interest in the brain is some kind of thresholding on voxel intensity. Therefore the *critical threshold* is the principal parameter to be calibrated. The main goal of the experiment is finding a working range of this threshold, applicable (i. e. discriminating dementia) to all available inputs. As the full range of the intensity is 0–4095, we run the parameter in 40 steps of 100.

With the described set of parameters and their steps, the overall number of the workflow instances per a single input data set is $4^4 \times 40 = 10240$, yielding more than 1 million of computations on all inputs altogether.

2.2   Visual Form — The Demo GUI

The demonstration is done using a simple graphical interface (Fig. 1), crafted specifically for this purpose. There are three logically distinct parts forming the interface:

- *Controls for job selection* allow to specify parameter ranges (Sect. 2.1) to query. The effect of changing the selection, e. g. restricting the threshold values, is rendered immediately by the other GUI components.

---

[1] http://twiki.ipaw.info

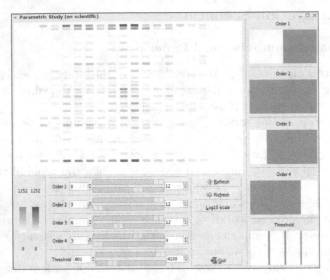

Fig. 1. Application GUI

– *Occurrence diagram* of queried jobs is an approx. 20×20 array, where the x
  axis maps to the age of the subject while y is hippocampus volume[2]. Each cell
  of the array is split up into "green" (non-demented) and "red" (demented)
  subject sections; the number of corresponding jobs (which processed data of
  subject of this age and dementia classification, and computed this volume) is
  visualized using color saturation. An attached color scale bar shows absolute
  numbers of jobs, up to several thousands per cell, typically. Array cells are
  selectable with a mouse.
– *Parameter value histograms* show the actual distribution (i. e. number of jobs
  again) of values of the five studied parameters corresponding to the *selected
  cells* of the occurrence diagram. Properties of these distributions can give
  clues for further changes in parameter selection.

2.3   Analysis Step by Step

In this section we describe the steps of the demonstration, as they are shown one
after another, the phenomena observed in each one, as well as partial conclusions
made.

Working Range of Threshold. We start with a full range of all the parameters, displaying all the jobs of the experiment. The resulting occurrence diagram
is blurred, showing almost regular distribution of green and red color.

According to the conclusions of [6] there should be a clear horizontal separation between red and green regions. We select the intermediate region (hippocampus volume 6.3–6.6 cm^3) on the diagram, which should be empty if [6]
holds and the automated measurement works reliably, and we start examining

---

[2] The region in brain which volume is related to dementia according to [6].

distribution of the parameters there. The histogram of the threshold parameter shows low occurrence of mid-range values (1000–2500) while both lower and higher values occur rather frequently.

We conclude that the range of 1000–2500 is the working range of the threshold. The conclusion is confirmed by restricting the job selection to this range — a visible separation of the green and red regions appears.

Sensitivity to Alignment Parameters. Now the diagram shows also an anomaly — a strange sharp vertical bar (i. e. a failure to discriminate dementia) at the subject age of 82. For the time being we exclude it (ignore the region), and we focus on further improvement of the separation.

Further experiments with the restriction of the threshold parameter do not help anymore. Therefore we keep its range of 1000–2500, as well as the selection of hippocampus volume 6.3–6.6 cm^3, and we focus on the warping order parameters. While the values of the third and fourth ones are distributed regularly, there is a visible domination of low values for the first and second ones. We deduce that there is a certain number of unaligned input images which require higher-order warping to get matched. If the warping order is restricted, the resulting softmeaned image is blurred, yielding the thresholding method to be unusable in general. Moreover, the sensitivity to the warping order is higher for the first two images. When the selection of these two values is restricted, the separation in the occurrence diagram improves visibly.

Defective Input. Now we focus on the visible anomaly of the sharp vertical bar. Its strict vertical orientation indicates a fixed patient age, therefore suggesting that it may have occurred for a specific input data only. We select the central (i. e. failing) part of the vertical bar and query for occurrence of input files in this area. Domination of one input set indicates that the hypothesis is likely. Visualization of this specific four files reveals the reason — an image taken by error from a completely different experiment.

2.4   Batch Job Submission

After finding the defective input we query for all jobs that are affected by it, and mark them as invalid. The defect disappears from the diagram.

We retrieve the full specification of the affected jobs, and after replacing the reference to the defective input we submit the fixed specifications. The processing takes some time but we can observe its progress[3].

3   Experiment Setup

3.1   Job Provenance Service

JP [1] was developed to keep tracks of job execution in a Grid environment. Since references to input and output datasets as well as arbitrary application-

---

[3] The bottleneck is *execution* of the jobs on our testbed which accepts approx. 100 jobs per minute. Our measurements [5] show the raw JP input throughput is about 10× higher.

specific attributes can be easily recorded with the jobs, the records gathered by JP form a natural provenance of the datasets. JP provides efficient means to store but also to search through such a provenance. Capabilities of JP were already demonstrated to data provenance community by participation on two previous Provenance challenges [2].

JP consists of two services — JP *Primary Storage* (JPPS) which keeps all job records permanently, and JP *Index Server* (JPIS), which is created, configured, and populated on demand, according to particular users' needs. This feature is highly exploited in the described demonstration.

One of the most important aspects of JP is the capability to be a core of application specific job management tools. As we shown in three independent studies ([3,4,5]), JP helps the user to see a grid job as a scientific experiment and to focus on the application layer. In the mentioned studies JP also acts as a generic engine to build a custom job management GUI. Such a graphical application is relatively thin layer on top of JP and can be highly customized for a particular need of experimental scientist (to support specific workflows and views). One of these studies was also focused on overall throughput, where the target load of millions jobs per day was successfully achieved ([5]).

3.2 Job Implementation

Unlike in Provenance Challenges, the internal structure of the image processing workflow is not important in our demonstration. Therefore we understand the whole workflow as a single job furthermore.

For the purpose of the demo (1 million of jobs in a reasonable time), the actual payload of the jobs is faked — the jobs refer to 100 pre-computed images, and the principal result (hippocampus volume) is generated pseudo-randomly in a distribution that allows "discovering" the phenomena described in Sect. 2.3. This artificial approach does not affect the main message of the demo — JP is able to deal with millions of provenance records, whatever was the way of obtaining them.

A core of the distribution is the formula

$$threshold \cdot warp\_sensitivity + threshold^3 \cdot (1 - warp\_sensitivity)$$

where *warp_sensitivity* is a number in the range 0–1 expressing how much a specific data set is affected by a given warping parameter settings. For its lower values the cubic term prevails, therefore the working range of the threshold, where the computed hippocampus volume is close to the real one, is fairly wide. On the contrary, for higher values of *warp_sensitivity* the formula is almost linear, hence requiring a specific threshold setting to yield the right result.

Job execution is monitored by L&B [7], application-specific tags (patient id, threshold, warping parameters, computed hippocampus volume etc.) are recorded in terms of L&B *user tags*. Full job records, including the application-specific attributes, are stored into JP shortly after their termination.

3.3   Testbed

The computations are run on a 16 CPU cores machine[4], hosting multiple virtual machines and being managed by PBS. L&B server and both JP services were run on common "off-the-shelf" machines.

Due to the simplified job payload the limiting speed factor turned to be the processing of jobs in PBS. Besides the need of careful setup of L&B in order to avoid disk congestion, as well as a known but addressable bottleneck of not reusing an open ftp connection [5], we did not observe any serious performance problems.

4   Related JP Extensions

4.1   Direct JPIS Database Access

The described parametric study became a pilot application for a new interface to JP Index Server — direct SQL database access. Unlike the web-service interface of JPIS that was used in previous demonstrations, this time the GUI communicates directly with the database engine underlying JPIS. Structure of the database tables that are meant to be accessed directly is documented and it will become another JPIS public interface. Compared to the limited (by intention) querying functionality of the WS interface this approach gives the user the full capability of SQL and it lets her optimize the queries. In the specific case we benefit of the GROUP BY clause counting occurrences of age/hippocampus volume quickly.

On the other hand, certain performance and security issues emerge. Ill-specified queries can generate unacceptable load on the database. As this access mode is intended mostly for single user JPIS instances, we don't consider the performance issues serious this time. However, the standard, fine-grain access control layer of JPIS, implemented on the WS interface, is bypassed, allowing the user to see all JPIS data. The emerging security problems must be addressed, probably by implementing the finer access control on JPPS too.

We are also considering an OGF-DAIS[5] compliant interface that would combine the portability of WS access with the expressiveness of SQL.

4.2   Application-Specific JP Type Plugin

The application also demonstrated the use of the *type plugin* concept in JP. JPIS database can store, besides literal values of the attributes, also their shrunk "database" form. This approach does not imply any general restriction on full attribute values (they can contain even large binary data) while still allowing efficient queries on the database form executed directly by the SQL engine, e. g. to index the columns appropriately. In general there is no 1:1 mapping between

---

[4] http://meta.cesnet.cz/en/resources/hardware.html#manwe4
[5] http://forge.gridforum.org/projects/dais-wg

full and shrunk values, therefore further filtering on the full values must be performed once they are retrieved with an SQL query. However, the result set of the query is not so large typically.

A JP type plugin is a library, linked into JPIS at run-time, performing the "full to shrunk" attribute value mapping. In addition, declarations of SQL column type for a specific attribute can be defined, and full-value comparison function provided.

Specifically the plugin for this experiment data rounds the "age" attribute to the nearest even value, truncates "hippocampus volume" into buckets of size 0.3, and it transforms real value of "clinical dementia rating" to boolean. Then a single query

```
select age,volume,cdr,count(*) ... group by age,volume,cdr
```

populates directly all the cells in the occurrence diagram (Sect. 2.2) within approx. 1–2 s.

4.3   Configuration Extensions and Database Schema Changes

The original database schema of JPIS allows multiple values of a single attribute for a single job. Therefore the attributes are stored in separate tables. However, on approx. 1 million of our job records, the "group by" query shown in Sect. 4.2 accessing multiple tables ran more than 1 minute, not being acceptable for interactive use.

Therefore we further extended the configurability of JPIS to distinguish between *single-* and *multiple-value* attributes. The latter ones are stored as before, however, the shrunk database form (Sect. 4.2) of the former ones are aggregated all in a single table, allowing more efficient queries. Our core "group by" query speeds up by a factor of almost 100.

5   Highlights and Conclusions

We show a specific usage of Job Provenance, a generic customizable system focused on work with huge number of provenance records. On the scenario of a hypothetical parametric study, involving more than a million of computational jobs, JP capabilities of interactive queries over such number of records are clearly demonstrated.

The described queries yield execution of fairly simple SQL statements processing approx. 1 million of tuples, so that their interactivity is not a surprising result nowadays. Our main message is demonstrating the capability of JP to record full information on job execution, to harvest the data required for the specific application (they represent a tiny fraction of the primary data), and to reprocess and make them available in a form suitable for interactive work (reasonable sized SQL database in this specific case). The demonstration also became a pilot application of the new direct JPIS database access interface.

From the application point of view, the queries represent non-straightforward transformations of the parametric space, therefore they can reveal unforeseen behaviour, pattern, and other phenomena that might have remained hidden with a straightforward visualization of the experiment results. Similarly, eventual defects, incorrect inputs etc., which would distort the experiment outcome, are also detected.

References

1. Dvořák, F., et al.: gLite job provenance. In: Moreau, L., Foster, I. (eds.) IPAW 2006. LNCS, vol. 4145, pp. 246–253. Springer, Heidelberg (2006)
2. Křenek, A., et al.: gLite job provenance—a job-centric view. Concurrency and Computation: Practice and Experience 20(5) (2007) doi: 10.1002/cpe.1252
3. Křenek, A., et al.: Multiple ligand trajectory docking study —semiautomatic analysis of molecular dynamics simulations using EGEE gLite services. In: Proc. Euromicro Conference on Parallel Distributed and network-based Processing (2008)
4. Schovancová, J., et al.: VO AUGER large scale Monte Carlo simulations using the EGEE grid environment. In: 3rd EGEE User Forum, Clermont-Ferrand, France (2008)
5. Křenek, A., et al.: Experimental evaluation of job provenance in ATLAS environment. J. Phys.: Conf. Series (accepted, 2007)
6. Head, D., et al.: Frontal-hippocampal double dissociation between normal aging and Alzheimer's disease. Celebral Cortex 15(6), 732–739 (2005)
7. Matyska, L., et al.: Job tracking on a grid—the Logging and Bookkeeping and Job Provenance services. Technical Report 9/2007, CESNET (2007),
http://www.cesnet.cz/doc/techzpravy

A Provenance-Based Fault Tolerance Mechanism for Scientific Workflows

Daniel Crawl and Ilkay Altintas

San Diego Supercomputer Center, UCSD, 9500 Gilman Drive,
La Jolla, CA 92093 USA
{crawl,altintas}@sdsc.edu

Abstract. Capturing provenance information in scientific workflows is not only useful for determining data-dependencies, but also for a wide range of queries including fault tolerance and usage statistics. As collaborative scientific workflow environments provide users with reusable shared workflows, collection and usage of provenance data in a generic way that could serve multiple data and computational models become vital. This paper presents a method for capturing data value- and control- dependencies for provenance information collection in the Kepler scientific workflow system. It also describes how the collected information based on these dependencies could be used for a fault tolerance framework in different models of computation.

1 Introduction and Background

Scientific workflows provide many advantages to the scientific community including provenance support. The lifecycle of scientific workflow provenance starts with workflow design and execution. The collected information can be used for evaluation of the results as well as for mining different patterns during workflow design. Different workflow users need information about different phases of the workflow. These concepts are shown in Figure 1.

Collection of Provenance Information. Provenance collection related to a scientific workflow is three-fold. Firstly, since workflow developers often change a workflow while experimenting with different computational tools and multiple scientific datasets, provenance recording can start during the design phase of the workflow. Capturing these user actions is important since it records what did and did not work, as well as how the workflow developer came up with the final workflow. The collection of provenance information continues during the experiment preparation (parameter binding) and execution of the workflow. The third aspect of collecting scientific workflow provenance that is often ignored is collection after the workflow results are published. One can verify the scientific impact of the workflow based on the citations for these results and statistics on how they are used.

Usages of Provenance Information. The collected provenance data is useful in many contexts, such as querying input/output associations, verifying results, etc. Different types of provenance information analysis based on the design and one or more runs of

J. Freire, D. Koop, and L. Moreau (Eds.): IPAW 2008, LNCS 5272, pp. 152–159, 2008.

the same workflow are listed in Figure 1. The collected information on the workflow design could be used both to analyze it and to visualize the evolution of the workflow as demonstrated in the Vistrails system [1]. In addition, provenance information on data-dependencies could be used for smart reruns and fault tolerance.

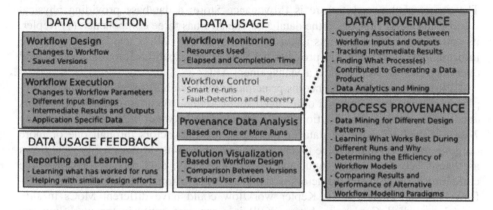

DATA COLLECTION

Workflow Design
- Changes to Workflow
- Saved Versions

Workflow Execution
- Changes to Workflow Parameters
- Different Input Bindings
- Intermediate Results and Outputs
- Application Specific Data

DATA USAGE FEEDBACK

Reporting and Learning
- Learning what has worked for runs
- Helping with similar design efforts

DATA USAGE

Workflow Monitoring
- Resources Used
- Elapsed and Completion Time

Workflow Control
- Smart re-runs
- Fault-Detection and Recovery

Provenance Data Analysis
- Based on One or More Runs

Evolution Visualization
- Based on Workflow Design
- Comparison Between Versions
- Tracking User Actions

DATA PROVENANCE
- Querying Associations Between Workflow Inputs and Outputs
- Tracking Intermediate Results
- Finding What Process(es) Contributed to Generating a Data Product
- Data Analytics and Mining

PROCESS PROVENANCE
- Data Mining for Different Design Patterns
- Learning What Works Best During Different Runs and Why
- Determining the Efficiency of Workflow Models
- Comparing Results and Performance of Alternative Workflow Modeling Paradigms

Fig. 1. Different usages of provenance data

Users of Provenance Information. Users of provenance data include the workflow developer and workflow user, scientific dashboards that help execute and monitor a workflow, and interfaces that use this data. To best serve different users, provenance recorders should provide for customized data collection through parametric interfaces.

This paper presents a method for capturing data-dependencies for provenance in the Kepler scientific workflow system, and describes how these dependencies could be used for a fault tolerance framework. Our fault-tolerance model targets different users of a workflow system. It provides mechanisms to detect errors that would be useful for workflow developers, workflow users, and programming interfaces that execute a given workflow. The level of information that needs to be collected for error-recovery is different for every workflow. Further, workflow systems could execute multiple models of computation (MoC), and the fault tolerance mechanism must work with each. To the best of our knowledge, no scientific workflow system supports these requirements for failure-detection and recovery.

In the rest of this paper, we explain a provenance collection approach in the Kepler scientific workflow system [2] and show how the collected information could be used in a fault-tolerance system that supports the requirements mentioned in the previous paragraph. We demonstrate this approach in a scientific workflow example using a part of the GEON LiDAR Workflow (GLW) [3].

2 The Kepler Provenance Framework

The Kepler scientific workflow system [2] is developed by a cross-project collaboration to serve scientists from different disciplines. Kepler provides a workflow environment in which scientists can design and execute workflows through a user interface or in batch mode from other applications. A *Provenance Recorder* that has plug-in interfaces for new data models, metadata formats and storage destinations was designed to serve the multi-disciplinary requirements of the broad user community. The *Kepler Provenance Framework* (KPR) was presented in [4]. An extended architecture that allows for binding different data models to KPR, collection of application-specific provenance data and using results through a dashboard has been created [5]. The center of this architecture is Provenance Store: a database providing physical storage and an API to access the database. The API has three components: (1) Kepler, its actors, and external scripts use a Recording API to collect and save provenance information; (2) a Query API provides different query capabilities for dashboards, and query actors in Kepler; and (3) a Management API.

KPR uses separation of concerns principle to work with different MoCs [4, 6]. Kepler workflows are composed of a linked set of *Actor*s executing under MoC. Actors encapsulate parameterized actions and communicate between themselves by sending *Token*s, which encapsulate data or messages, to other actors through one or more output ports. Ports that receive tokens are called input ports. MoCs specify what flows as tokens between actors' input and output ports, e.g., data or messages, how the communication between the actors is achieved, when actors fire, and when the workflow can stop execution. A Kepler workflow could have different MoCs in *subworkflows* called *Composite Actors*. KPR is a separate entity in the workflow and records provenance by communicating with the execution engine.; the information recorded depends on the MoC semantics. This can only be achieved using a data model that matches the set of observables about workflow run in a particular MoC.

2.1 Classifying Data-Dependencies

The KPR records workflow assertions and observables, including data-dependencies: data written by an actor may depend on some combination of previously read data. We categorize data-dependencies between output and input data as either *value-dependencies* or *control-dependencies*. A value-dependency occurs when an output data's *value* depends on the *value* of previously read data. For example, consider the two actors show in Figure 2. The Filter actor outputs the previously read token if the value is above a threshold. Each token written by this actor has a single value-dependency: the previously read input token. In Figure 2(a), this actor reads two input tokens T1 and T2. Only the value in T2 is above the threshold and is output in T3. The value-dependency for T3 is T2.

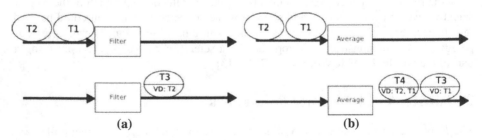

(a)   **(b)**

Fig. 2. Input and resulting output tokens for (a) Filter and (b) Average actors. The output tokens contain a list of value-dependencies (VD).

The Average actor outputs an average of all previously seen inputs. In this case, each output token is value-dependent on all input tokens. In Figure 2(b) the actor first reads T1, then outputs T3, which is only value-dependent on T1. Next, the actor reads T2 and outputs T4, which is value-dependent on both T2 and T1.

A control-dependency occurs when the arrival of input data causes the actor to execute and subsequently produce output data. As described above, the MoC determines when actors execute; in several the execution schedule is based on when input data are present. Many actors therefore use an input "trigger" port to determine when to execute. Since data read from this port are discarded, i.e., the *value* is not used by the actor to produce output data, the distinction between value- and control-dependencies is important for many use cases of provenance.

2.2 Recording Data-Dependencies

The KPR provides methods for recording data-dependencies, either automatically by the runtime system or manually by the actor developer.

Our method of automatically tracking dependencies is inspired by taint propagation, a technique commonly used to detect security vulnerabilities in applications [7,8]. For example, Perl's "taint mode" prohibits any data outside the application to affect something else outside the program [9]. Perl marks each variable assigned from an external input, e.g., files, web services, etc., as tainted and propagates taint to other variables when they are used in expressions with tainted variables.

To capture value-dependencies during workflow execution, the ids of tokens read by an actor are propagated "through the actor" to the produced tokens. (All tokens created during a single workflow execution are assigned a unique identifier). A token is a container for base classes such as Integer or String, and each is instrumented with a list of token ids on which its value depends. The list is created when the object is extracted from a newly read input token and updated when the object is used in an expression. For example, the assignment operator replaces the destination object's dependencies with those in the source, and the addition operator adds the source dependencies to the destination's list.

We also provide an API to capture dependencies for situations in which automatically propagating dependencies is impossible. This can occur, for example, when an actor reads from an external data source such as a web service.

In addition to value-dependencies, control-dependencies may exist between an output token and one or more previously read input tokens. KPR records a control-dependency between each output produced and each input read by an actor during the same firing cycle. A value-dependency between an output and input implies a control-dependency between the same tokens. The converse, however, is not always true. For example, consider the Ramp actor. It has two inputs: "trigger" and "step". Data must be available for both before the actor can execute. The value read in the step input increases or decreases the actor's output value. A control-dependency exists for an output token and the previously read trigger and step inputs. However, only the value in the step input is used to calculate the output; a data-dependency does not exist between the output and the trigger input.

3 Scientific Workflow Doctor: Using Provenance Data for Fault Tolerance

This section describes a fault tolerance framework using the data-dependencies recorded by the KPR. Scientific workflows commonly access a diverse set of resources such as, databases, and file systems. A scientific workflow system therefore must provide mechanisms to gracefully handle resource failures. Further, these mechanisms should be compatible with advanced modeling constructs, such as data-dependent routing, loops, and parallel processing.

Fault tolerance is provided with a composite actor called *Checkpoint*. When a sub-workflow within a *Checkpoint* produces an error event, all execution within the *Checkpoint* is stopped. *Checkpoint* handles the error itself, or passes it up the workflow hierarchy. This is similar to exception handling in text-based programming languages.

Workflow errors are detected and signaled with user-defined expressions called *port conditions*. A *port condition* can be specified for any port and is evaluated when the actor reads from the input port or writes to the output port. If the *port condition* evaluates to false, an error event is signaled. *Port conditions* are analogous to pre- and post-conditions in procedural languages and provide great flexibility for the workflow designer since they may be attached to any port in the workflow. A *port condition* uses the incoming or outgoing token's value, along with mathematical and logical operators. For example, it could check if a numerical token was above a threshold.

Actors also signal errors during workflow execution. An error API is provided for developers to generate error events based on actor-specific conditions, such as when a web service actor's request times-out.

A *Checkpoint* composite actor contains a primary sub-workflow and optionally alternate sub-workflow(s). Data read by the *Checkpoint's* input ports are first passed to the primary sub-workflow. When an error occurs in the primary sub-workflow, *Checkpoint* either re-executes the primary, or runs an alternate sub-workflow. The maximum number of times to retry the primary or an alternate sub-workflow is configurable. Once the retry limit is exceeded, the error is sent up the workflow hierarchy to the nearest enclosing *Checkpoint*.

When *Checkpoint* re-executes a sub-workflow, it resends all data read by the sub-workflow up to and including those that led to the error. The data to be resent are queried from *data-dependencies stored in the provenance database*. An actor generates an error based on the values of one or more input data. These data were written by upstream actors, which in turn created them from a set of input data. *Checkpoint* follows the data-dependencies, starting at the error, back to the data read by the *Checkpoint*'s input ports. These data tokens are sent again to the sub-workflow along with any data tokens received after it in their original order.

Figure 3 shows an example workflow containing a *Checkpoint* actor, based on the GLW [3], which allows geoscientists to analyze and interpolate Light Distance and Ranging (LiDAR) datasets. A geoscientist first selects a region to be analyzed from a web portal. The workflow retrieves the LiDAR point cloud matching the selected region from a database, which is then interpolated using GRASS [10]. GRASS outputs an ASCII grid, which must be converted to binary using Feature Manipulation

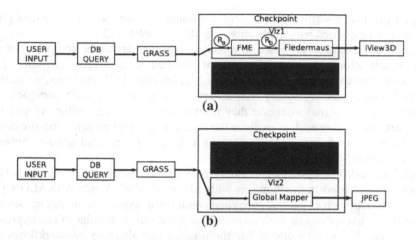

Fig. 3. GLW with fault tolerance. (a) During normal operation, the workflow executes *Viz1*. (b) If FME or Fledermaus in *Viz1* fail, Global Mapper creates a 2D image.

Engine[1] (FME) before Fledermaus[2] can read it. Fledermaus outputs the data into a format that the geoscientist can then load in an interactive 3D viewer. FME and Fledermaus are executed in the sub-workflow *Viz1*.

Since both FME and Fledermaus are web services, they may not always be available. If one fails, we would still like to provide a visualization of the selected LiDAR region. An alternative imaging tool is Global Mapper[3], shown in *Viz2*, which converts the ASCII grid data to a JPEG image.

The *Checkpoint* actor executes *Viz1*, unless FME or Fledermaus cannot be reached. When this occurs an error is signaled and *Checkpoint* runs *Viz2*. Any regions to be processed by FME or Fledermaus are instead processed by Global Mapper. R_a and R_b in Figure 3(a) represent the locations of these regions in the workflow. R_a has not been converted to binary by FME so can be sent directly to Global Mapper. However, R_b has been converted. In this case, *Checkpoint* uses the data-dependencies stored in the provenance database to find the ASCII data that led to R_b. The ASCII data can then be processed by Global Mapper. Since the datasets processed can be very large, references are passed between actors and saved in the provenance database instead of the actual data.

4   Related Work

Provenance in scientific workflow systems has become a major research track. Data-dependencies are analyzed and mapped into a data model for different systems [11,12]. Information collected on these is used to answer users' queries on different workflow aspects. Data-dependencies have also been used for a smart re-run system

---

[1] A GIS data conversion system (http://www.safe.com/).
[2] An interactive 3D visualization system (http://www.ivs3d.com/products/fledermaus/).
[3] A GIS visualization system (http://www.globalmapper.com/).

in Kepler [4]. In the Virtual Data System, provenance is used to reproduce data products, and can be queried with application-specific semantics [12].

Techniques have been proposed to record provenance about the computations occurring inside actors. The registry system of Wootten *et al.* records assertions of internal actor state executing a service-oriented architecture [13]. However, no method is given for automatically adding state assertions to actors. The RWS approach [14] annotates actors to signal whenever they reset to an initial state. Unlike our solution, this requires modifying each actor since the reset event is sent on actor-specific conditions. To our knowledge, no workflow provenance system distinguishes between value- and control-dependencies.

Scientific workflow systems commonly provide fault tolerance mechanisms [15], but most are not used in combination with advanced MoC. While ASKALON [16] allows constructs such as parallel loops and conditional statements, it does not support user-definable exceptions or fault-recovery for actor errors. Similar to our approach, Bowers *et al.* [17] propose embedding the primary and alternate sub-workflows in a control-flow template. However, these templates are directed by a finite state machine, which cannot be used to execute process networks [6]. The Ptolemy backtracking system [18] provides an incremental checkpoint and rollback mechanism. This is complementary to our approach, which deals primarily with stateless actors and provides user-definable fault-detection and recovery. Similar to *port conditions*, Karajan [19] performs matching on user-defined regular expressions attached to input ports. However, there is no mechanism to retry previously executed parts of the workflow.

5 Conclusions and Future Work

This paper discusses methods to identify value- and control- dependencies in the Kepler Provenance Framework. Additionally, we describe how the collected data-dependencies can be used to provide failure recovery in a scientific workflow system.

We will extend our fault tolerance system in several ways. Combining it with the Ptolemy II backtracking system will allow stateful actors to restart. Further, we are building more expressive port conditions by adding conceptual semantics. This will allow conditions such as "all Celsius temperatures (read or written by actors) must be above 5 degrees". We are also investigating other techniques to capture dependency information.

Acknowledgements

The work in this paper is supported by DOE SciDac Award No. DE-FC02-07ER25811 for SDM Center, NSF Award No. DBI 0619060 for REAP, and NSF Award OCI-0722079 for Kepler CORE.

References

1. Freire, J., Silva, C., Callahan, S., Santos, E., Scheidegger, C., Vo, H.: Managing Rapidly-Evolving Scientific Workflows. In: Proceedings of International Provenance and Annotation Workshop, pp. 10–18 (2006)

2. Ludäscher, B., Altintas, I., Berkley, C., Higgins, D., Jaeger-Frank, E., Jones, M., Lee, E., Tao, J., Zhao, Y.: Scientific Workflow Management and the Kepler System. Special Issue: Workflow in Grid Systems. Concurrency and Computation: Practice & Experience 18(10), 1039–1065 (2006)
3. Jaeger-Frank, E., Crosby, C., Memon, A., Nandigam, V., Arrowsmith, J., Conner, J., Altintas, I., Baru, C.: A Three-Tier Architecture for LiDAR Interpolation and Analysis. In: Proceedings of International Workshop on Workflow Systems in e-Science, pp. 920–927 (2006)
4. Altintas, I., Barney, O., Jaeger-Frank, E.: Provenance Collection Support in the Kepler Scientific Workflow System. In: Proceedings of International Provenance and Annotation Workshop, pp. 118–132 (2006)
5. Altintas, I., et al.: Provenance in Kepler-based Scientific Workflow Systems. In: Microsoft e-Science Workshop, poster (2007)
6. Goderis, A., Brooks, C., Altintas, I., Lee, E.A., Goble, C.: Composing Different Models of Computation in Kepler and Ptolemy II. In: Proceedings of the International Conference on Computational Science (2007)
7. Myers, A.: JFlow: practical mostly-static information flow control. In: Proceedings Symposium on Principles of Programming Languages, pp. 228–241 (1999)
8. Haldar, V., Chandra, D., Franz, M.: Dynamic Taint Propagation for Java. In: Proceedings of Computer Security Applications Conference, pp. 303–311 (2005)
9. Wall, L., Christiansen, T., Orwant, J.: Programming Perl, 3rd edn. O'Reilly, Sebastopol
10. Mitasova, H., Mitas, L., Harmon, R.: Simultaneous spline interpolation and topographic analysis for lidar elevation data: methods for open source GIS. IEEE GRSL 2(4), 375–379 (2005)
11. Miles, S., Groth, P., Branco, M., Moreau, L.: The Requirements of Recording and Using Provenance in e-Science Experiments. Journal of Grid Computing 5(1), 1–25 (2007)
12. Zhao, Y., Wilde, M., Foster, I.: Applying the Virtual Data Provenance Model. In: Proceedings of International Provenance and Annotation Workshop, pp. 148–161 (2006)
13. Wootten, I., Rana, O., Rajbhandari, S.: Recording Actor State in Scientific Workflows. In: Proceedings of International Provenance and Annotation Workshop, pp. 109–117 (2006)
14. Ludäscher, B., Podhorszki, N., Altintas, I., Bowers, S., McPhillips, T.: From Computation Models to Models of Provenance: The RWS Approach. Concurrency and Computation: Practice & Experience 2(5), 507–518 (2007)
15. Plankensteiner, K., Prodan, R., Fahringer, T., Kertesz, A., Kacsuk, P.: Fault-tolerant behavior in state-of-the-art Grid Workflow Management Systems. TR-0091, CoreGRID (2007)
16. Fahringer, T., Prodan, R., Duan, R., Nerieri, F., Podlipnig, S., Qin, J., Siddiqui, M., Truong, H., Villazon, A., Wieczorek, M.: ASKALON: A Grid Application Development and Computing Environment. In: Proceedings of International Workshop on Grid Computing (2005)
17. Bowers, S., Ludäscher, B., Ngu, A., Critchlow, T.: Enabling Scientific Workflow Reuse through Structured Composition of Dataflow and Control-Flow. In: IEEE Workshop on Workflow and Data Flow for Scientific Applications (2006)
18. Feng, T.H., Lee, E.A.: Real-Time Distributed Discrete-Event Execution with Fault Tolerance. In: Proceedings of IEEE Real-Time and Embedded Technology and Applications Symposium (2008)
19. Laszewski, G., Hategan, M.: Workflow Concepts of the Java CoG Kit. Journal of Grid Computing 3(3-4), 239–258 (2005)

A First Study on
Clustering Collections of Workflow Graphs

Emanuele Santos[1], Lauro Lins[1], James P. Ahrens[3], Juliana Freire[2],
and Cláudio T. Silva[1,2]

[1] Scientific Computing and Imaging Institute, University of Utah
[2] School of Computing, University of Utah
[3] Los Alamos National Lab

Abstract. As workflow systems get more widely used, the number of workflows and the volume of provenance they generate has grown considerably. New tools and infrastructure are needed to allow users to interact with, reason about, and re-use this information. In this paper, we explore the use of clustering techniques to organize large collections of workflow and provenance graphs. We propose two different representations for these graphs and present an experimental evaluation, using a collection of 1,700 workflow graphs, where we study the trade-offs of these representations and the effectiveness of alternative clustering techniques.

1   Introduction

As workflow systems get more widely used, the number of workflows and the volume of provenance they generate has grown considerably. In fact, large collections of workflows have recently become available through Web sites that enable users to publish and share workflows [13, 19]. Yahoo! Pipes [19], for example, allows users to interactively create data mashups (represented as workflows) through a Web-based interface. Although Yahoo! Pipes has been online for a little over one year, there are already several thousand "pipes" stored on their servers.

The availability of large collections of workflows, such as the ones being held at workflow-sharing sites and in provenance repositories, creates new opportunities for exploring and mining this data. In this paper, we explore different techniques to cluster workflows. The ability to group similar workflows together has many important applications. For example, clustering can be used to automatically create a directory of workflows, similar to DMOZ (http://www.dmoz.org), that users can easily browse. Clustering can also be used to provide a better organization for search results. For example, Yahoo! Pipes provides basic search capabilities through keyword-based interfaces. But because the results are displayed as a long list, users have to go through the list and examine the results sequentially to identify the relevant ones. By clustering the results into distinct groups, users can have a more global and succinct view of the results and more quickly identify the information they are looking for.

The problem of clustering workflows, however, remains largely unexplored. This paper is, to the best of our knowledge, the first study on using clustering

J. Freire, D. Koop, and L. Moreau (Eds.): IPAW 2008, LNCS 5272, pp. 160–173, 2008.
© Springer-Verlag Berlin Heidelberg 2008

techniques for workflow graphs. We explore different representations for these graphs as well as distance measures and clustering algorithms. We perform an experimental study, using a collection of 1,700 workflow graphs, where we examine the trade-offs of these configurations and the effectiveness of alternative clustering approaches.

The remainder of this paper is organized as follows. In Section 2, we review basic clustering concepts and discuss different choices for designing clustering strategies for workflows, including alternative representations for workflows and distance measures. We present our experimental evaluation in Section 3 and describe preliminary results that indicate that clustering strategies can be designed that are both scalable and effective for workflow graphs. We conclude in Section 4, where we outline directions for future work.

2   Clustering Workflows

Clustering is the partitioning of objects, observations or data items into groups (clusters) based on similarity. The goal is to group a collection of objects into clusters, such that the objects within each cluster are more related to one another than to those in different clusters.

Clustering techniques are widely applicable and have been used in many different areas (see [10] for a survey). These areas include, but are not limited to: document retrieval [2, 4], image segmentation [12, 18] and data mining [5]. Clustering has also been applied in the context of business workflows to derive workflow specifications from sequences of execution log entries [7].

To cluster a set of elements, three key components are needed: a model to represent the elements; a (dis)similarity measure or a distance metric; and a clustering algorithm. In this section we describe different alternatives for each of these components when the object of clustering is a workflow graph.

2.1   Alternative Workflow Representations

Data representation refers to the set of features that will be available to the clustering algorithm. A workflow can be defined as a network of tasks structured

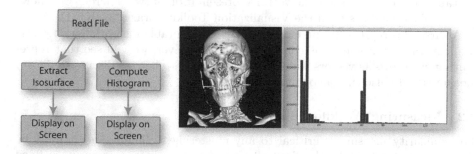

Fig. 1. On the left: a graph representation of a workflow in the visualization domain and on the right its generated data products

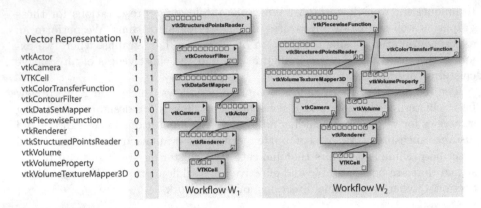

Fig. 2. Vector representation of two different VTK (Visualization Toolkit) workflows. The workflow on the left does isosurface extraction and the workflow on the right does volume rendering.

based on their control and data dependencies. Workflows can be represented as directed graphs, where nodes correspond to modules that perform computations and edges correspond to data streams, as shown on the left of Figure 1. For clustering purposes, we can select different features from these graphs. For example, a possible representation of this graph is to capture only the names of modules and the (unlabeled) edges between modules. More complex representations can be obtained if we take into consideration the parameter values and the input and output ports of each module.

For the clustering strategy to be effective, the data representation must include descriptive features in the input set (*feature selection*), or that new features based on the original set be generated (*feature extraction*). In the representation above, the selected features are the labeled workflow graphs, which is an example of a structured feature. Another way of representing a workflow is as a multidimensional vector [14], which is very popular in the information retrieval literature [1]. In our case, the dimensions in the vector space are defined by the union of all the possible module names the workflows in the input set may contain. Figure 2 illustrates the vector representation of two different workflows that combine modules from the Visualization Toolkit library (VTK) [11].

At first, this representation may seem not very suitable for workflows because the structural information is completely lost. However, we will see that representing workflows as vectors will have its advantages when we discuss similarity measures and clustering algorithms.

2.2 Measuring Workflow Similarity

The similarity measure is critical to any clustering technique and it must be chosen carefully. Usually, the similarity measure is a distance measure defined on the feature space. If we model workflows as graphs, graph-based distance measures can be used, such as edit distance [15], subgraph isomorphism [16], and Maximum Common Induced Subgraph (MCIS). Consider for example MCIS. The distance measure d_{MCIS} derived from the MCIS of two graphs G_1 and G_2 is defined as [3]:

$$d_{\mathrm{MCIS}}(G_1, G_2) = 1 - \frac{|\mathrm{mcis}(G_1, G_2)|}{\max\{|G_1|, |G_2|\}}$$

Intuitively, the larger a MCIS of two graphs is, the more similar the two graphs are. Notice that if two graphs are isomorphic, their MCIS distance is 0 and if they do not have any common subgraph, their MCIS distance is 1. Bunke and Shearer [3] also demonstrated that the MCIS distance satisfies the properties of a metric. The problem with this measure is that it is computationally expensive and for a large collection of workflows, that can be a limitation.

When workflows are represented using the vector space (VS) model, other distance metrics can be used (e.g., Euclidean and Euclidean squared distances). A widely-used distance metric for VS is the cosine distance d_{VS} between two vectors v_1 and v_2, defined as:

$$d_{\mathrm{VS}}(v_1, v_2) = 1 - \cos\theta = 1 - \frac{v_1 \cdot v_2}{\|v_1\|\|v_2\|}$$

Figure 3 shows a concrete example of how d_{MCIS} and d_{VS} are computed for two structurally different graphs. Note their different behaviors: while MCIS is able to capture the (structural) difference between the workflows, the cosine distance is not. This example highlights the importance of selecting an appropriate representation and distance measure.

The input set can be represented directly in terms of the dissimilarity between pairs of observations. This can be done by means of a matrix of dissimilarities, which is a $N \times N$ matrix M, where N is the number of observations and each element m_{ij} contains the distance between observations i and j.

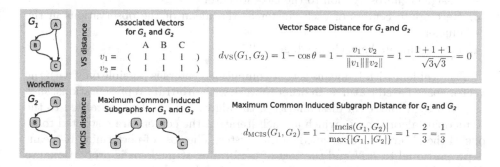

Fig. 3. Vector Space (VS) distance and Maximum Common Induced Subgraph (MCIS) distance for workflows G_1 and G_2. Notice that the VS distance does not capture structural differences (i.e., VS distance equals zero) and that although the path $A \to B \to C$ is a common subgraph of G_1 and G_2, it is not an induced subgraph of G_1.

2.3   Clustering Algorithms

There are many different approaches to clustering data. Roughly speaking, the cluster algorithms can be classified as hierarchical or partitioning (see [10] for a more comprehensive taxonomy of clustering techniques). Partitioning algorithms produce only a single partition of the input set while hierarchical methods produce a nested series of partitions. One of the most popular partitioning methods is the K-means algorithm. K-means partitions the input set N into K clusters in such a way that it minimizes the intracluster dissimilarity or equivalently maximizes the intercluster dissimilarity [8]. Intracluster dissimilarity D_{intra} is defined as:

$$D_{intra} = \frac{1}{2} \sum_{k=1}^{K} \sum_{m \in k} \sum_{n \neq m \in k} d(x_m, x_n)$$

and intercluster dissimilarity D_{inter} is defined as:

$$D_{inter} = \frac{1}{2} \sum_{k=1}^{K} \sum_{m \in k} \sum_{n \in k' \neq k} d(x_m, x_n)$$

Summing both dissimilarities, we obtain the total point scatter T of the input set, which is independent of cluster assignment:

$$T = D_{inter} + D_{intra} = \frac{1}{2} \sum_{m=1}^{N} \sum_{n=1}^{N} d(x_m, x_n)$$

Because it is not practical to compute this by exhaustive enumeration, K-means works in a iterative greedy descent fashion, as described below:

1. Specify the initial K cluster centers
2. Assign each observation to the closest center
3. Recompute centers of each cluster as the mean of the observations in the cluster
4. If assignments have changed, go to 2.

The problem with K-means is that computing centers is possible only with the vector space based features. In order to work with arbitrary representations, such as given by a matrix of dissimilarities, the algorithm can be generalized to the K-medoids algorithm, in which at each iteration the centers are restricted to be one of the observations assigned to the cluster. The cost of performing K-means is proportional to KN and the cost of performing K-medoids is proportional to KN^2, which is computationally more expensive.

The advantage of these methods is that they converge rather quickly and are very easy to implement. The disadvantages of both K-means and K-medoids are the choice of the parameter K and the fact that they are very sensitive to the initialization. Because of that we often need to run these algorithms a few times in order to get the best cluster configuration. Another problem is that they do not present an order relation inside each cluster, and when this is important, using a hierarchical clustering technique is a better option.

Hierarchical clustering algorithms, as their name suggests, build hierarchical representations such that the clusters at each level of the hierarchy are formed by merging two clusters at the next lower level. So, at the lowest level, each cluster has a single object and at the highest level, there is only one cluster containing all the objects. Then, there are $N - 1$ levels in the hierarchy. Hierarchical methods require neither an initialization nor a parameter K. However, they do require the specification of a dissimilarity measure between groups of objects, based on the pairwise dissimilarities among the objects in the two groups.

Depending on the strategy chosen to build the hierarchy, the algorithms can be classified as agglomerative (bottom-up) or divisive (top-down) [8]. In the agglomerative approach, the process is started at the bottom, and recursively at each level two clusters with the smallest intercluster dissimilarity are merged to form the next level, which will have one less cluster. Divisive approaches, on the other hand, start at the top and recursively at each level a cluster is divided into two new clusters such that they present the largest intercluster dissimilarity. These recursive processes can be represented by a rooted binary tree. Figure 7 illustrates the results of running K-medoids on an input set containing 50 workflows, using the two dissimilarities measures described above. The last column of the spreadsheet on the left shows the agglomerative representation for each dissimilarity measure.

3   Experimental Evaluation

Our goal in this experimental evaluation is to assess the effectiveness of different approaches to clustering workflows. In particular, we study the trade-offs between a graph-based and a vector-based representation for workflows, and compare different clustering algorithms. Before discussing our results, below we describe the dataset we used in the experiments.

3.1   The Dataset

The workflows used in this study were generated by thirty students during a scientific visualization course. Over the semester, the students were asked to design workflows to solve different visualization problems (e.g., generate an isosurface visualization of a skull or create a vector field visualization of the salinity of a river). All these tasks were performed in VisTrails [17], a workflow development tool that captures provenance of workflow evolution [6], i.e., all refinements and parameter explorations performed by users during workflow design. For each assignment, the students turned in a file containing detailed provenance of their work, including all different workflow variations they created to solve the problems in the assignment. They were instructed to tag the actual solution workflows with a meaningful label, so that these could be (easily) identified by the instructor and TAs.

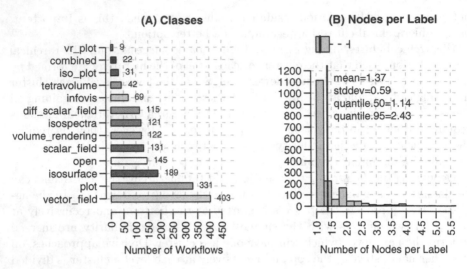

Fig. 4. (A) The initial 13 classes used to partition $\mathcal{W}$ and the number of workflows in each class. (B) Box-plot, histogram and some statistics for the distribution of the number of nodes per number of labels in $\mathcal{W}$.

To assemble our dataset $\mathcal{W}$ we extracted from the files only the workflows identified with a "solution" tag: a total of 1730 workflows. We also classified these workflows, so that we could have reference data to evaluate the quality of the resulting clusters. The classification was done as follows. Based on the assignment problem and the tag provided by the student, we classified each workflow by the type of problem they were supposedly solving. For example, a workflow for assignment 1 tagged as `Problem 1` was classified as `isosurface`, since problem 1 in this assignment asked the students design a workflow for extracting isosurfaces of a 3-dimensional object. For some problems, a specific technique was not required, the workflows created for these problems were classified as `open`. Figure 4 (A) shows the 13 classes we used and the number of workflows in each class.

The workflows in $\mathcal{W}$ contained all information necessary for running them: modules, connections, dependencies, parameters, parameter values, etc. For clustering purposes we use a simplified representation for the workflows that preserves only the module names and connection information: we abstract a workflow as a directed simple labeled graph. More formally, a workflow W is a triple $W = (N, A, \ell : N \rightarrow L)$, where N is the set of modules or *nodes*, A is the set of *arcs*, which is a subset of all ordered pairs in $N \times N$ and ℓ is a function assigning one *label* in the set L to each node in N. Simple graphs have no loops, so pairs (x, x) are not allowed in A.

Although $\mathcal{W}$ contained 1730 workflows some of their graph representations were exactly the same (i.e., *isomorphic graphs*). This was expected to happen since many workflows in $\mathcal{W}$ were designed to solve the same problem. So, for our purposes, instead of using $\mathcal{W}$ we used its subset $\mathcal{W}'$ that consisted of the 1031 different (i.e., *non-isomorphic*) graphs in $\mathcal{W}$.

3.2 Deriving Clusters

Based on the workflow abstraction described in Section 3.1, we used the representations, the dissimilarity measures and the algorithms detailed in Section 2 to cluster the workflows in $\mathcal{W}$. Throughout this section we will use the term MCIS to refer to the structural representation and dissimilarity configuration and VS to refer to the vector-space and cosine distance configuration.

We constructed two distance matrices M'_{mcis} and M'_{vs} for $\mathcal{W}'$ based on the MCIS and VS distance measures. These matrices were used as inputs for the clustering algorithms we experimented with: K-medoids and hierarchical (agglomerative) clustering algorithms were used for both VS and MCIS; and K-means was applied to the VS configuration.

For K-medoids and K-means, to select an appropriate value for K, each configuration was executed 50 times for each specific value of K, with K varying from 2 to 20. For each execution we computed the D_{intra} and D_{inter} cluster dissimilarities and picked the best values, which for the final results were $K = 8$ in the VS configuration and $K = 9$ in the MCIS configuration. The criterion used for choosing the values of K is illustrated in Figure 7, which shows its usage in preliminary results: we examine the values of $log D_{intra}$ as a function of the number of clusters K and search for a "kink" in the plot to choose the most interesting values of K for both configurations [8].

3.3 Effectiveness of Clustering

By examining visualizations of the clustering results, including the ones shown in Figures 5 and 6, we can observe that, for the most part, workflows that belong to the same class are grouped together for both VS and MCIS configurations. There are, however, classes that are spread out across (many) different clusters. As Figure 5 shows, most workflows in the vector_field and infovis classes are grouped in in the first and second clusters (the first two bars, starting from the bottom). However, workflows classified as being vector_field are also found in other clusters.

While trying to understand the heterogeneity of some of the clusters, we came across an interesting and unexpected finding: our classification based on assignment problem and student-specified tag was not accurate for all classes. We selected some of the workflows classified as vector_field but that ended up in different clusters (A and B)—which we refer to as vector_field1 and vector_field2. We also selected two workflows in cluster A which belong to different classes: vector_field1 and isospectra. Then, we compared them, side-by-side. The visual difference results for the two workflow pairs, displayed in Figure 6, show that: vector_field1 and vector_field2 have no modules in common; and vector_field1 and isospectra have a very similar structure, which differs in a single module. The workflows were actually correctly grouped.

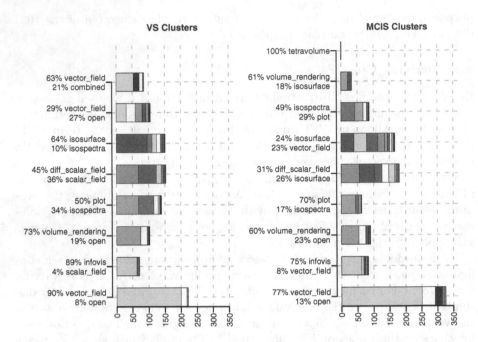

Fig. 5. Clustering $\mathcal{W}'$ using the VS and MCIS distances. The percentages of the two "initial" classes (see Figure 4(A)) that had the most number of workflows inside each cluster are reported. The bars were manually ordered trying to align similar color patterns. The colormap is also the same as used in Figure 4(A). Notice how the first 4 bars (bottom to top) present a similar pattern. *This figure is best understood if viewed in color.*

This indicates that clustering can be an effective means to organize workflow collections.

Although the results produced by K-medoids give some insight into the different types of workflows in our dataset, they do not provide much information about the relationship between workflows in each cluster. To understand these relationships, we used an agglomerative representation to inspect the behavior of both distance measures in more detail. Figure 7 shows, side by side, the results from MCIS and VS using K-medoids and agglomerative clustering. The relationship between the workflows in a cluster are easily seen by looking at the structure of the agglomerative trees. Interesting observations can be drawn from these trees. Notice in both trees that there is a cluster with a single observation (stemming from the root): they correspond to the same workflow. This workflow is an outlier because it contains a single module that does not appear frequently in other workflows in our dataset.

This hierarchical representation can also help in the selection of an appropriate value for K. Depending on the distance metric used, the best values for K can be different. When running K-medoids on a subset of $\mathcal{W}$ containing 50 workflows, $K = 6$ was chosen for MCIS and $K = 4$ for VS. These values are highlighted

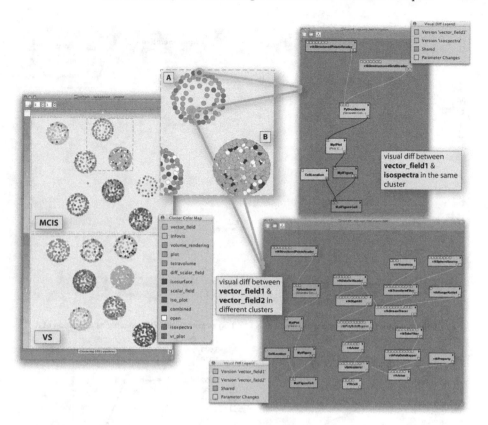

Fig. 6. Clustering results for 1031 workflows. On the spreadsheet (left) are the results of K-Medoids for MCIS (K=9) and for VS (K=8). The visual difference between representative workflows are shown on the right. They explain why observations classified as `vector_field` are in different clusters and why `isospectra` and `vector_field` observations were assigned to the same cluster. *This figure is best understood if viewed in color.*

in the plots on the right of the figure. Note that the both hierarchies in the figure have a number of subtrees that is similar to the K we selected for each configuration.

3.4 Workflow Representations: Graphs vs. Vectors

Figures 5 and 6 show an interesting pattern: the different representations and associated distance measures lead to similar clusters. Consider for example, the first four bars (bottom-up) of the two solutions in Figure 5 have a similar color pattern and size. Given that one representation captures the graph structure and the other is completely unstructured (i.e., it considers a workflow as a bag of words), this result was surprising to us.

To compare in more detail the graph-based and vector-based representations for workflows, we plotted the values of the distance matrices M'_{mcis} and M'_{vs}.

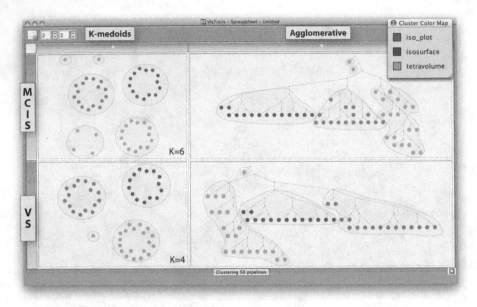

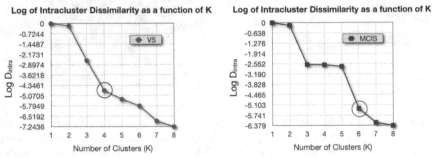

Fig. 7. Clustering results for 50 workflows. The groups formed by K-medoids are indicated in the agglomerative views. The plots below the spreadsheet show log D_{intra} as a function of the number of clusters (K) for each measure, where the chosen values of K are highlighted. The curves were translated to 0 at K=1.

Figure 8 shows a plot of the values in these matrices. Notice that the plot of the MCIS distances does not start from zero. This happens because the d_{mcis} is zero only if it is applied to a pair of isomorphic graphs and by construction there are no such pairs in $\mathcal{W}'$. The same does not occur to the VS plot: d_{vs} can be zero even when the graphs are different (see Figure 3 for an example). Note that this plot shows that the distances capture by these two distinct measures are similar.

We also compared the clusters produced by the two configurations: we used the Jaccard similarity coefficient [9], which is a well-known index for comparing two partitions of the same set. The larger this number is, the more similar the partitions are. Let $C_{vs}^{K=8}$ and $C_{mcis}^{K=9}$ denote the clustering results produced by the VS and the MCIS configurations, respectively. The Jaccard index for

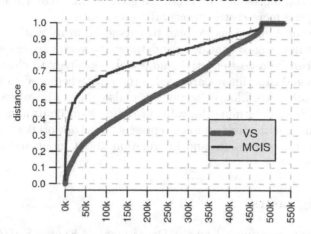

Fig. 8. For the 1031 workflows of $\mathcal{W}'$ we computed 530965 $(= 1031 \times 1030/2)$ VS and MCIS distance values. Ordering (independently) all these values for the two distance measures resulted in the above plot.

partitions $C_{vs}^{K=8}$ and $C_{mcis}^{K=9}$ was 0.328. To better understand what this number means, we checked if a partition of $\mathcal{W}'$ that matched $C_{mcis}^{K=9}$ as well as $C_{vs}^{K=8}$ could be found by chance. We then computed the Jaccard index between $C_{mcis}^{K=9}$ and 1000 randomly generated partitions of $\mathcal{W}'$, with $K = 9$. The mean value of the Jaccard index on this experiment was 0.08 and the maximum value was 0.082, very distant from the number obtained for the MCIS and VS clusters. This supports our hypothesis that the VS and MCIS configurations are correlated.

These results suggest that labels in $\mathcal{W}'$, the only information used by VS, capture a certain amount of the graph structure. To gain insight into this, we examined the distribution of labels across workflows (see Figure 4 (B)). A label appears in 1.37 workflows on average, with a standard deviation of 0.59. Thus, for our dataset, the number of labels is a good estimation to the number of nodes in a workflow (e.g., in 50% of our workflows the number of nodes was at most 1.14 times the number of labels). Also, empirically, we have observed that for the workflows in our dataset, the number of possible connections between modules is small, and it is constrained by the module labels. Intuitively, there is a large number of module pairs, but very few are compatible and can be directly connected.

4   Conclusion

We have presented a first study on clustering workflow graphs. We explored different representations for these graphs, studied the trade-offs of these representations, and assessed the effectiveness of alternative clustering techniques. Our experimental results show that clustering can be effective to organize large collections of workflows. We have also observed that for our dataset, using a vector-space based representation produced good results—comparable to results obtained using the more costly structural representation.

There are several directions we plan to pursue in future work. Although our preliminary results suggest that, for our dataset, the vector space representation for workflows can be a cost-effective and scalable strategy to cluster large collections, additional experiments are needed to verify whether a similar behavior is obtained in other workflow collections. We also plan to investigate more systematic methods to determine the value of K (for K-medoids and K-means) as well as experiment with more complex representations of workflows, for instance, that capture parameter values and information about input and output ports for the modules.

Acknowledgments

Our research has been funded by the Department of Energy SciDAC (VACET and SDM centers), the National Science Foundation (grants IIS-0746500, CNS-0751152, IIS-0713637, OCE-0424602, IIS-0534628, CNS-0514485, IIS-0513692, CNS-0524096, CCF-0401498, OISE-0405402, CCF-0528201, CNS-0551724), and IBM Faculty Awards (2005, 2006, 2007, and 2008). E. Santos is partially supported by a CAPES/Fulbright fellowship.

References

1. Baeza-Yates, R.A., Ribeiro-Neto, B.A.: Modern Information Retrieval. ACM Press/Addison-Wesley (1999)
2. Barbosa, L., Freire, J., da Silva, A.S.: Organizing hidden-web databases by clustering visible web documents. In: Proceedings of the 23rd International Conference on Data Engineering, ICDE 2007, pp. 326–335. IEEE, Los Alamitos (2007)
3. Bunke, H., Shearer, K.: A graph distance metric based on the maximal common subgraph. Pattern Recognition Letters 19(3-4), 255–259 (1998)
4. Cutting, D.R., Karger, D.R., Pedersen, J.O., Tukey, J.W.: Scatter/gather: a cluster-based approach to browsing large document collections. In: SIGIR 1992: Proceedings of the 15th annual international ACM SIGIR conference on Research and development in information retrieval, pp. 318–329 (1992)
5. Ester, M., Frommelt, A., Kriegel, H.-P., Sander, J.: Spatial data mining: Database primitives, algorithms and efficient dbms support. Data Mining and Knowledge Discovery 4(2-3), 193–216 (2000)
6. Freire, J., Silva, C.T., Callahan, S.P., Santos, E., Scheidegger, C.E., Vo, H.T.: Managing rapidly-evolving scientific workflows. In: Moreau, L., Foster, I. (eds.) IPAW 2006. LNCS, vol. 4145, pp. 10–18. Springer, Heidelberg (2006)
7. Greco, G., Guzzo, A., Pontieri, L., Sacca, D.: Discovering expressive process models by clustering log traces. IEEE Transactions on Knowledge and Data Engineering 18(8), 1010–1027 (2006)
8. Hastie, T., Tibshirani, R., Friedman, J.: The Elements of Statistical Learning: Data Mining, Inference and Prediction. Springer Series in Statistics. Springer, Heidelberg (2001)

9. Jaccard, P.: Étude comparative de la distribution florale dans une portion des Alpes et des Jura. Bulletin del la Société Vaudoise des Sciences Naturelles 37, 547–579 (1901)
10. Jain, A.K., Murty, M.N., Flynn, P.J.: Data clustering: a review. ACM Computing Surveys 31(3), 264–323 (1999)
11. Kitware. The Visualization Toolkit (March 15, 2008), http://www.vtk.org
12. Makrogiannis, S., Economou, G., Fotopoulos, S., Bourbakis, N.: Segmentation of color images using multiscale clustering and graph theoretic region synthesis. IEEE Transactions on Systems, Man and Cybernetics, Part A 35(2), 224–238 (2005)
13. MyExperiment (March 15, 2008), http://myexperiment.org
14. Salton, G., Wong, A., Yang, C.S.: A vector space model for automatic indexing. Communications of ACM 18(11), 613–620 (1975)
15. Sanfeliu, A., Fu, K.S.: A distance measure between attributed relational graphs for pattern recognition. IEEE Transactions on Systems, Man and Cybernetics (Part B) 13(3), 353–363 (1983)
16. Ullmann, J.R.: An algorithm for subgraph isomorphism. J. ACM 23(1), 31–42 (1976)
17. The VisTrails Project (March 15, 2008), http://www.vistrails.org
18. Wu, Z., Leahy, R.: An optimal graph theoretic approach to data clustering: theory and its application to image segmentation. IEEE Transactions on Pattern Analysis and Machine Intelligence 15(11), 1101–1113 (1993)
19. Yahoo! Pipes (March 15, 2008), http://pipes.yahoo.com

Exploiting Provenance to Make Sense of Automated Decisions in Scientific Workflows

Paolo Missier, Suzanne Embury, and Richard Stapenhurst

School of Computer Science, University of Manchester
{pmissier,suzanne,stapenr5}@cs.man.ac.uk

Abstract. Scientific workflows may include automated decision steps, for instance to accept/reject certain data products during the course of an *in silico* experiment, based on an assessment of their quality. The trustworthiness of these workflows can be enhanced by providing the users with a trace and explanation of the outcome of these decisions. In this paper we present a provenance model that is designed specifically to support this task. The model applies to a particular type of sub-workflow that is compiled automatically from a high-level specification of user-defined, quality-based data acceptance criteria. The keys to the effectiveness of the approach are that (i) these sub-workflows follow a predictable pattern structure, (ii) the purpose of their component services is defined using an ontology of Information Quality concepts, and (iii) the conceptual model for provenance is consistent with the ontology structure.

1 Introduction

Modern experimental science is increasingly data-intensive: a typical *in silico* experiment involves the coordinated execution of a number of processes that produce, consume, transform and analyse data. Automating these processes bears the promise of increasing the rate at which new scientific results can be produced. At the same time, however, scientists are also responsible for making sure that the data produced by these experiments is sound and scientifically of good quality. Let us mention two of the factors that may contribute to the production of invalid output from an e-science experiment. The first is the increasing reliance on public data and service resources that are contributed by multiple parties within a scientific community; the problem is that these contributors do not routinely offer guarantees of data quality control (or service accuracy). Because of this, low quality in the input may be expected. And secondly, errors can be introduced due to the inherent complexity and variability of the scientific experiments that produce the data. Some of these problems have been surveyed and classified for the case of transcriptomics and proteomics data, for example [6]. When these errors go undetected, because of a lack of appropriate quality controls either by the experimenter, or by the data provider, user scientists face the risk of inadvertently using using poor data that may invalidate the conclusions drawn from their own experiments.

J. Freire, D. Koop, and L. Moreau (Eds.): IPAW 2008, LNCS 5272, pp. 174–185, 2008.

In this paper we argue that, when the experimental process is implemented as a workflow, the analysis of provenance trails collected from workflow executions can play an important role in supporting the experimenters' claim of their results' soundness. By the term *workflow provenance* we mean metadata that is collected during the execution of the workflow, in order to enable various types of *post-mortem* analyses on its outcome. In particular, we are going to exploit provenance metadata to explain and justify the quality-based decisions made by a completely automated workflow on the user's behalf, in particular regarding which data elements are deemed acceptable based on their quality estimates. This problem is complicated by the potentially arbitrary nature of the processors that compose the workflow, as well as of the workflow structure. As has been noted [5], black-box processors that are not further annotated limit the ability to use the provenance log for explanation purposes, and similarly, an arbitrary workflow structure imposes a generic presentation model.

We do not propose a general solution to this problem. Instead, our approach is focused on a specific type of quality-based decision processes, and stems from three key design principles. Firstly, we take the stance that quality assurance in the workflow context is described by a process in its own right, which can be deployed as a part of the workflow itself, or as a sub-workflow. We call such process a *quality workflow*. Secondly, quality workflows are automatically generated from higher-level specifications, in a model-driven fashion, making their structure and their composing services *predictable*. And finally, the services that compose a quality workflow are described as part of an ontology of Information Quality concepts. As we will see in Section 3, this allows us to create a data model for provenance that follows the structure of the ontology. This uniformity of representation has at least two advantages. Firstly, we can query the provenance model using the ontology as a schema; and secondly, we can describe the relationships among elements in the provenance model in terms of semantic properties among their corresponding classes. The combination of these three design principles make it possible to exploit provenance to provide users with a high-level, "semantic" view of quality-based decisions, in a way that would not be possible when dealing with arbitrary workflows.

Based on these premises, in the paper we present a detailed provenance model that is specifically dedicated to analysing quality workflows. We view this as only one specific case of an otherwise general confluence between model-driven workflow design, semantic annotation of services, and provenance modelling. Note that the examples used in the paper are set in the context of e-science workflows; also, the implementation of the provenance model described in the paper uses the Taverna workflow language [7,10], part of the myGrid suite of middleware tools for e-science[1]. Neither of these is a limitation, however: the notion of quality workflows is completely general and applicable to other domains, and the provenance model does not contain any Taverna-specific element.

Concerning related research, we fine that the idea of semantic provenance models that are tailored to special-purpose workflows is not yet common in the

---

[1] http://mygrid.org.uk

literature, although various mature systems provide interesting ways to visualize provenance, i.e., VisTrail [3]. In fact, the ability to query provenance information at different levels of abstraction is listed as one of the many *desiderata* for provenance systems by Chapman and Jagadish [4] (it is listed as number IX).

The recent work on the *Zoom* provenance query prototype by Biton *et al.* [2] is relevant, in that it advocates a tailoring of provenance views to the needs of specific users, rather than just giving access to the enormous bulk of the raw logs in all their detail. We see their work as complementary to our own. We allow users to ignore the detail of the quality assessment aspects of the workflow (which could be packaged up into a "composite module", to use the terminology of Biton *et al.*) until query time. At this point, the provenance browser provides an abstract view over provenance, that is based not on a user-specified view, but on the high-level model from which the quality sub-workflow was produced. Clearly, a number of abstract views of workflows could be supported by adopting mechanisms similar to those suggested in [2].

2   Quality-Based Decision Processes

The quality assurance problems that motivate our work could, in principle, be alleviated by convincing data and service providers to deploy their own quality assurance procedures during data generation, maintenance, and provisioning. Besides being impractical, however, this proposition assumes that standardised quality estimation procedures can be developed. This, however, often contrasts with the very nature of interesting e-science data, which results from cutting-edge research conducted using new and experimental techniques that tend to change rapidly, not lending themselves well to standardisation.

Even when the data provider makes appropriate, objective quality metrics available, the user scientists are still faced with a decision problem, namely whether to accept or reject certain data based on its quality characteristics. Although the determination of data acceptability is based on objective metrics, the user's perception of whether the data is fit for use, given its quality characteristics, also plays a part: some types of error, or approximation, can be tolerable for some types of applications, but not for others, and different users may attach different importance to quality.

2.1   Example

To make these considerations concrete, consider a real-life case study in the domain of qualitative proteomics [1], i.e., concerning the identification and functional characterization of proteins from a cell sample. The experiment includes an *in vitro* portion whereby a mass spectrometer is used to quantify the peptide masses in the sample, followed by an *in silico* portion where the observed masses are matched against theoretically computed masses for a large collection of known proteins. The critical step in the latter portion of the experiment, denoted Identify Proteins in the Taverna workflow fragment of Fig. 1, is the

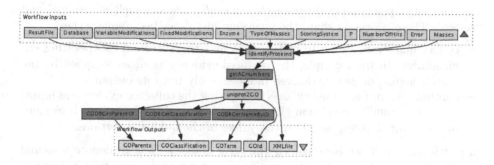

Fig. 1. A simple proteomics workflow with a potentially imprecise search processor

invocation of the matching service. We can view this service as a dedicated search engine that operates on sequences of peptide masses. The results of the search invariably include partial matches as well as exact matches. Although some of these matches may turn out to be false positives, the experimenter has no simple way to make that determination. Ideally, a quality-based data acceptance criteria would be able to accept/reject individual matches based on their likelihood of being a false positive.

To help determine the reliability of each reported match, implementations of this service (Imprint is the homegrown service used in our example) typically do provide additional metadata along with the match, including for example the *Hit Ratio*, i.e., the number of peptide masses matched, divided by the number of peptide masses submitted to the search (additional metadata that is required in this example is omitted for simplicity). Recent research [11] has shown a strong correlation between a simple score model for matches based on this and other readily available indicators, and the likelihood of false positives. By using this predictive score model to rank the output of the matching service, in combination with a user-defined threshold, experimenters have an effective way to make their quality acceptance criteria formal and automatically computable.

2.2 Structure of the Decision Process

The previous example highlights the main elements of a quality-based decision process that is applied to a dataset, in this case a collection of protein matches: first a set of objective metadata elements, i.e., the *Hit Ratio*, is collected in order to compute a predictive quality model (the match score). We will refer to the metadata elements as *quality evidence*, and to the quality model as *quality assertion*. Then, a threshold is applied in order to partition the ranked protein matches into the two classes "accept" and "reject" –this is an example of a *quality condition*. Note how the process combines purely objective elements, namely the evidence, with a predictive model, the assertion, and with a subjective element, namely the threshold. Generalising from the example, in [9] and [8] we have formally described a broad class of quality processes that take an input dataset and compute a partition of the dataset into *quality classes*, such as "accept" and "reject". These processes share the structure just described, namely they:

- collect quality evidence from the data and the surrounding operating environment. In the example, the required evidence is either supplied by the search engine, or can be derived independently from its output;
- compute one or more quality assertions, using the collected evidence as input;
- evaluate a quality condition that assigns one quality class to each element in the input dataset, based on the values of the quality assertions.

In particular, in [9] we have coined the term *Quality View* to denote a formal specification of such a quality process. The process is abstract in that it does not include any indications regarding its implementation. A Quality View specifies three types of functions, one for each of the steps listed above, namely (*i*) annotation functions that associate quality evidence metadata to the input dataset; (*ii*) quality assertion functions that associate quality assertions to the data based on the evidence, and (*iii*) quality actions that compute a quality classification based on the assertions.

2.3   Compiling Quality Processes to Workflows

Quality Views are defined as part of a workbench for Information Quality management, called *Qurator* [9]. Using Qurator, e-scientists may define their own quality metrics for specific types of data as quality assertion functions, and then specify Quality Views in order to apply those metrics to the data. Quality Views are most useful when they are deployed as filters within larger, user-defined processes. For this reason, Qurator includes a compiler that translates Quality Views into workflows, specifically targeted at the Taverna workflow system. An example of such a *quality workflow*, designed to work with the example protein identification workflow of Fig. 1, is shown in Fig. 2.

The compiler assumes that all the annotation and assertion functions that are part of the Quality View have been implemented as Web Services. With this assumption, those functions translate simply to Taverna processors that perform service invocations. Specifically, the example workflow includes one annotation processor, `InprintOutputAnnotator`, and three quality assertion processors, for instance `PIScoreClassifier`. The action step at the end evaluates an expression on the values of any of the assertions computed by these processors, for instance "HitRatio > 0.67 and PIScoreClassifier = 'high' and ...". Data elements that do not satisfy the condition are placed in the "reject" output of the processor, which is typically not connected to any other processor. Thus, this mechanism can be used in particular to filter out protein identifiers that rank too low, when a user-defined threshold is used in combination with the score model described in Section 2.1.

2.4   Role of Provenance

As this example shows, quality workflows may have an impact on the outcome of a workflow, for instance by removing the likely false positives. It is therefore

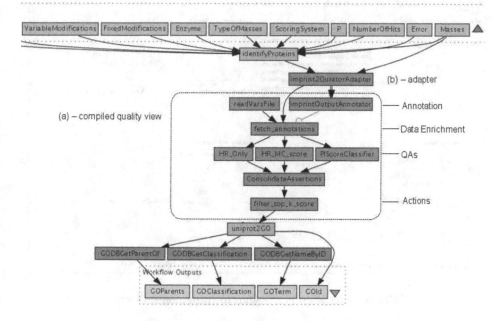

Fig. 2. A quality workflow deployed as part of the proteomics experiment

important for users to understand the effects of the quality workflow on the output of its original workflow. For this, the Qurator workbench includes a provenance component that is specialised to operate exclusively on quality workflows, providing users with a high-level trail to explain how a certain decision was reached. Specifically, the component supports the following tasks, among others:

- visualize the partitioning of the input data set into quality classes, as defined upon evaluating the action condition;
- for each data element, visualize the entire trail of transformations that contributed to its quality classification. This includes quality assertion values that were used in evaluating the condition, the names and types of the quality assertion functions, the values for their input quality evidence, and the annotation functions used to compute the evidence;
- visualize the different quality classification outcomes obtained over a series of workflow executions, highlighting the differences among the quality workflow settings (e.g. the action condition). Is a certain data element consistently rejected or accepted, for example? or is its acceptance particularly sensitive to a threshold configuration?
- compute descriptive statistics over the series, for instance by counting the number of times that each data element was rejected/accepted.

The ability to address these issues is particularly important, when one considers that the Qurator workbench provides users with ways to rapidly deploy and test new quality workflows, leading to the inexpensive generation of experiment

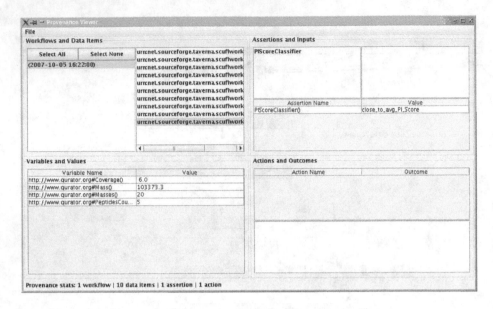

Fig. 3. Screenshot of the Qurator provenance viewer

variants. The screenshot in Fig. 3, taken from the current implementation of the provenance component (part of the Qurator workbench), shows an example of user presentation of quality provenance.

3   The Quality Provenance Model

In this section we describe in detail the data and query model for quality provenance that supports the tasks outlined above. Its design exploits the layered structure of the quality workflows, that corresponds to the abstract process steps of the Quality View they are compiled from.

3.1   Semantic Definition of Quality Processors

In addition to generating quality workflows with a predictable structure, Qurator offers a second advantage to the provenance component: all the elements of a Quality View (data, quality metadata, and processors) are assigned a *semantic type*, i.e., a reference to a class in an ontology of Information Quality (IQ) concepts. To illustrate, consider Fig. 4, where the main concepts are shown along with their properties[2]. The leftmost part of the figure shows some of the domain-independent ontology classes: an Annotation function computes values that are instances of Quality Evidence classes, using instances of Data Entity as input. Similarly, a generic Quality Assertion is based upon Quality

---

[2] This is a vastly simplified fragment of the ontology. For a complete account, please see [8].

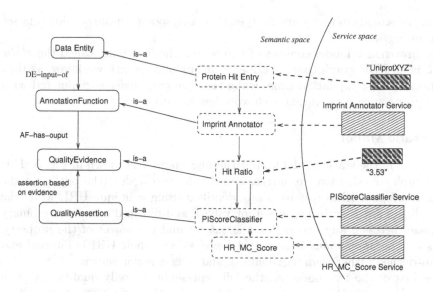

Fig. 4. A fragment of the Information Quality ontology with semantic typing of services

Evidence values. On its right are specializations of each of these generic classes to domain-specific sub-classes, in this case associated to protein identification data (Imprint is the name of the specific protein matching tool used in the main workflow). Together, these classes and properties belong to a "semantic space" of symbols that can be used to give meaning to objects in the "service and data space", on the right in the figure. In this space we find specific implementations of the functions as Web Services, as well as actual values for data and metadata elements (the patterned boxes).

When a Quality View is compiled into a quality workflow, entities in the service and data space are annotated with references to classes in the semantic space. As we will see shortly, by creating a data model for the provenance component that follows the structure of the ontology we are able to view provenance metadata as instances of the ontology classes. This uniformity of representation has at least two advantages. Firstly, we can query the provenance model using the ontology as a schema; and secondly, we can describe the relationships among elements in the provenance model in terms of semantic properties among their corresponding classes, leading to a presentation model for provenance that is close to the scientist's intuition of the intended workflow behaviour.

Since the IQ ontology is specified using the OWL Semantic Web language[3], these design decisions lead naturally to RDF[4] as the data model of choice for provenance. This is in accordance with common Semantic Web practice, whereby we can assign a semantic type to arbitrary RDF resources (by means of the pre-defined RDF(S) property rdf:type). In particular, some of the instances of the

---

[3] http://www.w3.org/TR/owl-guide/
[4] http://www.w3.org/RDF/

provenance schema have a semantic type that corresponds to the ontology classes shown in Fig. 4.

The provenance model consists of two parts. The first part, called the *static model*, is an RDF graph that describes elements of a quality workflow, as they are specified at compilation time, while the *dynamic model* is populated with actual provenance data during each workflow execution.

3.2   Static Model

A fragment of the static model for our running example is shown in Fig. 5. This RDF graph contains two resources, namely the two nodes (the ovals) on the left in the figure. RDF resources are identified using a unique URI, while the square boxes are *literals*, i.e., constant values, and directed arcs denote binary properties between any two nodes, the *subject* and the *object* of the property. Nodes can be *anonymous* (also called *b-nodes*), i.e., their URI is internal and system-defined rather than user-defined, and thus it is not shown.

The first of the two nodes on the left represents the only quality action in the workflow, i.e., `filter_action`, and it carries the definition of the action expression that is used to identify the "accept" data elements. The second is the root of a sub-graph that represents one of the quality assertion functions, along with its input and output variables, having semantic type `PIScoreClassifier`. Similarly, each input variable is an RDF resource too, consisting of a name (the literal) and a semantic type, i.e., a reference to a Quality Evidence class.

3.3   Dynamic Model

The static model is common to all executions of the same workflow. A *dynamic model* for quality provenance, also an RDF graph, is populated during each workflow execution, and contains references to the static model. Its purpose is to capture the values of the variables involved in the workflow, i.e., those that appear in the static model, as well as the effect of the quality actions. Each new execution of the same quality workflow results in the generation of a new dynamic model (for the same static model).

From a technical standpoint, the mechanism for collecting provenance information for the dynamic model exploits Taverna's ability to accept third party monitoring components and to send notifications to them for a variety of events that occur during workflow execution. Using this notification pattern, the quality provenance component monitors the activity of individual processors in the quality workflow, as well as the content of the messages they exchange.

With reference to our example, Fig. 6 represents a fragment of the dynamic model corresponding to the static model of Fig. 5. The b-nodes in the middle represent a variety of workflow elements. Second from top is the workflow execution node with a unique identifier (i.e., the resource `PP6...`) that serves as a reference for the other nodes, which are related to it through the `workflow` property. This common reference defines the scope for all the resources associated

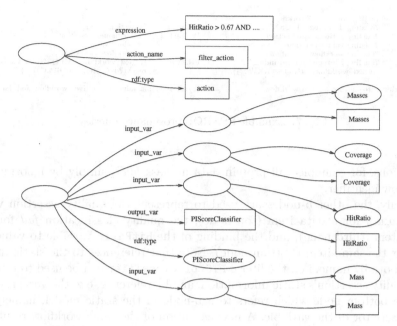

Fig. 5. Compiler-generated static model for quality provenance

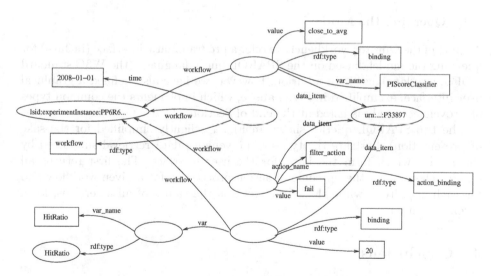

Fig. 6. Dynamic provenance model populated from workflow execution

with a single execution. It ensures, for example, that we can retrieve the entire
quality provenance graph for one execution independently from that of other
executions (using a query with the constraint that the workflow be the same for
all resources returned), while at the same time allowing for queries over multiple

```
SELECT      ?action ?outcome ?workflow              SELECT      ?assertion ?value
WHERE {     ?binding data_item "P33897" .           WHERE {     ?v var_name ?assertion .
            ?binding action_name ?action .                      ?v value ?value .
            ?binding value ?outcome .                           ?v workflow ?workflow .
            ?binding workflow ?workflow .           FILTER      (regex(?workflow, "4IPQF26RXW2")) .
            ?binding rdf:type "actionBinding" .                 regex(?data_item, "P26153")) . }
FILTER      (regex(?workflow, "4IPQF26RXW2")) . }
```

(1) all action outcomes for a given workflow   (2) all assertion values for a given workflow and data item

Fig. 7. Example SPARQL provenance queries

executions, for example "all protein data in class *fail*", simply by ignoring the workflow identifier.[5]

Briefly, the other b-nodes are used to represent the quality assertion value *close_to_avg* for a data item (top node), the quality classification *fail* for the same item (third node), and the binding of the `HitRatio` variable to value 20, still for the same item (bottom node). Note that references to the static model occur both by name, i.e., the literal `PIScoreClassifier` can be used to retrieve the quality assertion's static information, and by reference, e.g. the `var` property for the bottom node which refers to a b-node in the static model, namely for the descriptor of the variable. A new execution of the same workflow results in a new set of b-nodes, with references to the same static model nodes.

3.4   Querying the Model

As part of the Qurator workbench we offer a programmatic interface (in Java) for querying the model, based on the SPARQL query language (the W3C standard RDF query language[6]). In addition, however, we have also defined a graphical user interface, exemplified in Fig. 3 above, which implements the common types of provenance analysis listed at the end of Section 2.

The two SPARQL queries shown in Fig. 7 (slightly simplified for the sake of presentation) illustrate the types of provenance data retrieval supported by the model, which form the basis for the user interface. The first returns all quality classes, i.e., the outcome of action processors, for a given workflow and for each data item, while the second returns the values of all assertions, for a given data item.

4   Conclusions

In our previous work [9] we have proposed the notion of a *quality workflow* in the context of the Qurator workbench for managing information quality in e-science. In this paper we have described a focused, application-oriented process

---

[5] Recent extensions of RDF, namely for *named graphs* (http://www.w3.org/2004/03/trix/), can also be used to partition a large RDF graph according to a given scope.

[6] http://www.w3.org/TR/rdf-sparql-query/

provenance model, called *quality provenance*, that can be associated to quality workflows. The model benefits from the automated generation of quality workflows by means of a compiler, and from the use of an ontology of information quality concepts – both of which are pre-existing Qurator features.

Several broad-scope provenance models have been proposed in the literature. Oblivious of any workflow semantics, these models capture a generic and low-level form of provenance. In contrast, in our approach we narrow the scope of provenance analysis, in return for the ability to present users with a high-level explanation of the processors that are within the scope. Although we have developed this idea in the context of quality-based decision processes, we believe this to be a viable approach that can be generalised to other types of pattern-based workflow structures.

References

1. Aebersold, R., Mann, M.: Mass spectrometry-based proteomics. Nature 422, 198–207 (2003)
2. Biton, O., Cohen-Boulakia, S., Davidson, S., Hara, C.: Querying and managing provenance through user views in scientific workflows. In: Procs. International Conference on Data Engineering (ICDE) (April 2008)
3. Callahan, S.P., Freire, J., Santos, E., Scheidegger, C.E.: VisTrails: visualization meets data management. In: SIGMOD Conference, pp. 745–747 (2006)
4. Chapman, A., Jagadish, H.V.: Issues in building practical provenance systems. IEEE Data Eng. Bull. 30(4), 38–43 (2007)
5. Davidson, S., Cohen-Boulakia, S., Eyal, A., Ludascher, B., McPhillips, T., Bowers, S., Kumar Anand, M., Freire, J.: Provenance in scientific workflow systems. Data Engineering Bulletin 30 (December 2007)
6. Hedeler, C., Missier, P.: Database Modeling in Biology: Practices and Challenges. In: Quality management challenges in the post-genomic era., Artech House (2007)
7. Hull, D., Wolstencroft, K., Stevens, R., Goble, C., Pocock, M.R., Li, P., Oinn, T.: Taverna: a tool for building and running workflows of services. Nucleic Acids Research 34, W729–W732 (2006)
8. Missier, P.: Modelling and Computing Information Quality in e-science. Ph.D thesis, School of Computer Science (2008)
9. Missier, P., Embury, S.M., Greenwood, M., Preece, A.D., Jin, B.: Quality views: Capturing and exploiting the user perspective on data quality. In: VLDB, Seoul, Korea, pp. 977–988 (September 2006)
10. Oinn, T., Addis, M., Ferris, J., Marvin, D., Senger, M., Greenwood, M., Carver, T., Glover, K., Pocock, M.R., Wipat, A., Li, P.: Taverna: A tool for the composition and enactment of bioinformatics workflows. Bioinformatics, 3045–3054 (November 2004)
11. Stead, D.A., Preece, A., Brown, A.J.P.: Universal metrics for quality assessment of protein identifications by mass spectrometry. Molecular & Cellular Proteomics 5(7), 1205–1211 (2006)

Using Explicit Control Processes in Distributed Workflows to Gather Provenance

Sérgio Manuel Serra da Cruz[1], Fernando Seabra Chirigati[1], Rafael Dahis[1],
Maria Luiza M. Campos[2], and Marta Mattoso[1]

[1] PESC - COPPE
[2] PPGI - IM/NCE
Federal University of Rio de Janeiro (UFRJ)
P.O. Box: 68511, Rio de Janeiro, RJ, 21941-972, Brazil
{serra,fernando_seabra,rafaeldahis,marta}@cos.ufrj.br,
mluiza@ufrj.br

Abstract. Distributing workflow tasks among high performance environments involves local processing and remote execution on clusters and grids. This distribution often needs interoperation between heterogeneous workflow definition languages and their corresponding execution machines. A centralized Workflow Management System (WfMS) can be locally controlling the execution of a workflow that needs a grid WfMS to execute a sub-workflow that requires high performance. Workflow specification languages often provide different control-flow execution structures. Moving from one environment to another requires mappings between these languages. Due to heterogeneity, control-flow structures, available in one system, may not be supported in another. In these heterogeneous distributed environments, provenance gathering becomes also heterogeneous. This work presents control-flow modules that aim to be independent from WfMS. By inserting these control-flow modules on the workflow specification, the workflow execution control becomes less dependent of heterogeneous workflow execution engines. In addition, they can be used to gather provenance data both from local and remote execution, thus allowing the same provenance registration on both environments independent of the heterogeneous WfMS. The proposed modules extend the ordinary workflow tasks by providing dynamic behavioral execution control. They were implemented in the VisTrails graphical workflow enactment engine, which offers a flexible infrastructure for provenance gathering.

Keywords: workflow, provenance, scientific workflow, distributed computing.

1 Introduction

Scientific experiments are increasingly being conducted using workflow specifications controlled by workflow management systems (WfMS). Obtaining provenance data for scientific experiments with the help of these systems is becoming very attractive. However, provenance capture mechanisms are still an open issue [1]. Innumerous WfMS are available to support scientific workflow execution [1] [2] [3]. Each system has specific features to address different workflow requirements. It is very

J. Freire, D. Koop, and L. Moreau (Eds.): IPAW 2008, LNCS 5272, pp. 186–199, 2008.
© Springer-Verlag Berlin Heidelberg 2008

likely that workflows belonging to the same experiment use different WfMS. Each WfMS has its own provenance model and capture mechanism. Such heterogeneity imposes many challenges for provenance data representation and integration. Several efforts are underway to minimize this heterogeneity, such as the Open Provenance Model (OPM) [4] and the series of Provenance Challenges.

Scientific workflows are characterized by data intensive analyses. These data driven workflows also need control structures to specify how the data flow should be directed [5] [6] [7]. Often, these data analyses are time consuming and need to execute on remote parallel processing environments, such as cluster machines and grids. Several grid WfMS [3], such as Pegasus [8], P-GRADE [9] and Triana [10], have been proposed to offer high performance execution. However, not all tasks of a scientific workflow need to be executed on a high performance environment. Local WfMS have been designed with rich graphical interfaces to be interactively used. For example, they provide visual tools to follow the workflow execution steps. Local and centralized control based WfMS (e.g. Taverna, [11], VisTrails [12] [13], and Kepler [14]) are characterized by a single workflow execution engine, enacting the whole execution of a given scientific workflow.

A distributed workflow is characterized by a distributed execution where some of the workflow tasks are best executed locally, while others remotely. This is a typical scenario for many applications, such as bioinformatics. Local task execution is well supported by current centralized WfMS. However, they present limited capabilities to allow for remote executions. Usually, the WfMS presents some modules that help the invocation of a remote execution environment for executing one single task. When it is necessary to run a sub-workflow remotely, WfMS language mappings are required. Using one single workflow language/engine to run tasks of the same workflow along these local and distributed environments is currently an open issue.

In summary, a distributed workflow execution involves a lot of heterogeneity, i.e., execution under different workflow engines and heterogeneous provenance capture mechanisms. Provenance gathering based on central control can lose track of these remote tasks. Provenance gathering is usually tightly coupled to the workflow engine in charge of execution monitoring. Moving from one workflow system to another imposes at least two challenges. The first is related to the workflow design - in general, scientists are focused on composing and constructing a particular workflow within one single WfMS; designing parallel executions of processes may involve heterogeneous workflow models. The second relates to provenance gathering – currently, most WfMS register provenance in their own schema, often encompassing specific grid features or application domain attributes. Even if all systems adopt the same provenance schema, e.g. OPM [4], integrating its instances is not trivial.

One possible solution is to diminish the dependence of the workflow definition on the WfMS. This could be achieved by uncoupling the provenance gathering system from the WfMS, and also by having some control-flow of execution independent of the WfMS workflow specification language. By plugging control-flow and provenance gathering modules along the workflow original tasks, the workflow specification can be executed almost independently of the current WfMS and provenance can be gathered uniformly.

In this paper, it is proposed a small set of generic workflow-level control modules that can be used to design a scientific workflow to be executed by heterogeneous

WfMS. These control modules are close to basic workflows patterns proposed in [15]. They aims to improve remote workflow execution by allowing WfMS to face a dynamic execution behavior without losing track of the provenance gathering process in distributed environments. Such approach is a step towards the above-mentioned challenges on independent distributed workflow execution and provenance gathering.

This paper is organized as follows. Section 2 discusses scientific workflow controls and distributed provenance gathering. Section 3 presents the execution control modules. Section 4 shows an implementation of these modules on VisTrails WfMS. Section 5 concludes the paper.

2   Provenance Gathering in Distributed Scientific Workflows

In this section, we discuss the problems of having to move from one WfMS to another. Initially, we stress that control flow does matter in scientific workflows. Then, we discuss the problems of having different control structures in WfMS specification languages and address its impact on provenance gathering.

2.1   Control Flow in Scientific Workflows

Even though control is not the main characteristic of a scientific workflow, they do matter and are essential in many experiments [5] [3] [6] [7]. Workflow control patterns have been proposed by Aalst et al. [16] as a common framework to help on the heterogeneities of the several workflow specification languages. We used a subset of these control-flow patterns to design our proposed control modules. Our goal is to have a meta-workflow specification language that eases migration from one WfMS to another.

According to the taxonomy of Yu and Buyya [3] for Scientific Workflow Systems for Grid Computing, a DAG-based workflow structure can be categorized as sequence, parallelism, and choice, whereas a scientific non-DAG workflow also includes iteration structure. Control structures play an important part on this taxonomy that represents generically scientific workflows

Goderis, Brooks, Altintas, Lee, and Goble [6] stress the importance of combining different models of computation in one scientific workflow. They show examples of combining sequential pipelines with iteration and choice control flow process similar to a finite state machine that evaluates guards on all outgoing transitions. Similarly, Bowers, Ludaecher, Ngu and Critchlow [5] say that control-flow modeling, such as "if-then-else and switch-case statements, and iteration with multiple entry and exit points", are often necessary for engineering fault-tolerant, robust, and adaptive workflows. They also say "that modeling control-flow using only dataflow constructs can quickly lead to overly complex workflows that are hard to understand, reuse, reconfigure, maintain, and schedule." They present a similar approach to our proposal. They have designed a set of templates to represent control structures as actors in the Kepler WfMS [14]. Our approach differs from [5] and [6] in the sense that they present control structures for one specific WfMS, while we are focusing on general control-flow structures to simplify sub-workflow remote execution. In addition to reuse, we aim at gathering remote process provenance with the help of these control structures.

Tudruj, Kopanski and Borkowski [7] also state the importance of general dynamic control flow, but focus on synchronization of parallel execution. Similarly to our proposal they have presented a set of generic control structures and proposed the use of a monitoring middleware. However, we do not want to interfere on the execution of tasks on a remote distributed environment. So, our focus is more on remote-distributed provenance gathering rather than synchronization control.

2.2 Provenance Gathering in Heterogeneous WfMS

WfMS have been designed as distributed or centralized execution control. While distributed WfMS, like Pegasus [8], P-GRADE [9] and Triana [10], focus on high performance and resource scheduling, rather than provenance gathering, centralized control based WfMS (e.g. Taverna, [11], VisTrails [12] [13], Kepler [14]) are focused on semantic issues in workflow design and provenance gathering. However, centralized WfMS are characterized by having a single workflow execution engine, enacting the whole execution of a given scientific workflow. For instance, VisTrails provides visualization facilities and provenance of the whole exploration process, capturing the evolution of a workflow. Despite these facilities, VisTrails, in its current public version, lacks support in connecting to distributed environments and does not allow inner activities loops. Kepler has some predefined control-flow modules that can be plugged in the workflow specification. However, if a sub-workflow needs to be executed under a different WfMS, these Kepler's actors will no longer apply.

If you need to change from one environment to another, from local execution to a grid, you may send tasks of a sub-workflow to be remotely executed one by one. In this way, you can keep the local WfMS in charge of the execution control, but this can deteriorate performance severely. Another option is to recode the sub-workflow with the grid WfMS language, then this sub-workflow will execute under the grid WfMS and take advantage of the remote grid resources without coming back and forth to the local WfMS. Alternatively, if you send general control modules along the sub-workflow, you may send this augmented sub-workflow to run remotely and still be able to register provenance remotely and bring it back locally. Otherwise, if you rely on the provenance system of the remote WFMS, you will need to do conversions from one provenance model to another, and you may miss some provenance gathering not supported by the remote system and so on.

In this scenario, a typical scientific workflow may want to have its provenance recorded by a centralized WfMS, as well as to take advantage of high performance environments, such as the ones provided by grid WfMS. We aim at showing that having control independent from the WfMS gives flexibility to help in moving from one WfMS to another in a distributed environment, e.g. local and grid. These additional modules can further be used to record provenance remotely using the same representation model as the local WfMS, or OPM for example.

Having control modules explicitly defined can help on other workflow semantic issues. When control-flow specifications are based on patterns (standards), reusing parts of a workflow becomes easier. If control modules have a formal basis, several verifications can be done. For example, does the workflow terminate? Does it conform to some correction rules? This can lead to a meta-workflow definition. It can be seen as a step towards a canonical model or a layer to where all workflow languages and provenance models can be mapped to and from.

3 Scientific Workflow Control Flows

In this section, we present our approach to provide scientific workflows with generic control-flow modules for the coordination of the traditional data flow operations. These structures enable the execution of distributed applications with scheduling dependencies more advanced than the simple data availability criteria, and where the data passing between activities need to be restricted due to processing errors, or data volume, or costs associated with transfers. Aalst et al. [15] [16] have identified many patterns that provide a systematic examination of the various perspectives that need to be supported by workflow languages. In short, the control-flow perspective captures aspects related to control-flow dependencies between various activities of a workflow. The data perspective deals with the information flow and variables scope, among others. The resource perspective deals with resource to activity allocation and delegation. Finally, the patterns for the exception handling perspective deal with many causes of exceptions and the consequent actions needed to overcome them.

This work is centered on the control-flow perspective, because control patterns define which activities of a given workflow should become enabled after the completion of other activities and in what order they will be executed by the scientific WfMS. It is also important to highlight that the control patterns are not concerned with how an enabled activity will be executed and whether it works as it is supposed to do. The control flow pattern considers each activity as a black box and the only observable behavior which the pattern is concerned about is when the activity becomes enabled and when it finishes executing.

WfMS like Taverna [17], Kepler [14] and VisTrails [12] [13] present a heterogeneous and limited set of control-flow elements, making it difficult to design a scientific workflow which often requires iterations, decision, conditions and registering of processes' data. One of the possible ways to bypass those shortcomings requires reprogramming the WfMS. However, modifying existing WfMS may be time consuming and error prone. Another way is to reuse generic control-flow modules, such as the ones we propose in this work. Table 1 shows these modules, the number of input/output ports and the corresponding workflow pattern as defined by Aalst et al. [16].

Table 1. Control flow modules x workflow patterns

Module	Number of input/output ports	Workflow pattern
Mux	1 (selector) + user defined / 1	Structured Discriminator
Demux	2 / user defined	Exclusive Choice
String Control	2 / 2	Deferred Choice
NumberControl	1 / 5	Multiple Instances Without synchronization
NumberCompare	2 / 1	Synchronization
If	4 / 1	Exclusive Choice

The proposed workflow controls are extensible components that allow the workflow to be redefined at run-time, offering it the ability to adapt automatically to changes without compromising the logic of the scientific experiment and its safety. These control modules can be embedded in a graphical workflow design interface, enabling workflow programming with run-time modifiable functionality and dynamic interactions between activities. Thus, the workflow tasks can move from one workflow engine to another without having to recode the workflow specification to match heterogeneous workflow specification languages. In addition, when control moves, provenance gathering can move along and be aware of the remote execution flow. This flexibility comes with some limitations, for example, the workflow execution scheduler is not aware of control flow and may provide poor optimization. However, when specific workflow coding prevents provenance gathering, trading performance might be an option. In the next section, we present the control flow modules and compare them with workflow patterns.

3.1 Control Flow Modules in VisTrails

In this work, we used the VisTrails WfMS [12] [13] to implement the proposed control-flow modules by adding dynamic behavior without harnessing the provenance gathering process of the WfMS. In VisTrails, the workflow tasks are known as modules and are coded in Python. VisTrails presents some implementation requisites, such as: (i) each module is defined as a class, which describes a given structure; (ii) modules are connected through input/output ports; (iii) input values come through input ports, and results are given in output ports; and (iv) all the connection and relationship between the modules must be defined and formalized inside the class. Modules in VisTrails, as in other WfMS, like Kepler [14], require a data type. Developers need to know the type of the data that are passing through them, despite the programming language used in their code. Thus, each port must have a defined type (e.g. string, float, integer, file or boolean). Modules with similar goals can be grouped as packages in order to simplify deploy and development, making their organization clearer.

3.1.1 Multiplexer and Demultiplexer

The Multiplexer module, or simply Mux, is important for decision making activities. Its functionality lies on the choice of a data piece, between a series, to continue in the execution flow. Mux module offers the possibility of choosing an input port; such feature is not directly available in VisTrails or in other WfMS. The pattern that best represents the Mux module is the "Structured Discriminator" [15]. This pattern describes a convergence between two or more input ports, resulting in just one branch. The activation of the output port depends on an input port, what happens in the Mux module. However, in the module, there is a condition (the selector) to choose the input port; while in the pattern, the first incoming branch to be enabled is the one to activate the outgoing branch; it does not depend on a condition. Besides, in the pattern, there must be a "Parallel Split" pattern before, which not necessarily happens with the module. In VisTrails, the Mux module implementation has two user-defined characteristics: the number of input ports and the data type required. Both of them increase the flexibility of the activity.

The Demultiplexer module, or Demux, does the opposite of Mux. It selects the path that a piece of data will take. In other words, it makes the decision of what subsequent part of the workflow will get a piece of data and process it. It is important to notice that the same feature presented by the Mux module (the selection of desired ports) is also created by the Demux module. This module would be an example of the "Exclusive Choice" pattern [15]. This pattern represents an incoming branch that diverges into two or more parts. Just one of the outgoing branches is enabled depending on a condition associated. This condition, in the Demux module, would be the selector, which chooses the output port.

The Demux module, in VisTrails, has only one input port for the incoming data, and another for the selector. Its implementation was done in the same way as for the Mux module; the difference between them is that, instead of choosing the number of input ports, in Demux the user chooses the quantity of output ports.

There is one problematic situation associated to this pattern which is related to the structure response when the condition does not match any of the output ports. In VisTrails, the Demux module displays a warning message when a condition is reached, and all the execution stops. Besides, there is no way more than one outgoing branch to be enabled, once the selector is an integer, and each integer corresponds to only one branch.

3.1.2 String and Number Controls

In some cases, the workflow needs to generate control signals produced through comparison of strings or numbers. A control signal behaves as a flag for the execution of other activities. For that reason, such controls are particularly important and may be considered as control structures. The flags are usually used for decision making; so, they can be used in scientific workflows for the same purpose. The StringControl module represents the "Deferred Choice" pattern [15]. In this pattern, an activity in the workflow is divided in two or more branches, and just one of them can be enabled; the other outgoing branches are withdrawn. StringControl module acts like such pattern, only one of the output ports can be enabled. However, there is just one difference between the StringControl module and the pattern, in the latter, the faster outgoing branch to make an activity is the one which will be enabled; in the module, it depends on the number of input ports connected.

In VisTrails, StringControl has two input ports to receive strings. The StringControl execution depends on the number of strings connected. If there is just one, the module will return the length of it by an output port (an integer value). However, if two strings are connected, the module will do a comparison between them returning "1" for greater, "2" for smaller and "0" for equal strings.

For number signals, two new modules were created. The first one, NumberControl, generates flags that indicate whether the number is zero, negative, positive, odd or even. These signals can be essential if a given workflow activity depends on the number type. The second one, NumberCompare, on the other hand, compares two numbers, signaling which one is greater or smaller, or if both are equal. These signals are similar to the ones generated by StringControl module.

The NumberControl module is correlated with a variant of the "Multiple Instances without Synchronization" pattern [15], where all output data are originated simultaneously. The NumberCompare module, in the other hand, represents the "Synchronization" pattern [15]. In this pattern, two or more incoming branches become just one outgoing branch, which will be only enabled after the complete activation of all the input data. In other words, there must be a synchronization between the incoming branches. This is what happens with the "NumberCompare" module, once the comparison between the numbers can only be done with both of them enabled in the module.

3.1.3 If

The use of conditionals are particularly important when scientists need to orchestrate data flows, specifying which will be the next data flow to run based on the control decision, such as: knowing if an expression is true, choosing data between two input ports, or for stopping a whole workflow execution. The pattern that represents the If module is the "Exclusive Choice" pattern [15], the same pattern of the Demux module. The two essential differences between the Demux module and the If module are: in the former, the scientist can connect as many input ports as they need, different from the latter, which has just two input ports; in the Demux, there is an integer selector to choose between many input ports, and in the If module the selector is a logical expression, where the scientists can create any condition they need.

Its implementation in VisTrails has four input ports: two of them are the data that will be chosen, which can be of any type supported by VisTrails. Another port is used to write the condition associated to the module: if the condition is true, the first data is passed through the output port; if false, the second one is chosen. The last input port, which is optional, is an extra code that the users can write before the condition; maybe, for the desired condition, they need to import some libraries, make some logical and arithmetic expressions, read from a file, and so on; for this kind of programming, they can use this input port. The only output port is the chosen data.

There is another use for the If module. The second input port is optional; if the user chose to put that port, the functionality of the module will be the one stated before. However, if there is no second input port, the module will put the first input port in the output port if the condition is true; if false, the module will raise an error, stopping the workflow execution.

3.1.4 Inner Loops

It is important for a given workflow to have a sequence of commands to be executed repeatedly. It means that the workflow will execute an activity several times in a cyclic execution. This type of sequence is called inner loop, and it is useful for some loop cases. The loops inside a module could be done using a programming language. However, the loop encompassing several modules cannot be done so easily for some WfMS, particularly DAG-based. For instance, VisTrails does not allow recursion in the workflow. But it offers a mechanism named parameter exploration, which allows a scientist to make repetitive executions of a given scientific workflow, using different parameters for the input ports. The loop originated through the parameter exploration represents the "Multiple Instances with a priori Run-Time Knowledge" pattern [15]. In this pattern, series of multiple instances of an activity are created, and the number of instances is known before the process starts. This is precisely what happens with the loop in VisTrails. The instances run concurrently and they are created sequentially.

In this way, a kind of loop is created, since all activities of the workflow are re-initialized several times. However, there are two crucial differences between this kind of loop and the real one. The first one is that the workflow, in the parameter explora-tion, is finalized before it returns to the beginning, what does not occur in the loop itself. The second one is related to the call of the loop; in some cases, the loop must be called inside the workflow, and not outside of it, as it is with the VisTrails feature.

In order to offer simple but effective inner loop specification, it is possible to use a composition of control flow modules to execute an inner loop in VisTrails. For in-stance, a scientific workflow may need to process five different files, each one in a separated execution. One feasible way to make an inner loop with control modules rely on the use of the Mux module and the Register, a module that writes the data in a pre-defined file. At first, the scientist has to define the number of input ports of the Mux and its data types. After that, the files can be easily connected to the Mux ports, and its output port can be connected to the Register module. The parameter explora-tion is used, in this case, to generate a series of workflow executions by changing the Mux selector and for each execution, the file processed in the subsequent part of the workflow is replaced by other file connected to the Mux through a user-defined linear interpolation of the selector, for example (Figure 1). So, the workflow will be exe-cuted for each value inside the interpolation.

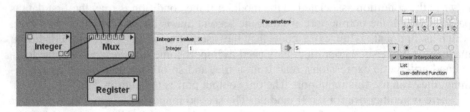

Fig. 1. VisTrails screenshot with control flow modules. On the left side, a part of the workflow is presented (the Integer module represents the selector); On the right side, using VisTrails' parameter exploration, a linear interpolation with the selector values is shown, and it generates an inner loop.

4   Execution Control on VisTrails

Due to modularity and flexibility of VisTrails open source WfMS, our execution control modules were easily added to VisTrails. In Figure 2 we highlight the execu-tion control modules incorporated in VisTrails through its interface. Preliminary tests showed the design power of including execution control previously not available in VisTrails. A bioinformatics workflow that requires execution control modules can now take advantage of VisTrails process provenance and its visual resources. In order to combine the control-flow modules, presented in Section 3, with remote parallel execution control, a parallel bioinformatics workflow was evaluated (Figure 2).

In a previous work [18], we designed a similar, but simpler, bioinformatics work-flow using Kepler WfMS. This bioinformatics workflow needs execution control such as If and NumberControl as well as remote parallel execution of Blast. The lack of remote parallel execution control in most WfMS motivated the development of our monitoring middleware named MidMon [18].

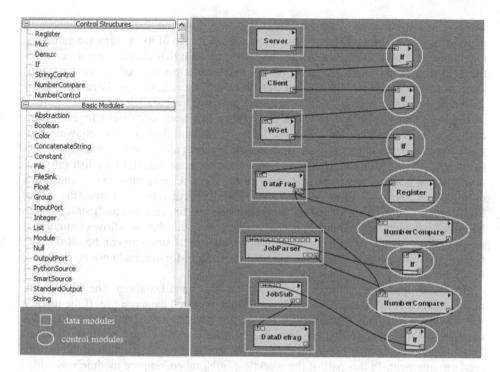

Fig. 2. Execution control modules on VisTrails. The highlighted processes in the left side (squares) are data intensive modules, from the MidMon middleware; the ones in the right side (ellipses) are control modules, from the "Control Structures" package.

MidMon is a lightweight middleware that presents a small number of structures to monitor the distributed execution of scientific workflow tasks. It was implemented with monitoring instrumentation middleware requirements in mind [19], providing a loosely coupled form of interaction with the WfMS. MidMon was designed as a multi-layer software, (*scientists desktop* and *distributed environment* layers) aiming to provide ease of use for scientific workflow developers, such as: being easily connected to a WfMS and monitor parallel applications; causing a negligible overhead on processing nodes and finally, taking advantage of remote machine job scheduling properties.

At the scientist desktop layer, the Server Monitor component allows scientists to monitor the status of distributed applications jobs. It receives unidirectional asynchronous monitoring messages submitted by Client Monitors on the distributed environment layer. The components of the distributed environment layer provide the ability for an execution thread to be diverged into several concurrent threads on a selective basis. Decoupling of monitors can allow greater scalability, lower message overheads and may be used on different network topologies.

In this work we redesigned the bioinformatics workflow using our control modules and MidMon modules to be executed using the extended VisTrails WfMS. The native VisTrails modules and our control-flow modules were coded in Python 2.5 and the MidMon Monitors in Java, so that new modules could be added to the workflow without major concerns. Unfortunately, VisTrails have no facilities to connect to distributed environments. Thus, in order to take advantage of its provenance gathering mechanisms it was also necessary to develop a module that enables remote connections to distributed environments. For the sake of simplicity, remote call modules were not represented in Figure 2. In our prototype, the BLAST package was represented as a one-step activity of the workflow and MidMon parallelized it.

Figure 2 shows MidMon modules inserted on the workflow design together with execution control modules in VisTrails. In short, the workflow runs as following. Initially, the Server Monitor is locally initiated. It receives asynchronous messages from the remote Client Monitor. Then, the Client Monitor is activated, to publish information's about remote processes and monitoring them. Considering the connection´s establishment between them, if the server finds difficulty to be started, the Client Monitor cannot be activated, and the workflow must be finished. So, an If structure can be added between both modules; if everything goes well, the workflow continues; if not, it will be ended. After the Client Monitor, another If structure can be introduced, because if a connection error was found, and the Client Monitor could not be activated, for example, the service cannot keep on.

The same approach can be done between the WGet and DataFrag. The WGet module connects through the Internet to download the required database file. If the module successfully downloads it, the service can go on; nevertheless, if an error condition is reached (e.g. the downloaded file is corrupted), the workflow must be finished. DataFrag module divides the file in little fragments that will run in parallel on the distributed environment. In this part of the workflow, a NumberCompare module was added in order to compare the number of fragments created with the user-defined number of fragments. After this, an If structure was introduced; it will check if both quantities of fragments were the same. The DataFrag module also produces log information that can be visualized inside VisTrails, through the Spreadsheet window. In order to store this information and make it accessible and usable later, we added a Register module (used in the section 3.1.4) after the DataFrag. In this workflow, the flexibility of the control structures can be confirmed, once it was not necessary to change the structure of the DataFrag module to control the fragments.

The JobParser module generates, for each fragment, a parallel job that will be submitted to the distributed environment by the JobSub module. Between the JobParser and the JobSub modules, another NumberCompare and If modules can be added; the former compares the number of fragments created by DataFrag with the number of jobs produced; the If enables the WfMS to monitor remote errors, more specifically, one job, for some reason, was not produced; so, it can finish the execution if some jobs were not created.

5 Conclusion

Workflow technology and distributed environments provide the keystone to leverage the continuing evolution of e-Science. In order to fully explore opportunities provided by these paradigms, it is important to track and monitor experiments to gain new insight about the scientific experiment. In this paper, it was presented a set of generic control-flow modules that can extend workflow design power by providing dynamic behavioral features. Control-flow modules allow scientists to use some of the workflow patterns described by Aalst [15] [16] by adding these modules on the scientific workflow specification to be executed by heterogeneous WfMS running on distributed environments.

The proposed control-flow modules can be plugged into the workflow during design-time, helping scientists to face challenges of distributed workflow development. First, it acts as documentation of the execution control workflow behavior, recording in a concise and explicit fashion the operational characteristics of the workflow. Second, by adding control-flow facilities to a distributed monitoring middleware it is possible not only to evaluate and monitor the activities of the workflow but also gather provenance from heterogeneous and independent environments with low programming efforts.

Our work shares the same generic motivation of Groth, Munroe, Miles and Moreau [20] that is supporting provenance in any type of execution environment. Groth *et al.* developed the "p-structure" in a way that provenance is created by actors within the workflow, independent from the workflow definition language and from the workflow execution engine. In a similar way, our proposed control-flow structures can be seen as control-flow actors within the workflow. These actors are independent from workflow engines. This is helpful when a local workflow needs to run a sub-workflow in a high performance environment, i.e., control specification does not need to change. Our work may be seen as complementary to the "p-structure" in a sense that these control structures can embed "p-structures" to record workflow decisions and iterations, in addition to its capturing of the actual causal connections according to execution.

Developing MidMon on top of VisTrails presented some additional advantages: it enabled scientists to monitor the submitted jobs status on their desktops and as by-products it preserves workflows' original features. It also allowed scientists to use a local centralized WfMS to connect and enact distributed activities, preserving the built-in facilities of provenance gathering. In addition, MidMon also complemented VisTrails tracking facilities, once VisTrails was not able to capture information about temporary and remote files created during distributed workflow execution.

By plugging these modules along the workflow specification we address the two challenges discussed at the motivation of this work. Using the control modules, design becomes less dependent of the WfMS specification language. Remote monitoring modules provide for parallel execution control in heterogeneous environments. Finally, these modules are the means of provenance gathering within a representation model that can be independent of the environment and the WfMS. The limitation of this approach is a verbose workflow specification due to several control processes that are not part of the scientific application domain. However, workflow view techniques [21] can hide these modules from the scientist. We are working on software component reuse techniques to help the automatic incorporation of these modules. Particularly in VisTrails, a "by example" tool for workflow design generation is under development. We intend to adapt it to recommend control modules that can help on workflow design, control and provenance gathering. Currently, other bioinformatics workflows are being analyzed to take advantage of MidMon combined to the proposed control-flow modules within VisTrails.

Acknowledgments

This work was partially funded by CNPq. Chirigati and Dahis are supported by CNPq and the UFRJ/PIBIC program.

References

1. Freire, J., Koop, D., Santos, E., Silva, C.T.: Provenance for Computational Tasks: A Survey. In: Computing in Science and Engineering, pp. 20–30 (May/June 2008)
2. Gil, Y., Deelman, E., Ellisman, M., Fahringer, T., Fox, G., Gannon, D., Goble, C., Livny, M., Moreau, L., Myers, J.: Examining the challenges of scientific workflows. IEEE Computer 40(12), 26–34 (2007)
3. Yu, J., Buyya, R.: A taxonomy of scientific workflow systems for grid computing. ACM SIGMOD 34, 44–49 (2005)
4. Moreau, L., Freire, J., Futrelle, J., McGrath, R., Myers, J., Paulson, P.: The Open Provenance Model, Technical Report 14979, ECS EPrints repository (2007)
5. Bowers, S., Ludascher, B., Ngu, A.H.H., Critchlow, T.: Enabling Scientific Workflow Reuse through Structured Composition of Dataflow and Control-Flow. In: ICDE Workshops, pp. 70–80 (2006)
6. Goderis, A., Brooks, C., Altintas, I., Lee, E.A., Goble, C.: Composing Different Models of Computation in Kepler and Ptolemy II. In: Proc. of the 2nd Int. Workshop on Workflow Systems in e-Science (WSES 2007) in conjunction with the Int. Conference on Computational Science (ICCS) 2007, Beijing, China, pp. 27–30 (2007)
7. Tudruj, M., Kopanski, D., Borkowski, J.: Dynamic Workflow Control with Global States Monitoring. In: ISPDC 2007, Hagenberg, Austria, July 5-8 (2007)
8. Deelman, E., et al.: Pegasus: Mapping Scientific Workflows onto the Grid. In: AGC 2004, Cyprus (2004)
9. Kacksuc, P., Farkas, Z., Sipos, G., et al.: Workflow-level parameters study management in multi-Grid environments by P-GRADE Grid portal. In: GC 2006 Workshop at SC (2006)
10. Churches, D., et al.: Programming Scientific and Distributed Workflow with Triana Services. Concurrency: Practice and Experience 18(10), 1021–1037 (2006)
11. Hull, D., Wolstencroft, K., Stevens, R., Goble, C., et al.: Taverna: a tool for building and running workflows of services. Nucleic Acids Research 34 (Web Server issue), 729–732 (2006)
12. Callahan, S., Freire, J., Santos, E., Scheidegger, C., Silva, C., Vo, H.: VisTrails: visualization meets data management. In: ACM SIGMOD, pp. 745–747 (2006)
13. Scheidegeer, C., Koop, D., Santos, E., Vo, H., Callahan, S., Freire, J., Silva, C.: Tackling the Provenance Challenge One Layer at a Time. Concurrency and Computation: Practice and Experience 20(5), 473–483 (2007)
14. Ludäscher, B., et al.: Scientific workflow management and the Kepler system. Concurrency and Computation: Practice and Experience 18(10), 1039–1065 (2006)
15. Russell, N., Hofstede, A., ter, A.W.M.P., van der Mulyar, N.: Workflow Control-Flow Patterns: A Revised View. Technical Report BPM-06-22, BPM Center (2006)
16. Aalst, W.M.P., van der Hosftede, A.H.M., ter Kiepuszewski, B., Barros, A.P.: Workflow Patterns. Distributed and Parallel Databases 14(1), 5–51 (2003)
17. Goble, C., Wroe, C., Stevens, R.: The myGrid project: services, architecture and demonstrator. In: UK e-Science All Hands Meeting (2003)

18. Cruz, S.M.S., Silva, F.N., Gadelha Jr., L., Cavalcanti, M., Campos, M., Mattoso, M.: A Lightweight Middleware Monitor for Distributed Scientific Workflows. In: 3rd WSES/CCGrid (2008)
19. Truong, H., Fahringer, T., Dustdar, S.: Dynamic Instrumentation, Performance Monitoring and Analysis of Grid Scientific Workflows. Journal of Grid Computing 3, 1–18 (2005)
20. Groth, P., Munroe, S., Miles, S., Moreau, L.: HPC and Grids in Action. In: Grandinetti, L. (ed.) Applying the Provenance Data Model to a Bioinformatics Case. IOS Press, Amsterdam (2008)
21. Davidson, S., Cohen-Boulakia, S., Eyal, A., Ludaescher, B., McPhillips, T., Bowers, S., Anand, M., Freire, J.: Provenance in Scientific Workflow Systems. IEEE Data Eng. Bull. 30(4), 44–50 (2007)

ES3: A Demonstration of Transparent Provenance for Scientific Computation*

James Frew and Peter Slaughter

Donald Bren School of Environmental Science and Management
University of California, Santa Barbara, CA 93106-5131, USA
{frew,peter}@bren.ucsb.edu
http://eil.bren.ucsb.edu

Abstract. The Earth System Science Server (ES3) is a software environment for data-intensive Earth science, with unique capabilities for automatically and transparently capturing and managing the provenance of arbitrary computations. Transparent acquisition avoids the scientist having to express their computations in specific languages or schemas for provenance to be available. ES3 models provenance as relationships between processes and their input and output files. These relationships are captured by monitoring read and write accesses at various levels in the science software and asynchronously converting them to time-ordered streams of provenance events which are stored in an XML database. An ES3 provenance query returns an XML serialization of a provenance graph, forward or backwards from a specified process or file. We demonstrate ES3 provenance by generating complex data products from Earth satellite imagery.

Keywords: ES3; provenance; instrumentation; passive; transparency.

1 Introduction

The Earth System Science Server (ES3) is a software environment for data-intensive Earth science. ES3 has unique capabilities for automatically and transparently capturing, managing, and reconstructing the provenance of arbitrary, unmodified computational sequences [1]. *Automatic* acquisition is critical to avoid the inaccuracies and incompleteness of human-specified provenance (i.e., annotation.) *Transparent* acquisition avoids the computational scientist having to learn, and be constrained by, a specific language or schema in which their problem must be expressed or structured for provenance to be available.

Unlike most other provenance management systems, ES3 captures provenance from running processes, as opposed to extracting it from static specifications such as scripts or workflows. ES3 provenance management can thus be added to any existing scientific computations, without modifying or re-specifying them.

---

* This work was supported by National Aeronautics and Space Administration cooperative agreements NNG04GC52A and NNG04GE66G.

J. Freire, D. Koop, and L. Moreau (Eds.): IPAW 2008, LNCS 5272, pp. 200–207, 2008.

2   Model and Methodology

ES3 models provenance in terms of processes and their input and output files. We use "process" in the classic sense of a specific execution of a program. In other words, each execution of a program or workflow, or access to a file, yields a new set of provenance events.

Relationships between files and processes are deduced by monitoring read and write accesses. This monitoring can take place at the levels of system calls (using strace), library calls (using instrumented versions of application libraries), and arbitrary checkpoints within source code (using automatically invoked source-to-source preprocessors for specific environments such as IDL [2].) Any combination of monitoring levels may be active simultaneously, and all are transparent to the scientist-programmer using the system.

ES3 provenance is the directed graph of files and processes resulting from a specific invocation event (e.g., a "job".) Nested processes (processes that spawn other processes) are correctly represented. In addition to retrieving the entire provenance of a job, ES3 supports arbitrary forward (descendant) and/or reverse (ancestor) provenance retrieval, starting at any specified file or process.

3   Implementation

ES3 is implemented as a provenance-gathering client and a provenance-managing server (Figure 1.) The client runs in the same environment as the processes whose provenance is being tracked.

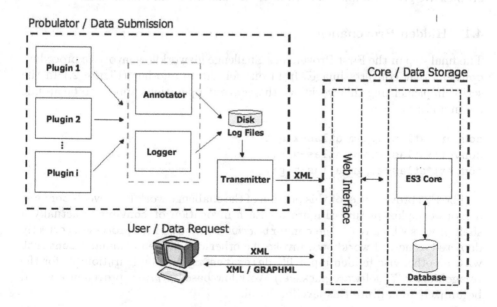

Fig. 1. ES3 architecture

The client is a set of *logger* processes that intercept raw messages from the various monitoring modes (*plugins*) and write them to log files. A separate *annotator* client optionally examines the files and directories being accessed by the instrumented processes and retrieves certain kinds of non-provenance metadata (e.g., README files and source code comments.) A common *transmitter* client asynchronously scans the log files, assembles the provenance events into a time-ordered stream, assigns UUIDs to each file and process being tracked, and submits a raw provenance report to the *ES3 core* (server.)

The ES3 core is an XML database with a web service middleware layer that supports insertion of file and provenance metadata, and retrieval of provenance graphs. File metadata allows ES3 to track the one-to-many correspondence between external file identifiers (e.g., pathnames) and internal (UUID) references to those files in provenance reports. Provenance queries cause the ES3 core to assemble a provenance graph (by linking UUIDs) starting at a specified process or file and proceeding in either the ancestor or descendant direction. The graphs are returned serialized in various XML formats (ES3 native, GraphML [3], etc.), and can be rendered visually by tools such as Graphviz [4] and yEd [5].

4   Applications

ES3 is particularly useful for elucidating "hidden" provenance—dependencies between files and processes that aren't explicitly stated in the workflows or scripts that invoke the processes—and for managing highly nested provenance graphs. We give examples of each of these capabilities in this section.

4.1   Hidden Provenance

The final step in the First Provenance Challenge [6] workflow invokes a procedure convert that converts images from one format to another (Figure 2.) In the script implementing this workflow, the convert operations appear to be atomic commands:

```
convert atlas-x.pgm atlas-x.gif
convert atlas-y.pgm atlas-y.gif
convert atlas-z.pgm atlas-z.gif
```

The ES3 provenance for this portion of the challenge workflow reveals convert a more complex picture (Figure 3.) Each invocation of convert is actually a shell process which reads the convert *script* as input. These processes, correctly depicted as nested workflows, invoke the otherwise hidden command convertb with an otherwise hidden input file delegates.mgk (a configuration file for the ImageMagick [7] software package.) Workflow-based *a priori* provenance would be unlikely to capture this level of detail.

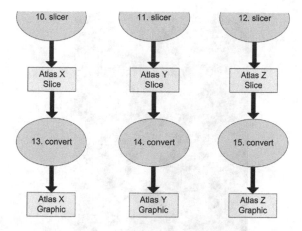

Fig. 2. convert operation in challenge workflow

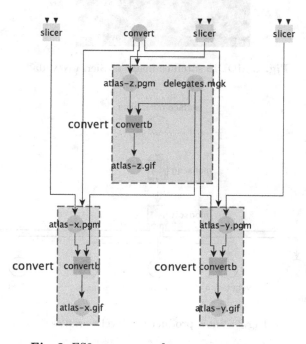

Fig. 3. ES3 provenance for convert operation

4.2   Nested Provenance

We use ES3 to track the provenance of a snow-covered-area data product, derived from satellite imagery of portions of the Sierra Nevada (California) mountain range (Figure 4.) The snow product involves processing steps implemented in IDL, C, and UNIX shell scripts, and the algorithms are under active development.

Fig. 4. MODIS satellite image of Sierra Nevada

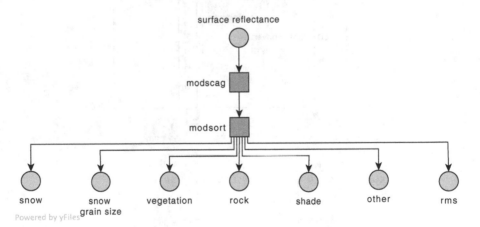

Fig. 5. Snow product top level workflow

Figure 5 shows an idealized top-level workflow for the product. A satellite image of surface reflectance (albedo) is processed by `modscag` into multiple estimates of the surface composition of each pixel. `modsort` select the best of these estimates for each pixel and creates a suite of output grids whose cell values are the percentage of snow (Figure 6) and other components present at the corresponding surface location, as well as estimates of snow grain size, classification error, and whether the input pixel was too deeply shaded by surrounding terrain to be usable.

Fig. 6. Fractional snow-covered area, Sierra Nevada

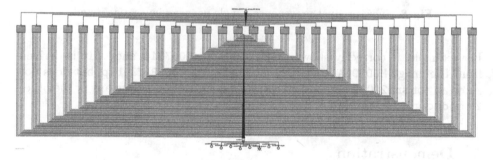

Fig. 7. Snow product provenance (`modscag` nesting expanded)

Requesting forward provenance for an actual satellite image (Figure 7) reveals that the `modscag` workflow step actually comprises 30 separate invocations of the `modscag` program (each of which uses different starting assumptions about surface composition), which `modsort` merges into a single set output files.

The ES3 request that yielded Figure 7 included a restriction to avoid expanding nested workflows. Relaxing this restriction for an entire `modscag` workflow would yield a provenance graph too complex for a printed page. Instead, Figure 8 shows the combined forward and reverse provenance for a single one of the 30 `modscag` program invocations. (Imagine variations on Figure 8 replacing all 30 processes in Figure 7 to get an idea of the complexity of a complete `modscag` "run.")

Note that since Figure 8 is a portion of a much larger provenance graph, it provides sufficient information for some provenance assertions but not others.

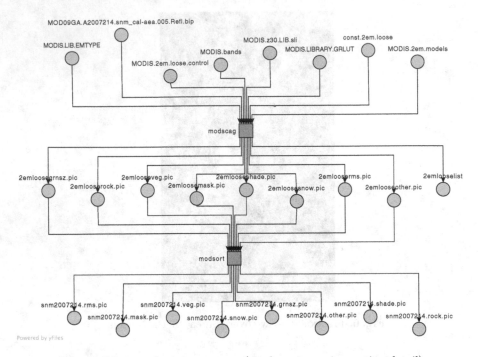

Fig. 8. Snow product provenance (single `modscag` invocation detail)

For example, it correctly shows that the file `snm2007214.snow.pic` is derived from the image `MOD09GA.A2007214.snm_cal-aea.005.Refl.bip`, but does not show any of `snm2007214.snow.pic`'s possible antecedents from any of the other 29 `modscag` invocations.

5   Demonstration

The ES3 client currently includes plugins for the `bash` shell and the IDL interpreted programming language. The ES3 server comprises Java servlets running in Tomcat. The ES3 demo runs on a standalone Linux host (optionally accessing a remote ES3 server) and includes sample shell scripts and IDL programs taken from production science applications. Demo users can run and modify the scripts (including adding and deleting applications), issue arbitrary provenance requests, and graphically explore the resulting provenance graphs and their attached metadata.

Acknowledgments. We thank Michael Colee for assembling and maintaining our computing environment, Greg Janée for advice and encouragement, Dominic Metzger for his work on the probulator, Thomas Painter for supplying the `modscag` test case, and Kathy Scheidemen for administrative support.

References

1. Frew, J., Metzger, D., Slaughter, P.: Automatic capture and reconstruction of computational provenance. Concurrency and Computation: Practice and Experience 20(5), 485–496 (2008)
2. The IDL Computing Environment for Data Visualization & Analysis from ITT, http://www.ittvis.com/idl
3. Brandes, U., Eiglsperger, M., Herman, I., Himsolt, M., Marshall, M.S.: GraphML Progress Report–Structural Layer Proposal. In: Mutzel, P., Jünger, M., Leipert, S. (eds.) GD 2001. LNCS, vol. 2265, p. 501. Springer, Heidelberg (2002)
4. Gansner, E.R., North, S.C.: An open graph visualization system and its applications to software engineering. Software—Practice and Experience 30(11), 1203–1233 (2000)
5. yEd - Java Graph Editor, http://www.yworks.com/products/yed
6. Moreau, L., Ludäscher, B., Altintas, I., Barga, R.S., Bowers, S., Callahan, S., Chin, G., Clifford, B., Cohen, S., Cohen-Boulakia, S., Davidson, S., Deelman, E., Digiampietri, L., Foster, I., Freire, J., Frew, J., Futrelle, J., Gibson, T., Gil, Y., Goble, C., Golbeck, J., Groth, P., Holland, D.A., Jiang, S., Kim, J., Koop, D., Krenek, A., McPhillips, T., Mehta, G., Miles, S., Metzger, D., Munroe, S., Myers, J., Plalc, B., Podhorszki, N., Ratnakar, V., Santos, E., Scheidegger, C., Schuchardt, K., Seltzer, M., Simmhan, Y.L., Silva, C., Slaughter, P., Stephan, E., Stevens, R., Turi, D., Vo, H., Wilde, M., Zhao, J., Zhao, Y.: Special Issue: The First Provenance Challenge. Concurrency and Computation: Practice and Experience 20(5), 409–418 (2008)
7. ImageMagick: Convert, Edit, and Compose Images, http://www.imagemagick.org

Neuroimaging Data Provenance Using the LONI Pipeline Workflow Environment

Allan J. MacKenzie-Graham, Arash Payan, Ivo D. Dinov,
John D. Van Horn, and Arthur W. Toga*

Laboratory of Neuro Imaging (LONI), Department of Neurology,
University of California Los Angeles School of Medicine,
635 Charles E. Young Drive South, Suite 225, Los Angeles, CA 90095-7334
{amg,apayan,ivo.dinov,jvanhorn,toga}@loni.ucla.edu

Abstract. Provenance, the description of the history of a set of data, has become important in the neurosciences with the proliferation of research consortia-related neuroimaging efforts. Knowledge about the origin, preprocessing, analysis and post hoc processing of neuroimaging volumes is essential for establishing data and results quality, the reproducibility of findings, and their scientific interpretation. Neuroimaging provenance also includes the specifics of the software routines, algorithmic parameters, and operating system settings that were employed in the analysis protocol. The LONI Pipeline (http://pipeline.loni.ucla.edu) is a Java-based workflow environment for the construction and execution of data processing streams. We have developed a provenance framework for describing the current and retrospective data state integrated with the LONI Pipeline workflow environment. Collection of provenance information under this framework alleviates much of the burden of documentation from the user while still providing a rich description of an images characteristics, as well as the description of the programs that interacted with that data. This combination of ease of use and highly descriptive meta-data will greatly facilitate the collection of provenance information from brain imaging workflows, encourage subsequent data and meta-data sharing, enhance peer-reviewed publication, and support multi-center collaboration.

Keywords: Provenance, Workflow, Neuroimaging, Grid, Pipeline.

1 Introduction

One of the fundamental challenges in neuroimaging, and in fact all biological sciences, involves devising ways to manage the enormous amounts of data currently being gathered. This challenge is compounded not only by the proliferation of collaborative efforts and the necessity of sharing data across multiple sites, but also of making that data openly available and useful to the scientific community

---

* Corresponding Author.

J. Freire, D. Koop, and L. Moreau (Eds.): IPAW 2008, LNCS 5272, pp. 208–220, 2008.
© Springer-Verlag Berlin Heidelberg 2008

at large. The scientific community has recognized the need for solutions that facilitate the process of tool and data exchange and numerous efforts are underway to achieve this goal [1]. Yet to be truly meaningful, the data obtained and the analytic tools employed must be adequately described and documented. The meta-data detailing the origin and subsequent processing of biological images is referred to as "provenance" [2].

Recently, leading computer scientists have recognized the unique issues associated with neuroimaging datasets that often exceed several tens of gigabytes in a full set of raw data. Simon Miles, Luc Moreau, Mike Wilde, Ian Foster, and others proposed a provenance challenge to determine the state of available provenance systems [3]. The challenge consisted of collecting provenance information from a simple neuroimaging workflow [4] and documenting each systems ability to respond to a set of predefined queries. Some of these existing provenance systems have previously been proposed as mechanisms for capturing provenance in neuroimaging, though they have not been widely adopted [5]. The main difficulty appears to be the need of a system to capture provenance information accurately, completely, but with minimal user intervention. Minimizing an individuals burden for providing the details on provenance, as well as facilitating a comprehensive data and process tracking system, will dramatically improve compliance, thereby freeing the user to focus on performing neuroimaging research rather than exhaustively documenting provenance.

In the biological sciences, a description of how data was obtained is crucial for assessing its quality and usefulness, as well as enabling analysis in an appropriate context. It is therefore imperative that the provenance of biological images be easily captured and readily accessible. In multiple sclerosis research, for example, increasingly complex analysis workflows are being developed to extract information from large cross-sectional or longitudinal studies [6]. This is also true of Alzheimers disease [7-9], autism [10], depression [11], schizophrenia [12], and even studies of normal populations [13]. The implementation of the increasingly complex processing workflows associated with these investigations requires the institution of quality-control practices to ensure the precision, reproducibility, and reusability of the results. In effect, provenance.

In a broad sense, provenance can be divided into two subtypes: data provenance and processing provenance. Data provenance is the metadata that describes the subject being imaged, how an image of that subject was collected, who acquired the image, what instrument was used, what settings or parameters were used, and how the sample was prepared. However, most scientific image data is not obtained directly from such measurements, but rather derived from other data by the application of computational processes. Processing provenance is the metadata that defines what processing an image has undergone; for example, how the image was skull-stripped, what form of image inhomogeneity correction was employed, how the volume was spatially aligned to a standard atlas space, etc. Even data that is presented as raw often has been subjected to reconstruction software or converted from the scanners native image format (k-space) to a more commonly used and easily shared file format [14]. A complete data provenance model would capture all this information, making the history of a complete set of data transparent, thus enabling seamless sharing across the neuroimaging community.

Certain neuroimaging data provenance may be gathered at the site where the data is collected, in the headers of image files or in databases that record image acquisition [15, 16]. A highly abbreviated form of this kind of provenance is often reported in method descriptions or even in the image files themselves [17]. However, this data is seldom propagated along with the images themselves, since it is commonly removed or ignored in the course of file conversion not being critical for further data processing.

Processing provenance can be obtained concerning any resource in the data processing system and may include multiple levels of detail. Two major models for collecting processing provenance have been described: a process-oriented model [18] and a data-oriented model [2]. The process-oriented model collects lineage information from the deriving processes and provenance is inferred from that processing and through an inspection of the input and output data. This mechanism is well suited for situations where individual data products are tracked within comprehensive frameworks and where the deriving processes can easily be reapplied to the original data to reproduce the data product. In the data-oriented model, lineage information is explicitly gathered about the set of data. This method may be better suited for situations where data sharing occurs across heterogeneous environments and intermediate data products may not be available for reproduction. This would be the case, for example, when neuroimaging data sets are shared between two or more collaborating laboratories.

The analysis of raw data in neuroimaging has become a computationally rich process with many intricate steps run on increasingly larger datasets [6]. Many commonly available software packages exist that provide either complete analyses or specific steps in neuroimaging data analysis. These packages often have diverse input and output requirements, utilize different file formats, run under particular computer environments, and may have limited abilities for certain types of data. The combination of these packages to achieve more sensitive and accurate results has become a widespread strategy in brain mapping studies, though requires much work to ensure valid interoperability between programs.

Simplicity of use cannot be overstated when developing software tools for the scientific community at large. Many outstanding software tools are not adopted due to difficult learning curves or because their use places too great a burden on the end user. One of the main requirements of a successful provenance system would be the simplicity and unobtrusiveness.

The LONI Pipeline was developed to facilitate ease of workflow construction, validation, and execution [19] freeing the user to focus on image analysis. In this article we describe a simple yet comprehensive provenance system that has been incorporated into the LONI Pipeline Processing Environment, placing little or no burden on the end user for documentation of processing provenance.

2   The LONI Pipeline Workflow Environment

The LONI Pipeline (http://pipeline.loni.ucla.edu) is a simple, efficient, and distributed computing environment, enabling software inclusion from different laboratories in different environments. It provides a visual programming interface for the design, execution, and dissemination of neuroimaging analyses. Individual executables are represented as modules that can be included, deleted, and substituted for other modules within a user-friendly graphical user interface. Connections between the modules that establish an analysis methodology are represented as workflows. The environment handles bookkeeping, controls the details of the computation, and information transfer between modules and within the workflow. It permits files, intermediate results, and other information to be accurately passed between individually connected modules. The DRMAA API (www.drmaa.net), backed by the Sun Grid Engine (http://gridengine.sunsource. net), acts as an interface to grid environments. Modules and workflows can be saved to disk at any stage of development and recalled at a later time for modification, use, or distribution.

2.1   Goals of the LONI Pipeline Environment

The overarching goals of the LONI Pipeline are to:

1. Graphical User Interface. Create a robust environment for scientific software tool interoperability, Grid integration and low-cost interactive user interface. For maximum portability, scalability and efficiency, this environment is built in Java and utilizes XML for storing and communication of meta-data, and descriptors for tools and services.

2. New Tool Discovery. Enable expert researchers to quickly design, test and validate novel experimental designs and to rapidly examine new data analysis protocols. This is achieved via dynamic, responsive and extensible graphical user interface.

3. Compatibility. Provide the necessary means for integration of LONI Pipeline XML workflow descriptions with other established graphical environments for scientific Grid computing. This functionality facilitates the translation of existent analysis paradigms from other environments to the LONI Pipeline and vice-versa.

The LONI Pipeline differs from many similar workflow environments. For instance, the LONI Pipeline does not require the use of an application programming interface (API) it considers all resources as well-described external applications that may be invoked with standard remote execution protocols. The LONI Pipeline XML description protocol allows any command-line driven process, web-service or data-server to be encapsulated into the environment by reference. There is no need to reprogram, revise or recompile external resources to make them usable within the LONI Pipeline. This is a deliberate design we have imposed to reduce the integration/utilization costs of including new resources within the LONI Pipeline environment. This approach provides the benefit of quick and easy management of large and disparately located resources and data. In addition, this choice significantly minimizes the hardware requirements for user-client machine (e.g., memory, storage, CPU). Finally, while the LONI Pipeline is primarily used in the context of neuroimaging, we wish to stress the important point that the Pipeline is agnostic to any particular scientific domain and can be used to manage workflows under any other scientific domain.

3   LONI Pipeline Provenance Architecture

To begin the discussion of how the LONI Pipeline manages provenance, we have defined some terms in order to prevent any ambiguity when software is discussed. To facilitate the current discussion we define the following terms; a binary is a pre-compiled program that is ready to run under a given operating system, a script is a simple program written in a utility language that is interpreted at runtime, and an executable is either a binary or script.

3.1   Data Provenance

As mentioned above, an important aspect of provenance is the description of the subject. Subject provenance includes birth and death dates (for post-mortem studies), in addition to the age of the subject at the time of the data collection (or death). Sex and species are captured, further qualified by strain and genetic manipulation in the case of non-human subjects. Treatments, such as disease induction in experimental models, drug treatment, and combinations of treatments can be documented in the schema. Subject name has explicitly been excluded in order to protect patient privacy (http://www.hhs.gov/ocr), SubjectID standing in as a unique identifier for a given subject. These elements are extensible, allowing for multiple treatments or clinical evaluations. Subject provenance has been described in a simple, yet flexible format in order to make it easily accessible to the community with a minimum of work to adapt it for specialized use. The description of how a set of data was acquired is of critical importance for data provenance. Different information is required from the user based on the kind of data acquired. For example, when collecting acquisition provenance about an MRI image, information about the acquisition type (2D vs. 3D), weighting (proton density, T1, T2, etc.), pulse sequence, flip angle, echo time (TE), repetition time (TR), inversion time (TI), matrix dimensions, step sizes, magnet field strength, coil used, equipment manufacturer and model are explicitly captured in the XSD. These elements are far from exhaustive, but are easily expanded and/or extended to accommodate other imaging modalities from diffusion tensor imaging (DTI) to positron emission tomography (PET). An XML schema document (XSD) describing the neuroimaging data provenance presented here is available to the public for use and discussion (http://provenance.loni.ucla.edu).

Table 1. Workflow Provenance. Outline describing the major elements of workflow provenance contained in a LONI Pipeline workflow file.

Example of a Computer Program

```
Workflow provenance
        Pipeline workflow
                Executable provenance
                        Environment
                        Options
                        Input files
                        Output files
                        Binary provenance
                                Binary configuration
                                        Configuration options
                                System configuration
                                        Architecture
                                        Operating system
                                        Compiler
                                        Libraries
                Script provenance
                        Shell
                        Script
                        Binary provenance
```

3.2   Processing Provenance

In our model, binary provenance describes how a piece of software was compiled. It comprises two parts, a description of the environment and a description of the binary itself. The environment description includes the operating system, environment variables, compiler used, and libraries installed. The binary description includes configuration flags and/or modifications made to configuration files or makefiles. Our goal is to provide the user with the ability to reproduce the binary exactly (Table 1).

A fundamental difference between executables is the hardware platform on which they were compiled. Differences in floating-point implementation across different architectures can have a profound impact on outcome of a calculation and have been widely publicized in the popular media [20]. The LONI Pipeline executable provenance description captures not only architecture, but also the specific processor and the flags that are enabled on it.

Capturing important details about the operating system is complicated, particularly for Linux and open-source Unix distributions, since each distribution contains many individually updated components. Essential information must be captured such as the operating system name, version, distribution, kernel name, and kernel version. For example, an application running on Ubuntu Dapper Drake (http://www.ubuntu.com) must have the following operating system metadata: Linux, 6.06, Ubuntu Desktop, #1 PREEMPT, 2.6.15-27-386; whereas an application built on the current Mac OS X Leopard platform must have the following operating system metadata: Mac OS, 10.5.2, n/a, Darwin, 9.2.0.

The compiler used and libraries linked during compilation are a crucial aspect of the environment. In addition to compiler name and version, a list of which updates have been applied is also captured. This section of the provenance metadata also records which flags were used when the compiler was invoked, architecture and optimization flags being of special interest. Libraries used for compilation are described similarly to the binary itself and are recursive.

Binaries also can be configured prior to compilation. Some packages are distributed in a format for use with the GNU build system or Autotools [21]. Modification of the configure script or the makefile can yield substantially different results after compilation. The LONI Pipeline executable provenance description captures flags to the configure script, modifications to configure scripts and makefiles.

Executable provenance need only be collected once, when a binary is compiled or when a script is written. This data is then included in the LONI Pipeline module description of the executable and thus is propagated with both the module and any workflows created with those modules.

Processing provenance describes the actual invocation of an individual executable or the invocation of an executable in the context of a series of steps or workflow. Recording the command-line that was used to invoke it captures arguments to the executable. The processing environment is described similarly to the environment for compilation, but also includes environmental variables that may modify the behavior of the executable.

Often image processing is complex and non-linear and cannot be represented in a simple script or directed acyclic graph. Data may converge along several lines of processing only to diverge again after a common step. These complex workflows are difficult to document, either for publication or later re-use. Capturing the provenance for these workflows is equally complex, not only requiring the execution order of the individual steps, but how those steps are related to one another, especially in the case of multiple lines of data being processed simultaneously. In order to address this issue we have used the LONI Pipeline Processing Environment (http://pipeline.loni.ucla.edu) [19] to capture not only executable provenance and description, but also the relationships between the executables.

Using the LONI Pipeline as an example of workflow software, we have designed the provenance framework to take advantage of context information that can only be kept while using workflow software. Specifically, the use of conditionals between executables, and loops can all be represented in a higher workflow language and associated with a series of executable events in the provenance. More generally, we want to be able to track how data is derived with sufficient precision that one can create or recreate it from this knowledge.

Continuing discussion and development of the LONI Pipeline Provenance Architecture can be found at http://provenance.loni.ucla.edu.

4   Provenance Validation

In order to document the utility of this model of provenance documentation, we performed a test to demonstrate the capacity to independently recreate a workflow and its output data using only the provenance documentation.

A workflow was created in the LONI Pipeline from binaries compiled on the LONI 306-node dual processor Opteron Sun V20z grid by the LONI system administrator and modules in the pipeline library constructed by the LONI Pipeline developers. Data and processing provenance was captured and recorded in a provenance file using only the mechanism described above.

A second workflow was constructed from scratch with modules defined by the authors for a second set of executables compiled for the LONI grid, also compiled by the authors. These executables were compiled using only the provenance information captured by the mechanism described above as a guide for compilation.

The workflows used for the test were simple neuroimaging workflows (Figure 1) with both sets of executables compiled using the same options. The workflows were then run on the LONI grid using the same input data. We compared the aligned images resulting from each workflow by subtracting them from one another and verified that the difference was 0 at every voxel (data not shown).

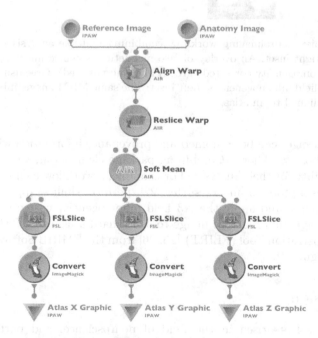

Fig. 1. A simple neuroimaging workflow derived from The First Provenance Challenge [3] in the LONI Pipeline Processing Environment

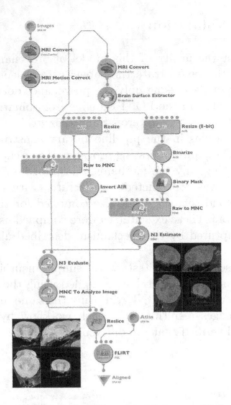

Fig. 2. A complex neuroimaging workflow combining multiple analysis and processing packages. Right inset: An overlay of two magnetic resonance microscopy (MRM) images, one inhomogeneity corrected (green) and one not (red). Greenish and orange areas represent field inhomogeneities. Left inset: The same MRM image, inhomogeneity corrected and aligned to an atlas.

Multiple packages can be combined and provenance information will be propagated with those workflows. Combining package elements allows the user the greatest flexibility for their analyses. For example, a workflow could correct motion artifact using tools from Freesurfer [22], perform skull stripping using the BSE [23], calculate and apply the N3 field inhomogeneity correction [24], and then align a magnetic resonance image to a standard atlas using FMRIB's Linear Image Registration Tool (FLIRT) [25, 26] from the FMRIB Software Library (FSL) [27] (Figure 2).

5   Discussion

Recent interest has arisen in the field of neuroscience, and particularly in neuroimaging, in identifying or creating standards to facilitate software tool interoperability. The NIMH Neuroimaging Informatics Technology Initiative (NIfTI; http://nifti.nimh.nih.gov) was formed to aid in the development and enhancement of informatics tools for neuroimaging. Though best known for the Data Format Working Group (DFWG) that has defined the NIfTI image file format standard, this effort has recently turned its attentions to how provenance metadata might be standardized. The Biomedical Informatics Research Network (BIRN; http://nbirn.net) is another high profile effort working to develop standards among its consortia membership, including the development of study data provenance.

Descriptions of data provenance have been used successfully in other fields of endeavor. For example, the Dublin Core Metadata Initiative (DCMI) is an organization dedicated to promoting the widespread adoption of interoperable metadata standards and developing specialized metadata vocabularies for describing resources that enable more intelligent information discovery systems (http://dublincore.org). This also includes meta-data related to workflow provenance.

The Collaboratory for Multi-scale Chemical Science (CMCS) project is an informatics toolkit for collaboration and data management for multi-scale chemistry [28]. CMCS collects pedigree information about individual data objects by defining input and output data and capturing pedigree chains describing the processing that the data has undergone (http://cmcs.org). The provenance data is explicitly defined in associations, placing the burden of documentation upon the user.

The Virtual Data System (VDS; formerly known as Chimera and incorporating Pegasus) [5] provides middleware for the GriPhyN project (www.griphyn. org), expressing, executing, and tracking the results of workflows. Provenance is used for the regeneration, comparison, and auditing of data derivations. Users construct workflows using a standard virtual data language (VDL) describing transformations (executable programs) that are executed by a VDL interpreter producing a derivation (the execution of a transformation). Data objects are entities that are consumed or produced by a derivation. In the VDS model, provenance is inferred from the processing by inverting the processing to associate the output data with the input data. This approach places very little burden on the user to document data provenance.

The myGrid project [29] provides middleware in support of computational experiments in the biological sciences, modeled as workflows in a grid environment. Users construct workflows written in XScufl language using the Taverna engine. The LogBook is a plug-in for Taverna engine that allows users to log their experiments in a mySQL database and browse, rerun, and maintain previously run workflows (http://www.mygrid.org.uk/wiki/Mygrid/LogBook). This provenance log contains the executables invoked, the parameters used, data used and derived, and is automatically produced when the workflow executes. This process-oriented provenance log is also inverted to infer the provenance for the intermediate and final set of data.

Within the neuroimaging community, the XCEDE (XML-based Clinical Experiment Data Exchange) schema [30] also provides for the storage of data provenance information. Provenance information manually captured includes hardware, compilation and libraries linked, operating system and software versions, and parameters used to generate and document results. XCEDE is a data-oriented system where the provenance metadata is associated with the actual data files.

The VisTrails scientific workflow management system [31] is an excellent example of an integrated workflow and provenance collection mechanism. The VisTrails workflow system focuses on capturing provenance in exploratory workflows and saving changes that occur over time. Processes and workflows are represented as python objects prior to execution and details of the execution are stored in a relational database automatically.

Efforts such as these examples have sought to capture data and workflow information sufficient to reproduce reported study findings and that enable cross-study comparison. Specific workflow description frameworks also exist in other fields that help to sequence data processing steps and that can be used to populate provenance descriptions. These frameworks are highly sophisticated tools that require substantial investment to learn and deploy. They do not provide a simple mechanism for the capture of provenance metadata from multiple packages, the capacity to represent complex, non-sequential analyses, nor at a sufficient level of detail to allow the reproduction of a derived set of data on a new platform. Hence the need for the development of a provenance framework that can easily be applied to complex neuroimaging analyses.

Future directions include the enrollment of LONI Pipeline workflows in a database, creating a processing and provenance database. Having a readily searchable database of commonly used (and rarely used) workflows would greatly aid investigators in recreating the conditions of a particular analysis, reproducing previous results and rerunning analyses with small modifications.

The concept of provenance can extend to knowledge of the behavior of executables, such as describing their function. The Brain Surface Extractor (BSE) [23], the Brain Extraction Tool (BET) [32], and MRI Watershed [22] are all brain extraction algorithms, however, their internal functions may not be evident to a naive user, especially since they are commonly referred to by their abbreviations. These tools can capture the expertise of algorithm developers, as well as the experience of experts at local institutions who have spent significant periods of time learning how best to apply specific tools to the analysis needs of the laboratory. The tools will inform the users of missing processing stages, suggest available and verified processing modules, and warn of incompatible data types.

6   Conclusions

We have used a combination of an executable provenance XSD incorporated into LONI Pipeline modules to capture processing provenance and description. One of the major strengths of this system is the capacity to easily recreate the processing applied to a file by viewing its provenance file, extracting the workflow, and then rerunning it in the LONI Pipeline. The LONI Pipeline can accommodate almost any form of workflow, the underlying architecture is application agnostic, not limiting the kind of science that can be examined within it. LONI Pipeline workflows can therefore serve to document workflow provenance in almost any field of endeavor.

In an era where digital information underlies much of the scientific enterprise and the manipulation of that data has become increasingly complex, the recording of data and methods provenance takes on greater importance. In this article, we describe an XML-based neuroimaging provenance description that can be implemented in any workflow environment. We envision the LONI Pipeline as fulfilling a role for neuroimaging similar to other frameworks in chemistry or high-energy physics. We believe that data and workflow provenance form a major element of the program that promotes data processing methods description, data sharing, and study replication.

Acknowledgments

This work was generously supported by a research grants from the National Institutes of Health through the NIH Roadmap for Medical Research (U54 RR021813), the National Center for Research Resources (U24 RR021760 [Mouse BIRN] and P41 RR013642), and the National Institute of Mental Health (R01 MH071940). The authors wish to acknowledge their deep appreciation to the members of the Laboratory of Neuro Imaging (LONI).

References

1. Murphy, S.N., et al.: A Web Portal that Enables Collaborative Use of Advanced Medical Image Processing and Informatics Tools through the Biomedical Informatics Research Network (BIRN). In: AMIA Annu. Symp. Proc., pp. 579–583 (2006)
2. Simmhan, Y.L., Plale, B., Gannon, D.: A survey of data provenance in e-science. Sigmod Record 34(3), 31–36 (2005)
3. Moreau, L., et al.: Special Issue: The First Provenance Challenge. Concurrency and Computation: Practice & Experience (2007)
4. Zhao, Y., et al.: A notation and system for expressing and executing cleanly typed workflows on messy scientific data. Sigmod Record 34(3), 37–43 (2005)
5. Zhao, Y., Wilde, M., Foster, I.: Applying the virtual data provenance model. In: Moreau, L., Foster, I. (eds.) IPAW 2006. LNCS, vol. 4145, pp. 148–161. Springer, Heidelberg (2006)
6. Liu, L., et al.: Multiple sclerosis medical image analysis and information management. J. Neuroimaging 15(4 suppl.), 103S–117S (2005)
7. Fleisher, A.S., et al.: Identification of Alzheimer disease risk by functional magnetic resonance imaging. Arch. Neurol. 62(12), 1881–1888 (2005)
8. Mueller, S.G., et al.: Ways toward an early diagnosis in Alzheimer's disease: The Alzheimer's Disease Neuroimaging Initiative (ADNI). Alzheimers Dement 1(1), 55–66 (2005)
9. Rusinek, H., et al.: Regional brain atrophy rate predicts future cognitive decline: 6-year longitudinal MR imaging study of normal aging. Radiology 229(3), 691–696 (2003)

10. Langen, M., et al.: Caudate nucleus is enlarged in high-functioning medication-naive subjects with autism. Biol. Psychiatry 62(3), 262–266 (2007)
11. Drevets, W.C.: Neuroimaging studies of mood disorders. Biol. Psychiatry 48(8), 813–829 (2000)
12. Narr, K.L., et al.: Asymmetries of cortical shape: Effects of handedness, sex and schizophrenia. Neuroimage 34(3), 939–948 (2007)
13. Mazziotta, J.C., et al.: A probabilistic atlas of the human brain: theory and rationale for its development. The International Consortium for Brain Mapping (ICBM). Neuroimage 2(2), 89–101 (1995)
14. Van Horn, J.D., et al.: Sharing neuroimaging studies of human cognition. Nat. Neurosci. 7(5), 473–481 (2004)
15. Erberich, S.G., et al.: Globus MEDICUS - Federation of DICOM Medical Imaging Devices into Healthcare Grids. Stud. Health Technol. Inform. 126, 269–278 (2007)
16. Martone, M.E., et al.: The cell-centered database: a database for multiscale structural and protein localization data from light and electron microscopy. Neuroinformatics 1(4), 379–395 (2003)
17. Bidgood Jr., W.D., et al.: Understanding and using DICOM, the data interchange standard for biomedical imaging. J. Am. Med. Inform. Assoc. 4(3), 199–212 (1997)
18. Zhao, J., et al.: Semantically linking and browsing provenance logs for e-science. In: Bouzeghoub, M., Goble, C.A., Kashyap, V., Spaccapietra, S. (eds.) ICSNW 2004. LNCS, vol. 3226, pp. 158–176. Springer, Heidelberg (2004)
19. Rex, D.E., Ma, J.Q., Toga, A.W.: The LONI Pipeline Processing Environment. Neuroimage 19(3), 1033–1048 (2003)
20. Halfhill, T.R.: The Truth Behind the Pentium Bug. Byte (1995)
21. Vaughan, G.V.: GNU Autoconf, Automake, and Libtool, 1st edn., p. 390. New Riders, Indianapolis (2000)
22. Dale, A.M., Fischl, B., Sereno, M.I.: Cortical surface-based analysis. I. Segmentation and surface reconstruction. Neuroimage 9(2), 179–194 (1999)
23. Shattuck, D.W., Leahy, R.M.: BrainSuite: an automated cortical surface identification tool. Med. Image Anal. 6(2), 129–142 (2002)
24. Sled, J.G., Zijdenbos, A.P., Evans, A.C.: A nonparametric method for automatic correction of intensity nonuniformity in MRI data. IEEE Trans. Med. Imaging 17(1), 87–97 (1998)
25. Jenkinson, M., et al.: Improved optimization for the robust and accurate linear registration and motion correction of brain images. Neuroimage 17(2), 825–841 (2002)
26. Jenkinson, M., Smith, S.: A global optimisation method for robust affine registration of brain images. Med. Image Anal. 5(2), 143–156 (2001)
27. Smith, S.M., et al.: Advances in functional and structural MR image analysis and implementation as FSL. Neuroimage 23 (suppl.1), S208–219 (2004)
28. Myers, J.D., et al.: A collaborative informatics infrastructure for multi-scale science. Cluster Computing-the Journal of Networks Software Tools and Applications 8(4), 243–253 (2005)
29. Oinn, T., et al.: Taverna: a tool for the composition and enactment of bioinformatics workflows. Bioinformatics 20(17), 3045–3054 (2004)
30. Keator, D.B., et al.: A general XML schema and SPM toolbox for storage of neuroimaging results and anatomical labels. Neuroinformatics 4(2), 199–212 (2006)
31. Freire, J., et al.: Provenance for computational tasks: A survey. Computing in Science & Engineering 10(3), 11–21 (2008)
32. Smith, S.M.: Fast robust automated brain extraction. Hum. Brain Mapp. 17(3), 143–155 (2002)

Provenance Tracking in an Earth Science Data Processing System

Curt Tilmes[1] and Albert J. Fleig[2]

[1] NASA Goddard Space Flight Center, Greenbelt, MD 20771, USA
Curt.Tilmes@nasa.gov
[2] PITA Analytic Sciences, 8705 Burning Tree Rd., Bethesda, MD 20817, USA
Albert.J.Fleig@nasa.gov

Abstract. NASA and other organizations involved with climate research have captured huge archives of earth observations. The sensors, spacecraft, and science algorithms for transforming and analyzing the data and the processing frameworks are evolving over time. Science Data Processing Systems (SDPSes) should capture, archive, and distribute provenance information of all externally received data and algorithms, as well as describing all internal processes used for data transformation. This will make the data sets produced by the systems easier to understand, enable independent scientific reproducability, and ultimately, increase the credibility of the scientific research that makes use of those data sets.

1 Introduction

Earth science data have been captured from remote sensing satellites for several decades now, and numerous national data centers hold vast quantities of such data. In addition to the initial raw data received directly from sensors, the data include calibration processes and geolocation determination. The data are used with a variety of scientific retrieval algorithms to produce derived geophysical products, and they undergo transformations to reformat, regrid, subset, etc. the data to massage it into forms useful for scientists to perform research. Over time, the systems that perform this long series of data transformations from observation through product generation evolve. New technologies are developed, later generations of spacecraft, sensors, and data processing frameworks have different characteristics. The science algorithms for transforming and analyzing the data also improve over time with our growing understanding of earth science and the overall climate.

Tracking the provenance of earth science data throughout this process is a difficult problem. Research that makes use of multiple data sets from multiple data sources housed in multiple archives distributed among multiple organizations or agencies with different standards and policies simply exacerbates the problem. Science data is being used in new ways not planned by the originators of a given data set. We now find value added services (such as SOAR[1]) are building new archives that have transformed data from other sources, and re-distributed the

J. Freire, D. Koop, and L. Moreau (Eds.): IPAW 2008, LNCS 5272, pp. 221–228, 2008.

data in a new form. Some of these systems even provide the capability to automatically retrieve data from a data archive on-demand and perform dynamic alterations, distributing requested data to an end user without retaining a copy of the data. Maintaining complete provenance information through a processing chain that includes ephemeral data from such a "virtual archive" can be even more complicated.

This paper will discuss some of the general concerns of science data processing, and provenance in the context of two specific science data processing systems in operation at NASA's Goddard Space Flight Center: the MODIS Adaptive Data Processing System (MODAPS) [3] and the OMI Data Processing System (OMIDAPS) [2]. MODIS, the Moderate Resolution Imaging Spectroradiometer, is an instrument on the NASA Terra spacecraft launched in 1999, and on the Aqua spacecraft launched in 2002. OMI, the Ozone Monitoring Instrument, is a Dutch instrument launched on the NASA Aura spacecraft in 2004. These systems will provide examples and serve as case studies.

2   Science Data Processing

2.1   Data Archiving

There are two parts of every data file in the data processing system, the actual **data** ("bunch of bits") and the **metadata** with information that describes or relates to the data.

The data files are assigned a unique identifier and stored in an archive system where they can be retrieved by that identifier. We refer to the smallest "chunk" of individually identified data as a *granule* of data. A granule could refer to a year, a month or a day of data.

For both MODIS and OMI, the level 0, or raw, data are provided to the processing systems in 2 hour granules. MODIS data is quite voluminous, so the Level 1/2 data are stored in 5 minute granules. These are canonicalized on even 5 minute boundaries, e.g. 00:00:00 - 00:05:00, 00:05:00 - 00:10:00, etc. MODIS Level 3 data are organized somewhat differently for each of three climate categories, Land, Oceans and Atmospheres. The MODIS Land Discipline organizes its data with a integerized sinusoidal projection on a latitude longitude grid. [4] There are 326 land tiles, identified by their horizontal and vertical tile coordinates. The Level 3 gridded data are stored on various temporal resolutions as well, typically including daily, 8 day, 16 day and 32 days of data.

OMI's purpose is to monitor atmospheric constituents (Ozone of course, but also several others), which it retrieves from measures of backscattered solar radiation. It also has a lower resolution and lower data rate than MODIS. For these and historical reasons, the data are organized into contiguous data on an orbit by orbit basis.

Each different type of data is assigned an "Earth Science Data Type" (ESDT) that identifies a set of data files. For example, OML1B for OMI Level 1B, or OMTO3 for OMI Total Ozone. The ESDT encodes multiple pieces of metadata, including the instrument, the level, the spacecraft (in the case of MODIS which has two instances currently flying), and the type of data.

2.2 Primary and Secondary Metadata

Depending on the data level, and the metadata associated with a particular granule, a unique identifier is constructed from a minimal set of metadata. For example, there is one OMI Level 1B granule for each orbit of data. For orbit number 123, the particular granule could be described with the tuple {OML1B, 123}. The Level 1B data from MODIS on Terra captured between 10:50 and 10:55 on Feb. 17, 2008 could be described with the tuple {MODL1B, 2008-02-17, 1050}. A MODIS level 3 land tile at tile coordinates (12, 17) of type MODVI (vegetation index) from data captured on Jan. 13, 2008 could be described with the tuple {MODVI, 2008-01-13, (12,17)}.

This *primary metadata* is a minimal set of metadata that can be used to find a particular granule of interest by searching an indexed database, resulting in a pointer to the data file of interest.

Secondary metadata is a much larger set. It can include any other information useful to the user of the data. This can include a large variety of information:

- Geographic information that can be used to limit a spatial search,
- Quality information ("Data is bad for some reason," "Granule is cloud obscured"),
- Instrument configuration information ("Instrument in spectral zoom mode," "Spacecraft maneuver in progress"),
- Extra information about the data files themselves: file size, checksum for data integrity verification
- Provenance information (Where did I get this file? How did it come to exist?).

Secondary metadata can also include data annotations added after processing, or by another organization. For example, after the data are processed, the science data quality can be assessed by independent QA group and the granules annotated with that assessment.

2.3 Reprocessing

Both MODAPS and OMIDAPS are operational systems that currently receive data from active satellites and run the various science algorithms continuously on newly acquired data. Science keeps marching forward however, and new research and analysis of the data yield new versions of the algorithms. The change could resolve a bug that introduces an artifact into the data, or simply improve the quality of the data. It can be complicated to assess the effect of the change on the data. Sometimes the algorithm is run in parallel on a significant quantity of data that are then compared to the older version. If the new version is substituted into the operational system, a discontinuity in trends can occur, affecting research that might depend on such a trend. Sometimes it is better to keep producing a dataset consistent with known problems than to produce an inconsistent data set.

For example, consider monitoring a long term trend. If a particular measurement is sufficiently *precise*, even in the absence of perfect *accuracy*, the trend may still be useful. If in the middle of such a dataset the accuracy suddenly improves, introducing a jump in the trend, the dataset may be less useful for monitoring the long term trend. The approach that MODAPS and OMIDAPS typically take is to periodically go back to the beginning of the mission and reprocess all the data with the best known set of algorithms, thus producing an improved and consistent data set. We refer to these periodic large scale reprocessing campaigns as a *collection*. MODAPS is currently completing production of collection 5.

All the science algorithms are carefully configuration controlled and versioned throughout the processing system. The metadata for every product always includes the version number of the algorithm that produced it within the system.

3   Provenance

Provenance refers to the source of information and the historical process that led to its existence. Provenance information is critical to end users trying to understand where a particular data file came from. To this end, the system records all aspects of the data production flow. This includes:

- The source of all externally supplied data files. This could include a reference to the specific file in another archive responsible for the stewardship [5] of that data file.
- The source of the algorithms used to transform the data within the system. "Source" here refers to the origin of the algorithm, but also important in understanding an algorithm is its source code. Where possible and legal, we store the source code in a controlled configuration management (CM) repository that tracks changes across multiple versions of the same algorithm. When used properly, the CM system can also store comments, bug report numbers, references to other papers, and other information that can help a researcher understand the reasons behind changes. possible and legal.
- Algorithm Design Documents. While the source code is the most up to date form of an algorithm, it is seldom the best way to understand the scientific functioning of the algorithm. Where possible, we also store or reference any design information which describe the mathematical basis and physical science behind the algorithms in the form of formulas, text, diagrams, tables, and graphs. These can also reference peer-reviewed science journal articles or other information about the algorithm. Our goal is to store or reference anything that can help someone understand the algorithm better.
- A complete description of the processing environment. This includes things as basic as what particular computer ran the program and what hardware resources it had. It could easily be the case in the future that the exact same hardware might be found only in a museum, but listing the particular hardware could be useful to someone trying to analyze the data. More important than the hardware is the software in the environment. This includes the operating system and software library versions.

- A complete description of the processing framework. Just as we CM the science algorithms, every module that is part of the processing system is stored in a CM repository.
- A record of each job's execution. This is a list of all of the outputs of the production rule execution process, including runtime parameters (things like "Orbit Number," "Data Date," "Debug Mode," "Algorithm Control Flags") and a list of all input files. We also store extra information about the execution including the clock time it started and finished, CPU and disk resource utilization, etc. These can help in the analysis of data processing performance and optimization.

It is expected that other archives and suppliers of all artifacts (data, algorithms, documents, etc.) will capture, archive, and distribute their own provenance information in a well-defined manner. Ideally, this should provide a complete distributed provenance graph even back to information describing the spacecraft and instrument that captured the original observations. This provenance helps to put scientific results derived from the data into context and allows future researchers to understand the entire data flow. Currently, questions like "Was the ozone input to the weather model derived from back-scattered ultra-violet or microwave radiation measurements?" require a human to read natural language data descriptions, visit various web sites, and/or call up scientists personally to manually determine the provenance of the dataset.

3.1   Scientific Reproducibility

While provenance information is nice to have for a researcher trying to understand a data set and algorithm, especially for climate research using remote sensing data, it is critical for scientific reproducibility. Many systems recognize this ideal and strive to store sufficient information that a dedicated (sometimes very dedicated) researcher who is able to expend sufficient effort could theoretically construct a system capable of reproducing the data. Other systems can reproduce the latest version of the data, but do not support obtaining older data.

Our goal is to make it not just possible, but *easy* to reproduce any data file that gets distributed from our system. To that end, we archive all versions of fully integrated algorithms. As a next step, we plan to distribute a processing framework that can access the integrated algorithms directly and interact with our system to download the information needed to replicate the environment and re-run the algorithms. Additionally, since the integrated algorithms are available and encapsulated provenance information is available, so that remote users can use their local execution framework to reproduce any of our files within their own systems. This provides complete scientific reproducibility and allows an independent verification and validation of all data provided by our main system. Providing this capability can increase the *credibility* of the science results that use the data.

3.2   Process on Demand and Virtual Archives

As algorithms improve and are inevitably changed over time, older data sets become obsolete and the expense of storing all data physically on disk outweighs their historical value. Typical archives keep previous versions of data around long enough to analyze its differences with current data, then remove it in favor of the new data. Those archives also store the metadata (including provenance information) colocated with the data, and deletion of the data often causes deletion of metadata and provenance information as well.

Our system also removes old data files, but, as described above, we retain sufficient provenance information to reproduce deleted data sets if needed. This functions as an extreme form of compression where the provenance information suffices to re-create a file. The provenance is a proxy for the physical contents of the file.

The next logical step, already implemented on MODAPS, is *Process on Demand*. Some MODIS products are very large, and less widely used (Level 1B), while others are much smaller and more widely used (Level 2 and above). The Level 1B products are created in normal processing and used as inputs to Level 2. After keeping them around for 30-60 days for the most interested users to retrieve, they are removed from the archive. Since the system retains the ability to re-create them as needed, users can order the older files from the archive whereupon the files are scheduled for reprocessing. Depending on the level of requests, the system can use a small amount of processing capability as a stand-in for a very large amount of disk.

Since archive space has historically been a very limiting factor, science teams make very considered, deliberate and often limiting choices when deciding which official data products to produce and archive. *Process on Demand* allows a "virtual" archive of many more products thereby relaxing some of the self-imposed limitations. This approach has led to the development of "services" that can transform data dynamically to very specific forms requested by users [1]. It is important that such services don't overlook the intensive verification and validation functions performed by the science teams, and that complete provenance information is captured, even for dynamically created, ephemeral data products served from a virtual archive.

3.3   Provenance Problems

As noted above, systems often store provenance information in the metadata along with the data files, and when the data are removed, so is the metadata. Someone later researching a science paper with results citing a specific data set may find that not only are the data no longer available, but also there is no information about how that data set was produced.

When data files used in production come from external providers, our provenance information can refer to that source, but it must also refer to the specific file so that it can be retrieved from that provider. If upstream providers don't archive or distribute sufficient provenance information for significant inputs, they can become a "dead end" in the graph.

The example above described a (very simplified) scenario where science leads to an algorithm, which is coded into software, which is used to process data. Sadly, this ideal seldom matches reality. We often find software evolving in new directions that simply aren't retroactively captured in design documents and published papers. Keeping the entire provenance chain up to date requires dedication and discipline.

Sometimes provenance information is captured, but the information is restricted. Hardware and software designs provide a competitive advantage, so some organizations are reluctant to release proprietary information in the processing chain. In particular, due to past problems with distribution of satellite and rocket technology the U.S. International Traffic in Arms Regulations (ITAR) is particularly restrictive of certain types of information. Even where the information isn't particularly sensitive, the default ITAR position is to restrict data, and sometimes it is simply easier to avoid the procedural burden to get permission to release information.

Most systems attempt to capture provenance information, but we have found that it is often incomplete, and represented in non-standard forms that can be difficult to follow. Often it is reduced to a phone call to the scientist asking "Where did you get this data, and what did you do to it?" Based on personal discussions, we have found that capturing and distributing good, usable provenance often simply isn't a priority for scientists. They are more than willing to talk about provenance and explain their methodologies with colleagues, but sometimes don't see the usefulness of incorporating provenance into the production system.

Even if provenance is captured, archived, and distributed, some systems can't (or won't) reproduce older datasets. They can rely on an error prone, manual process to attempt to reproduce data previously released.

4   Conclusion and Future Work

Access to complete provenance information is essential for many aspects of the use of Earth science data. It is possible to build science data processing systems that automatically capture the provenance information with little impact on resources, operations or the participating scientists involved in creating the data. This will make it possible for users to know how a data set was made, reproduce the results of the initial processing, and understand differences over time periods even after the original producers are no longer available for consultation.

With complete provenance a user will know what input data was used for any product including details of where it came from and what version it was. The user will be able to know what exact algorithms were used to make a product, what exact input data was used, what exact system the data was produced with and what processing system it was made on. This will improve the credibility of the data set and make it possible to determine whether differences over time of a remotely sensed data set come from true geophysical changes or are artifacts of the production system.

We are working on development of methods to distribute the processing framework used to make a product in such a way that remote scientists can access the algorithms that were used, interact with our system to download the information needed to replicate the environment, and run time parameters and reproduce the results or modify any component and asses the impact of the change.

Complete provenance requires that input data obtained from external sources also comes with its own provenance. We are working on identifying tools, content, and standards for this and on encouraging other data sources to provide this information. We note with concern that there is not a current commitment in the science community to require adequate stewardship to maintain and support complete provenance even if it is available. We also note that the requirement for the scientists providing processing algorithms to also provide complete documentation of the final version of their process does not receive adequate support.

It is our hope that by showing that all of the needed information can be easily captured if available and that it can assure data reproducibility we can encourage further development in these areas.

Acknowledgment

The authors thank the many individuals comprising MODIS and OMI teams for making development of MODAPS and OMIDAPS successful. Some of the information presented here was taken from a number of documents and web sites throughout the two projects.

References

1. Halem, M.: Service Oriented Atmospheric Radiances (SOAR): A Community Research Tool for the Synthesis of Multi-Sensor Satellite Radiance Data for Weather and Climate Studies. In: Proc. 3rd Intl. Conf. on Web Information Systems and Technology (2007)
2. Tilmes, C., Linda, M., Fleig, A.: Development of two Science Investigator-led Processing Systems (SIPS) for NASA's Earth Observation System (EOS). In: Proc. IEEE Geoscience and Remote Sensing Symposium, pp. 2190–2195 (2004)
3. Masuoka, E., Tilmes, C., Ye, G., Devine, N.: Producing Global Science Products for the Moderate Resolution Imaging Spectroradiometer (MODIS) in the EOSDIS and MODAPS. In: Proc. IEEE Geoscience and Remote Sensing Society (2000)
4. Wolfe, R., Roy, D., Vermote, E.: The MODIS land data storage, gridding and compositing methodology: LEVEL 2 Grid. IEEE Trans. on Geoscience and Remote Sensing 36, 1324–1338 (1998)
5. Diamond, H., Bates, J., Clark, D., Mairs, R.: Archive management: the missing component. In: Proc. 20th IEEE/11th NASA Goddard Conf. on Mass Storage Systems and Tech., pp. 40–48 (2003)
6. W3C Semantic Web Activity, http://www.w3.org/2001/sw/

A Python Library for Provenance Recording and Querying

Carsten Bochner, Roland Gude, and Andreas Schreiber

Simulation and Software Technology
German Aerospace Center
51147 Cologne, Germany
{Carsten.Bochner,Roland.Gude,Andreas.Schreiber}@dlr.de
http://www.dlr.de/sc

Abstract. In many application domains the provenance of data plays an important role. It is often required to get store detailed information of the underlying processes that led to the data (e.g., results of numerical simulations) for the purpose of documentation or checking the process for compliance to applicable regulations. Especially in science and engineering more and more applications are being developed in Python, which is used either for development of the whole application or as a glue language for coordinating codes written in other programming languages. To easily integrate provenance recording into applications developed in Python, a provenance client library with a suitable Python API is useful. In this paper we present such a Python client library for recording and querying provenance information. We show an exemplary application, explain the overall architecture of the library, and give some details on the technologies used for the implementation.

1 Introduction

The recording and analysis of the provenance for data (i.e., a suitable documentation of the process that led to the data [1,2]) resulting in IT based processes in science and engineering gets more and more important. Such kind of documentation is required or wanted in a variety of application domains, for example in aerospace engineering, medical applications, climate research, or other e-science applications. In some cases, the detailed documentation of processes that led to certain data is required by official regulations.

Since the recording of provenance gets more important in many application domains, it is essential that the overhead for adding the ability to record and query provenance from within application must be as low as possible. This is important to reduce the effort needing to enable existing application for provenance recording which might convince more developers and even scientists to do so. Therefore the availability of suitable libraries for commonly used languages with a high-level API is useful.

As an example, in science and engineering the high-level programming language Python [3] is being used in more and more complex applications. These

J. Freire, D. Koop, and L. Moreau (Eds.): IPAW 2008, LNCS 5272, pp. 229–240, 2008.

applications from industry, research labs, and universities are either implemented in Python completely or are provided with an Python programming API for controlling, extending, or embedding them. Especially, scientists in the fields of mathematics, physics, or engineering are often not interested or even willing to learn and use modern object-oriented languages such as Java, C++, or C# just to configure or extend existing applications.

Having a Python API and a correlative client library implementation for provenance recording and querying has two major fields of application. The first is, to enable existing applications written in Python with provenance recording and, as a special case, the customization of provenance recording on end-user level (e.g., by using an embedded Python interpreter). The second use case is the rapid development of (simple) tools for analyzing already recorded provenance information.

The rest of this paper is organized as follows. In Section 2 we will explain the application context of our work and discuss the advantages of the Python language. In Section 3, we present an overview and the architecture of the Python Provenance client-side library and in Section 4 we give some details on the implementation. Finally, in Sections 5 and 6 we present future work and conclusions.

2   Motivation

Currently, more and more scientific applications are being developed in Python or provided with a Python API. Examples are computational codes written in languages such as C or Fortran with Python APIs for convenient integration in working environments and steering the computation, simulation environments which integrates numerical codes, data management systems which manages input and output data of computation, or Grid environments which are able to distribute computation on a wide range of computing resources. In many cases, computational intensive parts of application codes are still written in C, C++, or Fortran whereas Python is used as a very high level language for configuration of these code, the setup of the overall computing workflow, or for managing the involved data. Very often these applications are multidisciplinary coupled computations, where simple Python scripts are used to implement the coupling scheme for steering the computation.

An example, where provenance-enabling Python applications is important is the German national D-Grid community project AeroGrid [4]. In AeroGrid, a Grid infra-structure for the aerospace research community is being created. The goal of the AeroGrid project is to provide a productive Service Grid for researchers from industry, national research labs, and universities who are collaborating in design and simulation phase of future products. In AeroGrid, the basic grid middleware services of the D-Grid infrastructure (The Globus Toolkit and UNICORE 6) are being used.

One of the project objectives is to enable the user interfaces and the infrastructure to record provenance information about the involved data. The integration of a provenance service means calculations performed in AeroGrid are automatically documented and traceable. Recording provenance information, i.e. complete information on the individual processing steps applied to data, improves the reliability of results for AeroGrid users. For example, during the design of turbine engines many variants of design are being simulated by a number of design engineers using a variety of internal and external computing resources. To get reliable and traceable results for each data file of the different variants, user information of involved engineers, detailed information of used computing resources, changes in parameter settings, as well as information about the used simulation codes are being recorded in a provenance data base.

The main user interface in AeroGrid is the data management client Data-Finder [5], a lightweight application software for managing technical and scientific data. It was developed to manage large amounts of data, and allows data to be stored using a number of different storage interfaces (e.g., WebDAV, FTP, GridFTP, Amazon S3, SRB, OpenAFS, or TSM). The structure of the data and descriptive metadata are stored in XML format on the central server and can be edited using the standardised WebDAV protocol. The DataFinder user interface consists of a platform-independent user client that allows users to navigate through the existing data, search for data, create and manage metainformation for all data, and execute scripts stored locally or on the server. The DataFinder client was developed in Python and the Qt GUI library and can be extended with Python easily.

Since the DataFinder is implemented in Python, integrating provenance recording can be done easily using a suitable provenance client library with a Python API.

The advantages of Python for applications in science and engineering are manifold [6,7], but it is an important prerequisite that Python is a general-purpose programming language without any restrictions and available on any platform with an ANSI-C compiler. It supports multiple programming paradigms (functional, object oriented, and imperative programming) and has many libraries and modules for a variety of tasks. But most important is the clear and highly-readable syntax which allows one to learn Python in very short time and which makes Python code very maintainable.

The rest of this paper presents a Python client library for recording and querying provenance information based on specifications developed in the EU Grid Provenance project [8].

3   Overview of the Python Library for Provenance

3.1   Fundamentals of the EU Grid Provenance Concept

The recording and querying of data and the interaction between Provenance-aware applications and a provenance store rests upon the following definitions [2]. The Provenance architecture uses an service oriented architecture (SOA) style, where a *provenance store* acts as Web Service for storing and querying the process information.

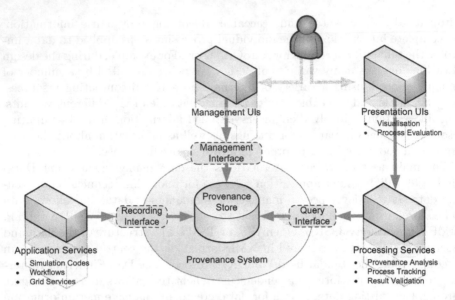

Fig. 1. Main concept of the EU Grid Provenance project

Every service involved in a data process is defined as an *actor*. The interaction between these actors is based on messages which take the form of SOAP messages for Web services. The interaction between actors characterizes the composition of the application workflow and is defined as a *process*.

In order to store and represent the provenance and process, different data models have been defined in the EU Grid Provenance Project. The elementary data model is the *p-assertion* which represent some step of process, while the *Process Documentation* data model represents the whole documentation of the process.

After the provenance of a process is recorded and stored in a provenance store a querying actor can ask for this provenance by sending a provenance query request to a provenance query engine, which is typically implemented by the provenance store [9]. Processing the query request the query engine must decide which p-assertions correspond to the request. Therefore the query must specify this factors and the provenance concept allows different search languages to do so. For executing queries a provenance store categorizes recorded p-assertions in a larger data structure, called the *p-structure*. This structure can be understood as a navigable schema or hierarchy of the provenance store. The p-structure is exposed to the querying actor through query interfaces of the provenance store. Figure 1 gives an overview of the main system concepts of the architecture defined in the EU Grid Provenance project.

A client-side library (CSL) is a collection of functions that allows applications to communicate with the services of the provenance store [10]. Furthermore a CSL should allow application developers to apply the rules of the provenance architecture easily. This should be enabled by a CSL that provides a clear and easy to use API with simple interfaces and data structures.

By developing a reusable library with an easy to use interface many details of this communication can be hidden from an application developer, thus reducing development cost of provenance-aware applications. Such a client-side library needs to implement the defined record and query protocols of the target Provenance store. In this case the client-side library mainly implements:

- **Process documentation recording protocol** - Definies the SOAP message communication between a recording actor and the provenance store [11]).
- **Query protocol** - Specifies the SOAP message communication between a querying actor and the the provenance store [9].
- **XPath protocol** - Definies the XPath-based profile of the provenance queries [12].

Furthermore, the client-side library needs to communicate with the provenance store using a defined technology binding (like the SOAP binding defined in [13]).

Currently two implementations of the provenance store are available. One store was developed by IBM for the EU Grid Provenance project and requires an installed Globus Toolkit. As the requirements are very extensive this store is not used in this project. The IBM store is a prototype implementation.

PReServ is the second provenance store and is developed by the University of Southampton. Currently prototype version 0.31 with WSDL 25 is available and used as reference store in this project [14].

3.2 General Architecture Overview

As the PReServ comes with a Java client-side Library [15], this Java CSL was used as a first reference for the design and implementation of the Python CSL. Therefore both architectures are mainly based on a similar layered model [15]. This model consists of three layers (see figure 2), with two API-layers offering interfaces for the server / the client, and one utilities or adaptions layer mapping this APIs to each other. The reason for this model is the complexity of the server API, which can not be used reasonable by application developers. Therefore the server API is mapped to a simpler client API, allowing application developers an easy access to the features of Provenance.

Client API. The top layer is the client API. This layer is exposed to the users of the library.

The client API offers interfaces to interact with the Provenance store, hold content of recordings (i.e. PAssertions) and queries. For querying the Provenance store currently the XQuery XML query language is supported, as defined in the PreServ XQuery interface [14]. Future versions of this Python CSL and the PReServ Provenance store might also support security, documentation style helper and policy helper.

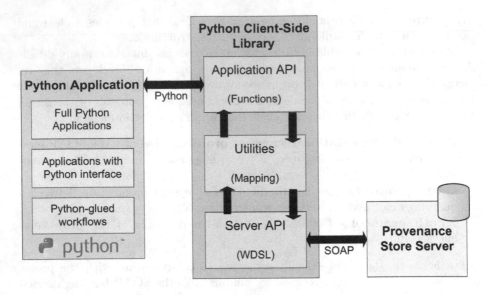

Fig. 2. Layer model of the Python CSL

The client API is used directly by application developers, which want to make their Python application provenance-aware. Hence the client API should contain simple and clear interfaces and data structures. Furthermore these interfaces need to be very robust and should not be subject to changes. The client API is defined using pyProtocols (see 4.1). The client API uses the utilities layer for mapping its services to the Service API.

Utilities. The middle layer is an adaption layer which maps the server API to the client API. This utilities layer or adaption layer implements the interfaces (or adapters) of the client API and contains several utility and helper classes for mapping the relatively simple client API to the complex server API. Furthermore several test modules have been integrated to ensure the correctness of the Python CSL implementation. The adaption layer consists out of pyProtocol adapters (see 4.1) which map a specific server APi to the client API.

Server API. The lowest layer is the server API. This layer directly communicates with a certain provenance store implementation. The interfaces of the Provenance store web services are defined in several WebServiceDefinition Language (WSDL) files. A WSDL uses the XML schema and can be understand as a contract between the service and the communicating component and mainly defines services, ports, operations and messages. The Python CSL contains Python stubs automatically generated from the WSDL files with the wsdl2python tool of the Zolera SOAP Infrastructure (ZSI) Python library. Currently the Server API module of the Python API consists mainly of four files:

- ProvenanceService_client
- ProvenanceService_server
- ProvenanceService_services
- ProvenanceService_types

The server API is specific for each supported provenance store implementation. Current files enable the communication with the PReServ Provenance store [14] according to the defined WSDL files of version 0.25.

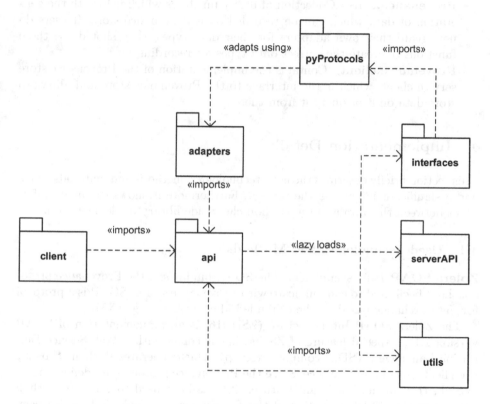

Fig. 3. Overview of the relation between the Python Provenance-CSL packages

3.3   API Description Overview

This section gives an overview of the API of the Provenance-CSL. See also figure 3 for the relations between packages.

- **Provenance** - Base package. It is only used as a collection of all the other parts.
- **Provenance.api** - This package contains the package users should utilize for their application. It is a collection of all parts of the Provenance-CSL which might be useful for a typical user.

- **Provenance.interfaces** - This package contains the interface-definitions for all types used in Provenance-CSL. Users will need this solely if they wish to define new adapters.
- **Provenance.adapters** - This package contains predefined adapters for several data types and interfaces.
- **Provenance.serverAPI** - This package contains the data types and stubs which are generated by wsdl2py. Users will usually not work with this package directly.
- **Provenance.utils** - Collection of utility functions which help with the generation of data which can be recorded on a Provenance store. If users do not create their own adapters for their data types, they should use these functions to create the correct data types for recording.
- **Provenance.client** - Contains the implementation of the Provenance store service client, which is the interface to the Provenance store and allows to store data on it or query it from there.

4   Implementation Details

This section briefly describes the used technologies, methods and materials which had a significant impact on the project. Furthermore it shows the main differences between the Java and the Python client-side library implementation.

4.1   Used Technologies and Methods

Zolera SOAP Infrastructure. The SOAP-bindings of the Provenance protocols have been used to communicate with Provenance stores. SOAP is a protocol for data exchange based on the eXtended Markup Language (XML).

The Zolera SOAP Infrastructure (ZSI) [16] is an implementation of SOAP version 1.1. A special feature of ZSI is that it comes with a Web Service Definition Language (WSDL) compiler wsdl2py, which generates Python stubs for the client-side of a web service. Since the Provenance protocols are defined using WSDL, this was an important feature. ZSI has been used to generate Python code from the WSDL definition of the Provenance protocols. It has also been used for all SOAP communication.

Python Enterprise Application Toolkit. The Python Enterprise Application Toolkit (PEAK) [17] is a collection of Python modules which adds useful features for component based design to Python. Its subpackages *importutils* and *pyprotocols* have been used to enable lazy loading and automated protocol adaption.

Lazy loading is a technique that allows the importing or loading of a library on demand. The *importutils* package of PEAK allows to define modules as *lazy modules*. It is completely compatible with the normal Python importing mechanism.

Unlike other object oriented programming languages, Python makes no use of anything like interfaces. In some object oriented programming languages (i.e. Java), interfaces are used to describe the methods a class has to provide in order to implement an interface. As an alternative concept, PyProtocols introduces protocols and protocol adaption to Python. Protocols are used to describe the behaviour of objects by defining which methods have to be supported and which members (i.e. variables, types) have to be provided in order to support the object. A really valuable feature of PyProtocols is the automatic adaption mechanism, which allows automated adaption from one data type *d1* which supports a protocol *p1* to support another protocol *p2* if an adapter from *p1* to *p2* has been defined.

An example of this adaption mechanism in the Provenance context is the following: Provenance records usually have a sink and a source. Both are complex types which usually contain a URL. By defining an adapter from strings which match the URL pattern to the complex type behind sink and source, it is now possible to use strings whenever the complex type is expected. In that case PyProtocols will automatically convert the strings to the expected complex type. This technique eases the usage of the generated code and the library.

For instance if a developer wants to use the Python CSL to store messages defined by his internal data types on a Provenance store, all he has to do is to define an adapter from his data type to the corresponding P-Assertion interface of the CSL. If he wants to record something on the store now, he can send the designated information to the store by simply supplying the Python CSLs recording API with instances of his data type. By defining adapters for the return types to his own data types, he would also be able to receive his own internal data types from a Provenance store using Provenance-CSL. Section 4.2 shows example code of how to define custom adapters.

4.2   Examples

The following source code shows examples for illustrating some basic provenance concepts.

Lazy-loading of all necessary modules and initializing a client-side access to a provenance store:

```
from provenance.api import *
cl = client.Client(http://localhost:8080, tracefile=sys.stdout)
```

Example of recording some complex provenance information (error handling code omitted)

```
viewKind = "isSender"
subj = utils.createSubjectId(1, dataAccessor, "parametername")
objlist = [utils.createObjectId(
    utils.createInteractionKey("http://sink", http://source"),
    pAssID, 'anything', 'dataAccessor', 'parameter', 'isSender')]
keys,response = self.cl.record([
        [utils.createActorState(a_content_0, doc_style),
         utils.createRelationship(subj, rel_type, objlist),
         utils.createInteraction(m_content_0, doc_style),
         utils.createInteraction(xml_content_0) ],
```

```
[utils.createActorState(a_content_1),
 utils.createActorState(a_content_2),
 utils.createInteraction(m_content_1, doc_style) ],
[utils.createRelationship(subj, rel_type, objlist)]
          ], viewKind, sink, source)
res = interfaces.IRecordAck(response)
```

Example of data querying using an XQuery expression

```
queryString = "for $n in $ps:pstruct return $n"
response = self.cl.query(queryString)
result = interfaces.IQueryAck(response)
```

Afterwards variable ''"result"'' contains an XML structure containing all pstructs available in the store.

The following code represents an example of extending data types using adapters. Here the adapter allows using type string when type address is expected.

Example of extending data types

```
class IAddress(IZSITypeCode):
    """ interface for string typecodes """
    def getAsString(self):
    """ returns a String with the Value of the Stringlike. """
    IString = protocols.protocolForType(basestring,[])


class AddressAdapter(object):
    protocols.advise(instancesProvide=[IAddress],
                     asAdapterForProtocols=[IString])
    def __init__(self, string):
        self._delegate = serverAPI.Address(string.__str__())
    def getAsString(self):
        return self._delegate.__str__()
    def toTypeCode(self):
        return self._delegate
```

5   Current and Future Work

5.1   Current State

The Python client-side library currently supports recording of P-Assertions on a PReServ Provenance store using the Provenance protocols of version 0.25. Querying the store using the XML XQuery language is possible. The concept of P-Headers has not been implemented yet. The current implementation features a complete set of utility functions for easy creation of P-Assertions and records and everything that is necessary for that. All interfaces which are necessary for recording have been defined as well as interfaces for the result types. Several interfaces have been defined to be context sensitive (i.e. is an Endpoint used as a sink or as source).

Adapters for all wsdl2py-generated types to the appropriate recording interfaces have been defined as well as adapters for a wide range of simple Python data types (like strings, lists and dictionaries) to support several recording interfaces. Adapters for the results of recording operations to the appropriate interfaces have been defined as well.

5.2   Future Work

Future works will focus on two main goals. First, current Python CSL will be adjusted to support upcoming new releases of the PReServ Provenance store and its changed WSDL definitions and functionalities. Therefore especially the package Server.API needs to be overworked, as this is always designed for a certain provenance store implementation. Further changes might become necessary, if the intent to change the current concept of an integrated XML database will be realised in the new PReServ release. In this case, the use of XQuery might become obsolete and a different query protocol must be integrated. Furthermore this process of adapting to a new PReServ version will be used for a redesign of the Python CSL and further quality assurance.

As the current version of the Python CSL is a proof of concept, not all protocols and functions of the provenance architecture [2] are supported. Therefore the second goal of our future work is the support of further functionality, including aspects as p-headers, security and different query protocols. This work will be subsequent to the fulfilment of our first goal and thus already support the new PReServ store version.

6   Conclusions

This paper presented a Python implementation of a provenance client-side library, which is currently able to record provenance information and to query provenance stores. The Python API as well as details on the implementation have been described.

Having this library eases the task to add provenance-awareness to existing or new Python applications. Especially, this includes applications written in other programming languages which have a Python API for extending or embedding. In particular, if the application has an embedded Python scripting functionality, end users could add provenance recording on their own or, at least, customize or extended existing provenance recording capabilities. Using the querying API, users can also use the Python CSL to rapidly develop specific analysis tools in Python.

Acknowledgment

This work has been supported by the German Federal Ministry for Research and Technology (BMBF) under Grant 01IG07006A.

References

1. Moreau, L., Groth, P., Miles, S., Vazquez-Salceda, J., Ibbotson, J., Jiang, S., Munroe, S., Rana, O., Schreiber, A., Tan, V., Varga, L.: The provenance of electronic data. Commun. ACM 51(4), 52–58 (2008)
2. Groth, P., Jiang, S., Miles, S., Munroe, S., Tan, V., Tsasakou, S., Moreau, L.: An Architecture for Provenance Systems. Technical report, University of Southampton (2006)
3. The Python Website, http://www.python.org
4. The AeroGrid Project Website, http://www.aero-grid.de
5. Schlauch, T., Schreiber, A.: Datafinder - a scientific data management solution. In: Ensuring the Long-Term Preservation and Value Adding to Scientific and Technical Data, PV 2007, Oberpfaffenhofen, Germany (2007)
6. Dubois, P.F.: Ten good practices in scientific programming. Computing in Science and Engg. 1(1), 7–11 (1999)
7. Jackson, K.R.: PyGlobus: a Python interface to the Globus Toolkit. Concurrency and Computation: Practice and Experience 14(13-15), 1075–1083 (2002)
8. The EU Grid Provenance Website, http://www.gridprovenance.org
9. Miles, S., Moreau, L., Groth, P., Tan, V., Munroe, S., Jiang, S.: Provenance Query Protocol. Technical report, University of Southampton (2006)
10. Jiang, S.: Client side library. Architecture tutorial. Technical report, University of Southampton (2005)
11. Groth, P., Tan, V., Munroe, S., Jiang, S., Miles, S., Moreau, L.: Process Documentation Recording Protocol. Technical report, University of Southampton (2006)
12. Miles, S., Moreau, L., Groth, P., Tan, V., Munroe, S., Jiang, S.: XPath Profile for the Provenance Query Protocol. Technical report, University of Southampton (2006)
13. Munroe, S., Tan, V., Groth, P., Jiang, S., Miles, S., Moreau, L.: A SOAP Binding For Process Documentation. Technical report, University of Southampton (2006)
14. The PReServ Website, http://twiki.pasoa.ecs.soton.ac.uk/bin/view/PASOA/SoftWare
15. Jiang, S., Moreau, L., Groth, P., Miles, S., Munroe, S., Tan, V.: Client Side Library Design and Implementation. Technical report, University of Southampton (2006)
16. The Python Webservices Project Website (including ZSI), http://pywebsvcs.sourceforge.net
17. The Python Enterprise Application Kit (PEAK) Website, http://peak.telecommunity.com

Requirements for a Provenance Visualization Component

Markus Kunde, Henning Bergmeyer, and Andreas Schreiber

Simulation and Software Technology
German Aerospace Center
51147 Cologne, Germany
{Markus.Kunde,Henning.Bergmeyer,Andreas.Schreiber}@dlr.de
http://www.dlr.de/sc

Abstract. The need for interpretation of provenance data increases with the introduction of further provenance related IT-systems. The interpretation of data only becomes intuitively with providing good and efficient visualization possibilities. During the development of general provenance visualization techniques, provenance users are classified into groups regarding their view to provenance information. The end-user requirements are evaluated on an abstract level to have a basis for research. Different intentions of end-users regarding provenance are identified and put into relationship with standard visualization types. Examples for standard visualization types are given and a brief forecast to future achievements is made.

1 Introduction

The importance of recorded provenance data will become clear during the evaluation of possible fields of application (see [1,2,3]). It is imaginable that in the next years the usage of tools including provenance technology will become mandatory in domains where the trust of information is highly crucial. Besides the recording of provenance data the interpretation of it plays a central role regarding any assertions about the past, present or future. The work represented by this paper is made up of development and evaluation of general, abstract concepts for visualization of provenance data. This analysis depends on a general approach, which can be used as a basis concept for provenance visualization in applications. The target of these visualization concepts is to provide an overview about possible general visualization alternatives.

The paper is organized as follows. Section 2 presents the motivation behind this work. In Section 3, a general user classification is made, regarding the scope of view to provenance data. Section 4 describes the transformation of user requirements into abstract types and their allocation to general visualization types. A functional classification of abstract user questions is presented. Visualization examples represent current standard visualization possibilities. In Section 5, brief examples of other projects are presented to give a first insight of possible application areas. Section 6 describes the current state of work and gives a forecast

J. Freire, D. Koop, and L. Moreau (Eds.): IPAW 2008, LNCS 5272, pp. 241–252, 2008.

to future achievements. Finally, in Section 7, a conclusion is presented including a brief evaluation of current and expected future outcomes.

2   Motivation

At the moment, the introduction of provenance on the market of IT-systems is still continuing. As the number and quality of concepts including provenance increases, further investments in the evolution of it will be made. The idea of storing provenance data grows as the concepts become more concrete and specific. This evolution comes upon its boundaries where application domain experts want to use these concepts. Storage of provenance data is one part of the whole topic, whereas the interpretation of data to get useful information is the other one.

With respect to the interpretation of provenance data the development of a provenance visualization concept becomes difficult in the manner of having a general approach for the visualization technique on the one hand and not to loose the connection to specific requirements of a concrete application domain on the other hand. The main intention of this work is to build-up general visualization concepts and their evaluation regarding concrete requirements. The advantage for the provenance community is based on the fundamental discover and development of different visualization techniques and their evaluation regarding possible application domains.

3   User Classification

The idea of analyzing provenance information depends on several circumstances like the application area of the concrete implementation and the individual task of a user of this application. The evaluation approach of these different intentions is to identify general user roles in the manner of different views to data and information and to group them together into generic user classes. Regarding the evaluation of a possible division the identified user groups are derived from the user requirements document of the EU Grid Provenance project [3].

In the context of user groups and provenance information a division between user and system provenance data is made. The term user provenance is used for workflow related provenance information. In this case the interaction-sequence with the involved user(s), the intermediate and end results and other direct workflow related information is important. The term system provenance is related to IT-system internal components and their relationship together. The exact relationship between IT-system specific components and their message exchange is mentioned with this term. The following list represents the identified abstract user roles and gives a brief explanation of each classification:

– **General User.** The general user should only see the user provenance information that is connected to workflows. The general user is involved in the configuration of the workflow. Only provenance information directly related to the own work-surrounding field is needed. The main intention is to rely on the outcome of a workflow and to check the authentically of these results.

- **Designer.** The designer role has main access to all user related provenance data, independent of the origin, which appears in the context of the monitored system. The designer is interested in the behavior of the workflow as well as the interaction between services or the connection with the outside world.
- **Manager.** A manager can see the owned user and system provenance data. The manager monitors the provenance usage on a whole to ensure the correctness of the individual services. This role is intended to support the interpretation steps and to ensure the quality of the provenance system.
- **Administrator/Developer.** The role of the administrator or developer is designed to capture the whole provenance data, which is available in the connected provenance stores. The purpose of this role is to build-up the provenance architecture and to ensure the correctness of the provenance system.

4   Generalized User Requirements

For the development of visualization concepts, a clear understanding of users need and users view regarding provenance information is mandatory. For evaluation of a general visualization concept, a derivation of user requirements for a special application must be made in order to have a universal assertion as a basis for these concepts. This is done by derivation of abstract types of identified user requirements. These types present the general intent of a user regarding provenance visualization. Besides the types of user requirements there is a need for a definition of an abstract layer of all provenance questions in relation to their point of interest.

4.1   Types

The derivation of types of user requirements into a more abstract view in order to display a general division of non-concrete user requirements is formed in the context of what element is the basis for visualization. Visualization is based on one element, the point of interest with additional information, with respect to the provenance data. The fundamental user requirements are extracted from [6]. The general approach for the derivation of the types was a two-way strategy. At first a bottom-up approach was used for a pre-selection of types. The pre-selection then was transformed into type-categories. Finally, a top-down approach was used to divide the user requirements into each type-category. In a further step, these types can be assigned to general visualization types, which were used as an essential for developing concrete visualization-concepts (see also 4.3).

Table 1 displays the abstract types of user requirements in which a user requirement can be arranged with a very brief denotation of each type.

Table 1. Types of user requirements

Type	Denotation
Process	In the center of the users view the process plays the central role. The approach of a workflow has to be evaluated. Involved actors as well as their connection are important. The sequence of the process steps is in the center of inspection.
Results	The intermediate or end results of interactions are in the center of users view. The outcome as well as the input has to be evaluated.
Relationship	In this case the relationship of interactions or actors is important and has to be evaluated. It is mandatory to reconstruct the evolution process of a result for reliance, in order to evaluate the results properly.
Timeline	If the time is important to observe, finding bottlenecks or trying of improvement of the workflow is one of the targets. Reconstructing the evolution of results or the behavior of actors to each other can be evaluated.
Participation	The evaluation of the correctness of the participants is important in the context of trust of the data. This type is very similar to the type Relationship, but there is another intention. The reconstructing of evolution processes is less important than the trust of all participated actors, which is mentioned with this type.
Compare	The comparison of two subjects deals with the differences between them. In the case of a comparison between one subject and a reference subject, the correctness of the subject can be proven.
Interpretation	This type represents a collection of individual questions, which cannot be classified into one of the other types. This type is represented with an individual visualization view depending on the special question of the end-user. Typical examples for these types are user requirements tend to develop new cognitions onto existing information.

4.2 Classification

As the division into types of user requirements is made to have an abstract division for assigning to basic visualization possibilities, a classification of the user requirements in the context of the user questions (listed in table 2) can be made. A classification of user requirements represents a functional division of user requirements. This division can be used to evaluate the fundamental provenance data, which is needed in order to give an answer to the user questions. Table 2 lists each classification and gives the abstract question behind it. Each user requirement related to the interpretation of the provenance should belong to this classification.

At first glance, there is interference between the classification and the division into types of the user requirements. The division into these two fields is made because of the different view of each field. The division into types is made in context of a possible visualization-panel in opposition to the classification, which context is the intention of user's question.

Table 2. Classification of user requirements

Classification	Abstract Formulation
Question of origin	What data was used in the generation of a data item?
Question of inheritance	What data items and information were generated using a given data item?
Question for participants	Which actors (users, applications, versions of tools, etc.) were employed in the generation of a data item?
Question for dependencies	Which resources from other projects/processes have been used in the generation of a data item?
Question for progress	In what stage of a processing chain is a given data item (for data items of the same type)? Has the process the data item is part of been finalized?
Question for quality	Did the process the data item is part of reach a satisfactory conclusion by some given regulations or criteria?

4.3 Visualization

At this point a rough assertion of visualization concepts is displayed (regarding process in [5]). This listing is made with the intention to have contrasting visualization domains, which are asserted to standard visualization concepts. These were fundamental for the ongoing project.

The general approach regarding the development of visualization concepts is represented by four steps. At first the user requirements are categorized into types. Secondly, existing standard visualization types are evaluated. The next step contains a matching between the user requirement types and the evaluation of standard visualizations. Regarding the results of the previous steps the concrete visualization concepts are developed.

Table 3 lists generic visualization types, allocates them with user requirements types and requirement classifications and briefly describes them. The type 'Interpretation' is missing in table 3. It is arguable if interpretation is carried out in every visualization type but primarily interpretation is completed by the user.

4.4 Visualization Examples

In this section few visualization examples are displayed (in addition to [7]). They depend on the division of visualization assertions and represent a first assertion of provenance information and their representation in standard visualization types, which will be evaluated to final visualization concepts. Each visualization example, representing only a first abstract sketch, evaluates the visualization technique in the context of one point of interest. After development of the final concepts, a complete evaluation of each visualization proposal will be made. The manipulation of information (e.g. zoom function of detail depth, filtering or sorting) is not considered in the sketches, but will be considered in the final visualization concepts. Regarding the detail level and scope of each individual visualization technique a visualization map (describes the behavior and relationship

Table 3. Visualization assertions

Visualization Type	Description	Related Type	Related Classification
Process diagram	The process diagram highlights the workflow with its actors, interactions and results into the center of users view.	Process Results Participation	Participants Dependencies Progress
Difference diagram	The difference diagram displays the difference between the compared objects (process, actor, interaction).	Compare	Quality
Dependency diagram	The dependency diagram displays the connection of the chosen elements (e.g. actors, interactions). It presents the behavior and the relation between income and outcome to each other.	Results Relationship Participation	Origin Inheritance Participants Dependencies
Timeline diagram	The timeline diagram displays all interactions between actors in the context of their relationship in a timeline. This diagram is similar to the process diagram, but in this diagram qualified connections are displayed.	Process Results Relationship Timeline Participation	Origin Inheritance Progress
Spreadsheet representation	The spreadsheet representation gives the most space for doing interpretation of the data. In order to have full freedom for sorting and filtering elements, this is the most flexible but also the most unclear representation strategy.	Process Results Relationship Timeline Participation Compare	Quality

of visualization concepts to each other) will be developed with respect to the scalability of the visualizations.

All visualization examples describe the three-way handshaking (or a part of it) used in information technology or related fields.

Flow Chart (Related to Process Diagram). The flow chart diagram represents the visualization of the complete workflow in the context of having actors interacting to each other and related data. This diagram type is intended for representation of interactions. The key points of interest are: process sequence, combination of actors and interactions, who interact with whom?, input and outcome of an actor, data transformation. The complete three-way handshaking is displayed in the example with focus on actors and data.

Data Flow Diagram (Related to Process Diagram). The data flow diagram represents the visualization of the complete workflow in the context of having actors interacting to each other and related interaction sequences. This diagram

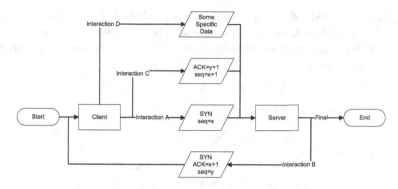

Fig. 1. Sketch of flow chart visualization type

type is intended for representation of actors and their interactions. The key points of interest are: information flow sequence, interaction-call sequence, who interact with whom?, factual process sequence. The complete three-way handshaking is displayed in the example with focus on actors.

Difference Diagram (Related to Difference Diagram). The difference diagram compares a workflow or data with comparable data. Differences are highlighted. The key points of interest are: comparison of two objects (processes, data, actor states, interactions). The complete three-way handshaking is compared with a reference workflow. The difference is highlighted in the example.

System Context Diagram (Related to Dependency Diagram). The system context diagram displays a central point (e.g. a workflow, interaction, actor or data) and the relation to any other part. This diagram type is intended for representation of relationships and states. The key points of interest are: effecting

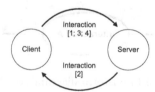

Fig. 2. Sketch of data flow diagram visualization type

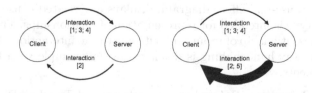

Fig. 3. Sketch of difference diagram visualization type

relationships achieved, effecting relationships published, input and outcome of an actor. The complete three-way handshaking is displayed in the example with focus on one actor and its relationships to other involved elements regarding the direction of their impact.

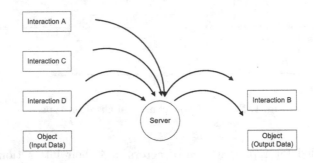

Fig. 4. Sketch of system context diagram visualization type

Brainstorm Diagram (Related to Dependency Diagram). The brainstorm diagram represents any related content regarding a central point. It displays all elements which have an effect to the central point or where the point has an effect to. This diagram type is intended for representation of relationships. The key points of interest are: relationship of input and outcome (data, interactions, actors). The complete three-way handshaking is displayed in the example with focus on one interaction and its relationships to other involved elements.

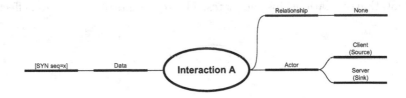

Fig. 5. Sketch of brainstorm diagram visualization type

Fishbone Diagram (Related to Dependency Diagram). The fishbone diagram, also known as cause-and-effect diagram, displays any related causes to a point. This diagram type is intended for representation of relationships. The key points of interest are: relationship of input and outcome (data, interactions, actors). The complete three-way handshaking is displayed in the example with focus on the impact of elements.

State Chart Diagram (Related to Dependency and Timeline Diagram). The state chart diagram displays all states of an actor during the life-cycle of a

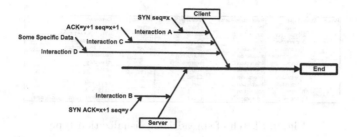

Fig. 6. Sketch of fishbone diagram visualization type

workflow. The key points of interest are: actor states, transforming interactions, transformed data, time-context. The complete three-way handshaking is displayed in the example with focus on state changes and their 'appearance-chain'.

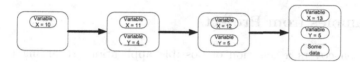

Fig. 7. Sketch of state chart diagram visualization type

Sequence Diagram (Related to Timeline Diagram). The sequence diagram represents the sequence of interactions of related actors in the context of a timeline. This timeline can be qualified or unqualified. This diagram type is intended for representation of interactions and states in a time-context. The key points of interest are: time-context of process, involved actors, executed interactions, input and outcome data. The complete three-way handshaking is displayed in the example with focus on actors and interactions.

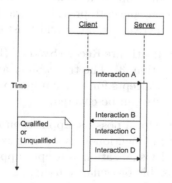

Fig. 8. Sketch of sequence diagram visualization type

ProcessStep	Type	Interaction-Name	MessageSource	MessageSink	Content
1	Interaction	Interaction A	Client	Server	SYN seq=x
2	Interaction	Interaction B	Server	Client	SYN ACK=x+1 seq=y
3	Interaction	Interaction C	Client	Server	ACK=y+1 seq=x+1
4	Interaction	Interaction D	Client	Server	some specific data
5	Relationship	Interaction B	Interaction A		causedBy
6	Relationship	Interaction C	Interaction B		causedBy
7	Relationship	Interaction D	Interaction B		causedBy
8	Actorstate	Interaction A	Client		X=10
9	Actorstate	Interaction B	Server		X=11; Y=4
10	Actorstate	Interaction C	Client		X=12; Y=5
11	Actorstate	Interaction D	Client		X=13; Y=5; [some specific data]

Fig. 9. Sketch of spreadsheet visualization type

Spreadsheet (Related to Spreadsheet Representation). The spreadsheet representation displays a scheduler collection of provenance datasets with the possibility of filtering or sorting of the results. This representation type is intended for detailed information research. The key points of interest are: Displaying all relevant information (interactions, relationships, actor states, time-context). The complete three-way handshaking is displayed in the example.

5   Examples from Projects

This section covers a selection of possible applications regarding provenance visualization. These examples already use the provenance system or are a proper candidate for employment. As it is obvious all applications use the provenance technology in a different way. In some cases provenance is used to understand the behavior of the IT-system (e.g. TENT) while other systems' usage is (partly) based on provenance (e.g. ENCHR, VisTrails).

C3-Grid. The main goal of the C3-Grid project is to do research about the earth system for understanding the behavior and dynamic of the whole and each subsystem [4]. The verification of the model and the data of this simulation is one possible application point for a visualization concept based on the result of this project.

TENT. TENT [8] is a software integration and workflow management system that simplifies work by building up simulation process chains in distributed environments. The visualization concepts provide a graphical way for evaluation of the workflows regarding increased quality and trust of the outcome [9].

ENCHR. The 'Electronic Healthcare Record System' (ENCHR) is a solution for an unbound healthcare situation [3]. The traceability and trust of each result is mandatory. With adequate concepts for a visual interpretation of this evolution a fast and correct consequence can be covered.

OTM. One further example for a possible application is the 'Organ Transplant Management' (OTM), already mentioned as a prime example in the provenance project [3]. A sophisticated visualization concept supports the tasks regarding the diversified group of possible provenance users.

VisTrails. The software 'VisTrails' is a good example to explain the need of good visualization concepts for interpretation of provenance data [10]. One intention of the software is to support an expert in data exploration, the systematic tracking of workflow evolution and to comprehend the steps made. The software shows the advantages of a good visualization concept supporting data interpretation.

6   Current and Future Work

Currently, the analysis of user requirements is done and its division into abstract types and its classification. Possible end-users are identified and grouped into different user roles. First assertions about standard visualization types, matching to the abstract intends of the users, are made and evaluated [5]. During next project phases the existing standard visualization types are being evaluated in more detail to enhance them into concrete visualization concepts [5]. New Visualization approaches are being developed regarding modern visualization techniques, such as tree maps, magic lens, network visualization and others. These visualization concepts will be evaluated regarding users' requirements.

7   Conclusions

The need for interpretation and visualization of provenance data increases step-by-step by the ongoing development of provenance technology and its introduction in real IT-systems [11]. The increasing number of application areas surrounds the usage and analysis of provenance data from application domain experts. Regarding this evolution the analysis of provenance data should become more easy and intuitive; considering the background of each application domain and the intention of the operating end-user. In this paper a first insight into the visualization of provenance data is given. A classification of user and requirements is made and a first assertion about possible visualization types is presented. With respect to other research projects [2,3], which evaluates the need and a concrete application for querying and exploring of provenance data, this paper describes an approach for visualization of these steps, taking a further step in the direction to end-users.

Acknowledgments. This work has been supported by the German Federal Ministry for Research and Technology (BMBF) under Grant 01IG07006A.

References

1. Groth, P., Jiang, S., Miles, S., Munroe, S., Tan, V., Tsasakou, S., Moreau, L.: An architecture for provenance systems. Technical report, Provenance Consortium (2006)
2. The Pasoa Website, http://www.pasoa.org
3. The EU Grid Provenance Project Website, http://www.gridprovenance.org

4. The C3-Grid Website, http://www.c3grid.de
5. Fry, B.: Visualizing Data, 1st edn. O'Reilly, Sebastopol (2007)
6. WorkPackage2: Grid provenance user requirements document. Technical report, Provenance Consortium (2005)
7. Deora, V., Contes, A., Rana, O.: Tool for Navigating Provenance Information. In: Provenance Challenge Workshop, Cardiff University (2006)
8. Schreiber, A.: The integrated simulation environment TENT. Concurrency and Computation: Practice and Experience (13-15), 1553–1568 (2002)
9. Kloss, G.K., Schreiber, A.: Provenance implementation in a scientific simulation environment. In: Moreau, L., Foster, I. (eds.) IPAW 2006. LNCS, vol. 4145, pp. 37–45. Springer, Heidelberg (2006)
10. Freire, J., Silva, C.T., Callahan, S.P., Santos, E., Scheidegger, C.E., Vo, H.T. (eds.): Managing rapidly-evolving scientific workflows, University of Utah (2006)
11. Miles, S. (ed.): Electronically Querying for the Provenance of Entites, School of Electronics and Computer Science, University of Southampton (2006)

Advances and Challenges for Scalable Provenance in Stream Processing Systems*

Archan Misra, Marion Blount, Anastasios Kementsietsidis, Daby Sow, and Min Wang

IBM T.J. Watson Research Center
Hawthorne, NY, USA
{archan,mlblount,akement,sowdaby,min}@us.ibm.com

Abstract. While data provenance is a well-studied topic in both database and workflow systems, its support within stream processing systems presents a new set of challenges. Part of the challenge is the high stream event rate and the low processing latency requirements imposed by many streaming applications. For example, emerging streaming applications in healthcare or finance call for data provenance, as illustrated in the Century stream processing infrastructure that we are building for supporting online healthcare analytics. At anytime, given an output data element (e.g., a medical alert) generated by Century, the system must be able to retrieve the input and intermediate data elements that led to its generation. In this paper, we describe the requirements behind our initial implementation of Century's provenance subsystem. We then analyze its strengths and limitations and propose a new provenance architecture to address some of these limitations. The paper also includes a discussion on the open challenges in this area.

1 Introduction

To enable an emerging class of *cyber-physical* computing applications, several stream computing platforms and middleware have been developed (e.g., Aurora [1], SPC [2]) to provide scalable, high throughput processing of sensor-generated data streams. In such systems, the arriving data are essentially *ephemeral*; to support low-latency processing of the data streams, stream operators perform only one pass over the arriving data, which are then typically discarded. In turn, this typically limits the forms of provenance in these systems to *process provenance*, i.e., determining which stream operators contributed to the generation of a particular data item.

Remote health monitoring represents an extremely important application domain for stream computing. To enable automated near-real time analysis of high volumes of medical sensor streams, we have been building, over the past year, an infrastructure, called Century [3], that permits the scalable deployment of online medical analytics. Stream analysis in the medical domain requires the Century infrastructure to support both process and *data* provenance, to support capabilities such as "offline dependency analysis" or "historical data replay". From a technical standpoint, data provenance imposes a

---

* This work was supported by the IT R&D program of MIC/IITA under the project/grant/funding number 2006-S-602-01 (Development of Stream-based Distributed Interoperable Health care Infrastructure Supporting Provenance and QoE).

J. Freire, D. Koop, and L. Moreau (Eds.): IPAW 2008, LNCS 5272, pp. 253–265, 2008.

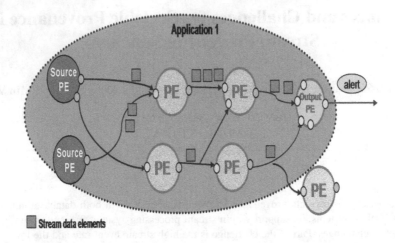

Fig. 1. Illustrating Data Provenance in a Stream Analysis Infrastructure. An application is represented as a directed acyclic graph (DAG) of nodes, with each node representing an operator or a Processing Element (PE). Provenance reconstruction involves determining the set of causative data elements belonging to streams that lie *upstream* of a particular data element.

novel challenge in data streaming systems, that of *stream persistence* [10,12]. At any point in time, given an output (e.g., a medical alert) generated by a stream processing graph, the Century Provenance system must not only recreate the processing graph that created the output, but also provide *all* the elements of the intermediate data streams that generated it. A data provenance solution for streams faces a couple of challenges:

- It must preserve the *high processing throughput* of the infrastructure, implying that the provenance solution cannot introduce significant additional processing overhead for every individual stream data element.
- It must *not impose a prohibitive storage load*, both in terms of the *volume of data*, as well as the *insertion rate* of data items requiring storage.

To support data provenance for such high throughput environments, we have previously introduced a model-based provenance solution, called Time-Value-Centric (TVC) provenance [17], which uses an explicit specification of the dependency relationship between input and output streams at every node (hereafter called a *Processing Element* or *PE*) in the processing graph. The notion of data provenance, involving the identification of multiple stream elements at upstream PEs belonging to a processing graph, is graphically illustrated in Figure 1.

This paper first describes some challenges with data provenance, based on our initial experiences with a TVC-based provenance solution for Century. The TVC approach does result in lower processing overhead, compared to the conventional annotation approach (which would require every element of every data stream to carry along a much longer set of stream elements as metadata). However, our experience reveals two new challenges for a pure model-based approach:

- Fundamentally, it has to contend with the increased *storage insert rate* that results from the need to persist the individual elements of *every* data stream occurring within a stream processing graph.
- The provenance model must reconcile and track potential discrepancies between the granularity at which stream data are produced and consumed by PEs within a processing graph. This discrepancy surfaces in extensible stream computing systems, where the data is not strongly typed, where the set of operators (PEs) is not closed and where different PEs choose to consume data at different granularities.

While both of these features need to be addressed, the issue of *much larger stream storage rates* is fundamentally more challenging and requires a change in the basic provenance model. The need to store both external and intermediate streams will impose an infeasibly high workload on commercial database systems. Accordingly, we shall propose a new hybrid provenance architecture, called *Composite Modeling with Intermediate Replay (CMIR)* that solves the problem of stream persistence by defining TVC-style dependency relationships only over a set of PEs (rather than at each individual PE) and by using *data replay* to recreate the data elements of streams internal to the PE set. We shall also discuss a set of open challenges and issues, with a goal of soliciting new approaches from the provenance community for tackling these challenges.

The rest of this paper is organized as follows. Section 2 provides an overview of the basic TVC primitives and their use in a representative analytic application, and then introduces two observed challenges. Section 3 introduces the suggested CMIR model for data provenance in stream computing platforms, and then describes the related technical challenges. Section 4 describes our current solution for resolving the granularity mismatch between output and input data elements. Section 5 then surveys prior relevant work and the paper concludes in Section 6 with a summary of the main points.

2   The TVC Model for Century and Resulting Limitations

The TVC model [17] specifies a set of primitives that are used to define a causative relationship between the data elements generated at the output port of a PE and the data elements arriving at its input ports. The TVC model differs from conventional annotation-based approaches for data provenance, which would need to embed a potentially large set of input data identifiers as metadata in every output data element (owing to the *statefulness* of stream operators, which implies that each output may be influenced by a large number of input data samples). TVC exploits the observation that the input-output dependencies for most PEs can be specified in terms of some invariants–while each output data element may have a variable set of causative input elements, this set may be indirectly determined through the application of these invariant primitives.

The TVC model supports the following primitives for dependency specification:

- *Time:* This primitive captures dependencies where an output data element is generated based on a past time window of past input data elements. For example, the notation $O_{m1}(t) \leftarrow I_{n1}(t - 10, t - 2)$ indicates that an output element generated at a time $t = 80$ on output port $m1$ depends only on those input elements that were timestamped with values in the interval $(70, 78)$, on input port $n1$.

- *Value:* The 'value' primitive defines a dependency in terms of predicates over the attributes of the input data elements. For example, a value primitive like $O_{m2}(t)$: $\{alertLevel = 1\} \leftarrow I_{n2}(t) : \{(systolic > 130)\&\&(diastolic > 100)\}$ indicates that an output element with 'alertLevel=1' depends only on *all* past input samples that satisfy the corresponding predicates over the (systolic, diastolic) attributes.
- *Sequence:* The 'sequence' primitive expresses dependencies in terms of the sequence number of arriving elements. For example, a sequence primitive $O_{m3}(t) \leftarrow I_{n3}(i - 30, i)$ indicates that an output element depends on the most recent 30 samples of input data.

A TVC dependency relationship may be composed by arbitrary conjunctions and disjunctions of these basic primitives. Moreover, for significantly enhanced expressiveness, the specifications allow each TVC term to specify a combination of (time, sequence, value) triples. Each element of such a triple has a unique 'order' term, which defines an evaluation order for these primitives, with the output sub-stream of a lower order primitive acting as the input stream for a higher order primitive. As an example, the dependency relation $O_{45}(t) \leftarrow I_{97}\{(t-1d, t, order = 2), (systolic > 130, order = 1)\}$ implies that the causative set for an output element of port 45 may be reconstructed by first obtaining the sub-stream of input elements on port 97 that have '$systolic > 130$' and then picking all the elements of this sub-stream that have been received in the last day. Figure 2 shows the specification of TVC primitives in a sample processing graph in Century.

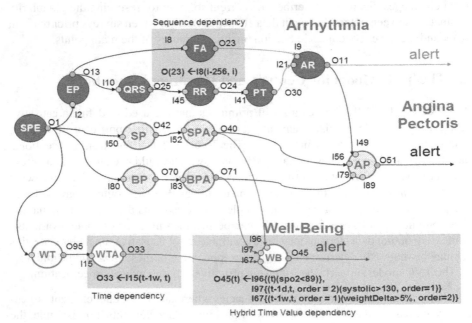

Fig. 2. Graph of a Representative Arrythmia Monitoring Application in Century. (The TVC-based dependency relationship for two PEs is explicitly highlighted.)

```
RetrieveCausativeData(Event e) {
ts= e.Timestamp; oport= e.phyOutputPort
{PE, logOutPort}= lookupDynamic(oport); // find the logical (PE,port) pair
tvcTerms = lookupTVC(PE,logOutPort); // find statically specified TVC terms
for (i ∈ InputPorts) {
    dataElements= retrieveElements(i); // retrieve incoming data elements
    /*use TVC to identify the causative subset */
    causativeInput= filter(tvcTerms, dataElements);
    causList.add(causativeInput);
} return causList;
}
```

Fig. 3. Data Provenance Reconstruction Algorithm

Assuming that all elements of all data streams are persisted, deriving the set of input causative data sample is a fairly straightforward process captured by the simple high level pseudo-code in Figure 3. Recursive application of this pseudo-code enables the reconstruction of data dependencies at progressively upstream points in the processing graph.

2.1 Challenges in the Practical Application of Model-Based Provenance

Applying the *generic* TVC description above to an actual stream computing environment, however, gives rise to two practical challenges:

– *Intermediate Stream Persistence and the Resulting Storage Load:* Streaming systems supporting data provenance require the data elements of *each stream* to be persisted. The TVC framework is no exception. Let $\overline{O_m, I_n}$ denote the stream flowing between output port m and input port n. To reconstruct the entire data provenance along the entire path for ECG in Figure 2, the system must store both the incoming ECG samples $(\overline{O_1, I_2})$ and all the intermediate streams $(\overline{O_{13}, I_8}, \overline{O_{13}, I_{10}}, \overline{O_{25}, I_{45}}, \overline{O_{24}, I_{41}})$. The persistence of high volume data streams is already known to be a potential performance bottleneck for state of the art database systems. In [12], the authors show both analytically and experimentally that the persistence of Electrocardiogram data streams with a state of the art database system could only scale up to a few hundreds of patients; capturing data provenance further acerbates the problem by causing a multiplicative increase in the stream insert rate on the backend storage system. Conceptually, we require an enhanced solution that can eliminate this requirement for storing every intermediate data stream.
– *Granularity Mismatch of Output and Input units for a Data Stream:* Consider a pair PE_1 and PE_2 of PEs where the output of PE_1 results in a stream that is one of the input streams of PE_2. In loosely-typed or extensible systems, it is entirely possible that the *granularity at which PE_2 consumes streaming elements differs from the granularity at which PE_1 generates streaming elements*. This difference may occur for two distinct reasons:
  • The 'data type' of the elements produced by PE_1 and those consumed by PE_2 need not be identical. In many systems that permit type extensions and

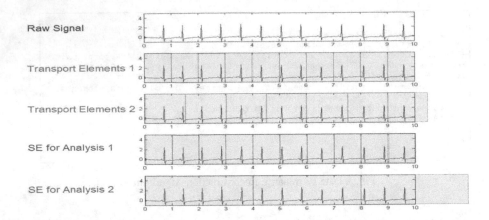

Fig. 4. Role of TEs vs. SEs in a generic stream-based analytic infrastructure. (The $TE \rightarrow SE$ mapping can be either one-one, one-many or many-one.)

inheritance (e.g., Tribeca [14]), and where stream bindings are based upon type-based subscriptions (e.g., SPC [2]), downstream PEs may bind to any output PE that produces the specific data type or its super-type (i.e., the consumed data is only *part* of the produced data element.) In most cases, the child PE merely consumes a sub-set of the data elements produced by a parent PE. As an example, PE_1 may be producing a person's 'vitalsigns' data type (which contains the elemental types: blood pressure (BP), heart rate and SpO2), while PE_2 may be using only the BP values; data reconstruction for a provenance query should then expose only the BP data.

- PE_1 may package multiple elements of a given data type into a single, larger transport element (TE), as this promotes more efficient transport of data within the processing runtime, by amortizing the transport-layer overhead over multiple data elements[1], especially when an individual data element may correspond to a sample of only a few bits. Figure 4 illustrates this for ECG signals that are collected in variable-sized TEs. This results in a potential incompatibility between the units of data produced by PE_1 and the unit of data consumed by PE_2. As an example of this, PE_1 may be an ECG PE that produces TEs containing a variable number of ECG 'samples', while PE_2 is a QRS detector PE that produces a QRS value based on the ECG samples in the last 60 seconds. Let's assume that PE_2 assumes an input rate of 1 TE (comprising 5 ECG samples) every 5 seconds, and therefore 12 TEs are used. Then, the TVC rule $O(t) \leftarrow I(i - 12, i)$ captures the provenance of QRS outputs in PE_2. What if we replace PE_1 with a PE_1' that uses a different rate, generating, say, one TE (comprising 1 sample) every 1 sec? How does this *innocent* change affect provenance? It is not hard to see that our TVC rule would now need to

---

[1] This issue does not arise in more restrictive systems, such as Aurora [1], where data units are both defined and transported as fixed tuples.

change to $O(t) \leftarrow I(i-60, i)$! Ideally, the provenance design should allow the TVC relationship specification to remain invariant of the specific granularity at which the data elements arrive at its input ports (as different 'parent' PEs can provide varying transport encapsulations of the data elements).

The above examples demonstrate that, in terms of data provenance, it does not suffice to focus our attention solely on models that describe the output/input dependencies *within* a single PE. Additional techniques are needed to capture the discrepancies that might arise between the units in which the data is produced by the parent PE and in which the data is consumed by the receiving PE.

3 Looking towards the Future: The CMIR Data Provenance Framework

We now propose a novel approach to provenance for stream-based environments that preserves the explicit model-based dependency specification of the TVC approach, yet does not require the persistence of all intermediate streams (but perhaps, only a smaller set of streams). The new approach, called *Composite Modeling With Intermediate Replay (CMIR)*, aggregates a cluster of PEs into a *virtual PE*, such that only streams that act as either input to or are output by the virtual PE are persisted. Moreover, the TVC relationships are then defined in terms of the output and input streams of the virtual PE, thus enabling the set of causative elements of input streams (of the virtual PE) to be determined for any given output stream element. The individual 'real' PEs, and their associated bindings, within such a virtual PE, are opaque to this model-based provenance framework, which treats the virtual PE as a 'black box'. The greater the size of the cluster, the smaller the number of streams that become 'external' to the virtual PE, thereby reducing the storage burden. Figure 5 illustrates the concept of CMIR-based provenance–in this case, the provenance relationships are captured over the *output and input streams of PE_{V1}*, a virtual PE defined by aggregating the 'real' PEs, $\{PE_1, PE_2\}$.

The process of virtualizing a group of PEs must also be supplemented by a mechanism that recreates, *on-demand*, the streams internal to the virtual PE, since data provenance inherently demands the reconstruction of data elements along the entire path of a specific processing graph. Our approach for this involves the use of a *replay mechanism*. To achieve this, one firstly requires the knowledge of the internal structure of the virtual PE, including the various real PE instances and the associated stream bindings. The dynamic provenance information must be extended to capture the association between the virtual PEs and the 'real' PEs.

The bigger challenge arises from the potential *statefulness* of the real PEs; such statefulness implies that the set of output stream objects produced by a PE will depend not only on its *fixed* processing logic, but also its current internal or external state. For CMIR, each individual PE must be *provenance-aware*–i.e., it must be responsible for checkpointing its internal state to the provenance store, and, conversely, for recreating its internal state based on such retrieved historical data. In the TVC model, the state of each individual PE is captured in provenance metadata externalized to the provenance infrastructure (typically, by annotating the state within the output stream elements).

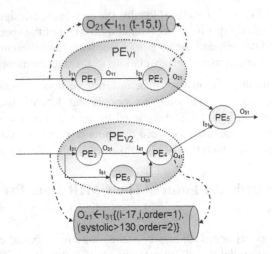

Fig. 5. The CMIR Framework and the Use of Virtual PEs

However, in the CMIR model, PEs internal to a virtual PE are not externalizing that metadata, so relevant state must be externalized in this way. In addition to such check-pointing, a CMIR based provenance system must also have a Replay component that dynamically instantiates, within the runtime, the set of PEs (along with their corresponding state evolution) corresponding to a virtual PE.

3.1 Challenges in CMIR-Based Provenance System Design

While the application of a CMIR-based solution for Century is still in its initial design phase, we are already aware of a few challenges that we must address. In particular, two very interesting open challenges are:

– *Models for Persisting State:* To support accurate replay of a PE's internal logic, the CMIR framework requires the persistence of the PE's internal state. Our initial thoughts are to have the provenance system treat this 'state information' as an opaque byte-stream, implying that each PE has the freedom to generate its own custom representation of its own state. It is, however, likely that the state information of the vast majority of PEs is likely to contain some common objects (examples of such likely state objects include command line arguments, the PE's load, the IDs of the individuals whose streams are being monitored, etc.); in such a situation, it may be worthwhile to define a more structured format for the object state. Moreover, it may also be desirable that this state representation lend itself easily to partial changes (as state change is often incremental), thereby allowing a PE to express its evolving state to the Provenance storage infrastructure in a more efficient fashion. *The issue of appropriate representation formats for such state information, which balance efficient storage and easy reconstruction, appears to be an open research question.*

– *Techniques for Composing Provenance Dependencies:* The use of virtual PEs within the CMIR framework implies the need for the system to be aware of the output-input dependency relationships at the virtual PE-level. Virtual PEs are, however, merely a runtime artifact of the provenance system; the basic TVC-style relationships will continue to be expressed for each individual PE (as individual PE developers shall specify the dependency logic of only their authored PEs). The provenance system must thus programmatically cascade the TVC relationships of individual PEs to derive the 'macro' dependency relationships of the virtual PE.

An interesting question that arises here relates to what types of dependencies are composable and what aren't. As a simple example, a time interval-based dependency primitive is composable in a fairly-straightforward fashion. If PE_1 has a time based relationship $O_{11}(t) \leftarrow I_{11}(t-10,t)$ and PE_2 has also a timed based relationship $O_{21}(t) \leftarrow I_{21}(t-5,t)$, then as shown in Figure 5 the composed rule for the virtual PE PE_{v1} is $O_{21}(t) \leftarrow I_{11}(t-15,t)$. However, other primitives of the basic TVC model do not lend themselves to such relationship cascading. For example, if PE_2 has a value-dependent relationship, such that $O_{21}(t)$ depends on the last 10 values generated by PE_1 with '$attr1 > 10$', while PE_1 has the same time based relationship as before, then the input-output relationship of the virtual PE *can no longer be expressed* using the primitives of the basic TVC model.

This example illustrates the central role that the choice of primitives in the dependency model have on the feasibility of deriving dependency relationships for the virtual PEs. Accordingly, we need to develop an enhanced *composable* provenance dependency model, such that its primitives, while being adequate expressive, are *'closed' (in set-theoretic terms)* under the operation of cascading. The issue of cascading is further complicated by the fact that, in many applications and scenarios, provenance is not used simply for backward reconstruction of data elements in a processing graph, but for *forward reconstruction* as well. As an example based on our own experiences with Century, a medical stakeholder who detects a faulty 'arrhythmia' analysis for a given patient may need to look 'downstream' and cleanse the system of faulty alerts generated as a result of this incorrect intermediate value. To support such 'forward provenance' semantics, the primitives of the provenance specification language must also be *reversible* (even if they are not very precise). *Overall, we believe that the development of a set of expressive provenance primitives, with the necessary composable and reversible properties, constitutes an important open problem for stream-based provenance.*

4   Resolving Granularity Differences between Stream Data Producers and Consumers

In Section 2, we illustrated how discrepancies in the granularity of stream elements produced by PEs, and the elements consumed by other PEs, directly influence our ability to accurately apply model-based provenance across PEs. One alternative to address this problem has already being hinted in Section 2. Instead of associating a single TVC rule for a particular PE, one can associate a set of rules, one for each output stream granularity (of the parent PE) that is known *a priori*. Unfortunately, this is a bad design choice for extensible stream systems, where new PEs, data types or stream encapsulations (containing the data type desired by a consuming PE) may become part of the stream computing infrastructure at any point; in such systems, the behavior of potential suppliers of specific data types cannot be predicted at PE design time. There are two other alternative, and better, design choices available:

- We may require the data types (and super-type) definitions to be *externalized* in a global type repository, with stream consumption by PEs being rigidly enforced to observe such type definitions. In such a system, a PE must indicate the *exact data type*, say DT_c, that it consumes on any input port, and the *runtime* must then ensure that this particular PE is able to receive only that exact data (i.e., for a parent PE that generates data elements belonging to data type DT_s that is a super-type of DT_c, the runtime must eliminate all extraneous data attributes and fields in DT_s, before making only DT_c available to the consuming PE). Such a strongly-typed system may become cumbersome for an open and extensible streaming infrastructure, where different organizations may define their own PEs, each of which may utilize multiple elements/fields within, or straddling different, data 'types'.
- Alternately, we can require the specification of a separate set of 'mapping functions' that perform the conversion between data elements of an output port and the data elements consumed by an input port. For flexibility, such mapping functions must be user-definable, thus supporting arbitrary mappings. Each stream binding (i.e., output, input) port combination is associated with one such function. Conceptually, such a mapping can itself be viewed as a TVC-style dependency rule, applied to an 'invisible PE' that simply transforms the data output by the stream's source to the data elements consumed by the stream's sink. This mapping function captures the discrepancy arising out of either inexact matches between the data 'types' or different TE encapsulations at the transport layer.

Either approach allows us to separate the TVC provenance logic (which uniquely captures the internal data dependencies of an individual PE) from the data element conversion logic (which is a function of the data formats and encapsulation, rather than a PE's *processing* logic). However, an implementation of either approach must choose between proactive vs. reactive conversion: the mapping from output to input element granularity may be performed either proactively (when elements are transported within the runtime) or reactively (in response to data provenance queries). Both approaches involve tradeoffs between the processing load and the resulting complexity of the data storage system, and thus require further investigation.

4.1 Granularity Resolution in Current Century Implementation

Century's current implementation is based on the second solution, namely the use of 'mapping functions' that convert output elements transported by the SPC runtime to input elements consumed by downstream PEs. In SPC, data is transported within the runtime in units known as Stream Data Objects ($SDOs$)–each SDO thus corresponds to a single TE. The provenance (TVC) specifications are themselves defined in terms of the elements (which we call *Stream Elements (SEs)*) consumed by a PE. Note that an individual SDO can contain both multiple elements of the same type (e.g., a batch

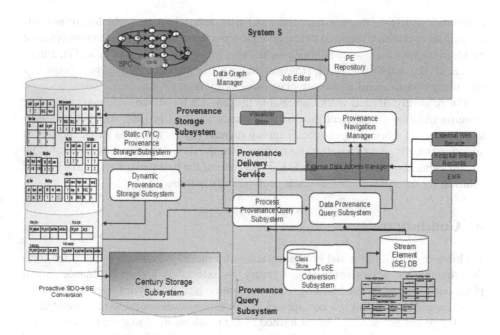

Fig. 6. Century's current TVC-based Provenance Architecture. Currently, provenance is tracked for a specified subset of PEs, and TEs are proactively converted to SEs prior to storage.

of ECG samples) or elements belonging to different data types (e.g., carry both 'QRS', 'ECG' and 'BP' data in the same SDO). Figure 6 shows the resulting component level architecture of Century's current provenance architecture design. To provide the needed SDO→SE conversion, Century currently requires the use of developer-specified 'conversion classes', stored in the class store.

5   Related Work

Provenance support for workflow-based systems has been investigated relatively recently, primarily in the context of scientific workflows. The Karma provenance framework [11] uses a publish-subscribe architecture for capturing and propagating process and data provenance for data-centric workflows in computational grids. Similarly, the PreServ provenance solution [9] provides a service for explicitly documenting and storing the process provenance in scientific experiments. More recently, the CoMaD provenance framework [4] for scientific applications presented an annotation-based approach reduces the volume of provenance information recorded for a workflow, by allowing provenance annotations on collections to cascade to child elements. All of these approaches involve explicit provenance annotations and are thus geared towards transactional systems, where events between workflow components have a much lower rate.

Data provenance has been explored more actively in the context of databases. The overview paper [15] classifies existing works into two categories, namely, the *annotation* [8,13] vs. the *non-annotation* [6] approaches, based on whether, or not, additional *meta-data* are required to compute the provenance of data. The data provenance problem without the use of annotations has also been studied by Cui et al. [7], Buneman et al. [5], and Widom [18]. However, none of the works mentioned here considers streaming environments or the associated scalability issues.

The relatively limited work on scalable provenance for stream-oriented computing systems includes an efficient *process* provenance solution in [16], which focuses on identifying and storing dependencies among streams (by encoding, as a tree, the IDs of ancestor streams of a derived stream), rather than the data dependencies for individual stream elements. Our earlier work in [17] was one of the first to explore a model-based solution for *data* provenance in stream computing platforms.

6   Conclusions

We have described the initial implementation of a model-based data provenance solution (using TVC primitives) within Century, an extensible, high-performance stream processing system we are building to support online health analytics over medical sensor streams. While a TVC based approach incurs much lower overhead than annotation-based approaches, its scalability is limited by the resulting need to store elements of *all data streams* in persistent storage. To overcome this practical limitation, we proposed a new provenance architecture, called *CMIR*, which implements model-based provenance over PE clusters, and uses data replay to recreate stream elements within the cluster. To support CMIR, the Provenance system has to implement new functions such as state persistence and recovery, cascaded replay of data streams and automated composition of provenance specifications for virtual PEs. This architecture also requires technical innovations for *a)* creating useful provenance primitives that are cascadable and reversible, and *b)* for mediating differences in the granularity of production and consumption of data stream elements. We are addressing these challenges in ongoing work.

References

1. Abadi, D., Carney, D., Çetintemel, U., Cherniack, M., Convey, C., Lee, S., Stonebraker, M., Tatbul, N., Zdonik, S.: Aurora: A New Model and Architecture for Data Stream Management. VLDB Journal 2(2), 120–139 (2003)
2. Amini, L., Andrade, H., Bhagwan, R., Eskesen, F., King, R., Selo, P., Park, Y., Venkatramani, C.: SPC: A Distributed, Scalable Platform for Data Mining. In: SIGKDD 2006 Workshop on Data Mining Standards, Services, and Platforms, pp. 27–37 (August 2006)
3. Blount, M., Davis II, J.S., Ebling, M., Kim, J.H., Kim, K.H., Lee, K., Misra, A., Park, S., Sow, D.M., Tak, Y.J., Wang, M., Witting, K.: Century:Automated Aspects of Patient Care. In: 13th IEEE International Conference on Embedded and Real-Time Computing Systems and Applications (RTCSA 2007) (August 2007)
4. Bowers, S., McPhillips, T., Ludascher, B.: Provenance in Collection-Oriented Scientific Workflows. Concurrency and Computation: Practice & Experience, special issue on the First Provenance Challenge (in press, 2007)

5. Buneman, P., Khanna, S., Tan, W.C.: On propagation of deletions and annotations through views. In: Proceedings of the ACM PODS Conference (2002)
6. Chiticariu, L., Tan, W.C.: Debugging Schema Mappings with Routes. In: Proceedings of the VLDB Conference (2006)
7. Cui, Y., Widom, J., Wiener, J.L.: Tracing the lineage of view data in a warehousing environment. ACM Trans. Database Syst. 25(2) (2000)
8. Geerts, F., Kementsietsidis, A., Milano, D.: MONDRIAN: Annotating and Querying Databases through Colors and Blocks. In: Proceedings of the International Conference on Data Engineering (ICDE) (2006)
9. Groth, P., Luck, M., Moreau, L.: A protocol for recording provenance in service-oriented grids. In: Higashino, T. (ed.) OPODIS 2004. LNCS, vol. 3544, pp. 124–139. Springer, Heidelberg (2005)
10. Hildrum, K., Douglis, F., Wolf, J.L., Yu, P.S., Fleischer, L., Katta, A.: Storage optimization for large-scale distributed stream-processing systems. ACM TOS 3(4), 1–28 (2008)
11. Simmhan, Y.L., Plale, B., Gannon, D., Marru, S.: Performance Evaluation of the Karma Provenance Framework for Scientific Workflows. In: International Provenance and Annotation Workshop (IPAW) (May 2006)
12. Sow, D., Lim, L., Wang, M., Kim, K.H.: Persisting and querying biometric event streams with hybrid relational XML DBMS. In: Proceedings of the International Conference on Distributed Event-Based Systems (DEBS), pp. 189–197 (June 2007)
13. Srivastava, D., Velegrakis, Y.: Intensional associations between data and metadata. In: Proceedings of the ACM SIGMOD Conference, pp. 401–412 (June 2007)
14. Sullivan, M., Heybey, A.: Tribeca: A System for Managing Large Databases of Network Traffic. In: Proceedings of the 1998 USENIX Annual Technical Conference (June 1998)
15. Tan, W.C.: Provenance in Databases: Past, Current, and Future. IEEE Data Eng. Bull. 30(4), 3–12 (2007)
16. Vijayakumar, N., Plale, B.: Towards Low Overhead Provenance Tracking in Near Real-Time Stream Filtering. In: International Provenance and Annotation Workshop, IPAW (May 2006)
17. Wang, M., Blount, M., Davis, J., Misra, A., Sow, D.: A Time-and-Value Centric Provenance Model and Architecture for Medical Event Streams. In: ACM HealthNet Workshop, pp. 95–100 (June 2007)
18. Widom, J.: Trio: A system for integrated management of data, accuracy, and lineage. In: Proceedings of CIDR (2005)

Using Provenance to Support Real-Time Collaborative Design of Workflows

Tommy Ellkvist[1], David Koop[2], Erik W. Anderson[2],
Juliana Freire[1,2], and Cláudio Silva[2]

[1] Linköpings universitet, Linköping, Sweden
[2] University of Utah, Salt Lake City, UT, USA

Abstract. Because designing workflows is a notoriously difficult task, it often requires multiple users to collaborate. In such scenarios, sharing workflow evolution provenance in a timely manner is critical. We present an environment where collaborating users can see each other's changes in real-time. The synchronization of workflow evolution provenance is automatic, immediate, and unobtrusive, allowing users to see collaborators' changes as they are made. This enables a richer and fuller method of collaboration. We present the interface and algorithm for the synchronization and discuss common scenarios where this mechanism has been utilized.

1 Introduction

Scientific workflows are often used as a means to create computational processes that solve complex scientific problems in diverse areas. The design of workflows in multi-disciplinary research areas such as bioinformatics and environmental modeling often requires cooperation between multiple experts in different geographic locations. Currently, there are few tools available to support the collaborative design of workflows. Users are often limited to exchanging workflow specifications over e-mail. This process can be slow and tedious. In some cases, it may be possible to divide the work in such a way that collaborators can work independently and then combine their work for a final result. However, this assumes that a modular design is possible; in reality, workflows are often created by trial and error with many inter-dependencies.

To support the collaborative design of workflows, we propose a mechanism that allows collaborators to simultaneously work on a task and see each others's changes in real-time. With a group of users who are working on the same task, the changes made by each user are automatically propogated to the rest of the group. Note that we *do not automatically merge* changes like version control systems. Rather, we display each change as a new branch of exploration and allow the user to switch between branches regardless of who created them. Using workflow evolution provenance, for example the change-based representation for a collection of workflows [3], we can visually display a tree containing all contributions. This lets collaborators share and receive updates in real-time, while

J. Freire, D. Koop, and L. Moreau (Eds.): IPAW 2008, LNCS 5272, pp. 266–279, 2008.

at the same time giving them the option to selectively ignore updates they do not care about. In this paper, we describe an architecture that supports this functionality. We present a new algorithm for synchronization and discuss how it can be used in practice.

2 Architecture

In order to support real-time collaborative design workflows, we need a provenance architecture that supports a collection of versioned workflows and a centralized provenance repository that all collaborators can access. We require a versioning system because each user needs to know how their collaborators' work relates to their own. More importantly, we need to protect the users' work; we should not blindly erase or update their own changes. A centralized repository is needed to manage all the workflows and to provide the means for notifying collaborators when changes occur. The combination of these two methods not only allows users to efficiently share collections of workflows, but also enables them to see the entire history of the workflow specifications as they develop in real-time, regardless of how many users collaborate on the project.

Workflow Evolution Provenance. Because we expect to encounter a large number of changes to a workflow specification, especially in a collaborative environment, it can be inefficient to store specifications for all different versions of the workflows. The change-based provenance model [3] provides a concise representation for workflow evolution history. This model captures the changes applied to a series of workflows, akin to a database transaction log. As a user modifies a workflow (e.g., by adding a module, changing a parameter or deleting a connection), the provenance mechanism transparently records each change action. We can then reconstruct any workflow specification by replaying the sequence of captured changes from an empty specification to the desired version.

The change-based model not only captures changes as a workflow evolves, but it also presents external changes to collaborators in a meaningful way. An important feature of this representation is that it can be visualized as a *version tree*, where each node corresponds to a workflow specification and each edge corresponds to the sequence of changes that transforms the parent specification into the child. Because the version tree captures *all* changes, users have great flexibility for exploring different alternatives without worrying about losing the ability to go back to a specific version. They can perform arbitrary undos and redos— any workflow version is easily recalled by selecting the corresponding node in the version tree. Additionally, users can easily see how their collaborators have taken different approaches to solving related problems and how their techniques relate to their own ideas. As discussed below, we leverage this layout to inform users of changes without forcing them to immediately consider or integrate those changes.

Centralized Repository. In order to efficiently capture and broadcast workflow changes, we use a relational database management system (RDBMS) for our centralized repository. We chose to use a RDBMS because these systems provide secure access protocols, support concurrent transactions from multiple users, and include trigger mechanisms for alerting users when the database is updated. These features are essential to ensure data consistency and to support real-times updates in our collaborative infrastructure. Other kinds of database systems that support these features could also be used in our infrastructure.

To use an RDBMS for our repository, we need to map the necessary provenance information to a relational schema. Because we use the change-based representation, a collection of related workflows is stored as a tree. This tree contains metadata and an ordered set of actions that correspond to user modifications to workflows. Each action, in turn, consists of a sequence of atomic operations. For example, a paste *action* that adds a set of modules and connections to an existing workflow contains a sequence of *operations*: add module, add connection, *etc.*. An operation, besides its data payload (e.g., module specification, connection specification, parameter value), includes metadata (e.g., the user who performed the action and annotations). Each of these entities (actions, operations, payloads) is stored in its own table, permitting a normalized (redundancy-free) representation. In addition to storing the changed-based representation of workflow evolution, the schema also supports explicit workflow specifications and workflow execution information. Execution information can be important when users are unfamiliar with the collection of workflows and wish to know which workflows are routinely used and which workflows were successfully executed.

3 Synchronized Design

One of the contributions of this paper is a new method for automatically capturing workflow changes performed by multiple users and alerting them about these changes immediately and unobtrusively. This allows users, in different geographically distributed locations, to collaboratively design and refine workflows, like in the scenario illustrated in Figure 1. We accomplish this by committing the local changes (performed by each individual user) to a centralized repository, sending the changes out from the repository to each collaborator, and adding the changes to each collaborator's local version tree. Note that we are not merging workflow specifications but synchronizing workflow evolution provenance. Each collaborator can continue their work and they need not even view the new changes. Before describing the implementation of our prototype, we describe the algorithm for synchronizing the version tree.

3.1 Algorithm

There are two key requirements for our algorithm. First, we need a way to save data from a local version tree to the centralized repository. Second, we need a way to load data from that repository to update the collaborators' local version trees. Below, we describe the mechanisms we developed to satisfy these requirements.

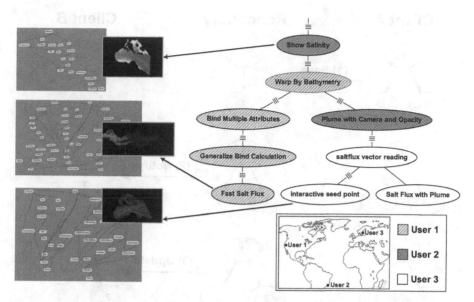

Fig. 1. A version tree containing a series of workflows that derive visualizations of the Columbia River Estuary. The visualizations have been created by collaborating users. Versions created by different users are represented using different colors.

Recall that the version tree is induced by a set of actions A. Each action $a \in A$ has a unique identifier derived by the function $id : A \rightarrow \mathbb{N}$, where id assigns the smallest unassigned integer to a new action. This function is trivially monotonic: given $a_1, a_2 \in A$,

$$id(a_1) < id(a_2) \iff a_1 \text{ was added before } a_2$$

We will leverage this property to easily determine what has changed in a given version tree. Specifically, let

$$N(A) = \max_{a_i \in V} id(a_i)$$

be the largest action id in a set of actions A. Then, for two sets of actions, $A_1 \subseteq A_2$, the set of new actions, ΔA, is

$$\Delta A = \{a \in A_2 \mid N(A_1) < id(a) \leq N(A_2)\}$$

This means that we can efficiently determine which actions a user requires to update his version tree. If a user has copied all of the actions in the database up to id N_D, then we only need to copy actions a_i with $id(a_i) > N_D$ from the database. Conversely, if a user has already saved all actions up to N_L to the database, only actions a_i with $id(a_i) > N_L$ need to be sent to the database. Figure 2 shows a simple example of the steps of the algorithm.

Relabeling. Determining the set of new actions is easy when one of the two sets being compared is a superset of the other. However, when multiple users are

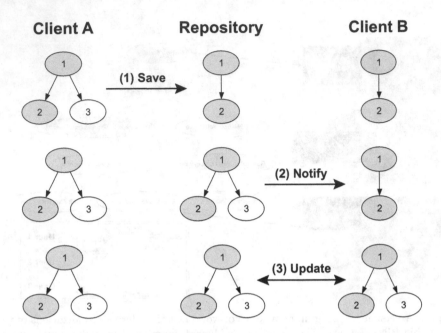

Fig. 2. The synchronization algorithm. Client A creates a new change (labeled as version 3). This new version is automatically saved to the repository (Step 1). Whenever the repository is updated, it notifies all clients of the new change (Step 2). All clients (including Client B) then incremenetally update themselves (Step 3).

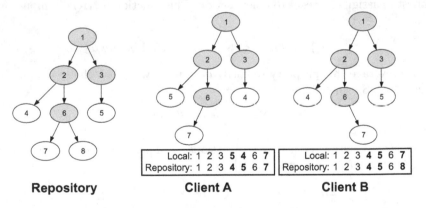

Fig. 3. Relabeling. Because two users may make updates at the same time or may temporarily lose their connections with the repository, the ids of their nodes may not correspond with the repository's ids. To solve this problem, each client stores the tree according to its own local ids and maintains a map to the repository's global ids.

collaborating, we might not be in this situation. Consider the scenario shown in Figure 3, where user A and user B made changes at the same time. Both clients will try to simultaneously save their actions to the database before being notified of the other's changes. In each of their local version trees, they both have actions with id 7, but these actions are not the same. Assuming A's request gets to the repository first, her action will be given id 7 while B's action will become id 8. Thus, after pushing out the other's updates, A and B will have the same tree except that the ids of the nodes may differ.

Since an update of the ids in the local version tree might interfere with a user's current work, we choose to maintain a set of local ids that can be mapped to the global repository ids. Specifically, we maintain a bijective map

$$M : id_{global} \leftrightarrow id_{local}$$

Let M_{local} denote the reverse mapping from global to local and M_{global} denote the forward mapping from local to global. All user operations will be accomplished using the local ids, but whenever we need to save to the centralized repository, we translate everything to the global set of ids. Figure 3 shows an example of this relabeling.

Beyond Actions. As described earlier, an action contains metadata and a set of atomic operations. The metadata and the atomic operations, in turn, contain their own ids and may also include references to other entities. Thus, the relabeling of an action needs to update these references as well. For example, each action stores both its own id (*action.id*) and its parent id (*action.prev_id*). If we update the id of the action referenced by *action.prev_id*, we also need to update the *prev_id* field. The same is true for child objects. Suppose the connection in an **add connection** operation references the two modules it connects by id. If we remap the id of one or both of those modules in an **add module** operation, we need to update the ids in the **add connection** operation as well. This requires an ordering that respects the properties being updated; we impose an explicit order on modules and connections so that all modules are relabeled before connections to ensure all references are updated.

Algorithm Specifics. We combine the method for determining new actions with our relabeling strategy to obtain robust algorithms for incrementally

---

Algorithm 1: Incremental Load Algorithm
Input: The local version tree V, id_V (the id function for V), the global-to-local id map M, and the centralized repository D.
Output: None. It updates both V and M in place.
LOAD(V, id_V, M, D)
(1) $max\_id \leftarrow$ Query V for the maximum id
(2) $A \leftarrow$ Query D for all actions with id $> max\_id$
(3)   **foreach** a in A:
(4)   Create a', a local copy of a
(5) $a'.id \leftarrow id_V(a)$
(6) $a'.prev\_id \leftarrow M_{local}(a.prev\_id)$
(7)   Add pair $(a.id, a'.id)$ to M
(8)   Add a' to V

Algorithm 2: Incremental Save Algorithm
Input: The local version tree V, id_D (the id function for D), the global-to-local id map M, and the centralized repository D.
Output: None. It updates both V and M in place.
STORE(V, id_D, M, D)
(1) $max\_id \leftarrow$ Query D for the maximum id
(2) $A \leftarrow$ Query V for all actions with id $> max\_id$
(3)   **foreach** a **in** A:
(4)   Create a', a global copy of a
(5) $a'.id \leftarrow id_D(a)$
(6) $a'.prev\_id \leftarrow M_{global}(a.prev\_id)$
(7)   Add pair $(a'.id, a.id)$ to M
(8)   Add a' to D

loading from and saving to a database. Algorithm 1 describes the loading algorithm and Algorithm 2 summarizes the saving algorithm. In each algorithm, we use either the database or local version tree to update the other depending on the direction, ensuring that new ids are assigned, existing ids are remapped, and the global-to-local mapping M is updated. Note that all entities are updated in place, copying only the (new) required information from one side to the other.

3.2   Implementation

We have implemented the synchronization mechanism on top of the VisTrails system (http://www.vistrails.org). The implementation consists of a client/server architecture shown in Figure 2. The server-side is a MySQL database that stores version trees. Users can create synchronization sessions through the user interface (see below). The standard VisTrails database schema has been extended to store information about synchronized sessions. This information includes the ids of synchronized version trees, user ids, IP addresses, and port numbers. A database trigger uses this information to notify clients when relevant updates are available. The notification is done by an external MySQL function that uses a socket to connect to the client. The message to the client includes the version tree id number so that the client can request the updates for that version tree. Note that messages about changes to a given version tree are sent to all users using that version tree, except to the user whose changes activated the trigger.

The client-side application is a modified version of VisTrails; the modifications include code for performing incremental updates and saves against the database and for receiving notification messages from the database. Because the system contains a controller object for each version tree, we use it to monitor these notifications and start update procedures. Because the controller is linked to the GUI, we also need to redraw the version tree whenever synchronization modifies the tree.

To setup synchronization, users need to select (or create a database) to serve as a centralized repository. This database must have the schema as outlined above and the synchronization triggers that send the update notifications. Once the database is in place, users connect to the database and select the version trees they want to share. After that, the synchronization (sync) mode can be enabled with the push of a button. From that point on, the version tree will be kept in sync with the central repository and the other users. To help distinguish between versions, those created by other users are shown in blue while a user's own versions are highlighted in orange.

3.3   Issues

Mutable Objects. The monotonicity of the version tree is required for the synchronization process. Change actions and operations are immutable: they are never modified after they are stored in the repository. Thus, the system only needs to check for *new* objects in order to perform synchronization. There are, however, *mutable* objects associated with actions for which this optimization cannot be applied. For example, VisTrails has *version tags* and *version annotations* associated with workflows that can be modified, and these modifications are not saved as actions. Version tags assign text labels to workflow versions while version annotations store general notes about the version. Because changes to these objects are non-monotonic (and destructive), *all* objects must be saved and loaded during each incremental load/save. Locally, we can keep a flag that indicates whether or not the entity changed so that we only need to save it when it does, but the same cannot be done for the global repository. Nonetheless, since the volume of mutable data is small, we copy all instances during an incremental load.

Integrating Changes. One nice feature of our synchronization framework is that it does not require the user to integrate another user's changes. However, consider the situation where two users (A and B) are working on a similar problem, and they have attacked different pieces of it from a common starting point. Each has seen that the other has made changes, but they wanted to finish their own piece. Later, when they decide to integrate these changes, user A can switch to B's version and make the changes applied in her own version. A more efficient alternative would be for user A to use the *analogies* mechanism [10] implemented in VisTrails to automatically apply the changes from one branch to another.

Local Parameters. Workflows may not always have the same meaning to all users, and they may disagree about certain parameter settings or methods used. For example, an input filename parameter may differ between two users because the users store the file in different disk locations. Currently, the only way to deal with such local parameter settings is to create a different version for each set of parameters. This means that a change in one user workflow will not propagate to the other version, which is not desirable. A solution to this problem could be to separate the shared workflow from the local settings creating a division of the workflow in some way.

Data Sharing. The ability to share data is an important part of collaboration. For workflows, you may want to share output data as well as input and intermediate results. This can be done with a data pool which maintains up-to-date data items created by the users. This would make it possible for users not only to see each other's results, but also use the data as inputs to other workflows. The COVISA project[12] implements this kind of data sharing. Users can exchange data and directly use them in their pipelines. Another system that implements the idea of a data pool is the *Data Playground*[4]. The Data Playground provides a workflow editor that is highly data centric, letting users view and import data while they compose workflows that in turn create new data items. This gives the users control over their data while they experiment with different data manipulation operations. The prototype only works for one user but it shows how a data centric view can be used in collaborative workflow design.

Module Packages. A requirement for users to be able to share workflow specifications is that they both use the same repository of module packages. Module packages contain sets of modules that perform similar functions, much like web services. If one collaborator is missing a module, a workflow containing that module can not be executed. For collaborations that require many different packages and libraries, an effective mechanism is needed for sharing. For example, through the use of public repositories or automatic methods for users to import module packages from other users as they are required. The packages are often platform specific and versioned, so finding the right package is not trivial. This requires packages to use a good version scheme, with possibly backward-compatible packages. There also needs to exist different versions for different platforms so that the users platform can be identified and the correct package used. Another way to handle module sharing is to use shared computing infrastructure, such as the TeraGrid (http://www.teragrid.org), which can provide a comprehensive set of packages.

3.4   Discussion

While there are many systems that provide mechanisms to deal with the difficulties associated with the collaborative modification of files, they are not built to handle structured information like workflows. For this reason, many workflow systems lack comprehensive version control for their workflow specifications.

Many systems have been developed with the singular purpose of providing version control. Software such as SVN [8], CVS [1], and Visual Source Safe [7] are optimized to robustly handle the version control requirements associated with source code. Unfortunately, when dealing with workflow descriptions, the standard merge operations common to text files are inadequate and require specialized processing. A second issue is that these systems require users to *manually* perform check-ins and check-outs in order to synchronize versions. Finally, users are often required to merge their changes with older changes, making it more difficult to explore new directions.

We address the shortfalls of standard version control with our method based on synchronizing workflow evolution provenance. Using this approach, workflow descriptions can be analyzed and modified to provide a truly multi-user, collaborative environment, in real time. These modifications provide the basis for version control of rapidly evolving, collaboratively created workflows. The intuitive system allows closer collaboration between users by immediately alerting all users of each other's changes.

4   Use Cases

Collaboration between two or more parties plays an important role in scientific discovery and in education. By carefully examining the working process of existing collaborative research projects, we have been able to design a system that not only respects individual working habits, but also strengthens and enhances the interaction among multiple users engaged in collaborative efforts. Here, we explore the benefits of real-time, synchronous collaborative workflow design.

Collaborative Design as a Teaching Aid. Many institutions of higher education offer a wide range of courses that utilize workflow systems. For example, in Scientific Visualization courses, the Visualization Toolkit [6] (VTK) is widely used to teach different visualization techniques to the students. Instructors use VTK to introduce various topics to the students *by example*, while the students use the library to explore the advantages and caveats associated with the various techniques they learn.

A first experience in using VisTrails to encapsulate VTK pipelines used in a Scientific Visualization course was very successful and showed that the reproducibility and sharing enabled by provenance is very beneficial in a teaching environment. However, even when using a provenance-aware system, a large amount of work was necessary to assist students with the various assignments. In these cases, the Teaching Assistant (TA) had to meet individually with each student to help solve the problems they had.

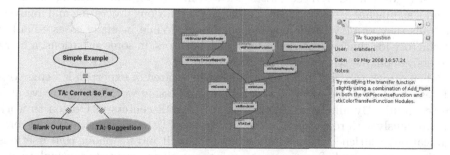

Fig. 4. An example of a TA session. The TA can highlight interesting versions in the students version tree as well as create new versions that explain some part of the workflow design.

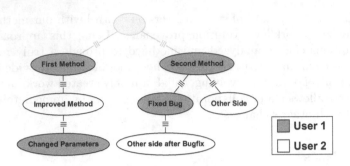

Fig. 5. An example of collaborative design. Here, two persons have built on each others workflow specifications, leading to incrementally better results.

By providing TA's with a system capable of synchronous, collaborative design of workflows, the time necessary to assist students can be greatly reduced. Instead of the students relying on restrictive office hours to get face-to-face help, they are able to get assistance from the TA as they work from their workstation (see Figure 4). This decreases the amount of time the students need to spend waiting for help and allows the TA to interactively explain the reason the student's workflow was incorrect. Coupled with an instant messaging (IM) program, this collaborative session greatly increases the number of people the TA is capable of helping in a given amount of time.

Collaborative Design in Multi-disciplinary Research. In today's scientific community, it is rarely the case that novel scientific discoveries can be made by a single person. Unfortunately, in many instances of close collaboration, the various domain experts are unable to work in the same location. These types of relationships benefit greatly from the ability to concurrently modify a given workflow description.

An example of the advantages gained from collaboratively designed workflows can be seen in collaborations between the authors at the University of Utah and researchers at the Center for Coastal Margin Observation and Prediction (CMOP).[1] CMOP scientists, located in Oregon and Washington, often spend a significant amount of time describing the various processing and analysis methods they employ to understand their data. While in many cases e-mail is satisfactory for sharing knowledge with collaborators, in some situations, a more immersive collaborative workspace is required.

When a task relating to a specific researcher's area of expertise is being considered, it is often necessary to synchronize processing workflows to arrive at a desired result. By allowing scientists at the CMOP centers in Oregon to work synchronously with researchers at the University of Utah, the critical task of communication is enriched. Instead of relying on e-mail and telephone conversations to ask important, and often time-consuming, questions, scientists can explore *and fix* each others processing and parameterization errors in real-time. This degree

---

[1] http://www.stccmop.org

of collaborative design reduces the number and severity of communication-based misunderstandings as well as increases the level of productivity of everyone involved in the project.

5 Related Work

This paper presents, to the best of our knowledge, the first proposal for an infrastructure that supports real-time collaborative workflow design.

There are existing mechanisms that can be used for collaborative design of workflows. One of the most general and common methods of real-time collaboration is through remote desktops like VNC [9]. By using this in the design of a workflow, users can see each others operations like dragging modules around and creating connections. But for more efficient modes of interaction, both users need to be in control simultaneously, and be able to choose whether to take notice of other users activities. In addition, provenance information would be lost, since it would not be possible to distinguish changes performed by different users.

A related area is that of collaborative visualization such as the COVISA project[12] and NoCoV [11]. COVISA enables several modes of collaboration like sharing data, sharing control of parameters and instructor driven collaboration where one user is in control of another user's pipeline. NoCoV enables users to collaboratively edit a pipeline consisting of instances of *Notification Web Services*. Both of these systems enables collaboration in the creation of the visualization pipeline but they do not support the exchange or existence of different versions of the pipeline.

The use of real-time collaboration has been explored in other areas. *Co-browsing* [2] enables multiple people to browse the by sharing a Web browser view and following links together. Similar to VNC, co-browsing is useful when a user wants to guide another through a browsing session. However, unlike VNC where the whole desktop is shared, in co-browsing users only share a browser view. Co-browsing can thus be more efficient, since only clicks withing a browser view need to be propagated to the users.

A more indirect way of sharing workflows is through public repositories, like myExperiment [5] and Yahoo! Pipes [13], that have become available recently. These repositories foster the re-use of knowledge. They provide search interfaces that allow the users to locate workflows that solve a particular task, and then integrate these workflows into their own. The synchronization infrastructure we propose could potentially be a useful feature offered by these sites.

6 Conclusion

In this paper, we described an infrastructure that supports real-time collaborative design of workflows. This infrastructure can be integrated with any workflow system that captures workflow evolution provenance. Our implementation of the synchronization mechanism on top of the VisTrails system shows that workflow systems can be a powerful tool for real-time collaboration. Users can collaborate efficiently and effectively, exploring different branches and taking advantage of each other's progress. Together with techniques for data sharing and remote execution, this enables efficient creation of complex workflows.

By leveraging the concise representation of workflows provided by the change-based provenance model, synchronization is efficient: only incremental changes need to be propagated to collaborating users. However, further experiments are needed to assess the scalability of the current implementation.

We believe that our provenance-based synchronization mechanism can be applied to applications other than workflows. Combined with techniques to visualize provenance information, this mechanism can serve as a powerful platform for collaborative design in general. Users can share their work effectively while inspecting each other's contributions. The application of our synchronization infrastructure in other areas of computational design is a direction we plan to pursue in future work.

Acknowledgements

Our research has been funded by the Department of Energy SciDAC (VACET and SDM centers), the National Science Foundation (grants IIS-0746500, CNS-0751152, IIS-0713637, OCE-0424602, IIS-0534628, CNS-0514485, IIS-0513692, CNS-0524096, CCF-0401498, OISE-0405402, CCF-0528201, CNS-0551724), and IBM Faculty Awards (2005, 2006, 2007, and 2008).

References

1. Cederqvist, P., et al.: Version Management with CVS, for CVS 1.11.6 (1993)
2. Esenther, A.: Instant co-browsing: Lightweight real-time collaborative web browsing (2002)
3. Freire, J., Silva, C.T., Callahan, S.P., Santos, E., Scheidegger, C.E., Vo, H.T.: Managing rapidly-evolving scientific workflows. In: Moreau, L., Foster, I. (eds.) IPAW 2006. LNCS, vol. 4145, pp. 10–18. Springer, Heidelberg (2006)
4. Gibson, A., Gamble, M., Wolstencroft, K., Oinn, T., Goble, C.: The data playground: An intuitive workflow specification environment. In: E-SCIENCE 2007: Proceedings of the Third IEEE International Conference on e-Science and Grid Computing, Washington, DC, USA, pp. 59–68. IEEE Computer Society, Los Alamitos (2007)
5. Goble, C.A., Roure, D.C.D.: Myexperiment: social networking for workflow-using e-scientists. In: WORKS 2007: Proceedings of the 2nd workshop on Workflows in support of large-scale science, pp. 1–2. ACM, New York (2007)
6. Kitware. The visualization toolkit (VTK), http://www.kitware.com
7. Microsoft Corporation. Managing projects with Visual SourceSafe. Redmond, Washington (1997)
8. Pilato, M.C., Collins-Sussman, B., Fitzpatrick, B.W.: Version Control with Subversion. O'Reilly Media, Inc., Sebastopol (2004)
9. Richardson, T., Stafford-Fraser, Q., Wood, K.R., Hopper, A.: Virtual network computing. IEEE Internet Computing 2(1), 33–38 (1998)

10. Scheidegger, C.E., Vo, H.T., Koop, D., Freire, J., Silva, C.T.: Querying and creating visualizations by analogy. IEEE Transactions on Visualization and Computer Graphics 13(6), 1560–1567 (2007)
11. Wang, H., Brodlie, K., Handley, J., Wood, J.: Service-oriented approach to collaborative visualization. In: Proceedings of UK e-Science All Hands Meeting 2006, pp. 241–248. National e-Science Centre (2006)
12. Wood, J., Wright, H., Brodlie, K.: Collaborative visualization. In: VIS 1997: Proceedings of the 8th conference on Visualization 1997, p. 253. IEEE Computer Society Press, Los Alamitos (1997)
13. Yahoo! Pipes (March 10, 2008), http://pipes.yahoo.com

Provenance in Sensornet Republishing

Unkyu Park and John Heidemann

Information Sciences Institute
University of Southern California
{ukpark,johnh}@isi.edu

Abstract. Sensornets are being deployed and increasingly brought on-line to share data as it is collected. Sensornet *republishing* is the process of transforming on-line sensor data and sharing the filtered, aggregated, or improved data with others. We explore the need for data provenance in this system to allow users to understand how processed results are derived and detect and correct anomalies. We describe our sensornet provenance system, exploring design alternatives and quantifying storage trade-offs in the context of a city-sized temperature monitoring application. In that application, our link approach outperforms other alternatives on saving storage requirement and our *incremental compression* scheme save the storage further up to 83%.

1   Introduction

Sensor networks have been proposed and deployed for study of scientific phenomena with levels of detail that was previously impossible [10, 12, 23, 25]. Research groups are using sensornets to study microclimates, animal habitats, or geology. To date, these deployments are undertaken by different research groups each to accomplish a specific objective. While many make their data available, reuse of data remains rare, and collaboration across multiple sensornets rarer still.

As sensornets become easier and more widely deployed, sharing data *across* sensors becomes increasingly important [20]. Several groups have recently begun exploring the role of the Internet in sharing sensor data [17, 20, 21], both to interconnect isolated sensornet patches, and to lower the barrier to sharing sensor data. In the limit, we see a world of *slogging* (sensor logging), where thousands of individual sensors each connect to the Internet to share data, analogous to how blogs share discourse. For example, WeatherUnderground.com allows "citizen scientists" to publish local weather conditions [13], while Sensorbase [7] and SensorWeb [21] provide frameworks for sharing sensor data, and for visualizing sensors and aggregates.

While individual sensors are sometimes of interest, the data becomes much more compelling when it is aggregated and processed. More than just visualizing individual sensors, we see a rich world where sensor values can be checked against each other, filtered, corrected, combined and divided, and indexed, not just by the sensor owners but potentially by anyone with access to the data.

Republishing is this process of transforming sensor data, and it can involve multiple steps and different users. As sensor sharing grows and republishing becomes more complex, tracking data back to its source is increasingly important. Understanding data

J. Freire, D. Koop, and L. Moreau (Eds.): IPAW 2008, LNCS 5272, pp. 280–292, 2008.

flow is important to track the evolution of data, to discover duplicate or supplementary data sources, to give credit and confidence to data sources for indexing, to interpret data properly and reproduce results, to uncover the causes of anomalies, and to troubleshoot and improve the transformation process.

Tracking data transformation is well established in scientific workflow and databases; in this paper, we propose *data provenance for sensornet republishing* which allows users to locate where the sensor data come from and to further identify how they are processed. We propose a novel, tuple-level linking scheme that tracks sensornet data as it is processed and republished (Section 3). To support fine-grain, tuple-level tracking, we compare several compression schemes in Section 4, showing that our *incremental compression* scheme saves the storage up to 83%. We also describe how our approach can support user-centric access control. We have implemented our approach and are evaluating it in the context of weather monitoring in West Los Angeles (Section 5).

2 Related Work

Sensornet/Internet Interaction: Several research efforts are exploring how sensornets and the Internet can interact [3, 11, 18, 20, 26]. We previously proposed an architecture to support sensornet sharing over the Internet [20]; this prior work is distinguished by the concept of *slogging*, the loose collaboration of many individually managed sensors; and by *republishing*, the idea that data will be processed and reprocessed in the Internet by different parties. In this paper we extend this prior work to explore how data provenance functions in the context of republishing.

Scientific Workflow: Data provenance is important in the field of scientific workflow. Close to our work is Kepler [1], supporting access and analysis of distributed, heterogeneous scientific data [14]. Many techniques have been proposed to support data provenance in scientific workflow, although details vary depending on the scientific domains [22].

Data provenance in sensornets differs from scientific workflow in several ways. First, data is often static in scientific workflow, or treated as static snapshots. Sensornets and our republishing instead focus on live data feeds and streaming processing; so our system for provenance must explicitly record the status of the changing stream. Second, ownership and access are often handled out-of-band in scientific workflow. We instead assume many users and so must integrate easy-to-use disclosure management with our provenance system. Similarly, scientific workflow can often make assumptions about storage of data in a local or shared file system; we instead assume data is located anywhere on the Internet with a web services-like protocol. Lastly, computations in scientific workflow are often quite heavyweight, often involving large supercomputers and taking hours or even weeks per job. We see sensornet republishing as usually very lightweight, so the cost of providing data provenance must scale accordingly.

Databases: Several researchers have considered provenance in the context of relational databases [5, 6, 9]. While we draw inspiration from their prior work, sensornets place several additional requirements on provenance. First, research efforts in databases mainly focus on capturing SQL-based transformations [24]; we instead wish to support transformations in republishing that include arbitrary, external programs not strictly described by SQL. We therefore capture the version of source code (or executable program) used in the transformation as part of our provenance scheme (Section 3.3). Second, database work in the area typically concentrates on provenance for a single database with centralized administrative control, while we assume a distributed environment with many data providers. In addition, the need to support distributed republishing motivates our plans for data disclosure management (Section 3.4). Lastly, databases support addition, deletion and update of information, but data provenance can be computed only for the current state of tables. Sensornets, on the other hand, rarely delete or update collected data, but constantly add new sensor data from live sensors and corresponding republishers. Assuming that data are inserted only, our provenance system can reconstruct old snapshots of the data by maintaining an explicit timestamp on provenance information. Therefore, we can trace the provenance of old results (Section 3.2).

Provenance Model: Recently community of data provenance researchers has begun to standardize provenance models. The Open Provenance Model (OPM) is proposed for provenance information to be interoperable via a compatibility layer [16]. It represents a provenance information with three entities and five types of dependencies among them. Our provenance approach records two basic provenance relationships; the derivation between republished data to source data and transformation of republished data (Section 3.2). These are a subset of OPM relationships, so our model can easily be converted to OPM if desired.

Our work goes beyond OPM, though, by considering the access control and disclosure of data and provenance information. We support user authorization for data sources and transformations through provenance tracking (Section 3.4). Separate steps of provenance chain can therefore have different privacy and permissions controls, and the global view of a provenance chain may vary according to the user's permissions in different data repositories.

Currently we provide basic provenance queries to locate sources of data and transformations applied to the data. These are relatively primitive compared to ones used in the Provenance Challenges [15]. We are planning to provide more sophisticated provenance queries through a sensornet search engine.

3   Data Provenance in Sensornet Republishing

We describe the definition and goals of data provenance in sensornets and how we can achieve those goals.

Our work builds on our model of sensornet sharing [20]. We assume many users independently maintain sensors, each attached to the Internet (perhaps indirectly over a wireless edge network). Analogous to blog hosting sites, these sensors *slog*, publishing data to one of many centralized *sensor stores*.

Users can also schedule computation to run on other Internet-attached computers; these *republishers* read data from a sensor store, compute some result (such as aggregation, statistics, interpretation, etc.), and then publish the data back to some other sensor store. As a special case of republishers, sensor search engines index data. We show the *publishing* and *republishing* examples in Section 5.1.

3.1 Definition and Goals of Sensornet Provenance

Data provenance is well established in many scientific domains; however the definition of provenance varies depending on the scientific domain [22]. In sensornet republishing, we define data provenance as information of the source and the transformation applied to the source. We explore our approaches to data provenance below (Section 3.2). The core of our sensornet provenance is a linkage between republished data and its source. In this paper we use this link to locate the sensor data stored in our sensor stores, but in principle it can also track any resource provided as a web service (Section 4.1).

The ultimate goal of sensornet republishing is to allow users to process and share transformed data. Data provenance should allow any end-user to follow back to the original source data, observing each step of processing. As in scientific workflow, provenance is useful for validation, both to assist in debugging a republisher and to confirm faulty source data.

Sensornet republishing and slogging also need to be able to assign "credit" for data generation and processing [8]; we expect provenance to help with this process. Collaborative processing systems from SETI@home [4] to Wikipedia and blogging all benefit because data generators can observe who uses their data; we are seeking to recreate this ecosystem for sensor data [20].

More than just encouragement, we seek to reproduce a link structure in sensornet data that mirrors the link structure in the web, with the intent that we can harvest this link structure to identify high quality sensor data, much as PageRank exploits links in the web [19].

Finally, data provenance provides attribution information that is useful in slogging to inform data disclosure. We expand on access control in Section 3.4.

3.2 Approaches to Provenance for Sensornet Republishing

We describe our approaches for sensornet provenance: what and how to record for provenance (annotation vs. inversion; content vs. link), provenance granularity (tuple- vs. table-level), and timestamping to handle changing streams of data.

Representation. There are two approaches to represent data provenance: annotation and inversion [22]. Annotation keeps the provenance information explicitly as metadata; on the other hand, inversion keeps the property of inverted transformation to find the source of derived data. The inversion is attractive if processing can be inverted to find the source of republished data, because it needs to keep only a single inversion function for the provenance. However our processing for sensor-data is arbitrary and cannot, in general, be inverted. We therefore choose *annotation* for sensornet provenance.

Given annotations, the annotation can either consist of a copy of source data, or a link to it and the transformation function. For small data items, copying source data to the republisher may be efficient. However, in some cases source data may be large, particularly for images, video, or audio. Thus a link to the source data is a good choice, because it is independent to the size of source data. In addition, over several steps, copying will accumulate many layers of data while linking is fixed in cost.

An additional advantages of linking is that a user following the provenance can discover not only the source data, but subsequent data generated later by the same source. It is also easy to trace back through multiple levels of republishings. This advantage is of particularly importance in streaming sensornet data where there is often new data, and where we wish to encourage repeated republishing.

Granularity. How much detail of data provenance should be provided for sensor republishing? Coarse-grained provenance keeps one record per transformation or republishing. It is useful to figure out the overview of the processing, but is not enough for tracking data tuples. Instead we provide fine-grained provenance – each tuple has its provenance – which can pin down the source data used for each republished data. However, a problem of fine-grained provenance is storage. The storage of fine-grained provenance increases according to the number of data while that of coarse-grained provenance does not. We provide fine-grained provenance while its provenance storage is managed to be small with our compression scheme. The details of compression scheme is described in Section 4.2.

Consistency. Sensornet data is often streaming, with new data arriving periodically. To truly reproduce a data transformation, data provenance must not only connect to a particular sensor, but also to a particular period of source data at that sensor.

Transformations are often expressed via user computations that are relative (for example, return the most recent five sensor readings). Provenance using this exact information would track a changing result as "most recent" changes when the sensor generates new data.

To manage changing data streams with potentially relative user queries, we embedded a timestamp with each data provenance record. This timestamp ties a query to a specific set of data at the source sensor store, regardless of when the link is later followed. Moreover, this timestamp approach supports data deletion. We soft-delete tuples by recording time of detection, allowing resolution of post-deletion references. The more details about the link are described in Section 4.1.

3.3   Tracking the Transformation

As we described in previous section, sensornet provenance allows users of the republished data to locate the source data for a transformation. Input data alone, however, does not fully define provenance. Data in our system is modified arbitrarily by some republisher—an arbitrary program running on some computer in the Internet.

To capture the republisher, we store transformation resource which includes a general description of republishing, source codes, and executable programs. We define transformation identifier to locate these transformation resources on the Internet (Section 4.1).

Our approach to tracking transformations has following benefits. First, it provides details transformations on every republished data. We store a simple identifier on every republished data as we do with the source data location; the specific transformation resource can be located by looking the identifier. Second, it is easy to distinguish data that are processed by different transformations. Because each transformation uses a unique identifier, the republished data can be grouped or selected according to transformations without looking the actual transformation resources.

3.4   Data Disclosure for Provenance

Our security model for sensor data allows the data generator to control data access. Data may be made publicly available, or access may be granted to individuals on a case-by-case basis [7]. This security model interacts with link-based data provenance because links may refer to data that a link-follower may not be able to access. To ease data disclosure, we integrate support for adjusting data disclosure into our data provenance system. When a user resolving a provenance encounters an access limitation, we generate a "letter of reference" about that user to pass to the data owner. This letter includes context about that user's activities, collaboration with other projects, other sharing activities, and how the user encountered the provider's data. He or she may then annotate or edit this information before sending it to the data owner who is responsible for controlling direct access to the source data. Our hope is that this information provides context to inform the owner of the data source, while the mechanism allows the requester to control what information they disclose.

4   Implementation

We have a prototype implementation of data provenance for sensornets. We use sensorbase.org [7] as our sensor store, and extend it to provide predecessor links. When a user creates a new table, we automatically create an additional column to store data provenance. We also have extended the sensorbase user interface to display data provenance; clicking on a predecessor link takes the user to the source data. APIs exist to extract this information and the transformation program. We use the existing sensorbase privacy model, and are in the process of automating support for data disclosure (Section 3.4).

We provide a PHP-based library that encapsulates this functionality and makes it easy for users to write republishers. We expect to provide bindings in other languages as well.

4.1   Predecessor Link

Our approach to data provenance in sensorbase provides exactly the information needed to track from derived data to its source data, potentially in another sensor store. As described in Section 3.1, we need the location of the source repository and table at that repository, the search used to retrieve the data from that table, and a timestamp to fix any temporarily relative portions of the query.

We encode this information into a URI-compatible link, the *predecessor link*, and use Web Services to access sensorbase [2]. The template of predecessor link is shown in Table 1. In a link, we directly encode the SQL-based search query, and any search parameters as arguments. We add a UTC-based timestamp corresponding to the query time,

Table 1. Predecessor Link Template

sb://<location of wsdl>?s=<service name>&a1=<arg 1>...an=<arg n>&t=<timestamp>&x=<xid>	
<location of wsdl>	This is the url of wsdl file which has the web service description. (message format, available service and etc) The actual url of wsdl is "http://<location of wsdl>"
<service name>	This indicates the service name to get the data. Currently we have a "getData" service to retrieve the data.
<arg 1>...<arg n>	These are arguments for the service. the "getData" service takes five arguments which are "attributes", "tables","condition", "from" and "delta".
<timestamp>	The timestamp of the link is created.('YYYY-MM-DD HH:MM:SS' UTC)
<xid>	The identifier of program doing transformation (a url) on-site identifier format : http://⟨sensorbase⟩/transformation _view.php?project=<no>&program=<name>&version=<version>

allowing us to replay a relative query later while producing the same result (Section 3.2). We add the user's ID and password at link resolution time, allowing the data provider to control access by requiring each user to authenticate separately (Section 3.4). Finally, in addition to the information locating the source data, we identify the transformation program (Section 3.3).

A sample predecessor link is: sb://sensorbase.org/soap/sensorbase2.wsdl? s=getData&a1="datetime,temperature"&a2=p_97_temperature&a3='sensor id="sum-in"'&a4=0&a5=1&t="2008-02-24 12:00:00"&x="http://www.isi.e du/ilense/siss/tempread.html" which locates temperature data used in a repub-lishing. In this link, the user retrieves the *datetime* and *temperature* fields from the "sum-in" sensor. To deference this link, a user's system will retrieve the WSDL file (http://sensorbase.org/soap/sensorbase2.wsdl), and invoke the *getData* ser-vice with the five arguments (a1 through a5). The link also indicates when it was created and which program used the source data.

It is worth to note that transformation identifier is a URL which can represent the location of program, source code, or webpage describing the transformation. It is com-pletely possible that identifier points off-site resource located shown in above sample link. However, we provide a on-site resource management for accessing the transforma-tion resources on the sensorbase more efficiently. For example, an on-site identifier such as http://sum.isi.edu/sb/transformation_view.php?project=97&transfo rmation=tempread&version=0.4 indicates a program called *tempread* and its ver-sion is *0.4* which is used in project no *97*. The web interface shows not only the specific program used in the transformation but also other versions of that.

4.2   Incremental Compression

While self contained and easy to manage with existing tools, the links we described above are quite verbose and redundant. If used directly, link size would quickly over-whelm small sensor data and dominate storage consumption. We therefore employ *pe-riodic incremental link compression* to provide simple link definition with reasonable storage cost. We quantify storage costs in Section 5.3 and consider compression ap-proaches here.

Our goal in link compression is to take advantage of redundancy in repeated links. Often only a few parameters will vary, perhaps just query time. We considered at several alternatives: per-link compression, complete compression and periodic incremental compression. We chose periodic incremental compression to balance read and write cost.

A naive approach would be the *per-link compression*, where each link is passed through a conventional compression algorithm independently. While very simple to manage, this approach does not take advantage of the redundancy across links since that requires a compression dictionary that spans multiple links.

The *complete compression*, to exploit the redundancy across links, we maintain the compression dictionary over many links. An easy way of maintaining the pattern history is keeping it as an external file, although current dictionaries are optimized for run-time and not storage efficiency, so overall this approach consumes considerable fixed storage. Alternatively, we can rebuild the dictionary on-the-fly when it is needed. This approach requires additional run-time each link update, but it requires neither an additional storage nor maintenance of explicit history. The disadvantage with complete compression are the dictionary run-time cost is proportional to the number of saved data items, and loss of any item will invalidate the dictionary, requiring recomputation to rebuild all subsequent compressed links.

The system we adopt is *periodic incremental compression*—we avoid complete history by periodically checkpointing and restarting compression. This approach is robust to tuple loss and limits the computational cost of updates. We implemented periodic incremental compression with the widely-used LZW compression algorithm. Although subsequent compression algorithms (such as those in gzip and bzip2) improve performance somewhat, LZW provided good tradeoff between compression and ease of implementation. We evaluate our periodic incremental compression compared to other alternatives in Section 5.3.

5   Evaluation

We next consider several ways to evaluate our provenance system. Ultimately, we would like to show that sensornet provenance is useful to users. Such demonstration requires an extended period of use; at this point we can only summarize our use of it in one application with three stages of republishing (Section 5.1). We then focus on two design questions: first we compare the storage costs of different provenance approaches (Section 5.2), then we look at tradeoffs in our compression algorithms (Section 5.3).

5.1   Provenance Benefit

We explore sensornet provenance in the context of one application: collecting temperature data from a city-wide region. This application has several steps (Figure 1): first, we collect temperature from low-cost, off-the-shelf wireless sensors via computer-attached web cameras and publish both the image and the interpreted digits of temperature to a sensor store. Two different republishers can then examine this data and recover from common image interpretation errors, passing along either just the temperature digits

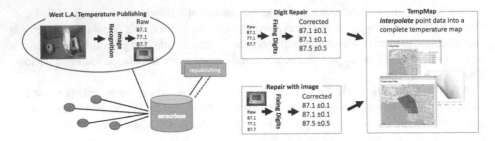

Fig. 1. West Los Angles Temperature Monitoring

(*digit repair*), or the digits and image (*repair with image*). Finally, we collect temperatures from a city neighborhood and interpolate a uniform grid of temperature with TempMap. We have been running this application with different numbers of sensors since March 2007, and currently have ten operational sensors.

Full evaluation of the benefits of provenance will require long-term experience with this application. However our initial experience is promising; we have found provenance important for helping evaluate and debug problems with both forms of digit repair. We also have occasional problems with sensors going off-line; drilling down to the raw data is essential to debug these problems. Finally, we expect it to be useful when peering through the TempMap data. If an abnormality is found on the map, provenance helps follow through to the sensor that is mis-reporting.

5.2 Provenance Design for Sensornet Republishing

In Section 3.2 we discussed alternative implementations of provenance, choosing annotation with incrementally compressed links. Here we compare our choice against two alternatives: copying the source data and using uncompressed links, and without preserving provenance. Our goal is to understand how these alternatives affect storage overhead.

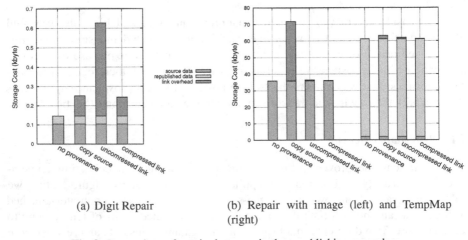

(a) Digit Repair

(b) Repair with image (left) and TempMap (right)

Fig. 2. Comparison of required storage in the republishing examples

Figures 2(a) and 2(b) show the amount of storage consumed in the three republishing examples. We break the storage down in three categories: source data, republished data, and provenance overhead. We show the data on two separate graphs because the storage cost of digit repair is much less than that with images or TempMap.

These graphs show differences in the three stages of the application. Simple digit repair has small source and republished data, just the temperature value. Repair with image has much larger source data because it includes a digital picture of the sensor in addition to the interpreted value. Finally, TempMap generates a large, uniform array of interpolated temperatures from a sparser source set.

First, we observe that copying the source works well when source data is small (digit repair and TempMap), but it becomes quite expensive when the source is large (repair with image). Uncompressed links, on the other hand, do quite well when sensor data is large (repair with image and TempMap), but the provenance overhead is quite large compared to small source and republished data (digit repair)—making storage four times more than the basic data. Finally, we observe that compressed links do quite well when the data is large. When the data is small, the storage of compression link becomes smaller that that of copying the source even for small source data. The compressed link takes the smallest storage in all three examples.

As a final point, we selected tuple-level, fine-grained provenance. While we did not implement table-level, coarse-grain provenance, the overhead of a per-table link would be nothing with large tables of data. Approximating that cost with the "no provenance" bar, we can see that the cost of tuple-level provenance is dwarfed by the cost of data in the large-data cases, but roughly doubles the cost of storage with small data (digit repair). In that case, incremental compression (explored next) is essential.

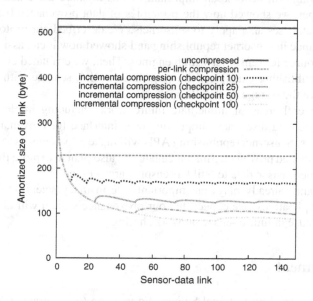

Fig. 3. Provenance storage with incremental compression

5.3 Redundancy across Predecessor Links

As we have just shown, links storage can dominate storage costs when sensor data is small. We therefore compare several compression alternatives, including independent, per-link compression and incremental compression with different levels of checkpointing.

Figure 3 shows per-link storage for a series of 0 to 150 predecessor links with these cases and without compression. First, we observe that per-link compression halves storage because each link must build its own dictionary table. In this case we do not take advantage of redundancy across links.

With incremental compression, we exploit compression dictionary across multiple links. For reasons described in Section 4.2, our incremental compression algorithm (LZW) is less efficient than per-link compression (gzip), so the first incremental link is less efficient. But the benefits of a shared dictionary quickly take over, making average links is the best with longer checkpoint periods. All incremental algorithms converge on different asymptotic efficiencies from only 90B/link with 100 links/checkpoint to 170B/link with 10 links/checkpoint. With less frequent checkpointing, read and write cost grows, therefore we need to balance efficiency with update speed. We selected 50 links/checkpoint as a reasonable trade-off, showing 80% savings in space which is slightly less than 100 links/checkpoint (83%).

6 Conclusion and Future Work

As data from sensornets are increasingly shared over the Internet, we expect that sensornet republishing will become an important means to share these abundant sensor data. In this paper, we showed how the principles of data provenance from scientific workflow and databases also apply to sensornets. We described our prototype system for data provenance in sensornet republishing and showed how it can assist debugging and serve as a source for sensornet search engines. Then, we evaluated our provenance system with republishing examples, showing that our link scheme with *incremental compression* save the storage up to 83%.

There are several areas of immediate future work, including implementation of provenance-aware data disclosure, improving user interface for provenance data and republishing APIs. Sensornet republishing APIs will make easy for users to write republishers with automated provenance management. We also plan to explore link structures among republished sensor-data to build a sensor search engine.

Data provenance already plays an important role in many scientific domains and data-oriented applications. We expect that our provenance system will also contribute to sharing and reuse in future sensor-network sharing.

Acknowledgment

This work is supported by National Science Foundation (NSF) grants CNS-0626702, Sensor-Internet Sharing and Search. Thanks to Sung Jin Kim and Junghoo Cho for helpful comments on our preliminary version.

References

1. Kepler project, http://kepler-project.org/
2. Sensorbase web service, http://sensorbase.org/help/web_services.php
3. Aberer, K., Hauswirth, M., Salehi, A.: A middleware for fast and flexible sensor network deployment. In: VLDB, pp. 1199–1202 (2006)
4. Anderson, D.P., Cobb, J., Korpela, E., Lebofsky, M., Werthimer, D.: Seti@home: an experiment in public-resource computing. Commun. ACM 45(11), 56–61 (2002)
5. Bhagwat, D., Chiticariu, L., Tan, W.-C., Vijayvargiya, G.: An annotation management system for relational databases. In: vldb 2004: Proceedings of the Thirtieth international conference on very large data bases, pp. 900–911. VLDB Endowment (2004)
6. Buneman, P., Chapman, A., Cheney, J.: Provenance management in curated databases. In: SIGMOD 2006: Proceedings of the 2006 ACM SIGMOD international conference on Management of data, pp. 539–550. ACM, New York (2006)
7. Chang, K., Yau, N., Hansen, M., Estrin, D.: Sensorbase.org - a centralized repository to slog sensor network data (May 2006)
8. Cuff, D., Hansen, M., Kang, J.: Urban sensing: out of the woods. Commun. ACM 51(3), 24–33 (2008)
9. Cui, Y., Widom, J.: Lineage tracing for general data warehouse transformations. The VLDB Journal, 471–480 (2001)
10. Eisenman, S.B., Miluzzo, E., Lane, N.D., Peterson, R.A., Ahn, G.-S., Campbell, A.T.: The bikenet mobile sensing system for cyclist experience mapping. In: SenSys 2007: Proceedings of the 5th international conference on Embedded networked sensor systems, pp. 87–101. ACM Press, New York (2007)
11. Gibbons, P.B., Karp, B., Ke, Y., Nath, S., Seshan, S.: Irisnet: An architecture for a worldwide sensor web. IEEE Pervasive Computing 02(4), 22–33 (2003)
12. Hull, B., Bychkovsky, V., Zhang, Y., Chen, K., Goraczko, M., Miu, A.K., Shih, E., Balakrishnan, H., Madden, S.: CarTel: A Distributed Mobile Sensor Computing System. In: 4th ACM SenSys, Boulder, CO (November 2006)
13. The Weather Underground Inc. Weather Underground (2006), http://wunderground.com
14. Ludäscher, B., Altintas, I., Berkley, C., Higgins, D., Jaeger, E., Jones, M., Lee, E.A., Tao, J., Zhao, Y.: Scientific workflow management and the kepler system: Research articles. Concurr. Comput.: Pract. Exper. 18(10), 1039–1065 (2006)
15. Moreau, L., et al.: Special issue: The first provenance challenge. Concurr. Comput.: Pract. Exper. 20(5), 409–418 (2008)
16. Moreau, L., Freire, J., Futrelle, J., McGrath, R.E., Myers, J., Paulson, P.: The open provenance model (2007)
17. Nath, S., Deshpande, A., Ke, Y., Gibbons, P.B., Karp, B., Seshan, S.: Irisnet: An architecture for internet-scale sensing services
18. Nath, S., Liu, J., Zhao, F.: Challenges in building a portal for sensors world-wide. In: First Workshop on World-Sensor-Web, Boulder, CO. ACM, New York (2006)
19. Page, L., Brin, S., Motwani, R., Winograd, T.: The PageRank citation ranking: Bringing order to the web (unpublished manuscript, January 1998)
20. Reddy, S., Chen, G., Fulkerson, B., Kim, S.J., Park, U., Yau, N., Cho, J., Hansen, J.H.M.: Sensor-internet share and search—enabling collaboration of citizen scientists. In: Proceedings of the ACM Workshop on Data Sharing and Interoperability on the World-wide Sensor Web, Cambridge, Mass, USA, April 2007, pp. 11–16. ACM, New York (2007)
21. Santanche, A., Nath, S., Liu, J., Priyantha, B., Zhao, F.: Senseweb: Browsing the physical world in real time (2006), http://research.microsoft.com/nec/senseweb

22. Simmhan, Y.L., Plale, B., Gannon, D.: A survey of data provenance in e-science. SIGMOD Rec. 34(3), 31–36 (2005)
23. Szewczyk, R., Mainwaring, A., Polastre, J., Anderson, J., Culler, D.: An analysis of a large scale habitat monitoring application. In: SenSys 2004: Proceedings of the 2nd international conference on Embedded networked sensor systems, pp. 214–226. ACM, New York (2004)
24. Tan, W.C.: Provenance in databases: Past, current, and future. IEEE Data Eng. Bull. 30(4), 3–12 (2007)
25. Werner-Allen, G., Lorincz, K., Welsh, M., Marcillo, O., Johnson, J., Ruiz, M., Lees, J.: Deploying a wireless sensor network on an active volcano. IEEE Internet Computing 10(2), 18–25 (2006)
26. Woo, A.: Demo abstract: A new embedded web services approach to wireless sensor networks. In: Proceedings of the Fourth ACM SenSys Conference, Boulder, Colorado, USA, p. 347. ACM, New York (2006)

Semantically-Enhanced Model-Experiment-Evaluation Processes (SeMEEPs) within the Atmospheric Chemistry Community

Chris Martin[1], Mohammed H. Haji[2], Peter Dew[2], Mike Pilling[1], and Peter Jimack[2]

[1] School of Chemistry, University of Leeds, Leeds, LS2 9JT, UK
{chmcjma,m.j.pilling}@leeds.ac.uk
[2] School of Computing, University of Leeds, Leeds LS2 9JT, UK
{mhh,dew,pkj}@comp.leeds.ac.uk

Abstract. The scientific model development process is often documented in an ad-hoc unstructured manner leading to difficulty in attributing provenance to data products. This can cause issues when the data owner or other interested stakeholder seeks to interpret the data at a later date. In this paper we discuss the design, development and evaluation of a Semantically-enhanced Electronic Lab-Notebook to facilitate the capture of provenance for the model development process, within the atmospheric chemistry community. We then proceed to consider the value of semantically enhanced provenance within the wider community processes, Semantically-enhanced Model-Experiment Evaluation Processes (SeMEEPs), that leverage data generated by experiments and computational models to conduct evaluations.

Keywords: Semantic Metadata, Provenance, Atmospheric Chemistry, Model Development.

1 Introduction

Progress in a wide range of scientific domains depends on complementary experimental and theoretical developments. Such scientific progress can be considered as the output of the Model-Experiment Evaluation Processes (MEEPs): The generic processes, within scientific communities, that leverage experimental and model output data to derive scientific insight. Example processes include: evaluating model data against experimental data and/or against alternative model data; and surveying models and data, across a community, to develop a benchmark model or model component. The efficiency and effectiveness of the MEEPs relies not only on the availability of data, experimental and computational model output, but also the availability and quality of data provenance. The demands of current applications (such as climate modeling, global warming, and energy demand) force the pace and drive the need for much closer integration between experimentalists and modellers. This integration over a global scale can only be facilitated in an economically feasible manner by the use of e-Science technologies.

This paper proposes new Semantically-enhanced Model-Experiment-Evaluation Processes (SeMEEPs) where semantic data and process provenance is captured or

J. Freire, D. Koop, and L. Moreau (Eds.): IPAW 2008, LNCS 5272, pp. 293–308, 2008.

leveraged by the MEEPs. In this paper we focus on one Semantically-enhanced Model-Experiment-Evaluation Process, the individual scientist who wants to evaluate a computational model against experimental results from the literature, and capture the provenance for this process. We propose that by capturing this provenance with a Electronic Laboratory Notebook (ELN), as opposed to a traditional lab-book, the provenance captured will be more complete and of a higher quality. A semantic data-driven workflow [1] is used by the ELN to capture provenance, with data and models treated as first class objects throughout the scientific process. We propose that by capturing provenance in this form of Semantic Metadata (SMD) existing processes can leverage provenance more easily and new processes will be enabled. In this paper we explore model development provenance capture with an ELN within the atmospheric chemistry community.

Our ELN captures provenance using a combination of automatic process capture and user annotation. We have adopted two guiding principles for the ELN's capture of provenance; Firstly minimise the changes in working practice required for scientists to adopt an ELN. Secondly ensure that complete provenance is captured, where complete is taken to mean; sufficient to enable a given piece of data to be reproduced.

Section 2 of this paper gives an overview of the atmospheric chemistry community focusing on the use of a community database, the Master Chemical Mechanism (MCM) [2], in the model development process. Section 3 describes the generic modeling process used to structure the semantic provenance captured by the ELN. Section 4 considers the implementation of a prototype ELN using semantic web technology (OWL and RDF). Section 5 discusses preliminary user-evaluation of the prototype ELN with members of the atmospheric chemistry modeling research group at Leeds University. Section 6 presents a review of relevant background literature and projects. Finally section 7 outlines our future work considering other community based SeMEEPs, which leverage the provenance captured by the ELN.

2   The Atmospheric Chemistry Community

The atmospheric chemistry community relies on the complementary efforts of experimentalists and modelers seeking to develop a better understanding of the chemical processes taking place in the atmosphere. This understanding is used to construct chemical mechanisms that quantitatively describe atmospheric chemistry. These chemical mechanisms are then used as components in climate and air quality models. The key community activities within the atmospheric chemistry communities include:

- determining fundamental parameters, rate constants and product yields, of reactions of atmospheric interest by calculation or experiment;
- gathering, evaluating and archiving these fundamental parameters;
- developing chemical mechanisms, using the fundamental parameters discussed above, that describe complex chemical processes taking place in the atmosphere;
- testing mechanisms by including them in atmospheric models and evaluating the model against in-situ atmospheric measurements or atmospheric simulation experiments, see figure 1 which presents a comparison of model output (model) and measured experimental values (measured) for the concentration of a chemical species (Methyl Glyoxal) of interest against time. It is this process that the ELN discussed in this paper seeks to capture the provenance for.

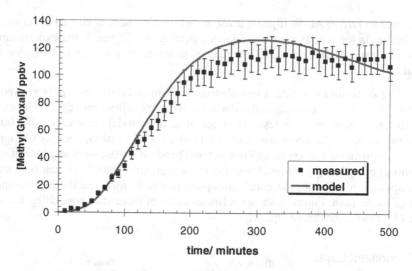

Fig. 1. Model-measurement comparison for Methyl Glyoxal

Currently informal processes are used that enable feedback and collaboration between each of these distinct activities. The activities of the atmospheric chemistry community are discussed in more detail in section 5.

The MCM is one example of an atmospheric chemistry mechanism, it is developed and maintained by the community and is widely used in laboratories around the world. The MCM is a structured list of fundamental chemical reactions and rate constants which is used to build specific chemical mechanisms for the lower atmosphere. Our work considers a modeller using the MCM within an atmospheric chemistry model to understand a set of in-situ atmospheric measurements, this is taken as an exemplar of a more generic modelling process describe within this paper in Section 3. Typically, within the atmospheric chemistry community, the provenance for this modelling process is recorded in an ad-hoc, unstructured fashion using a combination the traditional lab-book, word processor documents and spreadsheets. This approach to provenance capture leads to many issues such as archived data being rendered meaningless due to incomplete provenance and difficulty interpreting the work of other scientists as provenance remains a local and personal artefact.

3 The Modelling Process

We have taken the development of a model, to compare with experimental data, as the first of the Model-Experiment Evaluation Process to semantically enhance. This section describes a generic scientific model development process (see Figure 2) that we use to structure the SMD captured by the ELN. Our approach extends the work of Coles et al. for the capture of SMD for in-vitro chemistry experiments [3].

Our 3-layer mapping presents a hierarchical decomposition of the modelling process, each layer is considered from the abstract to the concrete below:

Experimental Layer: At the highest level model development is viewed as an *in-silico* experiment. In the top layer of the 3-layer mapping, see Figure 2, the experiment can be seen to take a high level modelling plan as an input and produce a conclusion as an output.

Modelling Iteration Layer: At a less abstract level model development is viewed as a network of modelling iterations. An iteration of the modelling process can be considered to take a plan, such as test the effect of setting model parameter x = 100 (the value proposed by the latest paper on x); produce a conclusion, such as changing x had no significant effect on model output; and produce a plan, such as proceed to test the impact of updating parameter y to the latest literature value. So it can be seen that the output of an iteration, the conclusion/plan, is able to form the input to another iteration, as the plan. Figure 2 shows a linear series of three such modelling iterations linked by shared conclusions/plans.

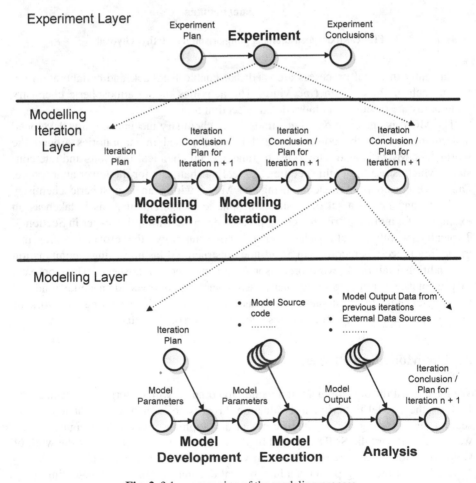

Fig. 2. 3-layer mapping of the modeling process

Modelling Layer: At a concrete level model development can be viewed as a network of modeling processes (Model Development, Model Execution, Analysis). In figure 2 the simplest case is presented; the model parameters are changed (Model Development), the model is run (Model Execution) and the model output is analysed to determine the impact of the parameter change and the fit with experimental data (Analysis). The Model Development processes takes an iteration plan (as discussed above) and some set of model parameters as an input, and produces a revised set of model parameters as an output. The Model Execution process takes the revised set of model parameters and the model source code as inputs and produces a set of model outputs. It has been assumed that versioning of model source code is managed separately by software version control software. The analysis process takes model output and other data sources (i.e. data from previous model runs or other external data repositories) as an input and produces an iteration conclusion/plan, as discussed above, as an output. There is clearly scope for more complicate networks of modelling processes, for example multiple analysis processes following a model execution.

A typical atmospheric chemistry model will depend on many parameters, including the chemical mechanism, input data sets and the environmental conditions including temperature, pressure etc. For the purpose of prototype development we have considered mechanism development to be the mode of model development. A scientist will iteratively develop a mechanism, by adding reactions, deleting reactions or editing the reactions themselves in an attempt to obtain a good model-measurement comparison.

4 Prototype Development

4.1 Methodology

Capturing the modelling process used by atmospheric chemistry modellers was the first phase of developing the ELN prototype. The process capture was facilitated by considering a modelling case study based on the development of a model for a field campaign that took place in Tasmania, SOAPEX [4]. The model in the case study was relatively simple, but also retained all the key characteristics of the more complicated models. The process for developing the SOAPEX model was then mapped, at the finest granularity of task description possible, to produce a process description for the case study. The importance of capturing process, at the finest granularity of task description possible, is that only with this level of detail is it possible to repeat an experiment (either modelling or laboratory based).

4.2 Provenance Specification

The case study process description was then examined to develop a provenance specification. This provenance specification was developed from an end user perspective, in the form of a set of provenance reports for the case study modelling process. The subsequent design and implementation of the prototype was guided by this provenance specification.

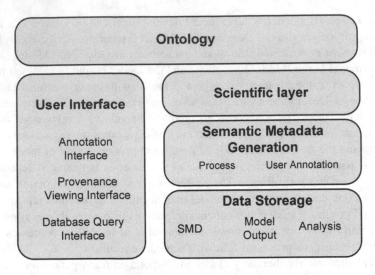

Fig. 3. ELN System Architecture

4.3 Architecture

Figure 3 shows the system architecture we have implemented in our prototype ELN. In this section the purpose of each architectural component is considered in turn: The scientific layer consists of the modeler's standard toolkit, this provides the ELN user with a familiar modelling process and allows them to view the ELN as a tool that is complementary to their existing working practices. The semantic metadata generation layer, interfaces with the scientific and user interface layers to automatically capture provenance for the modeling process and associated user annotations. This provenance is then expressed in a semantic form. The data storage layer provides archiving for SMD, model inputs and outputs, and analysis documents. The user interface enables the user to associate annotations with elements of their modelling process, access model input and output datasets, view provenance records in the form of standardised reports and query the SMD. The ontology is discussed in the following section.

4.4 Knowledge Engineering

Ontology was developed to describe atmosphere chemistry modeling experiments, the ontology provides a vocabulary for structuring the SMD captured by the ELN. The concepts represented in the ontology are sufficient to describe the experiments examined in the research. The ontology was developed in OWL using the Protégé ontology editor, building on the CombeChem ELN ontology [5] for *in-vitro* chemistry experiments.

As with the CombeChem ontology at the highest level concepts fall into two categories: Processes, for example at an abstract level a modeling iteration, as discussed above, and at a more concrete level changing a given model parameter; and Materials, in the CombeChem case physical chemicals etc., in our case more conceptual materials such as model output files etc. The domain specific elements of the ontology were identified with reference to the provenance specification, described above, and developed in conjunction with the domain scientists. Much of the ontology development effort centred on the domain specific ontology elements and understanding the set of processes conducting by atmospheric chemistry modellers.

4.5 Implementation

We now consider the implementation of each architectural component: The Scientific layer consists of the modeler's standard set of tools, for our prototype a FORTRAN atmospheric chemistry model and a diverse set of analysis tools. The Semantic Metadata Generation Layer captures provenance using file-based interactions and a number of python scripts, SMD is then generated as RDF, that adheres to the ontology described above. These RDF files store the provenance for entire experimental process. The semantic metadata generation layer has been developed using Java version 6.1 and the Jena library [6] enabling the system to be platform independent. The data storage layer is implemented as a MySQL database, future work will look at the additional use of a triplestore, for storeage of the SMD. Currently the user interface layer provides functionality for the user to annotate their scientific process and generate provenance reports; the provenance query interface remains subject of requirements capture.

We now consider the interaction of the system components during a typical modelling iteration:

- *Mechanism Development*: When starting a new model development project a unique global URI is automatically assigned to the experiment. The scientists can then proceed to develop the chemical mechanism including processes such as editing existing reactions or inserting a new reaction or set of reactions. The semantic metadata layer identifies any such changes to the chemical mechanism and drives the annotation interface to prompt the user for scientific justification for the changes. Once user annotation has been completed SMD is generated.
- *Model Execution*: The user then initiates the model execution; a number of model configuration and compilation processes and the model itself are executed. Input and output files for each model run are stored in a repository through JDBC-ODBC (Java Database Connectivity - Open Database Connectivity) enabling the experiment results to be quickly accessed or reproduced for future analysis. As each input or output file is added to the database it is allocated a resolvable URI that is referenced from the SMD.
- *Analysis*: The user performs their analysis of the model output; this can include comparison of data sources using graphing packages, or more complex processing and visualisation. The annotation interface, shown in figure 4, presents the user with the opportunity to record the data sources they have used, the type of analysis conducted and their conclusion and plans for the next modelling iteration. Full integration of semantic metadata generation layer into the analysis process, to automate capture of provenance, remains the subject of requirements capture.
- *Reviewing provenance records*: The user can generate provenance reports, for a given modelling process, from the SMD using the provenance viewer interface. These user-orientated provenance reports, conforming to the provenance specification outlined above, are generated by querying the SMD records using SPARQL [7] and formatted as plain text.

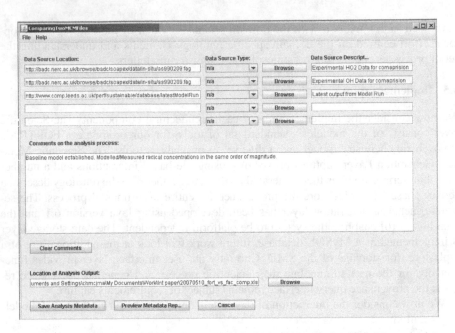

Fig. 4. Screen shot of provenance capture interface, for the analysis of model output data

5 Prototype Evaluation

5.1 Evaluation Methodology

To evaluate the ELN prototype system we adopted an approach that draws on the Scenario Based Development paradigm [8]. The mode of evaluation is very much formative [9], seeking to elicit user responses on topics including: the efficacy of the ELN prototype, the benefits and drawbacks of using an ELN and ways provenance could be used once captured by an ELN. The scenarios were developed by the informatics team, based on observation and personal experiences, without engaging the modellers who formed the evaluation panel in order to avoid prejudicing the evaluation.

The evaluation explored the scenarios and the prototype using elements of semistructured interview, discussion, prototype demonstration and user exploration of the prototype. This approach attempted to strike a balance between the interviewer's ability to respond to user feedback as it occurs and providing a structure that ensures important topics are addressed.

5.2 The Scenarios

Prior to the evaluation we developed problem scenarios, depicting the current processes of a modeller using a lab-book, and activity design scenarios depicting envisaged processes of a modeller using an ELN. These scenarios were developed for two cases:

- the capture of provenance at model development time (Case 1), for the individual scientist who wants to evaluate a model against experimental results from the literature;
- the use of provenance to help write a PhD thesis (Case 2).

Each scenario is a story that provides a description of: the actor involved (in our case a fictional PhD student called Helen developing atmospheric chemistry models using the MCM); contextual information on the setting (the modelling process being conducted etc.); the actions and interactions of the actor and the technological artefacts; and the actor's thoughts and feelings.

Although the prototype developed only supports scenario 1, we included scenario 2 in the evaluation in order to conduct a more thorough evaluation of the prototype. Asking the evaluators if the provenance, as captured by the ELN, would deliver benefits in a scenario they could easily envisage and relate to.

5.3 Evaluator Background

The first evaluator is responsible for the maintenance and development of the MCM. This type of work involves: extensive experimentation with mechanisms to model chamber experiments, reviewing the literature to update model parameters and identifying areas of deficiency in the MCM which new experiments would explore. The second evaluator is involved in modelling field campaigns using the MCM. This type of work involves; configuring the chemistry in a model, configuring model environmental conditions, managing the input of experimental data to the model including version control.

5.4 Barrier to Adoption of the ELN

From the very start of the first evaluation, when discussing the provenance capture scenario, it was clear a critical barrier to the adoption of an ELN was the effort involved in capturing provenance at modelling time:

"[in] your lab book you can write down what ever you want [but with an ELN] it is going to take time to go through the different protocol steps".

This concern was addressed by the prototype demonstration and user prototype testing, where the user was able to see the actual amount of user input required by the ELN. When asked if they would use an ELN requiring a similar amount of user input to the prototype the response was positive:

"Yeah, I think it would be a good thing. I don't think it is too much extra ... work."
Rather than viewing the prompts for user annotation as interruption to their normal work the user recognised the value of being prompted, stating it:

"is a good way to do it because otherwise you won't [record the provenance]."

A second barrier to adoption emerged due to the restricted focus of the prototype, on mechanism development provenance. In this case the ELN failed to meet the provenance requirements of a user for a particular modelling sub-process that is very important to their work causing reservations about the ELN's ability to meet their provenance needs. The prototype has yet to be developed to enable the user to "annotate model input files", and this became a theme that ran throughout the evaluation, being brought up as an issue repeatedly by the evaluator.

5.5 Perceived Benefits of Using an ELN for Provenance Capture

Both users intuitively grasped the benefits of recording provenance with an ELN and that the benefits would be realised after the time of modelling by a number of stakeholders:

"if someone else wants to look at ... [your provenance], that's great because the person can see exactly what you have done, where you have been and where to go next. And for yourself, if you are writing up a PhD ... [you can] ... see exactly what you've done whereas currently you have to rifle through lab-books to see exactly what you have done."

5.6 Using Provenance When Writing a PhD Thesis

A key focus of the evaluation of the scenarios for using provenance when writing a PhD thesis was to understand how a user may want to query an ELN archive. Many of the queries suggested were in the form:

"Show me the iteration/s where I ...[did some modelling process]."
Other queries, such as:
"Show me the history of reaction X"
"Show me the aerosol [or other reaction type] reactions I added to the original mechanism"

Had a different focus and require the ontology to be developed further to include the modelling of the various potential query return types. The queries suggested were large in number and diverse in nature, in future work the queries suggested will be analysed and prioritised to set the requirements for the an ELN query interface prototype.

6 Related Work

CombeChem and ELNs
One of the goals of e-Science is to enable the end-to-end scientific process from data generation to publication and long term archival. The CombeChem project [10] has demonstrated the advantages of using Semantic Web technology and in particular semantic provenance to describe and link diverse and complex chemical information across the end-to-end scientific process. The project successfully adopted a strategy of capturing semantic provenance (e.g. annotations) "at source", establishing schema and ontologies based closely on current operational practice in order to facilitate implementation and adoption. Provenance is expressed in RDF and held in a triplestore.

CombeChem uses an innovative, flexible, human-centric system based around an ELN and has been successfully used in a synthetic organic chemistry laboratory. Working closely with end users they discovered that a light touch and a high degree of flexibility were required for capture, representation and storage of provenance.

Similarly this applies to the modeling process discussed in this paper. Both Combe-Chem and our project address the challenge of designing a system that has to compete with paper on the basis of least perceived cost and minimal changes working practice of the scientist [11]. Experimental chemists must, by law, write a plan of the experimental process for safety purposes (in the UK this is the COSHH form). The Combe-Chem ELN use this experimental plan as the starting point for capturing provenance, leveraging the effort of user puts into a mandatory task without changing working practices. In a similar way, through the automatic capture of the modeling process, we have been able to minimize changes to working practices.

Summary of SOA Provenance Approaches

In recent years there has been considerable progress in the design of e-Science system based on service orientated architectures (SOAs), workflow and semantic annotations. The following provides a brief overview of the service-based provenance. For example Miles, Deelman et al. [12] argue that to have full provenance of data you not only record parameters, inputs, intermediary data, but also the abstract experiment refined into concrete execution by a "workflow complier". To do this they modify the Pegasus system which is a framework for mapping complex scientific workflows onto distributed systems [13]. A useful survey of data provenance in e-Science is given by Simmhan et al. [14]. They compared six systems of which the most relevant are CMCS (Collaboratorory for Multi-Scale Chemical Science) and MyGrid.

CMCS [15] is of relevance because it addresses multi-scaled chemical processes, in our work we consider chemical processes at two scales, the individual reaction and the atmospheric chemical mechanism. CMCS aims to support multi-disciplinary sciences but currently it is mainly focused on the combustion community. CMCS uses a SOA to manage heterogeneous data flows supplemented by provenance metadata for establishing the pedigree of data. In contrast to our work CMCS does not handle semantic metadata.

myGrid [16] provides semantically-enabled middleware for *in-silico* (computational laboratory) experiments, much of the work has focused on the bioinformatics research community. Within myGrid experiments are represented and manipulated as workflows composed of services (web services, local services etc.). myGrid leverages semantic web technologies to allow semantic description and discovery of workflows, central to this is the widely used ontology-based Taverna workflow system [17]. myGrid services include resource discovery, workflow enactment, and metadata and provenance management, which enable integration and present a semantically enhanced information model for bio-informatics and more recently in the neuroscience CARMEN project [18]. As workflow systems become established there is a growing need for scientists to be able to verify the correctness of their own experiments, or to review the correctness of their peers' work. Validation ensures results generated from experiments are meaningful. For example using the PASOA provenance system [19] and recently the idea of quality model has emerged [20]. The integration of atmospheric chemistry modeling tools and our ELN with a workflow system, such as Taverna, remains a subject for discussion with our users, who will determine if a workflow system meets their requirements for a model development system.

Socialisation and Provenance Using SOA

myExperiment is a Virtual Research Environment that seeks to enable collaboration between researchers and sharing of workflows and other digital objects [21]. It achieves this by adopting a social web approach which is tailored to the particular needs of the scientist. It aims to provide a 'workflow bazaar' for any workflow management system. myExperiment is distinctive in that it facilitates the sharing of workflows and these may come from multiple systems. myExperiment provides a potential means of sharing the modeling provenance records captured by the prototype ELN discussed in this paper.

SWAN [22] is a project that incorporates the full biomedical research knowledge lifecycle in its ontological model, including support for personal data organization, hypothesis generation, experimentation, lab data organization, and digital pre-publication collaboration. Its principal goal is to apply Semantic Web technology to enhance existing practices in a way that can (a) enhance the productivity of the community as a whole, (b) benefit each human constituency to ensure uptake and socialisation, (c) enable websites, individual scientists, and scientific laboratories to participate in virtual collaborations. Whilst SWAN can be seen to share similar high level goals to our work, enhancing working practices across a scientific community using semantic web technologies, a significant difference lies in the maturity of the two communities with respect to internet enabled collaboration. The SWAN community has a well establish online community, where as the atmospheric chemistry community is in the process of establishing itself within the web environment.

7   Conclusions and Future Work

The feedback from both the users involved in the evaluation was generally positive, whilst reinforcing our concern that adding work at the time of modelling to capture provenance is likely to deter users from adopting an ELN. The evaluation suggests that our prototype ELN does not place excessive burden on the user, due to the automation of much the provenance capture. The evaluators could see sufficient value in the provenance captured by the ELN, to envisage cases where it would be of benefit to themselves and other community members. Considering the PhD thesis scenario has enabled a starting point to be established to explore requirements for a provenance query interface.

The evaluation output presented above is in its preliminary stages, to complete the evaluation we intend to perform further evaluations, with individuals with different job roles such as experimentalists who perform some modelling to complement their experiments. We are also going to conduct in depth analysis of the evaluation transcripts to provide a more rigorous analysis of the evaluation results. We then plan to extend the prototype ELN to support a use of provenance scenario, such as a modeller reviewing their personal ELN archive when writing up their PhD, hopefully aided by the evaluation outcome.

Looking further ahead we will develop architecture for supporting a wider range of SeMEEPs across the atmospheric chemistry community, many of these SeMEEPs will draw on the provenance captured by the ELN. We will seek to understand and support the community evaluation processes, which typically involve experts with related interests forming working groups to evaluate data from a variety of sources. The goal of such evaluations is to develop and agree upon benchmark data, which the community can make use of or validate their results against. In the atmospheric chemistry community the data to be evaluated will have been produced by a combination of scientists involved in: undertaking experiments or theoretical calculations to determine the fundamental parameters of chemical reactions; those who build the chemical mechanisms using the fundamental parameters; scientists that perform experiments or develop models that are used to evaluate the mechanisms; and repository managers.

In current practice this evaluation process typically involves time consuming literature reviews, face-to-face meetings and is centred about a few key individuals. The information available to evaluators is often incomplete, only what is presented in academic publications so it is difficult to drill down to the under-pinning provenance.

Figure 4 presents envisaged SeMEEPs for the atmospheric chemistry community, from a modeller-centric perspective. The capture of model development provenance using an ELN, as discussed in this paper, is central to the wider community Se-MEEPs. A modeller can gather input to the modelling process from a variety of data sources, including a community semantic database of benchmark data, adding semantic annotations as required. As the modelling process progresses a modeller can store their model provenance and output in their personal ELN archive. Once a piece of modelling research has been completed and determined to be of sufficient quality it can then be stored in a laboratory (or research group) archive and made available to collaborating laboratories.

Once in a laboratory repository a provenance and model output can be used to support community evaluation processes. So the evaluation working group have the ability to semantically search and reason with the provenance of the modelling community they seek to develop benchmark data for. The evaluation work group also has access to experimental data and its provenance, although provision of this data and provenance is beyond the current scope of our work. The output of the evaluation work group is benchmark data based on an understanding of the experimental and model data, underpinned by complete and sound provenance. The benchmark data can then be incorporated in a community semantic database, which is in turn used in further model development projects. It is in this context of community evaluation, that the value of recording provenance with Semantic Web technologies will be truly tested.

In this paper we have discussed SeMEEPs in the Atmospheric Chemistry community, but as our work progresses we will seek to evaluate the suitability of SeMEEPs for application in other scientific communities. Our next target community is the geomagnetism community. This is an active international community that researches the origins and evolution of the Earth's magnetic field. As with the atmospheric chemistry community the research of the geomagnetism community relies on a mixture of field measurement (experiment) and computational simulation (modelling). The field measurements provide data about the record of the Earth's magnetic field preserved in various magnetic minerals through time (paleomagnetism). The computational simulation is based upon the numerical solution of Maxwell's equations coupled to the Navier-Stokes equations for the flow of conducting fluid in the Earth's outer core (known as magnetohydrodynamics, or MHD for short). There is a need to preserve the large amounts of disparate field data and reach agreement over what this

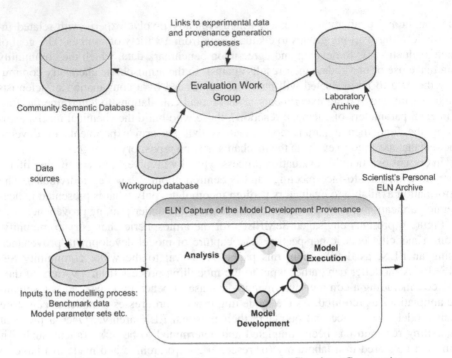

Fig. 5. Envisaged SeMEEPs for the Atmospheric Chemistry Community

raw data tells us about the historical evolution of the magnetic field. There are also a large number of different research groups who produce MHD codes to simulate the dynamo action that is believed to sustain the Earth's magnetic field. One key challenge for the SeMEEPs architecture will be to support the qualitative comparison of these MHD codes and facilitate the interpretation of the field data.

Acknowledgements. Many thanks to Jeremy Frey, Nick Gibbons and the CombeChem project at the University of Southampton for their support and input. Thank you to Andrew Rickard and Jenny Young at the University of Leeds for providing experimental data and assistance with use of the MCM. Also thanks to Roberto Sommariva for his help with the construction of SOAPEX model case study. This work has been conducted as part of an NERC e-Science PhD studentship.

References

1. Simmhan, Y., Plale, B., Gannon, D.: A Framework for Collecting Provenance in Data-Centric Scientific Workflows. In: Proceedings of the IEEE International Conference on Web Services. IEEE Computer Society, Los Alamitos (2006)
2. Saunders, S.M., Jenkin, M.E., Derwent, R.G., Pilling, M.J.: Protocol for the development of the Master Chemical Mechanism, MCM v3 (Part A): tropospheric degradation of non-aromatic volatile organic compounds. Atmos. Chem. Phys. 3, 161–180 (2003)

3. Frey, J., Hughes, G., Mills, H.: schraefel, m.c., Smith, G., De Roure, D.: Less is More: Lightweight Ontologies and User Interfaces for Smart Labs. The UK e-Science All Hands Meeting 2004. EPSRC, Nottingham, UK (2004)

4. Sommariva, R., Haggerstone, A.L., Carpenter, L.J., Carslaw, N., Creasey, D.J., Heard, D.E., Lee, J.D., Lewis, A.C., Pilling, M.J., ZÃ!dor, J.: OH and HO2 chemistry in clean marine air during SOAPEX-2. Atmos. Chem. Phys. 4, 839–856 (2004)

5. Hughes, G., Mills, H., Roure, D.D., Frey, J.G., Moreau, L., Schraefel, m., Smith, G., Zaluska, E.: The Semantic Smart Laboratory: A system for supporting the chemical eScientist. Org. Biomol. Chem. 2, 1–10 (2004)

6. Carroll, J.J., Dickinson, I., Dollin, C., Reynolds, D., Seaborne, A., Wilkinson, K.: Jena: implementing the semantic web recommendations. In: Proceedings of the 13th international World Wide Web conference on Alternate track papers \& posters. ACM, New York (2004)

7. Prud'hommeaux, E., Seaborne, A.: SPARQL Query Language for RDF, vol. 2008 (2005)

8. Rosson, M.B., Carroll, J.M.: Usability Engineering: Scenario-Based Development of Human-Computer Interaction. Morgan Kaufmann, San Francisco (2002)

9. Scriven, M.: Types of Evaluation and Types of Evaluator. American Journal of Evaluation 17, 151–161 (1996)

10. Taylor, K.R., Essex, J.W., Frey, J.G., Mills, H.R., Hughes, G., Zaluska, E.J.: The Semantic Grid and chemistry: Experiences with CombeChem. Web Semantics: Science, Services and Agents on the World Wide Web 4, 84–101 (2006)

11. Schraefel, m.c., Hughes, G., Mills, H., Smith, G., Frey, J.: Making tea: iterative design through analogy. In: Proceedings of the 5th conference on Designing interactive systems: processes, practices, methods, and techniques. ACM, Cambridge (2004)

12. Miles, S., Deelman, E., Groth, P., Vahi, K., Mehta, G., Moreau, L.: Connecting Scientific Data to Scientific Experiments with Provenance. In: Proceedings of the Third IEEE International Conference on e-Science and Grid Computing. IEEE Computer Society, Los Alamitos (2007)

13. Deelman, E., Singh, G., Su, M.-H., Blythe, J., Gil, Y., Kesselman, C., Mehta, G., Vahi, K., Berriman, G.B., Good, J., Laity, A., Jacob, J.C., Katz, D.S.: Pegasus: A framework for mapping complex scientific workflows onto distributed systems. Scientific Programming 13, 219–237 (2005)

14. Simmhan, Y., Plale, B., Gannon, D.: A survey of data provenance in e-science. ACM SIGMOD Record 34, 31–36 (2005)

15. Myers, J., Allison, T., Bittner, S., Didier, B., Frenklach, M., Green, W., Ho, Y.-L., Hewson, J., Koegler, W., Lansing, C., Leahy, D., Lee, M., McCoy, R., Minkoff, M., Nijsure, S., Laszewski, G., Montoya, D., Oluwole, L., Pancerella, C., Pinzon, R., Pitz, W., Rahn, L., Ruscic, B., Schuchardt, K., Stephan, E., Wagner, A., Windus, T., Yang, C.: A Collaborative Informatics Infrastructure for Multi-Scale Science. Cluster Computing 8, 243–253 (2005)

16. Radenkovic, M., Wietrzyk, B.: Life Science Grid Middleware in a More Dynamic Environment. In: On the Move to Meaningful Internet Systems 2005: OTM Workshops, pp. 264–273 (2005)

17. Missier, P., Turi, D., Goble, C., Oinn, T., De Roure, D.: Taverna Workflows: Syntax and Semantics. In: eScience 2007. IEEE Press, Bangalore (2007)

18. Watson, P., Watson, P.: e-Science in the Cloud with CARMEN e-Science in the Cloud with CARMEN. Parallel and Distributed Computing, Applications and Technologies. In: Eighth International Conference on Parallel and Distributed Computing, Applications and Technologies, 2007. PDCAT 2007, p. 5 (2007)

19. Miles, S., Groth, P., Branco, M., Moreau, L.: The Requirements of Using Provenance in e-Science Experiments. Journal of Grid Computing 5, 1–25 (2007)
20. Missier, P., Preece, A., Embury, S., Jin, B., Greenwood, M., Stead, D., Brown, A.: Managing Information Quality in e-Science: A Case Study in Proteomics. Perspectives in Conceptual Modeling, 423–432 (2005)
21. De Roure, D., De Roure, D., Goble, C., Stevens, R.: Designing the myExperiment Virtual Research Environment for the Social Sharing of Workflows Designing the myExperiment Virtual Research Environment for the Social Sharing of Workflows. In: Goble, C. (ed.) IEEE International Conference on e-Science and Grid Computing, pp. 603–610 (2007)
22. Gao, Y., Kinoshita, J., Wu, E., Miller, E., Lee, R., Seaborne, A., Cayzer, S., Clark, T.: SWAN: A distributed knowledge infrastructure for Alzheimer disease research. Web Semantics: Science, Services and Agents on the World Wide Web 4, 222–228 (2006)

Oceanographic Data Provenance Tracking with the Shore Side Data System

Michael McCann and Kevin Gomes

Monterey Bay Aquarium Research Institute,
7700 Sandholdt Rd, Moss Landing, CA, USA
{mccann,kgomes}@mbari.org
http://www.mbari.org/ssds

Abstract. The importance of tracking the provenance of electronic data becomes apparent when data set providers need to also provide metadata describing where the data came from. This need has driven the development of a practical oceanographic data provenance system at the Monterey Bay Aquarium Research Institute. MBARI's Shore Side Data System is designed to manage data collected, processed, and archived from oceanographic observatories. We describe the provenance tracking aspects of this system and the lessons learned from its implementation in an operational environment.

Keywords: Ocean Observatory, Data Processing, Data Provenance.

1 Introduction

Ocean scientists collect measurements of environmental parameters with a variety of instruments and platforms. Data produced by deployments of these assets are archived and later processed for scientific analysis. The collection, analysis, and archive of data is traditionally unique for each particular kind of asset. These *stovepipe* data systems make interoperability difficult and impede the goal of gaining a more complete and timely understanding of oceanographic processes. Operating these observational assets within the context of a managed observatory is one approach the oceanographic community is using to address this problem [1]. Having the data professionally managed within regional scale observatories provides opportunities for transformative uses as described in [2]. As part of the growing effort to establish oceanographic observatories the need for improving this situation is being recognized and systems have been developed employing various methods of provenance management.

Much of the research and development in provenance systems centers on the provenance of workflow systems in Service Oriented Architecture (SOA) and grid computing environments. Friere *et al.* describe the VisTrails system [3] where provenance tracking is integral to a data workflow/exploration/visualization system. It has been used to explore simulations of coastal oceanographic processes for the Columbia River system. Observational data are used as input for the simulations and provenance is tracked from there forward. The utility of VisTrails

J. Freire, D. Koop, and L. Moreau (Eds.): IPAW 2008, LNCS 5272, pp. 309–322, 2008.

is that workflow paths may be queried for and executed again on different input data and that it may be used in many domains. Chapman and Jagadish [4] propose eleven desiderata for provenance systems and relate how several real-world systems do in terms of meeting these desiderata. Comparison of these systems with the one described in this paper is provided in a discussion section below.

The Monterey Bay Aquarium Research Institute operates several oceanographic observation platforms for purposes of advancing knowledge in the deep waters of the worlds oceans. Data collected from these systems and the experience gained from their management led to the design and development of the Shore Side Data System (SSDS). One of the requirements stated for SSDS is to *capture and archive processed data products and associated metadata, maintaining known relationships between data sets.* This capability was designed and implemented for SSDS without awareness of the wealth of other work in the field of provenance. Putting this system to work for real world problems provides an experience case for device-to-dataset oceanographic observatory data provenance. In conjunction with MBARI's mooring system, the capability of SSDS to capture the provenance metadata from device to data set makes it unique among these other systems.

In this paper we describe the Monterey Ocean Observing System (MOOS) of which SSDS is a component, the SSDS data model, its application framework, and the operational procedures required for collecting *good* provenance information. We finish with comparisons and contrasts to other provenance systems.

1.1 Monterey Ocean Observing System

In 1999, MBARI began developing the components of MOOS [5], an advanced, integrated ocean observatory. Development focused on several themes:

- set common standards for power and data management,
- allow seamless reuse of instrumentation packages across a variety of platforms,
- permit very flexible geographic instrument location, and
- do all this at an affordable cost for both system acquisition and maintenance.

MOOS development now incorporates several major components, including observatory-scale science experiments, autonomous underwater vehicles (AUVs), standalone moorings with connected benthic components, an operational at sea software infrastructure (SIAM) [6], and a data management system (SSDS).

Fig. 1 is an artist's rendering of an actual observational campaign that took place in Monterey Bay in the summer of 2000 [7]. A variety of sensors were deployed on a diverse set of platforms including aircraft, ships, remotely operated vehicles, towed vehicles, moored and drifting buoys, and autonomous powered and gliding vehicles.

Immediately following this campaign most of the original data produced from the platform deployments were collated into a directory structure and descriptions were written using the Federal Geographic Data Committee (FGDC) Content Standards for Digital Geospatial Metadata [8]. The data and metadata

Fig. 1. Artist's rendering of intensive observational campaign to observe the waters of Monterey Bay with a variety of platforms. Data from these platforms are transferred to shore for processing and in some cases products are transferred back to shipboard teams.

descriptions are available on the MOOS Upper-water-column Science Experiment (MUSE)web site [7]. For most of us who have dealt with the management of oceanographic data this exercise was our first exposure to FGDC. The experience was useful as it helped guide the design and development of the data system that would satisfy the MOOS data handling requirements. For MUSE we had the personnel resources immediately following the field program to manually assemble all the deployment and processing information into FGDC descriptions for each data set. For future MOOS operations we wished to accomplish this task more efficiently and to do this we needed a central catalog for tracking deployment and data processing information.

1.2   Shore Side Data System

Following the definition of the MOOS goals, a workshop was held to help define the requirements for its Shore Side Data System [9] [10]. The high-level functional requirements of SSDS are to:

- Capture and store data from MOOS data sources
  (Includes files and streams)
- Capture information (i.e. metadata) about the stored data
  (Location, instrument, platform, data format, etc.)
- Capture and store data products
  (Derived products, quality controlled data, plots, etc.)

- Provide access to the original raw data
- Convert data to common formats for user application tools
  (Excel , Matlab, Ferret, ArcGIS, etc.)
- Present simple plots of any well-described data
- Capture and archive processed data products and associated metadata, maintaining known relationships between data sets
- Provide access to data and metadata through an application program interface (API) and a web interface

The SSDS development team consisted on average of two domain experts skilled in software development and two software engineers experienced in developing complex systems. We followed a modified Agile software development process [11] using Java, Enterprise Java Beans, Hibernate, and JBoss for the core components of the system. The system consists of two relational databases: one to store the original instrument data and another to store all the information about the data (the metadata). It is a mixed data system with much of the processed data existing outside the database in NetCDF [12] files stored on disk but accessible through the OPeNDAP [13] web interface. References to these data products and other resources are stored in the metadata database. Fig. 2 shows the overall architecture of SSDS. Data and XML descriptions of the data flow in from the Wet Side into a high-availability Ingest component. Data and metadata are accessible via web based services.

After about two years of development the SSDS had its first deployment with some components of the MOOS SIAM software with the Center for Integrated Marine Technologies [14] mooring in Monterey Bay. SSDS has continued to operate since then and we have adapted data streams from two other operational moorings and data file processing from our AUVs. [15]

1.3 Operational Details

The beginning of any observational data path is the definition of the instrument that produces the data. With SSDS this information is stored the Device table of SSDS's Metadata database. We use XML for the exchange of the device attributes. Fig. 3 shows one of the configuration panels from one our our tools for defining the device metadata.

For Programmable Underwater Connector with Knowledge [16] equipped instrumentation this XML can be embedded in the instrument. Upon first deployment on the system data and XML descriptions of the instrument's data flow into SSDS and are made available for shore side processing. Data and metadata are accessible via web based services. Our experience of writing the FGDC metadata for the MUSE campaign taught us that the human effort of writing fully described metadata would be huge for an observatory composed of hundreds of instruments producing data. Our goal with SSDS is to provide mechanisms to automatically capture data processing metadata such that all of our data sets are described with appropriate metadata.

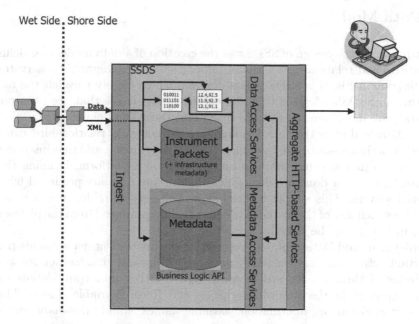

Fig. 2. The main components of the Shore Side Data System. Applications consuming data and producing derived data products read and write provenance metadata through the Aggregate HTTP-based Services and the Metadata Access Services.

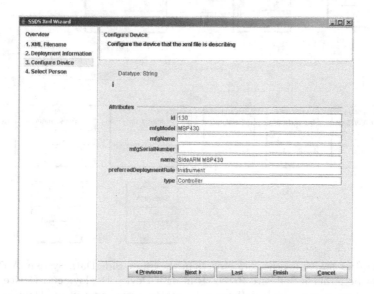

Fig. 3. Device metadata authoring tool. Details of the instrument and of its deployment are captured in advance of the deployment. Processing programs are then able to use this information to generate well described data sets.

2   Data Model

An early step in the design of SSDS was the creation of a data model that defines the entities and relationships within an operational oceanographic observatory. The diagram in Fig. 4 is SSDS's class diagram which closely parallels the table structure in SSDS's Metadata database. The main classes that are of interest for data provenance are the DataProducer and DataContainer classes.

For DataProducers that are Deployments parent-child relationships can be defined such that a sensor can be deployed on an instrument, and that instrument (along with other instruments) can be deployed on a platform. Defining these relationships is best done pre-deployment before any data are produced by the deployed system. This simple model has proven very durable. It is a general model for which any of the metadata about the data produced from the platforms shown in Fig. 1 may be stored.

Deployment and DataContainer records for the instrument deployments track important details that are needed by data processing and visualization software. Attributes of these classes are show in Fig. 5. Other important details (not shown here) are in the RecordDescription and RecordVariable classes. These classes contain parsing information, variable names, standard variable names,

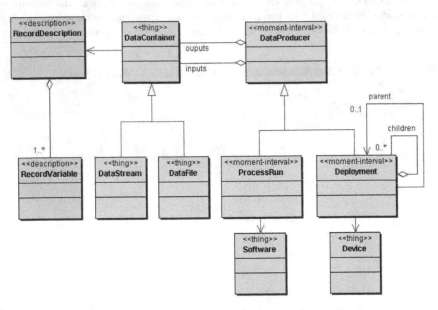

Fig. 4. Object model for the core objects in the Shore Side Data System. A DataProducer can be either a Software ProcessRun or a Device Deployment. Device Deployments may have parent-child relationships. DataProducers may output DataContainers. ProcessRuns have DataContainer(s) as input(s) and DataContainer(s) as output(s). A DataContainer is related to a single DataProducer and is described with a RecordDescription and a collection of RecordVariables. Each object has many attributes that define relevant who, what, where, when, and how information.

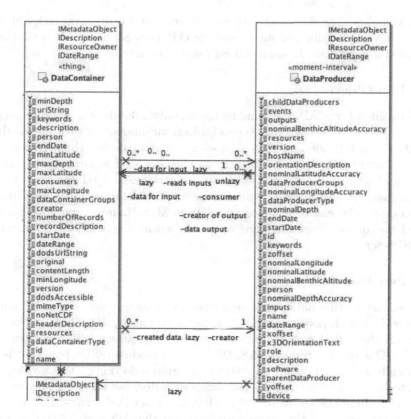

Fig. 5. Attribute details for the DataProducer and DataContainer classes

and units. Automated processing software has been abstracted such that one code base may be used to process output from any instrument. Our pre-SSDS data processing software was embedded with specific deployment and instrument deployment metadata making it cumbersome to maintain. Our current SSDS-enhanced data processing code base is much more flexible and easier to maintain as it retrieves all the information it needs from SSDS's Metadata database.

DataProducers that are ProcessRuns may have input DataContainers and their output DataContainers may be consumed by other ProcessRuns. Data from an observatory may go through several steps of processing before being provided to a scientist for analysis. SSDS can track all of these steps. There is no limit to the number of links in the chain of DataProducer-DataContainer.

3. Application Framework

To be successful as a data system SSDS had to meet the functional requirement of *providing access to data and metadata through an application program interface (API) and a web interface.* There are at least three different APIs to

SSDS Metadata: the Java Data Access Objects (optionally wrapped with Enterprise Java Beans for remote access), SOAP Web Services, and a simplified Representational State Transfer (REST)-style web interface.

3.1   Java Objects

In the Business Logic API surrounding the Metadata database a programmer can write Java code to use the Data Access Objects for interacting with the database directly through Hibernate. This approach is more attractive than writing SQL to interact with the database directly as business logic is incorporated in the DAOs making it easier to deal with the constraints and relationships within the database. It also abstracts out the underlying database technology so the database provider can be changed (MSSQL to MySQL, for example). This API is used for common core functions operating within the J2EE environment on the SSDS server.

3.2   Perl Module

Much of the routine data processing done in oceanographic research environments is done with powerful script languages such as Matlab, Python, Perl and Ruby. Of these Perl and Matlab are the most frequently used by people at MBARI. One of the products of SSDS is a Perl module (SSDS.pm) that is automatically generated during an SSDS build from reflection on the Java classes. (This technique may be used to generate native libraries for other languages as well.) This simplifies access to SSDS Metadata from Perl scripts. For instance, printing the names of the devices deployed on the 'M2 - May 2005' mooring deployment is done with this code:

```
#!/usr/bin/perl -w
#
# Print the child Deployments of mooring deployment name M2 - May 2005
#
use SSDS;
$ssds = new SSDS();
$ssds->ssdsServer('http://ssds:8080/');
my $dpAccess = new SSDS::DataProducerAccess();
my $dps = $dpAccess->findByName('M2 - May 2005', 'true', 'name', 'false');
my $children = $dpAccess->findChildDataProducers(${$dps}[0], 'name', 'false');
foreach my $child (@{$children}) {
    print "child deployment device name = " . $child->getDevice()->name(). "\n";
}
```

This little program produces output like this:

```
child deployment device name = OASIS3 Controller
child deployment device name = Garmin GPS
child deployment device name = Workhorse Long Ranger ADCP
child deployment device name = MicroCAT Serial CTD
child deployment device name = MicroCAT Serial CTD
child deployment device name = Biospherical PRR Spectroradiometer
```

```
child deployment device name = pCO2 Analyzer
child deployment device name = MBARI ISUS
child deployment device name = MBARI Metsys
child deployment device name = WETStar Fluorometer
child deployment device name = E-meter
child deployment device name = HydroScat-2
child deployment device name = Surface Inductive Modem
child deployment device name = HOBI HS2
```

Though we are showing just the name of the device deployment in the above example. all of the attributes from all of the objects are available to the script.

An example of how our operational software traverses the metadata structure to produce a fully described mooring data set follows.

Starting at a parent mooring deployment as in the one above do the following:

- Loop through all the child device deployments and find output data container references.
- Build structures of variable names and units from the RecordDescription for the DataContainer.
- Parse the records from the DataContainer and create a Climate Forecast [17] compliant NetCDF data set.
- Populate discovery level metadata by walking the deployment tree as necessary. For example, the nominal position of the mooring is an attribute of the mooring platform deployment and not of the individual instrument deployments. If the Deployment that produced the data does not have the information (e.g. nominal depth, latitude, longitude) then the code walks up the parent deployment heirarchy until it finds the needed attributes.

When the Perl script has completed generation of a new DataContainer it calls the SSDS DataProducerAccess functions to add (or update) a ProcessRun. The script has access to all the information that is needed to populate the attributes that help provide fully tracked provenance information. A key piece of information is the specific version of the code that generates the output DataContainer. This is done in coordination with our version control system and the $Id:$ expansion within the source code. The specific version is parsed from the source code and the Version attribute for the Software object associated with the ProcesRun is set to the value from the expanded $Id:$ line. Discipline is required in making sure to commit changes before running the software; otherwise the version number parsed from the file will not accurately reflect the actual version used for the processing.

3.3   Web Application

Having visibility into the relationships and attributes of all the objects in the SSDS Metadata database is essential for being able to maintain the integrity of the data. One such tool is SSDS Explorer, a Java web application that allows a user to navigate down device deployment trees and down chains of data processing. Along the way attributes and references to resources are made available for examination. An example view of an expanded tree is in Fig. 6. The highlighted output DataContainer, a netCDF file named tenMinuteM2_20050520.nc was produced from a run of the combineAll.pl script on 28 August 2007. There are two other scripts (DStoNetCDF.pl and combineTS.pl) that operated on the data after it was produced by a MicroCAT Serial CTD instrument deployment on mooring M2.

4   Operational Procedures

SSDS requires the definition of instruments and the data they produce before the instruments are deployed to collect data. Having tools (Fig. 3) and clearly documented procedures that complement rather than replace existing procedures facilitates the capture of instrument metadata. This is the first step for tracking data lineage and is required for its processing within SSDS. As SSDS provides value with self-described data files and automated time series plots there is additional motivation for people to provide the information the system needs. The life cycle of data within SSDS is as follows:

- Instrument is defined by creating Device record.
- Instrument is configured for deployment by writing Deployment, DataContainer, RecordDescription, RecordVariable XML.
- Instrument is deployed. XML metadata is ingested by SSDS, data packets flow into the Instrument Packets database.
- Automated DataStream processing software consumes the data packets producing a NetCDF file for each instrument's data. A DataProducer record is created linking the input DataStream to the output DataFile.
- Follow-on data processing runs consume instrument NetCDF DataContainers producing combined data sets and graphical products. Metadata from SSDS is extracted as needed to fully describe data in all the NetCDF data sets.
- User uses the data with all the needed information to assess its suitability for a particular use.

5   Discussion of Provenance Systems

As oceanographic observatories become established we can expect a variety of solutions to provenance management issues. The spectrum of problems and their solutions is wide. SSDS provides a solution to the management of provenance early in the life cycle of observatory data — between instruments and their configuration to the data sets produced by their deployments. Many of the provenance systems described in the literature operate "downstream" of where SSDS operates. They operate in workflow, SOA, and high-performance grid computing environments. SSDS operates in a less sophisticated environment where highly

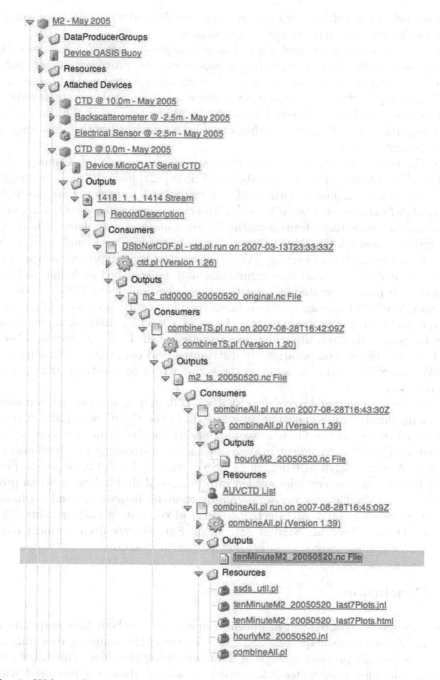

Fig. 6. Web application display of OASIS Buoy deployment's CTD Device output and the chain of ProcessRuns and Outputs that finally combine data from the other instruments into a gridded tenMinute NetCDF data set the. Ancillary output from the combineAll.pl ProcessRun are recorded as Resources.

diverse, but small volume data streams are transformed with relatively simple processing programs that are not computationally demanding.

In this environment we employ a *pay-as-you-go provenance* [2] system: as each process is executed a p-assertion [18] is constructed by provenance-aware software and is sent to the provenance store. As data sets are produced following this discipline, application software access the provenance store to generate metadata that assists in evaluating the usefulness of downstream data sets. This is a powerful capability, but it is not all that can be accomplished with a provenance management system.

Of the several provenance management systems reviewed [19], Chimera [20] and the Earth System Science Workbench (ESSW) [21] have the most similarity to provenance management within SSDS. Key to SSDS provenance are the *Software*, *DataProducer*, and *DataContainer* objects. Chimera has exactly the same concepts, but calls them *transformation*, *derivation*, and *data object*. Chimera, like SSDS, stores relationships between these objects in a relational databse. It specifies a Virtual Data Language (VDL) where details of all processing (derivations), including command line arguments, may be specified such that output data objects may be created by executing the derivation again. VDL also allows the specification of queries to search for derivations or the producers of specific data objects. Stored derivations may be re-executed on different input data, may be used to dynamically regenerate missing output files, and may be scheduled to run massive computations in distributed grid computing environments. ESSW, like SSDS, puts the onus on the script writer to construct and submit the p-assertion.

Chimera has been used to conduct analyses of data from millions of input files, producing another million output data files, from the Sloan Digital Sky Survey. Chimera handles all the file bookkeeping easing the headache that can be involved with data management in domains such as astronomy and high energy physics. A system such as Chimera or ESSW may be helpful in oceanography. Data from ocean observatories are fed into numerical simulations of ocean processes. These simulations are quite computationally demanding and do make use of Service Oriented Architectures and grid computing environments [22]. Driving Ocean Observing System Simulation Experiments from a robust data provenance management system is an attractive proposition.

6   Conclusion

The Shore Side Data System has been in operation for about four years and is meeting its functional requirements. A key feature of the system is its ability to track the specific processing steps of data processing pipelines. This capability provides detailed provenance information for all the data sets produced with SSDS enhanced software. This helps us create better described data sets with more efficient and simpler to maintain data processing software. The system is currently undergoing some refinements to improve its ability to maintain the metadata store and we are also simplifying the configuration steps so that it is easier for others to install and use. We are not done capitalizing on the data provenance tracking capabilities within SSDS. Future projects may fund the incorporation of workflow tools and better client processing integration. We want the barrier to be low for people and software to use the provenance aspects of the system.

One of the lessons learned from our efforts is that discipline is required at key steps of the data generation and processing processes. Accurate recording of instrument attributes is required in advance of the deployment of the instrument and once it is deployed the deployment information (time, location, and parent deployment device) is required at the beginning of the data processing path. Original data is processed by software whose source code is maintained in a version control system. As the data are processed the specific version number of the software components are logged. With this system we have reproducibility of derived data from the original data and exposure of specific processing techniques used at every step of the data path. A logical next step to consider is the integration of SSDS with an industry-standard provenance management system such that more benefits of provenance management may be realized.

Acknowledgements

This research was supported by the Monterey Bay Aquarium Research Institute through funding from the David and Lucile Packard Foundation.

References

1. Glenn, S., Schofield, O.: Observing the Oceans from the COOL Room: Our History, Experience, and Opinions. Oceanography 16(4), 37–52 (2003)
2. Baptista, A., Howe, B., Freire, J., Maier, D., Silva, C.T.: Scientific Exploration in the Era of Ocean Observatories. Computing in Science and Engineering 10(3), 53–58 (2008)
3. Freire, J., Silva, C.T., Callahan, S.P., Santos, E., Scheidegger, C.E., Vo, H.T.: Managing Rapidly-Evolving Scientific Workflows. In: Moreau, L., Foster, I. (eds.) IPAW 2006. LNCS, vol. 4145, pp. 10–18. Springer, Heidelberg (2006)
4. Chapman, A., Jagadish, H.V.: Issues in Building Practical Provenance Systems. Bulletin of the IEEE Computer Society Technical Committee on Data Engineering 30(4), 38–43 (2007)
5. MOOS: Monterey Ocean Observing System,
   http://www.mbari.org/moos/
6. SIAM: Software infrastructure and application for MOOS,
   http://www.mbari.org/moos/siam/siam.htm
7. MUSE: MOOS Upper-Water-Column Science Experiment,
   http://www.mbari.org/muse/
8. FGDC: Federal Geographic Data Committee, http://www.fgdc.gov/
9. Graybeal, J., Gomes, K., McCann, M., Schlining, B., Schramm, R., Wilkin, D.: MBARI's Operational, extensible data management for ocean observatories. In: The Third International Workshop on Scientific Use of Submarine Cables and Related Technologies, Tokyo, pp. 288–292 (2003)

10. The Shore Side Data System, http://www.mbari.org/ssds/
11. Agile software development,
    http://en.wikipedia.org/wiki/Agile_software_development
12. NetCDF: Network Common Data Form,
    http://www.unidata.ucar.edu/software/netcdf/
13. OPeNDAP: Open-source Project for a Network Data Access Protocol,
    http://www.opendap.org/
14. CIMT: Center for Integrated Marine Technologies, http://cimt.ucsc.edu/
15. Gomes, K., OReilly, T., Graybeal, J.: Issues in data management in observing systems and lessons learned. In: Proceedings of the Marine Technology Society/Institute of Electrical and Electronics Engineers Oceans Conference, Boston, Massachusetts (2006)
16. PUCK: Programmable Underwater Connector with Knowledge,
    http://www.mbari.org/pw/puck.htm
17. NetCDF Climate and Forecast (CF) Metadata Convention,
    http://cf-pcmdi.llnl.gov/
18. Moreau, L., Groth, P., Miles, S., Vazquez-Salceda, J., Ibbotson, J., Jiang, S., Munroe, S., Rana, O., Schreiber, A., Tan, V., Varga, L.: The Provenance of Electronic Data. Communications of the ACM 51(4), 52–58 (2008)
19. Simmhan, Y.L., Plale, B., Gannon, D.: A survey of Data Provenance in e-science. SIGMOD 34(3), 31–36 (2005)
20. Foster, I., Vockler, J., Wilde, M., Yong, Z.: Chimera: a virtual data system for representing, querying, and automating data derivation. In: Proceedings of 14th International Conference on Scientific and Statistical Database Management, 2002, pp. 37–46 (2002)
21. Frew, J., Bose, R.: Earth System Science Workbench: A Data Management Infrastructure for Earth Science Products. In: Proceedings of the 13th International Conference on Scientific and Statistical Database Management, Fairfax, VA, pp. 180–189 (2001)
22. Abbott, M., Sears, C.: The Always-Connected World and Its Impacts on Ocean research. Oceanography 19(1), 14–21 (2006)

The Open Provenance Model: An Overview

Luc Moreau[1], Juliana Freire[2], Joe Futrelle[3], Robert E. McGrath[3],
Jim Myers[3], and Patrick Paulson[4]

[1] University of Southampton
[2] University of Utah
[3] NCSA
[4] PNNL

1   Background

Provenance is well understood in the context of art or digital libaries, where it respectively refers to the documented history of an art object, or the documentation of processes in a digital object's life cycle. Interest for provenance in the "e-science community" [12] is also growing, since provenance is perceived as a crucial component of workflow systems that can help scientists ensure reproducibility of their scientific analyses and processes [2,4].

Against this background, the *International Provenance and Annotation Workshop* (IPAW'06), held on May 3-5, 2006 in Chicago, involved some 50 participants interested in the issues of data provenance, process documentation, data derivation, and data annotation [7]. During a session on provenance standardization, a consensus began to emerge, whereby the provenance research community needed to understand better the capabilities of the different systems, the representations they used for provenance, their similarities, their differences, and the rationale that motivated their designs.

Hence, the first Provenance Challenge [1] was born, and from the outset, the challenge was set up to be *informative* rather than *competitive*. The first Provenance Challenge was set up in order to provide a forum for the community to understand the capabilities of different provenance systems and the expressiveness of their provenance representations. Participants simulated or ran a Functional Magnetic Resonance Imaging workflow, from which they implemented and executed a pre-identified set of "provenance queries". Sixteen teams responded to the challenge, and reported their experience in a journal special issue [9].

The first Provenance Challenge was followed by the second Provenance Challenge [1], aiming at establishing inter-operability of systems, by exchanging provenance information. During discussions, the thirteen teams that responded to the second challenge found out that there was substantial agreement on a core representation of provenance. As a result, following a workshop in August 2007, in Salt Lake City, a data model was crafted by the authors and released as the *Open Provenance Model* (OPM v1.00) [8].

On June 19th 2008, some twenty participants attended the first OPM workshop, held after IPAW'08 [3], to discuss the OPM specification. Minutes of the workshop and recommendations [5] were published, and led to the current version (v1.01) of the Open Provenance Model [10].

J. Freire, D. Koop, and L. Moreau (Eds.): IPAW 2008, LNCS 5272, pp. 323–326, 2008.
© Springer-Verlag Berlin Heidelberg 2008

2 Scope

The *Open Provenance Model* (OPM) is a model for provenance that is designed to meet the following requirements:

- To allow provenance information to be exchanged between systems, by means of a compatibility layer based on a shared provenance model.
- To allow developers to build and share tools that operate on such provenance model.
- To define the model in a precise, technology-agnostic manner.
- To support a digital representation of provenance for any "thing", whether produced by computer systems or not.
- To define a core set of rules that identify the valid inferences that can be made on provenance graphs.

While specifying this model, we also have some *non*-requirements:

- It is not the purpose of OPM to specify the internal representations that systems have to adopt to store and manipulate provenance internally; systems remain free to adopt internal representations that are fit for their purpose.
- It is not the purpose of [8,10] to define a computer-parsable syntax for this model; model implementations in XML, RDF or others are being specified in separate documents.
- OPM does not specify protocols to store provenance information in provenance repositories.
- OPM does not specify protocols to query provenance repositories.

3 Technical Overview

The foundations of the Open Provenance Model can be traced back to the Second Provenance Challenge 'community agreement', summarized by Miles [6]. It is assumed that the provenance of objects (whether digital or not) can be represented by an annotated causality graph, which is a directed acyclic graph, enriched with annotations capturing further information pertaining to execution.

In OPM, provenance graphs consist of three types of nodes. *Artifacts* represent an immutable piece of state, which may have a physical embodiment in a physical object, or a digital representation in a computer system. *Processes* represent actions performed on or caused by artifacts, and resulting in new artifacts. *Agents* represent contextual entities acting as a catalyst of a process, enabling, facilitating, controlling, or affecting its execution.

Importantly, in OPM, a provenance graph is defined as *a record of a past execution* (or current execution); it is not a description of something that may happen in the future, nor a general recipe (workflow) that could be used to derive future data. OPM is a model of artifacts *in the past*, explaining how they *were* derived. Processes may be in the past, or can still be currently running. In no case is OPM intended to describe the state of future artifacts and the activities of future processes.

A provenance graph aims to capture the causal dependencies between the abovementioned entities. Therefore, nodes, whether artifacts, processes or agents, can be connected by directed edges that belong to one of the categories defined in the model. An edge represents a causal dependency, between its source, denoting the effect, and its destination, denoting the cause. Edges can express the following dependencies: an artifact was generated by a process; a process used an artifact; a process was controlled by an agent; an artifact was derived from another artifact; a process was triggered by another process.

A set theoretic model is proposed, and a set of inference rules are defined, allowing reasoning over causal dependencies. While the core model is timeless, it is permitted to annotate a provenance graph with time annotations, which themselves must satisfy constraints regarding causality.

4   Conclusion

The Open Provenance Model is work in progress, as indicated by the issues raised in the OPM Workshop [5]. We hope to capitalize on the community momentum, to keep on evolving the OPM specification into a well-founded data exchange format. It is proposed that OPM be used as a model for an inter-operability exercise, in a third Provenance Challenge. Serialisations are now being proposed for OPM, and libraries to manipulate provenance graphs are being implemented. All material related to OPM can be found from [11].

References

1. The Provenance Challenge Wiki (June 2006),
   http://twiki.ipaw.info/bin/view/Challenge
2. Davidson, S.B., Freire, J.: Provenance and scientific workflows: challenges and opportunities. In: SIGMOD Conference, pp. 1345–1350 (2008)
3. Freire, J., Koop, D., Moreau, L. (eds.): IPAW 2008. LNCS, vol. 5272. Springer, Heidelberg (2008)
4. Gil, Y., Deelman, E., Ellisman, M., Fahringer, T., Fox, G., Gannon, D., Goble, C., Livny, M., Moreau, L., Myers, J.: Examining the challenges of scientific workflows. IEEE Computer 40(12), 26–34 (2007)
5. Groth, P.: First OPM Workshop Minutes. In: Information Science Institute, USC (July 2008),
   http://twiki.ipaw.info/bin/view/Challenge/FirstOPMWorkshopMinutes
6. Miles, S.: Technical summary of the second provenance challenge workshop, King's College (July 2007),
   http://twiki.ipaw.info/bin/view/Challenge/SecondWorkshopMinutes
7. Moreau, L., Foster, I. (eds.): IPAW 2006. LNCS, vol. 4145. Springer, Heidelberg (2006)
8. Moreau, L., Freire, J., Futrelle, J., McGrath, R.E., Myers, J., Paulson, P.: The open provenance model (v1.00). Technical report, University of Southampton (December 2007), http://eprints.ecs.soton.ac.uk/14979

9. Moreau, L., Ludaescher, B. (eds.): Special Issue on the First Provenance Challenge, vol. 20. Wiley, Chichester (2007)
10. Moreau, L. (ed.), Plale, B., Miles, S., Goble, C., Missier, P., Barga, R., Simmhan, Y., Futrelle, J., McGrath, R., Myers, J., Paulson, P., Bowers, S., Ludaescher, B., Kwasnikowska, N., Van den Bussche, J., Ellkvist, T., Freire, J., Groth, P.: The open provenance model (v1.01). Technical report, University of Southampton (July 2008), http://eprints.ecs.soton.ac.uk/16148
11. The Open Provenance Web Site (August 2008), http://openprovenance.org
12. Simmhan, Y., Plale, B., Gannon, D.: A survey of data provenance in e-science. SIGMOD Record 34(3), 31–36 (2005)

Author Index